Dark Psychology

7 BOOKS in 1

The Art of Persuasion, How to influence people, Hypnosis Techniques, NLP secrets, Analyze Body language, Gaslighting, Manipulation Subliminal, and Emotional Intelligence 2.0

© Written by: Robert Dale Goleman – Daniel Brandon Bradberry – Travis Greene Carnegie – Katerina Griffith – Joseph Griffith – Caroline Empath – Power Laws – Jack Mind

Dark Psychology and Manipulation (Caroline Empathy)

Introduction	28
Chapter 1: An Overview to Dark Psychology versus Normal Psychology	32
Chapter 2: How to Use Dark Psychology to Manipulate Others	41
Chapter 3: Analyzing People through Body Language	45
Chapter 4: Emotional Intelligence	49
Chapter 5: Importance of Emotional Intelligence	59
Chapter 6: Mind Control	68
Chapter 7: Mind Control Techniques	77
Chapter 8: The Secrets of Neuro Linguistic Programming	83
Chapter 9: Manipulation and Persuasion	96
Chapter 10: Characteristics of Manipulators	107
Chapter 11: Hypnosis	121
Chapter 12: Brain washing	124
Chapter 13: Preventing Manipulation	127
Conclusion	132

Dark Psychology and Manipulation (Joseph Griffith)

Book Description   135

Chapter 1 What is Dark psychology?   139

Benefits of knowing your dark side   144

   Improved relationship   147

   Clearer perception   147

   Enhanced energy and physical health   147

   Psychological integration and maturity   148

   Greater creativity   148

      Center yourself   148

      Cultivate self-compassion   149

      Cultivate self-awareness   149

      Be courageously honest   150

      Record your discoveries   150

Chapter 2 Dark psychology Triad   151

Chapter 3 Manipulation   156

Techniques used by manipulators to gain control   158

   Gaslighting   158

   Projection   159

   Generalizations   159

   Moving goalposts   160

   Changing the subject   160

   Name-calling   161

   Smear campaigns   161

   Devaluation   162

   Aggressive jokers   162

- *Triangulation* 162
- *Using body language to your advantage* 163
- *Change your perspective* 164
- *Leverage your knowledge of others* 165
- *Beware of good timing and opportunity* 166

Unconscious Mind 168
Limbic Brain System 170
The Process of Mind Control 171
- *Step 1 – Understanding the target* 172
- *Step 2- Unfreezing Solid Beliefs and Values* 173
- *Step 3 – Reprogramming the Mind* 174
- *Step 4 – Freezing the New Beliefs and Values* 175

The relationship between mind control and emotional influence 176
Types of Mind Control 177
Stages of Hypnosis 179
- *Stage 1: Absorb Attention* 179
- *Stage 2: Bypass the Critical Faculty* 180
- *Step 3: Activate an Unconscious Response* 181
- *Stage 4: Lead to Your Desired Outcome* 182

Pattern Interrupts & Rapid Induction Techniques 182
Using Pattern Interrupt to Induce Hypnosis 184

Chapter 6 Dark Persuasion — 190

Elements of persuasion 190
Subliminal persuasion 191
Basic Persuasion techniques 192
- *Create a need* 192
- *Utilizing illustrative and words* 193

Tricks used by mass media and advertising — 193
Images — 193
Sound — 193
Dark Persuasion Techniques to Be on the Lookout For — 194
The Long Con — 194
Graduality — 195
Masking the True Intentions — 196
Leading Questions — 198
The Law of State Transference — 198
Why Analyze People — 201
How to Analyze People — 202
Establish a neutral baseline behavior set — 203
Identify deviations from neutral behaviors — 204
Identify clusters of deviations — 204
Analyze — 205
When to Analyze People — 205
How to defend from manipulators — 207
Act Fast — 209
Get Assistance Quickly — 210
Have Confidence in Your Instincts — 211

How to Influence People

Factors Influencing Human Behavior — 218
Abilities — 218
Gender — 219
Racial and Cultural Background — 219
Perception — 220
Attribution — 220
Attitude — 221

Chapter 1 Understanding influence — 222

Types of influence — 223
Negative influence — 224
Neutral influence — 224
Positive influence — 224
Life-changing influence — 225

Chapter 2 Reading Body Language — 226

Some regular non-verbal communication signs. — 227
Concentrate the Eyes — 227
Look at the Face – Body Language Touching Mouth or Smiling — 228
Focus on nearness — 228
Check whether the other individual is reflecting you — 229
Watch the head development — 229
Take a gander at the other individual's feet — 229
Watch for hand signals — 230
Inspect the situation of the arms — 230
Body parts — 232

Lower Body — 232

- Legs Touching — 232
- Pointing Feet — 232
- Smarty Pants — 232
- Shy Tangle — 232

Upper Body — 233

- Leaning — 233
- The Superman — 233
- The Chest in Profile — 233
- Outward Thrust Chest — 234

Hands — 234

- Control — 234
- Greeting — 235
- Holding — 235
- Shaping — 236

Face — 237

- Mouth — 237
- Negative Emotions — 238
- Not Enough Response — 238
- Using the Word "But" — 238
- Personal Space — 239
- Talking Too Fast — 239
- Not Listening — 239
- Slumping — 239
- Checking Your Phone — 239
- Face is Scrunched-Up — 240
- Not Making Eye Contact — 240
- Not Smiling — 240
- Glancing Around — 240
- Handshake Too Weak or Strong — 240

Chapter 3 How to Analyze Those around You — 242

- It helps you know your allies — 242

It helps avoid conflict	243
It allows you to appreciate diversity	243
It helps you fine-tune your goals	244
It helps you understand the motivations of people	244
It helps you understand a person's strengths	245
So why measure conduct specifically?	246
How to Master the Art of the First Impression	248

Chapter 4 Understanding the people and world around us   252

Sensation and Perception	252
Learning and Conditioning	255
Classical Conditioning.	255
Operant Conditioning.	256
Observational Learning.	256
Attention	256
Attention is Limited.	257
Attention is Selective.	257
Attention is a Fundamental Part of The Cognitive System.	257
Intelligence	258
State of Consciousness	261
Body Clocks.	261
Sleep and Consciousness.	261
Dreams and Consciousness.	262
Hypnosis and consciousness.	262
Drugs, And Consciousness.	262

Chapter 5: Steps to Increase Your Influence   264

Expertise	264
Information	264

Resources	264
Relationships	265
Attitude	265
Authority	265
Appreciate People	265
Show Abundant Passion And Enthusiasm	266
Stay Consistent	266
Find Solutions	267

Chapter 6: Sources of influence — 268

1. Personal Motivation	268
2. Personal Ability	268
3. Harness Peer Pressure	268
4. Find Strength in Numbers	269
5. Design Rewards and Demand Accountability	269
6. Change the Environment	269

Chapter 7: The Art of Influence and Persuasion? — 270

Practice repetition	270
Use imagination	271
Try to obtain a yes early	271
Build your confidence	271
Improve your listening skills	272
Learn how to integrate connection in all your persuasion endeavors	272
Learn how to give praises	273

Chapter 8: Powerful Verbal and Nonverbal Cues — 274

Analyzing People via Their Verbal Statements	275
Understanding the Relationship between Words, Behavior, and Personality	275

How Words Reveal Your Personality 275

Learn to Unclothe the Veil around Jokes 276

Stories Are Powerful 276

Common Word Clues You Need to Know 277

An Insight into How the Brain Process Words 278

Types of Nonverbal Communication 279

 1. Outward appearances 279

 2. Motions 279

 3. Paralinguistic 279

 4. Non-verbal communication and Posture 280

 5. Proxemics 280

 6. Eye Stare 280

 7. Haptics 281

 8. Appearance 281

 9. Relics 281

Chapter 9: Facial Expressions   283

Chapter 10: Distance in Communication   286

Chapter 11: Dark psychology and manipulation   291

The Dark Triad 292

 Manipulation Techniques 294

How to Use Dark Psychology to Manipulate Others 297

How to Deal with Manipulation 300

Chapter 12 Tips and Tricks for Reading and Analyzing People   304

Listen to What your Intuition is Telling You 304

Step by Step Tips for Reading Others 306

Emotional Intelligence 2.0

Book Description   312

Chapter 1 What is emotional intelligence, and why is it important?   318

Robust emotional vocabulary   319
Curiosity about people   320
You embrace change   320
You know your strengths and weaknesses   320
You are a good judge of character   321
You are hard to offend   321
Letting go of mistakes   321
Don't hold grudges   322
Neutralizes toxic people   322
Don't seek perfection   323
You disconnect   323
Limit caffeine intake   324
Get enough sleep   324
Stop negative self-talk in its tracks   325
Won't allow anyone limits your joy   325
Importance of emotional intelligence   326

Chapter 2 The Four Attributes of Emotional Intelligence   327

Self-management   327
Three steps of self-management   328
Step 1 Identify what you are feeling   328
Step 2 Determine the underlying cause   328
Step 3 Act   329
Tips to improve your self-management skills   330
Self-awareness   331
Tips on how to improve your self-awareness   334
Get out of your comfort zone   334

11

Identify your triggers 334

Don't judge your feelings 335

Don't make decisions in a bad mood 336

Don't make decisions in a good mood either 337

Get to the birds-eye view 337

Revisit your values and actions accordingly 338

Check yourself 338

Fill your blind spot with feedback 339

Social awareness 340

Ensure that the lens you are looking through is clear 340

Watch their body language 341

Listen carefully 341

Relationship management 342

Criteria for effective relationship management 344

    Decision 344

    Interaction with others 344

    An outcome 344

    Your needs 344

Chapter 3 Busting myths about Emotional Intelligence — 345

Emotional intelligence does not exist 345

It is all about empathy 346

It is not about awareness but behavioral change 346

Emotional intelligence is equated with other personality traits 347

Emotional intelligence predicts success 347

You either have EI, or you don't 348

You have to give up emotional intelligence to be mentally tough 348

There is no dark side to emotional intelligence 349

It does not influence our decisions 350

There is no correlation between emotional intelligence and physical wellbeing ... 350

Chapter 4 Steps on how to grow Emotional Intelligence — 351

Step 1 Tapping into your emotions ... 351

Note your emotional reactions to events throughout the day ... 351

Pay attention to your body ... 351

Observe how your emotions and behavior are connected ... 352

Avoid judging your own emotions ... 352

Notice patterns in your emotional history ... 353

Practice deciding how to behave ... 353

Step 2 Connecting with other people ... 354

Be open-minded and agreeable ... 354

Improve your empathy skills ... 355

Read people's body language ... 355

See the effect you have on others ... 356

Practice being emotionally honest ... 356

Step 3 Putting EQ to Practical Use ... 357

See where you have room for improvement ... 357

Lower your stress level by raising your EQ ... 357

Be more light-hearted at home and work ... 358

Chapter 5 Emotional Intelligence at school/workplace — 359

EI is the key to communication in the workplace and school ... 360

Emotional intelligence in hiring processes ... 361

Emotional intelligence in the globalized economy ... 362

Physical health ... 363

Attention ... 363

Clarity ... 363

13

Repair	363
Mental health	364
Actively seek change in your relationship	369
Look at challenges as opportunities instead of problems	370
Respect all the feelings you have for each other	370
Keep laughter in your love life	371
Pay attention to how you feel when your spouse or partner is not around	371
Listen to your body and not your mind	372
Heed the messages from your whole body	373
Take a chance on reaching out	374
What you need to feel loved vs. what you want	374
How to respond to a low EQ partner	375

Chapter 8 The interaction between EQ and Social Intelligence 376

Social competencies of EQ	377
Empathy	377
Types of Empathy	380
Cognitive Empathy	380
Emotional empathy	380
Compassionate empathy	381
How to improve empathy for a successful life	384
Social skills	384
Communication skills	384
Leadership skills	385
Persuasion skills	385
Conflict-management skills	386

Chapter 9 Understanding Emotional drain and dealing with them 387

Hopelessness	387

- *Crying often* 387
- *Insomnia* 388
- *Lack of motivation* 388
- *Detachment* 388
- **Things you can do if you are experiencing emotional exhaustion** 389
  - *Exercise* 389
  - *Breathing exercises* 389
  - *Meditation* 390
  - *Journaling* 390

GASLGHTING

Introduction — 395

Chapter 1. Gaslighting — 397

Chapter 2. Understanding the Ins and Outs of Gaslighting — 401

Chapter 3. How to spot a gaslighter — 410

Chapter 4. Cognitive Dissonance | How Manipulation Affects You — 412

    Effects of Manipulation — 415

Chapter 5. How Gaslighting Narcissists operate to make their Victim Think that they are Crazy — 421

    What Is A Narcissist? — 421
    Narcissism and Gaslighting — 422
        The Art of Making Others Crazy — 423
        Making People do What the Narcissist Wants — 425

Chapter 6. The Effects of Gaslighting — 427

    Recovering from Gaslighting — 427
    Are You Being Gas lighted? — 428
    Gaslighting tends to work in stages — 429

Chapter 7. Signs you are Being Manipulated with Gaslighting — 431

Chapter 8. Things Narcissists Say During Gaslighting. — 436

    Stuff Your Gaslighting Abuser Says — 436

Chapter 9. Empowering Ways to Disarm a Narcissist and Take Control — 439

Techniques to handle narcissists 439
    Get away 439
    Avoid the inner circle 440
    Avoid narcissistic injury 440
    Avoid exposing them 441
    Admire and listen to them 441
    Don't reject them 442
    Avoid showing weakness 442
    Give them an "out" 443
    Don't expect fairness 444
    They want to look good 444
    Understand their narcissistic supply 444
    An audience 445
    Status 445
    Sex 445
    Love 446
    Avoid flooding them with supply 446

Chapter 10. Ways to Stop a Gaslighter in Their Tracks — 447

Putting an End to Gaslighting 447
Change Is Possible 449
Born of Vulnerability 449
When the Narcissist Finds True, Secure Love 450
Breaking the Cycle 451
The Narcissist to who wants to Change 451
The Trouble with Emotional Abuse 453
Unmasking Emotional Abuse 453
What to Do If You're Being Abused 454

Don't Make Excuses for the Abuse ... 455

Chapter 11. A Match Made in Hell: Narcissists And Empaths — 457

What is an Empath? ... 457
Why Are Narcissists And Empaths Drawn to Each Other? ... 459
Is There a Future For This Relationship? ... 460
How an Empath Can be Severely Emotionally Damaged by a Narcissist ... 460
Points to Take From This Chapter ... 462

Chapter 12 – How to stop being manipulated by a gaslighter — 464

Clarify yourself ... 464
Do some ground exercise ... 464
Decide whether you want to continue the relationship ... 465
Reach out to a trusted loved one or friend ... 465
Take a Stand ... 466
Dealing with the Narcissist ... 466
Take a step back and analyze the situation. ... 466
Accept that the narcissist will not change. ... 467
Seek help. ... 467
Set boundaries. ... 467
Be realistic. ... 467
Remember that your value as a person does not depend on the narcissist. ... 467
Speak to them in a way that will make them aware of how they will benefit. ... 467
Find proof of or document any kind of abuse. ... 468
Do not fall for the narcissist's tactics again. ... 468
Leave. ... 468

Chapter 13- Narcissistic Personality Disorder — 469

Symptoms and characteristics of narcissistic personality disorder	469
Narcissistic personality disorder: causes	470
Narcissistic personality disorder: treatment	471
Criteria for Narcissistic Personality Disorder	472
Characteristics of narcissistic personality disorder	474

Chapter 14- Toxic Relationships Recovery — 478

How to Reduce Conflicts in Relationships	478
Forgiveness	478
Invest in Yourself	479
Experiment with other methods.	480
Find an Outlet	481
Research	481
Exercise	482
Challenge Your Comfort Zone	482
Self-soothing	482
Praise Yourself	483
Stop the Comparison	483
Time for Yourself	484
Therapy	484
How to Know When it's Time to Go	486

Conclusion — 488

Master Your Emotions — 491

Chapter 1: Emotions — 493

Chapter 2: How to Handle Your Emotions In Relationships — 497

- How emotions transform into stress — 493
- Fight or Flight — 493
- Living in a World of Stress — 494
- The Key to Personal Resilience — 495

Chapter 3: Methods for Mastering Your Emotions — 501

- Relaxation Training — 502
- Finding Happiness — 512
- Feeling an Emotion — 517
- Learning to Soothe Ourselves — 518
- Steps for Embracing Our Feelings — 519
- Numbness and Embracing Feelings — 520
- Facing Areas of Discomfort Gradually — 521
- Mindfulness — 525
- Awareness When We Are Emotionally Aroused — 527

Chapter 4: Embracing Our Feelings — 517

Chapter 5: The Benefits of Emotional Intelligence — 531

- What makes people talk without thinking? — 531
- 10 main benefits of having high emotional intelligence: — 532
- How Emotional Intelligence Can Really Help Out In Relationships — 534
- How To Determine Whether My Emotional Intelligence Needs Improvement — 538
- Strategies to Improve Emotional Intelligence — 539

Chapter 6: Communications Skills in the Workplace — 541

Chapter 7: Secrets of Building Healthy Social Relationships — 553

Chapter 8: Tricks & Techniques for Overcoming Negativity — 563

Acknowledge Your Feelings	572
Ask the Hard Questions	572
Journaling	574
Find Reasons to be Grateful	575
Focus on Your Strengths	576
Establish New Habits	577
Use Affirmations	578
Practice Mindfulness	579
Channel Your Thoughts into Something Positive	580
Consider Cognitive Behavioral Therapy	581

Chapter 9: Unleash The Empath In You! — 582

Why Practice Empathy?	584
Recognize Your Enemies	587
Be the Third Person	588
Tips to Improve Empathy	589
How to be Empathetic	590

Conclusion — 594

How to deal with Difficult People

Book Description — 597

Introduction — 598

Chapter 1 How to identify a difficult person: The big five — 601

Wrapping it up — 606

Chapter 2 Types of difficult people — 609

Perfectionists — 609

Dealing with a perfectionist subordinate — 610

- Avoid giving them large project scopes — 610
- Appeal to their sense of vanity and empathy — 610
- Appeal to their self-interest — 611

Dealing with a perfectionist colleague — 611

- Choose your battles wisely — 611
- Ask them what it is they would like to do differently — 612
- Stick to your guns — 612
- Keep distance — 613

Dealing with a perfectionist supervisor — 613

- Manage your manager — 613
- Push information their way — 613
- Be at peace with the fact that there is only so much you can do — 614
- Seek mentorship and support elsewhere — 614
- Jump ship when you have to — 614

Control Freaks — 614

- Get rid of turf wars — 616
- Stroke their ego — 616
- Stand your ground — 617
- Take note of the little things — 617
- Give a little — 618
- Ask questions — 618

If necessary, enlist the help 619

Narcissists 619

Gossips 620

Bullies 621

Slackers 621

Pessimists 621

The hostile or bossy 622

The Super-Agreeable 623

Critics 624

Liars 625

Everything is about them 626

They are verbally toxic 626

They paint themselves as victims 627

Often oblivious to the obvious 627

They count everything 628

Chapter 4 Identifying the complicated issue 629

Mitigating These Situations 630

Realistic optimism lens 630

The reverse lens 630

The long lens 631

How to manage your reactions 631

Leveraging self-control 632

Chapter 5 Developing Coping and Negotiation strategies 634

Method 1 Approach the problematic person 634

Step 1 Choose your battles carefully 634

Step 2 Take a pause 635

Step 3 Clearly state your needs with assertive communications 635

Step 4 Keep being polite 636

Step 5 Stick to the facts 636

Step 6 Minimize your interactions 637

Step 7 Talk to allies 637

Method 2 Change your mindset 637

Step 1 Realize that there will always be difficult people anyway 637

Step 2 Increase of frustration tolerance 638

Step 3 Examine your behavior 639

Step 4 Beware of your perceptions of others 639

Chapter 6 Steps on how to deal with a difficult person   641

Step 1: Listen 641

Step 2: Offer clear behavioral feedback 642

Pay attention first 643

Camera check 644

Step 3: Document 645

Step 4: Maintain consistency 646

Step 5: Establish consequences for when things don't change 647

Step 6: Work through the company's processes 647

Step 7: Don't poison the well 647

Step 8: Manage your self-talk 648

Step 9: Have the courage 649

Chapter 7 What do you do when all these do not work?   650

Be calm 650

Understand the other person's intentions 651

Get some perspective 651

Let them know where you are coming from 651

Establish a rapport 652

The power of utilization 653

Effective communication through the utilization 653

Stop the psych-jargon 655

Utilizing the gaping problem	656
Treat the other with respect	656
Stop to see where they are coming from	657
Trust them first	657
Pay attention to the positive	658
Have a new perspective	658
Focus on what can be actioned	659
Ignore	659
Employ kindness	660
Show compassion	660
Find something in common	661
Control what you can	662
Look at yourself	663
Overcome Your Fear of Conflict	663

Chapter 8 Expert techniques to handle difficult people — 665

Practice reflective listening	665
Consider their affect heuristic	666
Tap into the beginner's mind	667
Let go of fear	668
"Chunk" the problem	668
Remember, anger is natural	669
Keep your calm	670
Practice active listening	671
Repeat back what your customers say	672
Thank them for bringing the issue to your attention	672
Explain the steps you'll take to solve the problem	673
Set a time to follow-up with them, if needed	673
Be sincere	674

DARK PSYCHOLOGY
AND
MANIPULATION

HOW TO INFLUENCE PEOPLE:
GUIDE TO LEARNING THE ART OF PERSUASION, HYPNOSIS, BODY LANGUAGE, NLP SECRETS, MIND CONTROL TECHNIQUES, AND EMOTIONAL INTELLIGENCE 2.0

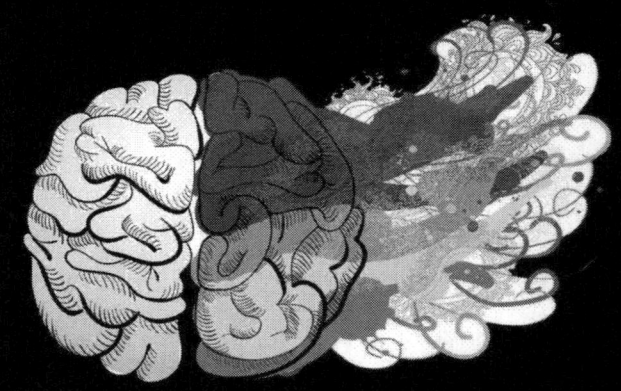

CAROLINE EMPATHY — POWER LAWS

Dark Psychology

and

Manipulation

How to influence People: Guide to Learning the Art of Persuasion, Hypnosis, Body Language, NLP Secrets, Mind Control Techniques, And Emotional Intelligence 2.0

© Written by : Caroline Empathy & Power Laws

Introduction

Next time you are in a public space look around you and examine the people that are walking about. What are they doing? Who are they with? In which direction are they going? If you can imagine that last time you went to your supermarket of choice, you can probably recall people pushing carts of food around the aisles. Maybe with their spouse and children, or with friends. Maybe alone. Each one of them has one thing in common: they want to buy their groceries for the week and get on with their day.

In that sense, the motivation behind their behavior is patently visible. A father walks over to the dairy section and grabs a gallon of %2 milk. He then scratches off the item from the grocery list and walks towards the next item. The grocery store is a nice metaphor for motivation in the real world. Everyone is doing something because they have some item that needs to be crossed out from a list. At times it will be easily doable, like getting a haircut. At other times it will be complex and time-dependent, like getting a Ph.D. in astrophysics.

Whatever the case, people have motivations. Everyone has a metaphorical grocery list they want to fulfill, whether they know what is on the list or not. There is where human psychology gets tricky. Some of us know what we want. Some of us don't know. Some of us are "open" to suggestions and recommendations. Still, others are constantly seeking for direction from others. Some of us know what our moral values and core beliefs are. Others do not. One second you can be reaching for the creamy peanut butter, and the next you are looking at the crunchy version. Or perhaps you drop peanut butter altogether and look towards the organic nut butter. Or perhaps you reach for the peanut butter and mixed jelly jar.

To understand what dark psychology is, we first need to establish what psychology is as a whole. Psychology is defined as the study of the human mind, especially in regard to the connection between thoughts and behaviors. Even in the times of the great Greek philosophers, scholars were fascinated by the workings of the mind and how it related to our actions and reactions.

Modern psychology was founded by a German doctor named Wilhelm Wundt. Wundt was a physiologist and philosopher, and his interest in these fields led to the development of his theories about the relationship between body and mind.

In 1879, Wundt founded the world's first psychology laboratory, located at the University of Leipzig. He was determined to prove that the inner workings of the mind could be measured and examined much like any other science experiment. He developed theories and experiments based on the following principles:

- *Voluntarism*- the process of organizing the mind
- *Reductionism*- the ability to isolate each part of the mind
- *Introspection*- the ability to perform detailed self-examination

Using these principles and a modified experiment from his days in physiology, Wundt developed a method of testing the psyche of his subjects. When he was medical doctor, Wundt had tested the reaction time of his patients to certain physical stimuli in a controlled environment, like a noise or a flashing light (the precursors to modern hearing or vision tests). Wundt wondered if he could test the mind in a similar fashion.

The result was an experiment in which Wundt had his subjects concentrate on a metronome, and then describe how the metronome made them feel. By detailing the sounds, sensations, and thoughts they had when focusing on the metronome ticking, Wundt was able to begin determining the way the brain is affected by controlled stimuli. He even attempted to measure the levels of chemical activity in the brain during and after these experiments.

While Wundt's work was primitive by the standards of modern psychology, it was groundbreaking enough for him to have trained over one hundred students in the budding field, and he inspired the next generation of psychologists; Sigmund Freud, who fathered psychoanalysis; Carl Jung, who expanded upon Freud's theories and developed analytical psychology; William James, who brought modern psychology to America; and Alfred Alder, who formulated the connections between emotional needs and social skills. These men created the body of work that would blossom into the many branches of psychology and psychotherapy we see today, including cognitive-behavioral therapy.

Dark Psychology is a branch of psychology that fascinates people across the globe who are interested in topics like understanding the criminal mind, better understanding the darker thoughts that control human behavior at all ages, and the conscious actions people take to influence others using psychological manipulation.

At its core, Dark Psychology is the specified study of the more wicked side to human nature: what defines it, how to observe it, where the lines are and how it can be utilized for both constructive and nefarious purposes. It covers mild uses like a clever car salesman who continuously has the best sales numbers on his team because he is able to read his customers and build an amiable connection with them based on observations to the severe uses like studying the mind of criminals who use their understanding of human behavior to victimize others.

Persuasion, manipulation, and other forms of influence are ubiquitous. You can pick up on some obvious signs here and there, but there are also hidden secret ways that others control you which you might never be able to fully comprehend.

Many reasons exist that can make you yearn to be a more persuasive person. Perhaps you feel as though you are already under the deep influence of others and you wish to break yourself free. Maybe you are the kind of individual that can easily fall for the charm of others and now is the moment for you to be able to better protect yourself against any types of influence that might happen to you.

Perhaps you are trying to sell something, maybe yourself or your brand, and you need to figure out how to get people to be more persuaded by you in order to help you achieve the things that you want in this life. No matter where you are or what you are trying to do, you have all the tools that you will ever need to be persuasive or influential with you already.

Before getting into this book, there are a few things that you need to know to be introduced to this topic, in order to get into the right mindset as you read through this text. First, understand that there are no two manipulators that are alike. There are no two easily persuaded people that are the same either. Though it might seem like this sometimes, especially since you can influence a group all at once, you can't let yourself fall into a thinking pattern where you place everyone in the same category.

What you also have to understand is that you should have an open mind with how you interpret the types of manipulation or persuasion that you will see as you read through the book, and afterwards in everyday life. We have tips and tricks to assist you be more persuasive, but look for your own methods as well. Apply the things we are talking about practically in a way that helps your life and with methods that are individual to your experiences and circumstances.

Remember, above all this takes practice. You won't be able to understand the human brain and be a persuasive person overnight. You will certainly be more aware of these kinds of things and the switch will be much quicker than you realize. Your perspective has likely started to change already. To really be an expert, you are going to have to put yourself out there in real situations and go through trial and error periods of trying to study other people. Don't blame yourself for not being aware of the ways that you have been manipulated in the past. Regret isn't going to do you any good in this journey, so it's best to leave those feelings of, "I wish I would have known this sooner," behind. All that you can do now is move forward, and we are going to help you on every step of the way!

Chapter 1: An Overview to Dark Psychology versus Normal Psychology

What Is Normal Psychology?

Normal psychology, otherwise called basic psychology, or simply psychology, is a study of the mind and behavior. Psychology (Greek - soul; Greek - knowledge) is a science that studies the behavior and mental processes of people and animals. The psyche is the highest form of the relationship of living beings with the objective world, expressed in their ability to realize their motives and act on the basis of information about him. Through the psyche, a person reflects the laws of the world. This is what psychology aims to understand.

Thinking, memory, perception, imagination, sensation, emotions, feelings, inclinations, temperament - all these moments are studied by psychology. But the main question remains - what drives a person, his behavior in a particular situation, what processes does their inner world entail? The range of issues addressed by psychology is wide enough. So, in modern psychology there are a large number of sections:

- General psychology

- Age-related psychology,

- Social psychology,

- Psychology of religion,

- Pathophysiology

- Neuropsychology,

- Family psychology

- Sports psychology, etc.

Other sciences and branches of scientific knowledge (genetics, speech therapy, jurisprudence, anthropology, psychiatry, etc.) penetrate into psychology. In order to live in harmony with himself and with the world around him, modern man needs to master the basics of psychology.

Psychology operates with the following methods:

1.) **Introspection** - observation of one's own mental processes, cognition of one's own life.

2.) **Observation** - the study of certain characteristics of a process without active involvement in the process itself.

3.) **Experiment** - an experimental study of a specific process. An experiment can be built on the modeling of activities in specially defined conditions or can be carried out in conditions close to ordinary activities.

4.) **Development study** - the study of certain characteristics of the same set of people (children, a tribe, etc.), which are monitored for several years.

As a science, psychology originated in the second half of the 19th century, having separated from philosophy and physiology. Psychology explores the mechanisms of the psyche unconscious and conscious of man.

A person turns to psychology in order to know himself and better understand his loved ones. Such knowledge is essential in seeing and realizing true motives of their actions. Psychology is also called the science of the soul, which at certain points in life begins to ask questions - "who am I?", "Where am I?", "Why am I here?" Why does a person need this knowledge and awareness? To stay on the road of life and not fall in one ditch, then in another. And having fallen, find the strength in yourself to rise and move on.

Interest in this field of knowledge is growing. By training the body, athletes necessarily come to psychological knowledge and expand it. Psychology is actively pouring into training and education, into business, into art.

A man is not only a storehouse of certain knowledge and skills but also a person with his own emotions, feelings, ideas about this world.

Today, knowledge of psychology is indispensable either at work or at home. To sell yourself or a product, you need certain knowledge. In order to have well-being in the family and be able to resolve conflicts, knowledge of psychology is also necessary. Understanding the motives of people's behavior, learning to manage their emotions, being able to build relationships, being able to convey their thoughts to the interlocutor - and here psychological knowledge will come to the rescue. Psychology begins where a person appears and, knowing the basics of psychology, many mistakes in life can be avoided. "Psychology is the ability to live."

What Is Dark Psychology?

We define Dark Psychology as the art and science focusing on mind control and manipulation. Psychology, as a general term, aims at studying and understanding human behavior. It is focused on our thoughts, actions, and the way we interact with each other. Dark psychology, however, just focuses on the kinds of thoughts and actions that are predatory in nature. Dark psychology examines the tactics used by malicious people to motivate, persuade, manipulate, or coerce others into acting in ways that are beneficial to themselves, and potentially detrimental to the other person.

The best definition for dark psychology is that it is the study of a human status in its connection to the people's psychological nature to prey upon other people. The entire humanity possesses a certain potential to victimize not only their fellow human beings but also other living creatures. Whereas, other individuals who might want to sublimate or restrain this kind of tendency, there are also others who opt to act upon some of these impulses. What dark psychology seeks to achieve is to make one understand those perceptions, feelings, and thoughts that end up leading to the predatory behavior of human beings. Dark psychology assumes this type of production is done for a given purpose and contains certain goal-oriented and rational motivation nearly all the time. The remaining portion of this time is essentially the dangerous victimization of other people with no purposive intent. In other words, we can perceive and define it by both religious doctrine and evolutionary science.

The point of dark psychology, as a subject, is to try to understand those thoughts, feelings, and perceptions that cause people to behave in predatory ways towards each other. Experts in dark psychology work under the assumption that the vast majority of human predatory actions are purposeful. In other words, most individuals who prey on others (99.99%) do it for specific reasons, while the remaining people (0.01%) do it for no reason at all.

The assumption is that when people do evil things, they have specific motivations, some of which may even be completely rational from their point of view. People do bad things with specific goals in mind and specific rationales for their actions, and only a tiny fraction of the population brutally victimizes others without a purpose that can be reasonably explained by either evolutionary science or some form of religious dogma.

You have heard many times that everyone has a dark side. All cultures and belief systems acknowledge this dark side to some extent. Our society refers to it as "evil" while some cultures and religions have gone so far as to create mythical beings to whom they attribute that evil (the devil, Satan, demons, etc.). Experts in dark psychology posit that there as some among us who commit the worst kinds of evil, for purposes that are unknown. While most people may do evil things to gain power, money, retribution, or for sexual purposes, there are those who do evil things because that's just who they are. They commit acts of horror for absolutely no reason. In other words, their ends don't justify their means; they cause harm for its own sake.

Dark psychology is rooted in 4 dark personality traits. These traits are; narcissism, Machiavellianism, psychopathy, and sadism. People with such traits tend to act in ways that are pointlessly harmful to others.

The skills and methods of influencing others can be quite different. They can be used both for constructive purposes and for various frauds. The characteristics of those who manage to influence people, no matter what is the "dark" in the dark psychology name.

People who successfully use dark psychology have understood fully all aspects of normal psychology. Thus, they understand themselves as well as others around them. They easily analyze others with this skill. They perceive the views, opinions and other information from those whom they wish to influence. Such a skill can be developed independently, and you will learn all about this in subsequent chapters.

Certain stories of deception of citizens with the help of dark psychology, like those that were told at the beginning of the book, were perceived as exotic, and the victims of this deception were considered unlimited simpletons. The bulk of fraudulent "exploits" using dark psychology as a special state of the psyche was not associated at all: the victim of dark psychological influence simply could not find an explanation for what happened.

As has been noted more than once, the specifics of dark psychology makes the active user "process" the client in a roundabout way. He does not give direct commands to do this or that but encourages a person to do it as if he is acting on his own initiative. The person comments, asks, consults and - gets his way.

Behind his behavior is a certain strategy. One of them is speculation. The phrase stands in such a way that some phenomenon, action or object is presented in it as if it was actually accepted. For example, they ask you: "Will you pay in dollars or bitcoins?" The question is innocent, but you have not yet said that you intend to purchase this thing at all. The question assumes that you have already made such a decision and it remains to solve the trifle - to pay in bitcoins or dollars, about which you begin to reflect.

I suppose that what was read caused the reader an ironic smile: a primitive ploy, visible, as they say, with the naked eye. Do not rush to conclusions. Let me remind you that the "seller" has already adjusted to you and leads you, your consciousness is no longer as critical as when reading these lines. This is the basis of analyzing people first, then thinking steps ahead of them, even about their own actions and reactions.

The essence of this technique is as follows: the dark psychologist makes up the text of the suggestion, and then "dissolves" it in a story of neutral content. During the conversation, the "user" in some way selects the words of suggestion and they turn out to be a brilliant trap for consciousness. He (or she) will change the volume of speech, pause in characteristic places, speed up or slow down the story.

There are other tools for highlighting words and phrases in order to consolidate them in the subconscious. The "user" can emphasize the right places in the story with gestures, facial expressions, touching your arm, shoulder, back. He can approach you sharply, turn around, turn away, etc. All these manipulations, if you follow them, are the basis of dark psychology. Now let's think about how often this is done to us against our will. And how this new knowledge is about to turn your life around. But first, it is worth considering the various personality types you should get ready to come across…

Understanding the Dark Triad and What It Means

This is a very important concept because it is going to help tie together some of the other aspects that we have discussed Dark Psychology. The name "dark triad" may sound like something that comes from a horror movie, but it is actually a legitimate psychological concept that is well recognized.

The dark triad is nothing more than an identification system for the three most destructive and harmful psychological personality traits a person can have. This chapter will take some time to detail each of the traits, including narcissism, psychopathy, and Machiavellianism. Let's take a look at each part and see what it means when it comes to dark psychology.

What Is Machiavellianism?

The first aspect of the Dark Triad that we will discuss is known as Machiavellianism. This aspect gets its name from the political philosopher known as Machiavelli. In his classical work "The Prince," the ideas, principles, and tactics that are used by those who seek to influence others are outlined. But how exactly does a Machiavellian person come across?

The hallmarks of this trait include a willingness to focus on your self-interest all the time, an understanding of the importance of your image, the perception of appearance, and even the ruthless exercise of power and cruelty rather than using mercy or compassion.

To keep it simple, people who have this trait are ones who always have a strategy when they approach life. The consequences and any ramifications about any action are going to be thought out and then assessed in terms of how they are going to impact the one who is carrying them out. The Machiavellian approach to the world is summed up with a simple question: "How will this action benefit me, and how will my public perception be impacted as a result?"

Machiavellian people are going to be masters of doing what is going to personally serve them well, while still being able to maintain the good public image that they want. This allows the manipulator to do what they want, while still getting people around them to still like them.

What Is Psychopathy?

The net aspect that we can discuss is psychopathy. This is going to refer to a psychological condition that involves a superficial charm, impulsivity, and a lack of commonly held human emotions, such as remorse and empathy. Someone who exhibits enough of these traits can be known as a psychopath. These individuals are seen as some of the most dangerous people because they are able to hide their true intentions, while still causing a lot of trouble.

People often associate the word "psychopath" with an image of someone who is mad and wields a machete. The reality is different, and this can make it more deadly. A true psychopath is more likely to be that charming and handsome stranger who is able to win over their victim before they ruin those victims' lives in the process.

Interestingly, some of the top people in business score high on psychopathy personality tests. But as time goes on, it is becoming more common to see psychopathy as more of a problem to the victim and to society rather than an issue in the psychopath's own life. Psychopaths are able to get to the top of anything that they choose because they don't have to worry about some of the compassionate indecision that other humans are going to experience.

What Is Narcissism?

The third aspect of the Dark Triad that we need to explore is narcissism. This is often thought of as the idea that a person loves themselves too much. This is close but quite the right definition for someone who is a narcissist. You can have self-love without being considered a narcissist.

Someone who is considered a narcissist is likely to have a range of traits that are there. They will have an excessively inflated self-worth, such as seeing that their life is extra special and one of the most important lives in all of history. If this has been inflated enough, they may see that they are the very most important in the whole world.

In the mind of a narcissist, they are not only special, but they are superior to everyone else. They consider themselves to be a better species of person, higher than what normal people would be. And because a narcissist believes this way, their behaviors are going to change. The behavior that you see in a narcissist is going to reflect the self-worth that the person has.

Some of the outward signs or manifestations of this aspect would include the inability of the person to accept any dissent or criticism of any kind. Even if they feel that someone is trying to criticize them, they are going to have a hard time dealing with this. This kind of person also feels the need to have others agree with them all the time and they like to be flattered. If you are around someone who seems to always have a need for constant praise, recognition, and approval, and if they seem to organize their lives in order to give them constant access to those who will fill this need, then it is likely that you are dealing with someone who is a narcissist.

These three aspects are going to come together to form the Dark Triad. When one person has all of these three traits in them, it can be a hard task to stay away and not get pulled into whatever plan they have. Being on the lookout for these can make a big difference in how much control you have in your own personal life.

Chapter 2: How to Use Dark Psychology to Manipulate Others

People around us may use dark psychology tactics every day to manipulate, influence, persuade and intimidate us to take advantage and get what they want. As you get to know that dark psychology includes the science and art of mind control and manipulation. Whereas psychology is different from dark psychology as it is the study of human behavior and our actions, interactions and thoughts are centered with them. Some people get confused and don't know the difference between psychology and dark psychology. However, if you want to manipulate others, you need to know how to use dark psychology.

Here are a different kind of people who know the tactics of manipulating others-

a) Manipulation is an art and you need to know the tactics to meet your needs first, even at someone else's expense. Though these kinds of people are known to be self-centered, and they are good when it comes to manipulating and intimidating others. These people are not bothered with the outcomes but they have an agenda of self before others, no matter what.

b) People who are good public speakers use dark psychological and persuasion tactics to maximize the emotional state of the listeners which leads to increase in the sale of their product (whatever they were selling to the audience). These people also know the moment and time of taking advantage of the emotional turmoil's of other people.

c) Some people meet clinical diagnosis, as they are true sociopaths. However, these people usually are intellectual, alluring but alongside they are impulsive. Just because these people do not have much ability to feel remorse and lack of emotionality, they build a superficial relationship and take advantage of innocent people by using dark tactics. They are not concerned about anyone's feelings and are least bothered with what others might do once the innocents know about their true face.

d) People in politics (usual politicians) use dark tactics to persuade people that they will do the needful and perform the activities in favor of the common people just to get a vote and to become the ruling party.

e) Some lawyers or attorneys focus solely on winning their case regardless of knowing the truth and even after knowing the truth, using dark manipulating tactics to get the outcome of what they want to win the case. They are not bothered about justice but are only concerned about their reputation and self-esteem.

f) People in corporate offices who are in a higher position and deployed as the companies regional head use dark psychological tactics to get compliance, higher performance, or greater efforts from their subordinates. They are not cared about 'what their subordinates deserve' or 'is their salary justified as per the work they are performing within the organization'.

g) People who are involved in the sales department are usually well aware of many of these dark influencing tactics to persuade and convince other people to buy whatever they are selling. They could even disguise the customers, as they are only concerned with selling their product and earning a profit.

Now that you got to know about different types of people who may deceit you by using these dark tricks, here are the different dark psychological tactics to manipulate the people and make them do what you want them to do-

1) If you want to sell your product and wish to manipulate your customers to make them surely buy your product, you can use a decoy option. You can use it as the third option. For example, if you are facing a troublesome situation to sell the more expensive of two products, by adding the third option you can make the expensive product more captivating and appealing. You just need to make sure that decoy option should be the same price for the more expensive option but assuring that it is less effective. It is a good strategy to increase the sale and enticing more customers towards your expensive product.

2) To win an argument, speak quickly so that the opponent has no other option left but to agree with you. If you speak faster, it will give the other person the less time to process what you are saying and they will agree with you. While you should do the opposite in case when the other person agrees with you, speaking slowly is better as it will give them the time to evaluate and analyze what you are saying.

3) You can copy the body language of people whom you want to manipulate. Imitating their body actions shall impress them and will make you closer to them and they may start liking you. If you subtly imitate the way the other person is talking, sitting, and walking, they would probably not notice that you are copying them and it may get them to do as per your wants.

4) Scaring the other people to make them give you what you want and need is one of the dark psychological tactics to manipulate people. Anxious people often respond positively to requests afterward as they may be occupied thinking about the danger they are surrounded with. It would make them feel scared and would do as your saying. In addition, sometimes, even if you will not say anything they will understand what you need and do what you would have spoken them to do for you.

5) To get people to behave ethically with you, you need to display an image of eyes. It means you should create your image as a person who watches, notice and observe the other person by posting a picture of eyes nearby. The other people could never take you like a side option and will return all borrowed items on time.

6) Tweak such an environment for the people so that they would act less selfish. For example, if you were bargaining in a coffee shop, needless to say, you would be less aggressive as compared to what you would be in a conference room. Usually, people tend to act less selfish when neutral items surround them, whereas if work-related objects occupy them, they incline towards more aggression and selfishness.

7) Try to keep your point complicatedly and do not make it very easy for the people to understand in a first move. To comply with people with your request, confuse them. For example- instead of keeping a price tag of your product for 4 dollars, make it 400 pennies, so that

people would first analyze how much dollars would 400 pennies make and if they bargain they will do that in pennies rather than in dollars. Or they may just think that the price given is a deal to go for.

8) If you help someone to achieve their goals or sort their problems out, the other person tends to return your favor, as they would feel obliged by what you have done for them. This way when the time comes, you may manipulate the other person and is one of the tactics.

9) Try to ask a question or request a person at a time when they are mentally drained and exhausted. They would never question the request or the chances of denial for your request are very less.

10) Always make the other person focus on their gaining not losing. Moreover, declare the price of your product at last after telling all the features and benefits of your product. For instance, if you are selling your car in 1000 dollars, always let the other person know about its features, specifications, and benefits first. Then declare its price. The benefits will entice the customer towards the car, and then the price shall not be a constraint.

11) Do not use verbs; try to use more nouns to change the behavior of the other person towards you. If you use nouns, it will reinforce the identity of the person for whom you may be using it. It will also indicate a specific group which shall be eloquent.

Chapter 3: Analyzing People through Body Language

Body Language Clues: The Basics

When you try to know more about your goal and how they view the world, body language is going to be so crucial. Too many times we get caught in the words that someone else tells us and we won't concentrate on the other indications they also give us. There is so much that can be disclosed by these body language clues, and it makes a large difference how effective you are in understanding and working with your goals.

Body language will refer to some of the nonverbal signals we use to interact with others. These nonverbal signals will take up much of the interaction we communicate every day. From the movement of our body to our facial expressions and everything in between, things we don't say can still share a ton of information during the process. Indeed, 60 to 65% of our interaction could be accounted for by body language and other nonverbal communications. So how do we learn to read this language to our own advantage? Let's begin by learning more about the various indications of body language, and how we can read this for our benefit. First off we have the facial expressions.

Think of a time, by the expression on your face, about how much data someone can convey. A smile is a nice way to show happiness or consent. A frown can imply the other way around. In some instances, facial expressions can show our real emotions about a scenario. While an individual may say he's okay, he looks like he's talking when he says this might talk otherwise. There are many feelings on our facial expressions, including:

1. Contempt

2. Desire

3. Excitement

4. Confusion

5. Fear

The expression that appears on the person's face helps us to determine if we trust and think anything the person says. In reality, one research discovered that the most credible of all facial expressions will be a small eyebrow raise and a slight smile. This is an expression that in many instances shows us to trust and friendliness.

The other type of body language cue will have to be the mouth. Mouth expressions and motions can be another vital component of body language reading. For instance, if you notice someone else chewing on his bottom lip, it may show that there are feelings of insecurity, fear, and worry. The individual can cover his mouth to be polite when he coughs, but sometimes the other person's disapproval. And smiling will be one of the best signals of corporeal language, but the smile and what it says about a person can be evaluated differently. Some of the stuff you can care about when reading someone else's mouth movements include;

- Pursed lips: If you see your goal tightened up, it's a sign of distrust, disagreement, and disgust.

- Lip biting: This is when you bite your lower lip, usually when you are stressed, anxious, or distressed.

- Mouth cover: Any moment someone wishes to conceal one of their emotional responses, they can cover their mouths in order to assist.

- Turned up or down: Even a slight shift in your mouth can be a subtle indication of how you feel right now. When your mouth turns up, it's a sign that you are hopeful or glad. It could be a grimace, disagreement, and even sorrow when the mouth turns down.

Another area to observe as body language cue is gestures. Gestures can be a very evident, direct sign of body language to be careful about. Waiving, pointing and fingering can be common and easy to understand gestures. Some may even be cultural. Some of the most popular gestures and the significances that come with them include:

- A clung fist: In most cases, this will show anger, but sometimes it can also imply solidarity.

- Up or down thumbs: This is used as a sign of approval and disapproval.

- The "all correct" gesture: This one will assist others to say you're fine in the United States. But it is seen in some other cultures as a vulgar gesture.

The next thing we have to do is look at the arms and legs of the individual you talk to. These can be useful if a lot of information is to be transmitted nonverbally. Crossing the weapons will often be a defensive maneuver. Crossing the legs away from another individual will also show a person's discomfort or a dislike.

Other subtle signals, including the large expansion of the arm, can sometimes help us to seem bigger and more comfortable while maintaining the arms close to the body. When you try to measure your body language a little, be careful about some of the following signals that your legs and arms will transmit to you from the target:

- Crossed arms: This will give you a signal that you're closed, safe and defensive. As a manipulator, you need to uncross the arms of the goal to make you feel comfortable.

- Standing on hips with your hands: This can be a good sign that the person is ready and controlled. This will sometimes be a sign of aggression.

- Clamp the hands so that they're behind the back: This will be a sign that your goal is angry, anxious or boring. You have to look at some of the other signals that come first.

- Tap fingers or fidgeting quickly: The other person is frustrated, impatient and even bored.

- Crossed legs: This is a good indication that someone feels closed or needs some privacy.

Posture is another thing you should look at. The way we hold our bodies will also be a significant component of body language. Posture refers to the way we hold our bodies and to a person's general physical shape. Posture can give a wealth of data on how someone feels and also suggests that a person's features are submissive, open or confident.

For instance, if you sit directly, it can show that an individual is concentrated and is attempting to look after what is going on. Sitting down with the body, on the other side, will show that someone is most of the time indifferent or bored. Looking at your goal will assist you to understand whether you are interested in what you do or say, or if you need to move on to find a different destination.

Whenever you attempt to read some of the languages of your body, attempt and find out some signals that your goal's position is attempting to tell you. Some of them are:

- Open posture. Open posture. This includes keeping the body's trunk exposed and open. This sort of

- Closed position: this one will require hiding the body's trunk and hitting the legs and arms. This posture will be more indicative of anxiety, discomfort, and depression in the objective.

Chapter 4: Emotional Intelligence

Emotional intelligence also referred to as emotional leadership or emotional quotient, is the ability of certain people to realize their emotions, as well as those of others, differentiate them, label, and readily manage or adjust depending on the situation or environment. These people typically remain calm despite the changes in the surrounding or negative impacts associated with a given case. Besides, they may apply the capability to help those affected by awkward feelings, therefore, making them feel at peace. Emotional intelligence is psychological, where one understands and handles any kind of emotion with ease while remaining calm.

Over the years, the definition of emotional intelligence was broken down into four sections: perceiving, utilizing, learning, and managing. The four abilities were all attributed to emotional intelligence with relative meanings behind them. Different models were created using these abilities, therefore, facilitating how thoughts and understanding of emotions interact. Studies show that people with more emotional intelligence tend to succeed more in various areas, including academics, careers, and talents. The ability has also been associated with providing great leadership and higher performance at work. More so, researchers agree that these people are healthy mentally as well as on their standard personality traits.

Since the introduction of emotional intelligence, different studies have been conducted with the objective of determining the actual factors driving an individual to manage emotions. Most of us react to varying feelings to some extent, depending on the severity or fun in it. However, higher emotional intelligence people have the ability to manage these emotions and have a minimal impact on their lives, even on extensive influences of a situation. With different groups of people, emotional intelligence has been seen to have different implications on the thoughts of these individuals. For instance, children and teens with high emotional intelligence tend to have good social interaction while those having lower abilities have the opposite. Adults with high emotional intelligence accompany an excellent self-perception socially while those with low emotional intelligence tend to become aggressive.

Features of Emotional Intelligence

Show of Authenticity

High emotional intelligence people, especially those who are more social, tend to stick to their principles and values. When sharing about themselves to others, they usually stand by their boundaries rather than sharing everything about themselves to others. As such, authenticity does not imply that you have to share all about yourself. However, you share about yourself to people who matter and those who understand you and appreciate your thoughts and feelings.

Demonstration of Empathy

These individuals tend to demonstrate empathy to people as they readily understand other people's feelings and thoughts. They, therefore, readily connect to others and agree on what is essential. Emotional intelligence enables them to develop more profound and more productive relationships with others. Instead of becoming judgmental and avoiding those who feel different, they comfort and make them feel important to society. Despite being empathetic, these people are cautious when it comes to decision making, therefore avoiding agreeing to every person's motive.

Apologetic and Forgiving

Another feature of emotional intelligence people is that they quickly understand their mistakes. They usually have the courage and strength to apologize even without errors, therefore, indicating value to a relationship. The same applies to forgive and forget, even in the most resentful situations. As such, having emotional intelligence provides a mind that readily forgives and free from your emotions from those who hurt you.

Being Helpful

As emotional intelligence entails understanding and managing your emotions and that of others, then helping them becomes part of what the ability accompanies. As one of the most significant rewards to others, helping becomes a habit to these people, and they never tire or discriminate against others. However, they help each person in need without asking too many questions. As such, it helps those who follow similar footsteps as well as building trust among people to help others.

Always Thinking About Feelings

Emotional intelligence primarily dwells on one's feelings which often change suddenly or slowly depending on the situation or environment. When an individual has a higher emotional intelligence capability, then he or she frequently thinks about different feelings and how it may impact others. They usually ask about common questions regarding their self-awareness, reflecting on everyday activities, and people who may be influenced by their emotions. As such, systematic thinking and learning about emotions provide insights used to their advantage in managing their feelings and that of others.

Benefit from Criticism

Nobody experiences fun when it comes to negative feedback, especially from people you trust and those close to you. However, these types of reputation are quite effective in life as they teach you a few lessons about a particular aspect. Besides, it enables you to learn more about how others think mainly about you and things to change and become better in what you do. Receiving these negative feedbacks may become a challenge to others, but those with the ability to check their emotions benefit a lot. With the use of emotional intelligence, these people can learn to manage their emotions and move around calmly without focusing on the thoughts of others.

Managing Emotions

People with Low Emotional Intelligence

When low emotional intelligence people are faced with any negative emotion, they tend to become violent or rather more reactive when compared to those with high emotional intelligence. For instance, when an individual with low emotional intelligence faces negative criticism, they may initially go into denial and withdraw from a given group to avoid shame. They become lonely and prevent any form of help offered towards them. In some cases, others may opt to use substances to keep their minds active and evade others and what they are feeling. Others may harm themselves by cutting, starving, purging, or engaging in dangerous behaviors. The primary drive to these activities is influenced by a lack of control of emotions which are usually hurting, such as criticism

People with High Emotional Intelligence

High emotional intelligence people have all it takes to absorb and express reasonably about how they feel about a particular sensation. For instance, when these group people are offended, they would initially pause before acting and think what their next word or rather the best harmless action to take. They would also acknowledge what the next person is feeling or have in mind before deciding on providing their contribution or conclusion of what will become. Thinking first is usually their first step to prevent escalating the problem or causing more harm to themselves and others. Another critical aspect of high emotional intelligence people is helping themselves and people affected by a given emotion. In this case, high emotional intelligence people act entirely different when compared to low emotional intelligence individuals.

Emotional Quotient (EQ) Vs. Intelligence Quotient (IQ)

Emotional Quotient, EQ, is the ability of an individual to readily learn, understand, handle, and control his or her emotions even in the most resentful situations. On the other hand, Intelligence Quotient, IQ, is the measure of one's intelligence usually expressed in a number. EQ enables an individual to focus on emotions which, in turn, acts as a management system to different emotions which may become harmful to others. More so, it involves other people's emotions, and an individual can readily manage these emotions without the need to sympathize. IQ measures the degree of intelligence calculated from standardized tests created to analyze human intelligence.

Components of Emotional Intelligence

Emotional intelligence is linked to different internal components of a person usually within the brain, which determines how one understands and controls emotions. In most cases, people who lack control of their emotions have been associated with mental problems. While others stating that lack of emotional control is attributed to the extent of the immediate feeling at hand. However, emotional intelligence has been proven to exist among different individuals and comprises the following components.

Self-Awareness

This is the ability to recognize and learn about your emotions as well as understanding the effects accompanied by your feelings. Becoming self-aware is determined by being able to monitor emotions, realizing emotional reactions, and identifying each emotion independently. Besides, you readily understand and figure out the interaction between your emotions and how you behave when that feeling occurs. That is, when you are an emotionally intelligent individual, you become aware of several aspects about yourself and others while keeping in mind about what is wrong and right. You can readily make a choice to do wrong or wicked despite how sad, angry, or hopeless you become.

Self-awareness also builds the ability to determine the strengths and limitations for quick development of measures to avoid negative impacts to an individual and to others. As a person, you can get access to new information and personal skills; therefore, you learn from others. People with a sense of self-awareness are usually humorous, confident, and aware of the perception of others. More so, they understand what it means to be emotional despite being an everyday behavior. As among the primary components of emotional intelligence, self-awareness provides a complete guide to an individual to quickly learn what to do when facing a given emotion, which may harm both them and another person when mishandled.

Self-Regulation

Another significant component of emotional intelligence is self-regulation, which entails the regulation and management of emotions. After becoming self-aware of your feelings and the accompanying impacts to others and yourself, you are required to have a governing force that enhances how you react during these situations. However, it does not imply that an individual has to lock away his or her real emotions and hide how they feel about others, but they should express them in an organized manner. That is, regulating how you express your feelings in an appropriate time and place.

People skilled in self-regulation are mostly flexible and quickly adapt to change as well as excellent in settling disagreements among people and diffusion of tension. More so, they are high in conscientiousness, thoughtful, and take responsibility for their doings. As a component of emotional intelligence, self-regulation plays a significant role in enabling an individual to quickly manage and handle all types of feelings, either positive or negative, without influencing others negatively.

Social Skills

Emotional intelligence also comprises of social skills which are the ability to interact with others correctly. Learning about your feelings and that of others, and being able to control is not enough to develop your emotional intelligence. Then, there is a need to implement these abilities into actions when interacting with others daily. When you indulge in daily communication with others and put into action this information, then you are at the forefront in managing your feelings and that of others. For example, managers in businesses have utilized the knowledge of social skills to interact with workers and clients, thus benefiting significantly in their careers.

Empathy

Empathy is the capability of comprehending other individual's feelings. It is also vital to emotional intelligence but provides more insight to an individual rather than recognizing the emotions of others. Empathy involves realizing emotions as well as reactions to these emotions, which primarily encompasses the help needed. For example, if someone is hopeless, sad, or emotional dependent, you are likely to sense these emotions and respond accordingly as if they are yours. You tend to provide extra care and concern, allowing other people to recognize power dynamics that influence relationships. Therefore, emotional intelligence enables you to become empathetic to others and give the needed support.

Intrinsic Motivation

Unlike others, people with emotional intelligence abilities are rarely motivated by external rewards, for example, richness, fame, or acclaim. These people usually work to meet their personal needs and objectives. They seek to ensure their internal satisfaction which, in turn, leads to rewarding their inner needs. Such individuals remain action-oriented by creating goals that are of higher standards and work to achieve. Also, they remain committed to performing their duties entirely when needed without failure. As such, the motivation allows for the achievement of essential goals in nearly everything they engage in no matter the complexity of the situation.

More Emotional People

More emotional people tend to have low emotional intelligence and therefore, become very reactive, especially on negative emotions. In this case, these people usually lack self-awareness, self-regulation, and other components of emotional intelligence. When someone is regarded as a more sensitive person, the chances are that they may become very reactive on occasions such as anger and become violent. When sad, they may end up becoming stressed, lonely, and eventually, being depressed. This group of people may, however, have some ability to control some of their emotions but limited knowledge about how they react to a given situation.

More emotional people may, at times, face difficulties on how they interact publicly, henceforth, cannot sustain relationships. Some of the characteristic features of more emotional people include the inability to understand other people's emotions, getting into arguments quickly, blaming others for their mistakes, and lack of empathy. Other features include difficulty sustaining friends, sudden outbursts of emotions, refusal to listen to other's views, and thinking people are usually oversensitive. More emotional people typically have no control over how they express their feelings or emotions. Therefore, they become too dependent on themselves without minding others.

Less Emotional People

Less emotional people are those individuals with the ability to control their emotions or feelings even when they are profound or negative. These individuals usually have a much higher emotional intelligence when compared to more emotional people. As highlighted above, less emotional people have the ability to suppress their emotions even in the states where these emotions seem unbearable. They may look calm and in peace even after a hurtful event. More so, they are relaxed and understanding and interact well with the general public, mainly with friends, family, and those close to them, such as coworkers.

When in an emotional state, for instance, these individuals typically respond to issues rather than react and understand the matter at hand. They are equipped with the five components of emotional intelligence as well as self-control and handle situations with their related selves. When faced with a more challenging situation, less emotional people rarely complain but work to find ways of solving the problem, which, in most cases, succeed with limited failure possibilities. As typical human beings, however, less emotional people also undergo similar impacts of negative emotions, but due to their emotional intelligence abilities, they readily get in control of their feelings and find ways to handle these situations without causing scenes.

Emotional Intelligence History

Emotional intelligence, the ability to control emotions, originally began in 1964, where Michael Beldoch wrote the term 'Emotional Intelligence' in the paper. In 1966, another article by B. Leuner, *Emotional Intelligence and Emancipation* also featured the term 'Emotional Intelligence.' Howard Gardner again mentioned the term in 1983 with an effort to describe IQ and other related types of intelligence. In this case, Gardner stated that various kinds of human IQ at the time failed to detail cognitive ability which, henceforth, introduced emotional intelligence in his study. Subsequently, the term began being used in multiple papers, journals, and thesis such as *A Study of Emotions: Developing Emotional Intelligence* written by Wayne Payne in 1985.

The term 'Emotional Quotient, EQ' surfaced in 1987 in an article written by Keith Beasley, which introduced a similar meaning to emotional intelligence. In the late 1980s, different models emerged to prove emotional intelligence in the context of controlling human feelings. Among them include the one created by Stanley Greenspan in 1989, another by Peter Salovey, and John Mayer in 1990. The term began becoming among the most commonly used. In 1995, the book, *Emotional Intelligence- Why It Can Matter More Than IQ* by Goleman, was published.

As such, the term became more popular in the 1990s with several models being developed by different scientists. However, emotional intelligence, like most findings, has received several critics, especially on its role in the business sector and the development of leadership skills. More advanced research in emotional intelligence entails the trait and ability of emotional intelligence. Trait emotional intelligence remains considered as a generic behavior passed from parents to offspring. Ability emotional intelligence is the practice learned by an individual, henceforth, gaining the technique of controlling their own emotions.

Chapter 5: Importance of Emotional Intelligence

Emotional Intelligence is linked to various aspects in one's life if not all. It can, therefore, be said that it can be linked to our careers, job performance, and even our success. The following are, therefore, the various ways which have depicted the importance of emotional intelligence:

Emotional Intelligence and Job Performance

Recently, there has been a rise in emotional intelligence awareness in management-focused literature together with leadership training summits. This gives us an indication that there exists a very strong relationship between job performance and emotional intelligence. It not only proves to exist but also has depicted an array of value in different areas. One's workplace is a representation of a social community that is very separate from their personal lives. This is also a place where increased appreciation of emotional intelligence has been on the rise allowing people to have an understanding of themselves and even others, be conversant with hard situations and communicating in a more effective manner. This, therefore, means that employing emotional intelligence at your workplace might greatly improve your personal and even other individuals' social capabilities.

Emotional Intelligence entails management of emotions which improves job performance, which in turn helps people to stay calm and think logically thus establishing good working relationships and achievement of goals. Apart from that, there is an evident relationship between emotional intelligence and how senior employees manage their juniors. A manager who has got a high emotional intelligence is well conversant with the stress management skills and also how recognize and manage the stress in other people. Therefore, if we put emotional intelligence in the stress management perspective, then the relationship between job performance and emotional intelligence is crystal clear. This is because one's commitment to their job is highly and positively impacted by stress management.

In many instances, emotional intelligence usually applies to all kinds of employees and not only those at the management level. The employees that are at the lower rank in the hierarchy of an organization and have a high emotional intelligence usually have got desires and abilities to establish and maintain good relationships at the workplace. Apart from that, these individuals are good in management and resolution of conflicts. This, therefore, means that they have the capability of sustaining relationships that exists in the workplace as compared to those with either low or moderate emotional intelligence. In the current job market, many organizations are undergoing revolution and changes in different sectors. This has made organizations to have the need of employees who can easily cope up with these changes and respond to them easily. This indicates that emotional intelligence is an important factor in job performance in both group and individual levels. This thus clearly describes the way in which emotional intelligence is of value.

Emotional Intelligence and Resilience

Emotional intelligence has proved to be a valuable tool in adversity as it has the potential of enhancing not only teamwork effectiveness and leadership abilities but it is also an important tool in enhancing personal resilience. The impact of emotional intelligence on the resilience of a person is the ability of that person to cope up with situations that are stressful. It has been clearly demonstrated by research that a person who has got high emotional intelligence usually easily overcome stressors and their negative impacts.

Focusing on leadership, a leader is usually expected to have increased responsibilities which usually are accompanied by potential stressors. In such a case, it is important for the person to have strong emotional intelligence in order to be resilient and battle with these stressful conditions. From research where investigations were done into the link existing between emotional intelligence and stress, it was found out that people who showed high emotional intelligence levels were not negatively affected by stressors. These participants did an emotional intelligence ability-based test before the threat level that was posed by the two stressors was rated. After that, they reported their emotional reactions the stressors before being subjected to physiological stress to also assess their responses. The findings of this research showed that emotional intelligence has a relationship with lower threats. This study, therefore, provides us with a valid prediction that stress resilience is facilitated by emotional intelligence.

From further research done, the relationship between high levels of emotional intelligence, the tendency to depressive behaviors and resilience was drawn. It was established that there was a positive correlation that exists between mindfulness, self-compassion, and resilience with the rate of burnout. In conclusion, individuals who have got high emotional intelligence levels were more resilient and could not easily fall into depression or burnout. Emotional intelligence has a strong link to the individual's advancement and also their performance. Evidence also suggests that there is a significant link between their resilience and their motivation to achieve. Apart from that, it also made a suggestion that resilience acts as a mediator between self-motivated achievement and resilience. Resilience, in this case, has got a perseverance component that acts as a motivation to motivation when facing obstacles. From the various research findings and theories, we have seen a strong relationship between emotional intelligence and resilience. We have clearly seen how one's emotional intelligence levels affect their resilience. This, therefore, has proved emotional intelligence to be very important.

Emotional Intelligence and Motivation

Emotional intelligence is a key component for motivation which in turn is very vital in the achievement of success. An emotionally intelligent person will always have an understanding of what they aspire and the necessary motivation skills that they would need to achieve these aspirations. There are four elements that are said to make up motivation; how we commit ourselves to the goals we set, how ready we are to utilize opportunities, self-drive to improve and how resilient we are. Motivation is said to be a psychological process that which we use to psyche ourselves into action in order to realize a desirable outcome. It doesn't matter the action we are doing, whether dedication of much time to work on a project or just changing the TV channel using a remote, without being motivated we cannot act.

This is because motivation energizes, arouses, sustains and directs performance and behavior. The motivation that usually comes from within, also known as intrinsic motivation usually drives us to the achievement of our full capability. A person who is emotionally intelligent has got both skills required to motivate themselves and those needed to motivate other people too. This is a very useful skill to possess especially if you are in a management position in your job. Self-motivation is the key to the achievement of one's goals. With self-motivation, emotionally intelligent people will always be capable of impacting the motivation of employees. The ability to determine the emotions and needs or concerns of others is a great skill to possess in relation to the determination of perfect methods of motivating individuals and teams.

From a study and research did, it was found out that the emotional intelligence of a first-year graduate was positively linked to their self-motivation to studying the respective course and choosing that course. Another study of senior employees with very high emotional intelligence found out that they are good in arguments, have good behavior and great work outcomes. It, therefore, means that a happy employee is a motivated employee. The capability to be conversant with anxiety and stress is a very useful emotional intelligence tool when it comes to motivation. From the above studies and research findings, it is clear that emotional intelligence plays a major role in one's motivation. Since motivation is a very vital tool in our actions, then emotional intelligence is also very important.

Emotional Intelligence and Decision-Making

Emotional intelligence plays a key role in both professional and personal development. It not only has an impact on the way in which we handle our behaviors and control our social complexities but also the approaches we take in decision-making. Having an in-depth understanding of the emotions you feel and the reason as to why you are feeling them can heavily impact your decision-making capabilities. This, therefore, means that if we carefully look into our emotions, then we can avoid making misleading and misguided decisions. Emotional intelligence is a very vital tool required in the prevention of making poor decisions based on our emotions whereby lower emotional intelligence can make you anxious and result in you making a poor misguided decision. This does not imply that we should keep emotions aside when making decisions but discovering these emotions which might not have any relationship with the problem and ensuring that they do not influence the decision that you are going to make. Negative emotions can be a stumbling block to decision making and problem-solving in either your workplace or even personal circumstances. Being able to recognize emotions that are becoming a stumbling block to making rational decisions and being able to effectively ignore the emotions will prevent their negative influence on your decision. This, therefore, means that decision making at this stage will be much favored as it will not be negatively influenced in any way.

From research done through observations and administering a series of questions, it was discovered that people and organizations reaped big benefits from a practical application of emotional intelligence in making decisions. This study had the aim of improving emotional intelligence awareness and how emotional intelligence skills can be employed in decision making. From the observations, it was discovered that having training sessions on emotional intelligence is one of the most effective ways to incorporate decision-making skills and also helps you to understand the possible consequences of poor decision-making.

Having an understanding of the causes and possible consequences of emotions gives you the freedom to manage and make a decision about the feeling. For instance, if you have an argument with your spouse the go to work without resolving it you will probably stay angry the whole day. Being angry at work, your colleague might make an offer to you but you dismiss it without even paying attention to it. This is a kind of emotional interference that can be very dangerous to your decision-making. If you have high emotional intelligence, then you can be able to identify this form of emotional interference and manage it thus avoiding making decisions that are emotionally driven. This, therefore, means that emotional intelligence is vital when making decisions.

Emotional Intelligence and Success

There are things which mean different to different people. As happiness is so is a success which everyone has a different version of defining it. But no matter no success is defined, it is clear that emotional intelligence plays an important part in its achievement. From history, most intelligent individuals are usually not attributed to greatest successes. This is because IQ is not sufficient on its own to enable one to succeed in life. In regards to this, you can be the most intelligent person but if you lack emotional quotient, you may fail to turn down people with negative thoughts about you and even manage stress. This shows that emotional intelligence is sometimes even more powerful as compared to IQ in life success. Your emotional intelligence is the actual thing that helps you to achieve your life objectives and realize great successes. Therefore, developing emotional intelligence would influence your achievements through contribution to your morale, cooperation and most importantly motivation by a great margin. In a workplace, the managers and employees who perform well as compared to others usually employ strategies that are associated with emotional intelligence in the management of conflicts, reduction of stress and thus achieving their goals. In the recent past, there has been blooming evidence of a range of activities said to constitute emotional intelligence are now vital in determining success.

This refers to success both in the workplace and also one's personal life. It incorporates applications that we associate with in our daily lives in relationships, businesses, and even parenting. Emotional intelligence guides one to easily manage their emotions in situations that are likely to provoke anxiety. These situations include when taking examinations at the university. It is also positively associated with success in social functioning and personal relationships.

In social relationships, success achievable with the employment of emotional intelligence skills to determine other people's emotions, then adopt their emotional states and thus regulate the way they behave. This briefly shows how important emotional intelligence is in achieving success in the different spheres of life.

Emotional Intelligence and Communication

One's ability to have the knowledge and understanding of their emotions might aid them to be aware and understand the feelings that other people are experiencing. This has got an impact on the way in which we communicate in our daily lives.

Considering communication in conflict resolution in the workplace, people with great emotional intelligence levels would most probably approach the conflict in the most reasonable way possible and negotiate together with others to finally come up with a reasonable outcome. On the contrary, a person with lower levels of emotional intelligence will not be able to solve the conflict in a reasonable calm manner thus might even end up without a solution at the end.

In the workplace, relationships are usually affected by the manner in which we can manage our emotions and also understanding the emotions of those around us. The capability to do this helps us in communicating without necessarily resorting to confrontation. If you have high emotional intelligence, then it is beyond doubt that you are equipped with conflict management skills and thus you will be able to put up a meaningful relationship guaranteed capacity to understand and address needs of those they engage with.

In recent years, emotional intelligence has been able to receive much attention that drives effective communication within individuals and even teams. On close examination of emotional intelligence as a reason for team success, you will find that it does not only do it drives the viability of a team but also affects communication quality in a positive way.

Achievement of successful communication in relation to successful negotiation and conflict has a very close relationship with high emotional intelligence levels. In this case, individuals with lower emotional intelligence would be so defensive in such stressful situations. This will instead escalate the conflict instead of managing it. If you have high emotional intelligence, then this means that you have got the necessary skills to ensure effective communication without resulting in a confrontation. From this, we can easily derive the importance and great contribution that high levels of emotional intelligence add to the achievement of effective communication.

Emotional Intelligence and Happiness

Just like any other word or felling, happiness seems something easy but actually getting to understand it is when you will realize that it is a hard nut to crack. This is because different people have got different instances and experiences that they describe them to mean happiness to them. Truly, happiness means different to different people but undoubtedly, emotional intelligence is a great requirement to have despite the kind of interpretation you prefer. Happiness is an emotional intelligence facilitator that contributes to each and everyone's self-actualization which positively impacts our happiness.

From a study where the relationship between different interpersonal relations and emotional intelligence was examined, it was discovered that individuals with high emotional intelligence scored highly in self-monitoring, social skills and taking empathic perspective. Apart from that, they also scored highly in affectionate relationships, satisfaction in relationships, and cooperation with their partners.

Emotional intelligence skills are very important when it comes to reducing stress, thus, in turn, will positively impact on one's happiness and wellbeing in general. Apart from the motivational value that it possesses, happiness acts as a monitor to the wellbeing of an individual. It is also a source of a positive mood to the manner in which the person copes up and meets daily needs, pressures and challenges.

Positivity is what actually encourages the emotional energy required in the increment of an individual's motivational levels which is responsible for getting things done. It actually helps one to be successful in what they are doing and even gets to the extent of telling them the extent of success they are actually achieving. From a study done by Furnham, it was realized that a large section of variance that is evident in the wellbeing and happiness of a person is determined by their emotional intelligence levels. This refers to their ability to stabilize their emotions, social competence, and even relationship skills. Although these emotional intelligence skills are not the only source of one's happiness, it is very vital to realize that they contribute and impacts our happiness up to 50%. This, therefore, prove it to be a very vital thing which should always be put into consideration.

Happiness has, therefore, proven to be closely linked to emotional intelligence if the research and studies detailed above are to go by. A person with high emotional intelligence will have the necessary skills to dodge any obstructions that might act as a hindrance to happiness. On the other hand, an individual who has low levels of emotional intelligence will not be able to cope up with these obstructions and end up always sad and stressed up. This thus proves emotional intelligence to be vital.

Emotional Intelligence and Goals

In life, each and every person has got goals and achievements that they hope to achieve someday in life. In order to achieve these goals, there are various conditions that usually impact it either positively or negatively. In this case, emotional intelligence also plays a key role in the achievement of these goals. Emotional intelligence will drive you to realize self-actualization which requires you to first get motivated. In order to have the motivation, you will need to be happy with whatever you do. This is because lack of happiness will challenge you in pursuit of the motivational levels that are required to achieve your goals.

In order to realize success and eventually achieve your dreams and goals, there is a need to employ emotional intelligence skills. If you have high emotional intelligence levels, you will definitely perform excellently in what you are doing in all aspects. The effectiveness of a person or a team in a certain process directly reflects their emotional intelligence skill level. Those with high emotional intelligence levels will perform well while those with lower intelligence levels would perform dismally and might never achieve their goals.

If we want to produce best results in what we do and achieve the goals we might have set, then all we need is a positive self-regard, effective skills to solve problems, skills to make informed decisions and informed self-awareness. All these are directly attributed to one's emotional intelligence. This, therefore, means that our levels of emotional intelligence dictate if we will achieve our goals or not. Low emotional intelligence will see you fail and never achieve the set goals. On the other hand, high emotional intelligence levels with required emotional skills are very important and they will positively contribute to the achievement of your goals in life.

Chapter 6: Mind Control

Mind control sounds like a devious plot in a movie, but you have most likely experienced it many times a day for many years and never noticed it. Mind control, or the idea of thought-reform, is a controversial theory and practice, but one that does not necessarily mean tricking and scheming. As a matter of fact, mind control can be as simple as subliminal suggestion used to steer one in the direction you want rather than the direction they were going autonomously.

There are many schools of thought in regards to mind control, but for this book, let's look at a common example of mind control to start. Color, smell, sight, sound, and taste are used on the consumer by every company selling a product to advance their customers and sales. When you enter your local grocery store, often there are fresh cut flowers at the entrance. Now, how often have you bought those flowers? Chances are, never, if maybe a time or two because you forgot a special occasion. Grocers use the presence of these flowers as a means of manipulating the subconscious of their customers. Fresh cut flowers are, well, fresh. Ripe. Pleasant. They subliminally convey they thought of freshness, and your local grocery store wants you to be thinking about all the fresh produce they have waiting for you. More often, these grocers make more on the sale of their fresh produce over name brand canned and frozen produce, and if you buy the produce they have available, more of your dollars go in their pocket as opposed to mass production companies.

Every day, you are exposed to one form of mind control or another. Product placement on television and in movies. The music you hear in a store or even an elevator. Friends that are so convincing, you can't help but agree, or you find yourself always saying yes to them.

Re-education is a very optimal, but controversial tool in mind control. The ability to re-educate another person's previous thought process or beliefs is possible, but can take time. At the heart of re-education sits repetition. I repeat, repetition. By repeating the same belief, idea, or thought to another person, repeatedly, you are impressing upon them the change from their own ideas towards your own. And this repetition leads to immersion in the idea or action you want them to follow. Being immersed in an idea, the idea in question always being repeated, the idea or goal always being spoken of, leads to the individual re-examining their previous feelings about the issue. Re-examining one's feelings often leads to them coming to a new conclusion. Your conclusion. You have just exerted a form of mind control on another individual, and now they agree with you.

Priming an individual is another effective way to get what you want. Some who see this activity negatively may refer to in as indoctrination, but the goal is not to necessarily start a cult. You are just trying to get others to agree with you, and are trying to use all the available tools you possess to your advantage. Priming involves softening a person towards you and your ideas, easing them into the thought that you know what is best. Softening can include hours of conversation, empathizing with them and showing them that you care or love them. You care about what happens, you understand them. Once you have a foundation of trust through understanding and priming, soft persuasion towards the new idea, belief, or action can be introduced. It is imperative that you have formed a mutual bond or respect with the person who you want to influence. And it is a given that change takes time.

A few techniques to help you on your path to persuasion using coercion may involve thinking for others, being specific in your logic and requests, creating a real sense of urgency, and stressing the importance of your goal or idea. When presenting someone with a change in long held ideas or requests, thinking for them takes the pressure of deciding off them. People often have enough on their mental plates as it is, you shouldn't be asking them to take on more, especially when you can do the heavy lifting for them. Explain exactly why they should see things your way, offering as many examples as possible as to the correctness to your idea, proof that what you want is not only right, but it is proven to be effective or accurate. Once you have specifically lined out why they should agree with you, tell them what is next and why things need to be done your way. Be friendly but as firm and confident in your pitch to them as you need be, and often discouraging questions until you are finished explaining your stance helps steer others in your direction. They often forget their questions or objections as they listen to you explain what you want, why, and what you think needs to happen next to achieve the goal. It is all about the goal.

While on the topic of your goals and what you want to achieve, it is imperative to stress the importance of what you want to achieve. If others are consistently being spoken with on how important the idea or goal is, and specifics on why it is so important, eventually they start to see your idea as more than just something you want, but an issue of utmost importance. Your thought or goal becomes something more, and it should be more to you too. It should be a movement. A goal doesn't have to be a social ideal to be a movement, you just need others to feel its importance as much as you do. Everybody wishes to be on the right side of history, no matter how big or small the issue is. And all it takes is someone to see your want as a matter that needs to be addressed or adjusted, and where there is one person who agrees with you, there are two, and more soon to follow.

So, your idea, goal, or thought is now more than just something you want. Other people want it too. And it is not just important, it is imperative. And it needs to happen now. Creating a sense of urgency is another effective form of utilizing mind control techniques to your benefit. Making urgent statements, or claiming that this situation is time sensitive will create an emotional response in those you wish to influence or persuade. A specific deadline needs to be in place, but the idea that this can't wait long needs to be an underlying sentiment. The quicker you get other people on board, the more important you convince them your want is, the more urgent they believe things are, the less resistance you will run into. Repeating equals results. The more information backing your idea or goal people are given, the more likely they will let you think for them and just go with the flow. The more urgent the matter is, the less time people have to ask discouraging questions or second guess their shift in ideas.

Being consistent is the core aspect of implementing mind control techniques to get what you want. Consistently repeating what you want, and be consistent when rejecting old ideas or goals. Be consistent when speaking about what needs to happen, when and why. These factors should be underlined, in bold print, repeated regularly, and the time sensitivity need to be stressed.

There is nothing wrong with being a little pushy to get what you want out of your life. Another great technique when using mind control is to ask small things of others, or asking for small changes in another's ideas, and then expanding from there. Let's use a raise from your employer as an example. If you want a decent increase in pay, don't ask for your top dollar pay increase. Ask for a small increase in pay based on your performance and loyalty. Your boss will agree (considering you are worthy of the raise to begin with) and think that they got off cheap keeping you happy. After you have reached the first step in reaching your ultimate pay goal, ask for more work. Let your employer know you are more than happy taking on more responsibility. You can possibly save them money if you are doing more work than before, they may not have to hire another employee to work weekends if you are willing to come in for a few hours on a Saturday. Now, you have a pay increase, but you have more responsibility. It only seems fair that you are paid a little more now that you are a more valuable resource for your employer to utilize. It's better they give you another slight pay increase to cover your knowledge and expertise in the workplace than bother trying to hire another employee to replace you. You see how simple it can be? Now, that isn't saying that you have a boss or employer this would work on, but if you are implementing the other tools you have in your fast-growing arsenal, you are now a very well-liked employee and co-worker who knows how to influence and persuade others to see things the way you do. Your employer may dislike the idea of paying you even more than before, but sometimes it's not just your work ethic that matters, sometimes it's what you bring to the table for everyone you encounter.

It is not easy to say no to someone who you feel a debt to. The final technique of mood control we should consider is generosity. You should always strive to give more than you take from others. When you give more of your time, your effort, your attention, to others, they appreciate it. They remember it. And, when the moment comes that you want something in return, it is much harder to say no, or disagree, or refuse to cooperate with another who has freely offered up so much to them. Even in circumstances or changes others may not want to agree or get on board with, if they know that you have been offered the same courtesy by you previously, they find it hard to go against you. It falls back to persuasion, influence, and reciprocation. Most often, those that you have committed your time and attention to will return the favor. Even if you are met with resistance by someone who you have given to, a gentle reminder of what you have done for them is often all that is needed to get them on board with what you want. Sometimes it isn't the loudest voice in the room that matters, but the most consistent and softest from the individual who has done the most to help others. That soft but firm voice can be yours, you only need to take your opportunities as they present themselves.

Who uses mind control?

Media Producers

Just as our five senses are our guides in life, they can also be our enemies and traitors. Our sense of sight and the visual processing areas of the brain are very powerful. We almost always dream visually, even if another sense is missing, and we usually picture someone we are remembering rather than associating some other sensory input with them. This makes imagery and visual manipulation a particularly powerful technique of media mind control.

Traditionally, media production was in the hands of companies and institutions. These manipulative entities were able to pioneer the use of visual, subliminal mind control. Examples include split-second pictures of a product or person inserted into a seemingly innocent movie. Such split-second images, which the person perceives as nothing more than a flash of light, are able to take powerful control of a person's emotions. They have been used as recently as 21st century Presidential elections.

Sound is another way in which a person is vulnerable to undetected mind control. Both experiments and personal experience will confirm this to you. Have you ever loved a song until it stuck in your head? How easy was it to get rid of? The sound had a powerful influence over you, even though you knew it was present. The power of audio manipulation is even greater when it is undetected. Experiments have shown that if restaurant customers are exposed to music from a particular region, they are more likely to order wine from that country. When questioned, they had no idea that something as simple as sound had steered their decision.

Lovers

People are always a product of the environment they are in, whether they want to be or not. The way people are raised directly affects the way they act in later life. Someone who is raised by alcoholics has a greater chance of becoming alcoholics in adult life, or they may choose never to drink at all. People who are raised in a house where everything is forbidden may cut loose and go a bit crazy when they are finally out on their own. People who are raised in total disorganization may grow up to be totally obsessive about household cleanliness.

Nurture affects people in other, less severe ways, too. Many people believe that Mom's meatloaf is the absolute best and no other recipe exists. People come from different religious and economic backgrounds. People have different beliefs about what is good and bad, what is acceptable and unacceptable. The problem comes when two people are trying to have a relationship, but neither wants to change their way of thinking. When that happens there is no relationship. There are just two people living together under the same roof.

Achieving success in love is just like achieving success in anything else. It is mostly a function of developing good relationships with other people in order to be better able to influence them. Those people who are successful in creating and keeping good, mutually satisfactory relationships with others usually enjoy much more success than people who do not do this. The ability to grow and maintain satisfactory relationships is a trait that is easier for some people. But even if the ability does not come naturally it is easy enough to learn. And Neuro-Linguistic Programming (NLP) makes this skill easier to learn by offering tools and ideas to enable almost anyone to learn the ability to develop great relationships.

Sales people

If a salesperson asks a regular customer to write a brief endorsement of the product they buy, hopefully, they will say yes. If someone asks their significant other to take some of the business cards to pass out at work, hopefully, they will say yes. If you write any kind of blog and ask another blogger to provide a link to yours on their blog, hopefully, they will say yes. When enough people say yes, the business or blog will begin to grow. With even more yesses, it will continue to grow and thrive. This is the very simple basis of marketing. Marketing is nothing more than using mind control to get other people to buy something or to do something beneficial for someone else. And the techniques can easily be learned.

Writers

Think of writing a guest spot for someone else who has their own blog. By sending in the entire manuscript first, there is a greater risk of rejection. Begin small. Send them a paragraph or two discussing them the idea. Then make an outline of the idea and send that in an email. Then write the complete draft you would like them too use and send it along. When asking a customer for a testimonial, start by asking for a few lines in an email. Then ask the customer to expand those few lines into a testimonial that covers at least half a typed page. Soon the customer will be ready for an hour-long webcast extolling the virtues of the product and your great customer service skills.

Everything must have a deadline that really exists. The important word here is the word 'real'. Everyone has heard the salesperson who said to decide quickly because the deal might not be available later or another customer was coming in and they might get it. That is a total fabrication and everyone knows it to be true. There are no impending other customers and the deal is not going to disappear. There is no real sense of urgency involved. But everyone does it. There are too many situations where people are given a totally fake deadline by someone who thinks it will instill a great sense of urgency for completion of the task. It is not only totally not effective but completely unneeded. It is a simple matter to create true urgency. Only leave free things available for a finite amount of time. When asking customers for testimonials be certain to mention the last possible day for it to be received to be able to be used. Some people will be unable to assist, but having people unable to participate is better than never being able to begin.

In Education

By educating impressionable children, society essentially teaches them to become "ideal" members of society. They are taught and trained in certain ways that fulfil the desires of the government and authorities, and most people don't even think twice about it.

Advertising and Propaganda

By putting advertising and propaganda everywhere, those in control are capable of eliminating people's feeling of self-worth and encourage them to *need* what is being sold, as opposed to just wanting it. This is essentially a subliminal strategy to make people feel poorly about themselves so that they will purchase whatever is being advertised to increase their feelings of self-worth.

Sports, Politics, Religion
The idea of these strategies is to "divide and conquer". Ultimately, each one has people placed into various categories, where they feel very strongly. As a result, they don't come together and support one another, but rather they are against each other. This means that they are divided, and so the authority can conquer.

Chapter 7: Mind Control Techniques

It's interesting to see that manipulation has been around for a long time, and that is not a new or imaginary concept. Understanding what the art of persuasion is really all about is vital, to help you to deal with it.

Here, we briefly look at the psychology of manipulation. This allows us to see where it might occur in our lives. It will also help you in identifying those who might attempt to manipulate you. It is not only about people who like to dominate. If we don't know it is happening to us, might be encouraged to act in ways that are incongruous to our normal personality and behavior. Learn how commerce can persuade customers into buying their goods and services. Recognizing such methods will help in dealing with the power of persuasion.

We like to believe that we are individuals who make sensible choices. In our personal journey of life, we do not always have full control, and we don't always realize this. As children, we are influenced by our parents and have little control over how we raised. Once in the education system, we are further manipulated. The teachers will tell us all about the social norms and what is expected of us in society. As adults, we are lured in by politicians trying to get their share of votes. Many are persuaded to vote for a party because of what they promise for the future, even if they don't necessarily believe in their policies. This gives such politicians power, and their decisions will affect our lives. Are we in full control of our lives, or are we merely influenced by those who know all the tricks of persuasion?

Later on, we will look at how to deal with various manipulative methods, even sometimes covert. First, you need to learn to recognize when you are being manipulated so you can counteract it.

Recognizing the Art of Manipulation

What then, in our everyday lives, do we need to be wary of?

Persuasive Language

The idiom that every picture tells a story is very true. Words can be so much more powerful as they inspire and encourage us, even to the point of manipulation. How many are the times you have been inspired by a good orator, whose daring speech motives you into action? Words even influence when we are lost completely in a great book. The art of words can be so influential in coercing us to believe something, even when our eyes tell us differently. Communication is a powerful tool, especially when it comes to making people do things.

- Advertisers and salespeople use language to convince their goods are just what we are looking for. Using words, such as:

Affordable; Easy to use; Safe; Enjoyable; Time Saving; Guaranteed to last.

Note how all these words make us believe they are confident in their own products.

- Politicians will use language, such as:

"We" - to encompass you in their world.

"Us" to make you feel a part of a team.

These are all communication tactics to make us feel included, so therefore important.

- Bullies use language along with aggressive behavior, to achieve their own selfish goals.

- Criminal predators, such as psychopaths, sociopaths and narcissists, are all people who learn the use of persuasive language. This is a means to get their own way and gain control over another person.

Techniques Used in Mind Control

Present day mind control is both innovative and mental. Tests demonstrate that basically by uncovering the techniques for mind control, the impacts can be diminished or disposed of, at any rate for mind control publicizing and promulgation. Increasingly hard to counter are the physical interruptions, which the military-mechanical complex keeps on creating and enhance.

1. **Education** — This is the most self-evident, yet still remains the most treacherous. It has consistently been an eventual tyrant's definitive dream to "teach" normally receptive youngsters, subsequently it has been a focal segment to Communist and Fascist oppressive regimes from the beginning of time. Nobody has been increasingly instrumental in uncovering the motivation of present day instruction than Charlotte Iserbyt — one can start investigation into this region by downloading a her book as a free PDF, The Deliberate Dumbing Down of America, revealing the job of Globalist establishments in forming a future planned to deliver servile automatons reigned over by a completely taught, mindful exclusive class.

2. **Promotions and Propaganda** – Edward Bernays has been referred to as the creator of the consumerist culture that was planned principally to focus on individuals' mental self-portrait (or scarcity in that department) so as to transform a need into a need. This was at first imagined for items, for example, cigarettes, for instance. Nonetheless, Bernays additionally noted in his 1928 book, Propaganda, that "purposeful publicity is the official arm of the imperceptible government." This can be seen most unmistakably in the advanced police state and the developing native nark culture, enveloped with the pseudo-enthusiastic War on Terror. The expanding union of media has empowered the whole corporate structure to converge with government, which currently uses the idea of promulgation arrangement. Media; print, motion pictures, TV, and link news would now be able

to work flawlessly to incorporate a general message which appears to have the ring of truth since it originates from such a significant number of sources, at the same time. When one moves toward becoming sensitive to recognizing the fundamental "message," one will see this engraving all over. What's more, this isn't even to specify subliminal informing.

3. **Prescient Programming** – Many still deny that prescient writing computer programs is genuine. Prescient programming has its causes in predominately elitist Hollywood, where the big screen can offer a major vision of where society is going. Simply glance back at the books and motion pictures which you thought were implausible, or "sci-fi" and investigate society today. For a nitty gritty breakdown of explicit models, Vigilant Citizen is an incredible asset that will most likely make you take a gander at "amusement" in a totally unique light.

4. **Sports, Politics, Religion** – Some may resent seeing religion, or even legislative issues, put together with sports as a technique for mind control. The focal topic is the equivalent all through: isolate and prevail. The systems are very straightforward: impede common propensity of individuals to participate for their endurance, and train them to frame groups bowed on control and winning. Sports has consistently had a job as a key diversion that corrals innate propensities into a non-significant occasion, which in present day America has arrived at silly extents where challenges will break out over a game VIP leaving their city, yet basic human issues, for example, freedom are chuckled away as immaterial.

5. **Food, Water, and Air** – Additives, poisons, and other nourishment harms actually modify mind science to make mildness and indifference. Fluoride in drinking water has been demonstrated to bring down IQ; Aspartame and MSG are excitotoxins which energize

synapses until they kick the bucket; and simple access to the inexpensive food that contains these toxins by and large has made a populace that needs center and inspiration for a functioning way of life. The vast majority of the cutting edge world is flawlessly prepped for uninvolved responsiveness — and acknowledgment — of the authoritarian tip top.

6. **Medications** — we can equate this to any addictive substance, however the mission of mind controllers is to be certain you are dependent on something. One noteworthy arm of the cutting edge mind control motivation is psychiatry, which expects to characterize all individuals by their issue, instead of their human potential. This was foreshadowed in books, for example, Brave New World. Today, it has been taken to considerably assist limits as a medicinal oppression has grabbed hold where about everybody has a type of confusion — especially the individuals who question authority. The utilization of nerve tranquilizes in the military has prompted record quantities of suicides. To top it all off, the cutting edge medication state currently has over 25% of U.S. youngsters on mind-desensitizing drugs.

7. **Military testing** — There is a long history associated to the military as the proving ground for mind control. The military personality is maybe the most pliable, as the individuals who seek after life in the military by and large resound to the structures of progression, control, and the requirement for unchallenged submission to a mission. For the expanding number of military individual scrutinizing their influence, an ongoing story featured DARPA's arrangements for trans cranial mind control head protectors that will keep them centered.

8. **Electromagnetic range** — An electromagnetic soup encompasses all of us, charged by present day gadgets of comfort which have been appeared to directly affect mind work. In an implicit affirmation of what is

conceivable, one scientist has been working with a "divine being head protector" to instigate dreams by adjusting the electromagnetic field of the mind. Our advanced soup has us latently washed by conceivably mind-changing waves, while a wide scope of potential outcomes, for example, phone towers is currently accessible to the eventual personality controller for more straightforward mediation.

Mind control is more common than most people think. It is not easy to detect because of its subtle nature. In many instances, it happens under what is perceived as normal circumstances like through education, religion, TV programs, advertisements and so much more. Cults and their leadership use mind control to influence their members and control whatever they do. It is not easy to detect mind control. However, when one realizes it, they can get out and start afresh.

Chapter 8: The Secrets of Neuro Linguistic Programming

Neuro-Linguistic Programming or NLP, as it is commonly referred to, is one of the most prevalent systems of mind control in the entire universe. It is applied by nearly everyone from politicians to marketers to media personalities, and it is very nasty to its main cores. John Grinder and Richard Bandler invented this famous method of mind control in the 1970s. It would later gain much popularity in the new age, occult, and psychoanalytic spaces back in the 1980s. Later on, in the 1990s and 2000s, NLP started to make inroads in the political, marketing, as the advertising markets. Over time, it has become so interwoven with the manner at which people are communicated to and even marketed. It is also very crucial to note that NLP has, to some extent, become a type of devilish and pernicious force in the entire global space, which has been studied by nearly everybody in the business spheres. Those who have mastered the techniques of this great dark psychology trait are known for owning a Rasputin-like capability of tricking persons into some incredible ways, nearly at all times.

Neuro-Linguistic Programming is used today for a variety of different things. It can be helpful in helping people overcome issues like anxiety, PTSD, and fears. These are only a very few issues that Neuro-Linguistic Programming can help with. While some people use it for good, others use it for darker desires.

We would love to say that the only place you will find NLP is in your therapist's office, however, we actually see it in everyday life. From your workplace to the ads on your social media accounts, you can actually see it everywhere. NLP does not only focus on what people say but more importantly focus on what people are doing. Our body language says more than our mouths ever could.

NLP has been under the debate of whether it is an actual science or if it is considered a pseudoscience. The debate still exists today, and it is hard to pinpoint this science due to the fact that it has not gone through the same rigorous testing as therapies such as CBT, Cognitive Behavioral Therapy.

There is a pretty broad range of techniques used within NLP and this also makes it difficult to lock down which pieces actually work. There have been some studies performed and oftentimes the results were inconclusive. In some it appears as if NLP had made a true improvement in subjects with psychosis, instability, and other unwanted traits. Others worked on looking at its effectiveness to help issues like PTSD and anxiety. The results came back exceptionally varied.

Neuro-Linguistic Programming has been around for more than forty years. For something to be around this long and continue to be used throughout many people's daily lives means there has got to be some validity to it, right? We see it used so widely on a commercial level and it certainly does have an impact.

It also has its place in the world of Psychology and Dark Psychology. Due to the fact that it is quite unstructured it is difficult to show true proof of its success. There are also a plethora of different idea and ways of executing NLP. For some, it is a very effective form of therapy that truly helps them lead better lives. For others, it may not benefit them at all. These people will need to look at more traditional therapies to work through their issues and lead a happier and mentally healthier life.

NLP History

NLP is, in a way, a method of mind control. It was developed by a team of people. However, the majority of the credit is given to, two California boys, John Grinder and Richard Bandler. In the 1970's, they decided to combine the works of Virginia Satir, a therapist for families, Friedrich Perls, a psychotherapist, and a hypnotherapist by the name of Milton Erickson. They wanted to take the heart of linguistic therapy and improve it. Find the pieces that truly worked and make something better.

The three people that they studied were chosen due to the fact that they had better results with their clients than most others in their field. In fact, people found their success to be odd and uncommon. Naturally, inquisitive minds wanted to know what these people had in common and why their methods worked so well. They studied them in live sessions and via video tape.

NLP is subtle. When we think about normal hypnotherapy, we think about people falling asleep and acting out strange and silly acts. Realistically, it is used for much more meaningful purposes. For example, people use hypnotherapy to help them stop smoking or to deal with traumas of the past that may have not been coped with. NLP does things a bit differently. It is much more suggestive and not so in your face.

In the beginning, Neuro-Linguistic Programming was thought to be as helpful as products like "snake juice" from the days of the old west. However, as the seventies turned into the eighties it became more and more accepted. Businesses were jumping on the bandwagon to learn about it so they could, in turn, use it to help them gain profits from consumers. In addition, everyone from therapists to political figures started to want the information on this type of "programming". It seriously started to blow up in terms of popularity.

Companies became interested in NLP because it can help them communicate more clearly. This helps to improve the performance of employees and the overall performance of the business. Businesses that use NLP have experienced better growth in their companies as a whole.

Not only can it help people become better negotiators it can also help them stay motivated. When you feel comfortable at work and you feel like everyone is giving it their all, it's easy to build a solid team. Being a confident leader that pays attention to tone, body language, and verbiage will help lead to better success. Implementing the practices of NLP can promote growth for companies.

As people started to employ these tactics, they started to notice changes in their teams. Boosts in morale and productivity. Now we see NLP happening around us every day. This is not necessarily a bad thing as people that practice NLP tend to be more self-aware. In turn, they tend to make better choices that are made from rationality rather than emotions

Pillars of NLP

There are four main points to NLP, they are referred to as the Pillars of NLP. They are Behavioral Flexibility, Rapport, Outcome Thinking, and Sensory Awareness. Each one is of equal importance as the others. Taking the time to look briefly at each one of these points gives a better understanding of NPL as a whole and how it can help you weed out the fakers in your life.

The first pillar is Behavioral Flexibility. Basically, this means to go with the flow. When people can see that the tactic they are currently using isn't working and adapt their behavior it can have great results. Being able to quickly change your perspective will allow more people to understand you.

The next aspect we are going to look at is Rapport. Creating a good rapport with someone is simply getting them to trust you quickly. In addition, it is the ability to form quick relationships with people. It is easy to build rapport by using common language, being polite, and showing empathy. There are many ways to build a good rapport with a person, these are only a few.

Then we move on to Outcome Thinking. It is exactly what it states, spending the time to think about the end result of what you want. Oftentimes, people get stuck on a certain point that is commonly negative. It consumes the thought pattern and can make choosing the correct route to where you actually want to go difficult. With outcome thinking you are always working toward an end goal. This can promote better decision making along the way.

Lastly, we have Sensory Awareness. Being aware of the surroundings contributes to knowing what is actually going on. When you walk into a public place and you take notice of the tone of the room, the colors surrounding you, the groups of people, it can be very enlightening. It can also help you easily understand how you need to behave in that situation.

The more you learn about these four pillars the more success you will have with NLP. They are the foundation and anyone who wants to learn NLP will spend a lot of time on each one. Gaining more knowledgeable helps you apply what you have learned to your daily life and the more protected you will be from the ones that want to manipulate you, control you, or cause other burdens in your life.

NLP has grown and changed over the years. What started out as focusing on what people's eyes were doing, the words they choose to use, and building quick rapport, turned into something much, much more. All sciences grow and change over the course of time and we imagine that this one will also continue to evolve.

After focusing on what the yes were doing, word choice, and rapport this therapy started to grow and focus on other aspects. In the 80's, the people using NLP were focusing on what it is that causes feelings inside of us. This helped therapists to figure out how to help someone deal with their individual problems.

More and more people started using the techniques found with NLP but they wanted to put different names to it. To say they had come up with it all on their own. When it comes down to it, no matter what you call it, NLP is the same across the globe. Today, it is used not only to help you have control and choices in how you react, but it can also help you figure out what other people are up to.

The people in the here and now that are using NLP have a variety of different reasons for doing it. Some of it is to help themselves become better people while for others it is about weeding out the rats in their lives. Businesses use it in team building and marketing techniques. Here again, we can see how vast the world of Neuro-Linguistic Programming really is.

It has been said that people who study Neuro-Linguistic Programming live freely. They have the ability to access all different types of situations and make choices in how they choose to proceed instead of being led by instinct and emotion. How you think, feel, behave, and speak can all be choices you make that can help you lead the best life possible.

NLP can be used throughout your daily life in a huge variety of ways. Some common reasons that people start using this are that they want to motivate other people, have control over their emotions, conquer their fears, communicate more effectively, and find success in life. There are many other reasons a person would take an interest in NLP.

If you are unsure of who you can trust in your crowd NLP can seriously help. Understanding behaviors and actions of people can help to clue you in on what's really going on around you. This falls into Sensory Awareness. It is startling what you can learn from looking at someone's body position and paying attention to things like their tone of voice. People really do tell you everything you need to know with very little conversation.

Whether you are at your job or heading for a late-night party downtown honing these skills can keep you mentally and physically protected against predators. Knowing NLP techniques can also inform you when other people are using it for darker desires. Many people use these practices to become their best selves, however, others have more nefarious intent.

Obviously, when you can adapt in a situation and make well-thought out choices you are going to be more successful. There is less of a chance that people will be able to take advantage of you. In addition, you will be able to better understand the people in your life. Weeding out the keepers from the trash is simpler when you can read the situation accurately and adjust so that you are working toward your desired outcome.

How Does it Work?

NLP may seem like enchantment or spellbinding. During treatment the subject dives deep into their oblivious personality and filters through layers and layers of convictions and discernments to wind up mindful of an involvement in early youth that is in charge of a standard of conduct. NLP takes a shot at the rule that everybody has every one of the assets they have to roll out positive improvements in their very own life. NLP strategies are utilized as a device to encourage these changes.

NLP Therapy can be sans substance. That implies the specialist can be viable without thinking about the issue in incredible detail. Consequently the specialist need not be told about the occasion or even the issue, in this manner guaranteeing protection for the customer. Other than this we likewise have a non-exposure understanding in which the communication between the customer and the advisor is kept secret.

NLP puts stock in flawlessness of nature in human creation. Henceforth NLP urges the customer to perceive their tangible sensitivities and use them to react to a specific issue. Indeed, NLP additionally accepts that the brain is fit for finding even fixes to illnesses and infections.

NLP procedures include noninvasive, medication free treatment that enables the customer to find better approaches for managing enthusiastic issues, for example, low confidence, uneasiness, absence of certainty, ruinous relationship designs (adapting to separation), and are fruitful inadequate mourning guiding.

NLP has its underlying foundations in the field of social science, created by Pavlov, Skinner and Thorndike. It utilizes physiology and the oblivious personality to change points of view and consequently conduct.

NLP is simply the investigation of astounding correspondence both with yourself, and with others. It was created by demonstrating astounding communicators and advisors who got results with their customers. NLP is a lot of instruments and methods, yet it is far beyond that. It is a demeanor and an approach of realizing how to accomplish your objectives and get results.

Dark Traits of Manipulative People

Among the groups of the Dark Triad there is a conglomeration of personality traits that are oftentimes, seen in criminals. It is not a surprise to realize that most criminals have quite a bit in common. Taking notice to these dark traits is a great way of figuring out if someone has malicious intent toward you or not.

There are a variety of different dark traits that we see on an everyday basis. You may know someone who is very spiteful. Anyone that does something they don't like will pay for it. Sometimes it will be petty retaliation, but it can explode into something much more dangerous, depending on who you are dealing with. Criminals tend to be spiteful, as they have malicious intent with their transgressions.

Another dark trait that you want to watch out for is egoism. When someone is so self-absorbed and focused on their own achievements that they will run everyone else around them into the ground, it is a major problem. Some criminals scramble their way to the top because of their giant egos and their ability to only care about themselves. Keeping an eye on a big ego can save you a lot of trouble, especially in relationships and business.

Have you ever met someone that had loose morals? You know that person that really doesn't have much regard for if what they are doing is right or wrong. Someone that even when they know what they are doing is wrong, does it anyway, and then just laugh it off. This is a personality trait referred to as moral disengagement. Obviously, the ability to commit a crime and not feel terrible about it is something common among criminals a pretty dark trait.

Earlier we discussed Machiavellianism. That person that will go to any means to get what they want. They are the ones that are the masters of manipulation. The justification for what they are doing is always solid. When trying to track down criminals these are some of the hardest to catch as they tend to also be some of the smartest out there. Even experts of NLP can have a hard time locking this trait down.

Entitlement or Psychological Entitlement are also dark traits that we commonly see in criminals and everyday adversaries. Unfortunately, the world's sense of entitlement has gone off the rails. Nowadays, it is natural to meet people that have a sense of entitlement and this can make it difficult to use this trait in determining somebody's true intent.

Self-interest is another trait that you need to watch out for. We all have tendencies to be selfish, however, for some people it is to an extreme. They simply do not care what other people feel or want. This is commonly seen by people boasting about how much money they have or their status. In addition, their self-interest could be used to motivate them in gaining betterment in finances or society. Those that are self-interested also tend to be extremely manipulative.

Then we have the narcissist. We spoke of the narcissist earlier, but their traits are very common among criminals. They have a need for attention and commonly and inflated sense of self. They will go to great extremes to prove that they are better than those that are around them. This could be in how they look, how they think, or how they act. The narcissist thinks that their ideas are the best and therefore criminal intent goes hand-in-hand with the narcissist.

Psychopathy means that you are lacking in the ability to empathize with people. They have an extreme lack of concern where others are involved. This dark trait can also lead to a lack of self-control and extremely impulsive behaviors. Obviously, when thinking about criminals, this trait rings true for many of the extreme horrors we have witnessed in the past.

The last dark trait that we think needs to be discussed is sadism. A sadist is a person that likes to inflict pain. In fact, they take pleasure in causing other people pain. This does not necessarily have to be physical pain. In fact, many sadists find joy and completely tearing you down mentally. A wide variety of criminal classes fall into this category and it is a common trait that we see in many of the people that are committing heinous crimes.

Behavior Imitation

Behavior imitation is something that can be used for good and for bad. Oftentimes, as children, we mimic the behavior of the people around us. It helps us to learn social norms. In addition, it helps us feel like we fit in to the crowd. Many traditions have been built off of people mimicking other people's behavior.

As we continue to grow up, we continue to imitate people around us. Here again, it makes us feel as if we belong. Additionally, it can help us build relationships and understand the people around us more easily. While, many people use behavior imitation for the right reasons there are many others who don't.

Criminals who are socially awkward have a tendency of acting like the people around them. It can make it harder to discern the good guys from the bad guys. It is a manipulation tactic that works quite well when people don't exactly know how to behave appropriately. While some people are very good at mimicking those around them it will be quite obvious when others are trying to do this. Cases of extreme social awkwardness will not allow the person to genuinely behave like those that are around them. This can be a tip to seeing what they may have planned next.

Another way that behavior imitation is prevalent with criminals is when they idolize someone or something. They will change their very persona to reflect that of which they have admiration for. A good example of this are people that still follow the ideals of Adolf Hitler. The new generation of Nazis mimic the ways of old because they still believe his blasphemous thoughts to be true. This is truly scary behavior imitation.

Body Language

A person's body language is one of the biggest tells in how they are feeling and what they may be planning. The way a person moves and behaves while in a conversation, out in public, and at home gives great insight to what's happening with them at that particular moment. Those who work on learning NLP techniques spend a ton of time studying about body language.

Body language is how we speak without using words. It can suggest that you are happy, sad, open to conversation, or completely closed off from everyone. Not only is it shown through your actual body but also through your eyes. Paying attention to the eyes is also an important part of NLP. There are some truths to be found in body language that may not be what the words coming out of someone's mouth are actually stating.

It has been found that we gather more information from a person's facial expressions, eyes, and body language than we ever could from their spoken words. So, learning how to read body language can help you in just about every situation you find yourself in. Learning how shady people act can help you in avoiding unwanted issues.

When you first start learning about body language, you will be able to easily identify some emotions. Obviously, we all know what it looks like when a person is happy or sad. The signs of this can be seen easily but finding out when someone is anxious or uncomfortable can be a bit more difficult.

Studying non-verbal cues will take you to every area of the body. For example, slightly dilated pupils may not be from a bright light but may in fact be due to arousal. If someone is constantly biting at their lip it could be a sign of stalling or higher levels of anxiety in the current situation.

How a person is standing or sitting also gives us some clues as to how they are feeling. A person with their arms folded around them is less likely to want to be approached. Whereas, an open stance with your hands on your hips means you are likely in control of the situation or you may be aggressive. Learning these types of things can seriously help improve your ability to pick out a troublemaker in a crowd.

Ever been in an area and realized someone was acting kind of shifty? You know, like moving around the room frequently and during conversations they are unable to hold eye-contact. Your ability to notice these this is because most people have at least some basic knowledge on how to read a person's body language.

Your posture also plays a key role in what your body is saying to other people. People who slouch and tend to wrap their arms around themselves are typical closed off. They may be feeling unwelcome or anxious. On the other hand, an open posture with your chin up and shoulders back is very welcoming. It shows that you are open to conversation, friendly, and approachable.

Not only does your body language help people decide how to approach you, theirs helps you decide about them. There is a plethora of different aspects to be considered with body language. The more you delve into NLP, the more pieces of body language you will pick up. It can seriously help when trying to identify those that are threatening and may have mal intent.

Language Imitation

Language imitation is another piece of NLP that should be taken into consideration. When we talk to someone, even if we speak the same language, it can be difficult for us to understand each other. Each individual has what is referred to as common language. Common language is simply the words a person uses frequently and understand better than others.

When you are in a therapy session or at work and you are listening to someone talk, understanding what they are saying can be hard. It can feel as if they are speaking in a different language. This doesn't work well for anyone as the person listening is actually learning anything. This is a major issue and can cause massive detriment to a company or a person's mental status.

Working to hear how someone talks, the phrases they use, and the tone that they have can help you succeed in language imitation. When you can speak in common language to the person or people you are addressing, you will be much more successful. Understanding will be promoted and what everyone gets out of what you have to say will be more beneficial.

Mimicking someone's language is more difficult than mimicking their body language. The more time you spend talking with a person, the easier it will be to pick up on their vocal habits. Someone that is very good at picking up other people's common language can be a danger if they have intentions of doing harm.

When we speak in a common language it promotes trust. Putting trust into someone that wants to use your language against you is obviously something you want to avoid. So, be careful when dealing with people that quickly change their voice to match those that are around them. The ones that pick up on little pieces of context and repeat them to gain sympathy, trust, or control. It may be hard to recognize, at first, but the more aware you become of your surrounding the easier this will be to spot.

Criminals tend to be good at this parrot like behavior. They understand that to get people to like you they absolutely need to understand you. If control is what someone is looking for this is a good place to start and get their hooks in. So, while language imitation can help you and your therapist or employees relate, it can also be used to manipulate situations in favor of the person using this tactic.

Chapter 9: Manipulation and Persuasion

What is Manipulation?

For many people, manipulation is a faraway phenomenon that happens to other people, and not to themselves. It is unlikely that you will be going about your day thinking about manipulation or worrying that others are manipulating you. Yet the truth of the matter is, manipulation is everywhere around us. It is in sales adverts that try to entice you to buy something that you do not need by convincing you that you do need it. It is in the puppy eyes of a lover or child trying to get something out of you. Manipulation is also at play when a passenger is trying to charm a flight attendant into getting a first-class upgrade. In short, manipulation is everywhere in your daily life. The only reason it goes unnoticed is because high chances are that you are not looking out for it. In many cases, it is often so subtle that even if you were looking for it, you would not notice it.

First things first, what is the textbook definition of manipulation? Merriam-Webster dictionary has various definitions for manipulation, among them: *to manage or utilize skillfully; to control by unfair means in order to gain advantage* and; *to change by unfair means in order to serve one's purpose.*

Well, if you are reading this book, high chances are that you're likely tired of having lost control and wish to have it back. Or maybe you're tired of hearing no and want to hear yes more regularly. This book will not be a manual on how to use manipulation to hurt or lie to others. It is more of a handbook on how to make the most out of your social interactions for your own benefit and possibly for the benefit of the people around you. It is not an encouragement to be deceiving to others, but rather a tell-all on the manipulation signs you have been missing and how you can take back your own power in your life.

How Psychology Correlate with Manipulation

Three psychological conditions that are associated with manipulation are narcissism, psychosis, and sociopathy. Before talking about how the different ways manipulators might attempt to influence others, we'll give some background on these underlying psychological conditions.

A narcissist suffers from narcissistic personality disorder, or NPD. As is true of many psychological measures, NPD can be seen as existing on a spectrum; people might have it to differing degrees.

The overarching characteristics of NPD include the following:

• A grandiose self-image that might exaggerate the sufferer's importance, talent, or achievements.

• A lack of empathy for other people.

• A strong need for admiration from others.

• Unrealistic fantasies of power, achievement, success, or idealized love.

• A belief in a unique or special status that can only be understood by an elite few.

• An expectation of special or deferential treatment.

• A general attitude of arrogance.

• An envy of others or delusional belief that he or she is subject to the envy of others.

• A willingness to exploit or manipulate others.

Obviously, this last characteristic is the most relevant to our purposes, but most of the others point towards the basic psychology of narcissism that so enables manipulation. The strong egocentric framing, the delusions of grandeur and the lack of empathy lead to a personality perfectly willing to pursue self-interested behavior at the expense of others.

Within the broader category of narcissists there is a spectrum of subtypes that ranges from exhibitionist narcissists to closeted ones. There are some who are unapologetically abusive and vindictive and others that are thoughtful and capable of remorse. The more fully a narcissist conforms to the above list of characteristics, the more likely they are to be considered a malignant narcissist; one capable of inflicting harm.

Antisocial Personality Disorder, or APD, is the clinical diagnosis for sociopathy. Like narcissism, sociopathy tends to be a long-lived condition, often permanent, and has extensive effects. To meet the clinical definition, an APD sufferer must demonstrate a conduct disorder by the age of fifteen which includes at least four of the following characteristics.

• Inability to maintain consistency in work or schoolwork.

• Ignored social norms. May engage in illegal behavior.

• A casual disregard for safety concerns, either concerning the self or others.

• Irresponsibility, as seen on the job or in a failure to honor obligations of a financial nature.

• Difficulty in maintaining monogamous relationships for over a year.

• Impulsive and lacking in ambition or planning, tending to proceed without clear goals.

• Easily irritated and aggressive or violent.

• A lack of concern with honesty. This might be demonstrated by continuous lying, conning people, reneging on debts, or using aliases.

These first two categories are similar in both their positive and negative characteristics. Either can be intelligent, charismatic or successful. At the same time, narcissists and sociopaths can both be controlling, irresponsible, and proceed with an exaggerated sense of entitlement. Both can be abusive and both tend to refuse to take responsibility for this behavior. They tend to produce justifications for their worst behaviors. On a core level, both tend to lack empathy, although they may be able to fake empathetic reactions when it benefits them.

Although they do have similarities, there are important distinctions between the two categories. In the Venn diagram of disorders, all sociopaths are narcissists, but not all narcissists qualify as sociopaths. They differ in motivations. Sociopaths tend to be more cunningly manipulative, because everything isn't personal for them. Narcissists are ego-driven, but for sociopaths, the ego isn't a factor. They can, in fact, be viewed as lacking a real personality. They can inhabit any persona that is convenient to a given situation. This makes sociopaths harder to identify. Their tactics shift relative to a situation. They may try to win the approval of others, but only if it acts in service of their goals. They can perform humility, seeming to show remorse, but again, this is strategic and based on an agenda. Sociopaths act with a higher level of planning and calculation. Even aggression might be premeditated.

Narcissists are more reactive. They may employ lies and attempt to intimidate, but are more likely to do it without a game plan, simply reacting to a situation driven by their overactive egos. A narcissist will work towards their own success or goal of achieving some measure of perfection. They are perfectly willing to exploit others as they pursue these goals, but the manipulation is secondary and directed towards personal interests and a self-centered worldview.

Both personality types are motivated by their own interests, but only narcissists truly care what others think of them. The admiration of others is gratifying. This introduces a codependent aspect to their personalities, making them capable of being manipulated themselves.

A third category of manipulative personality type worth discussing includes psychopaths. Psychosis is distinguished by a difficulty in distinguishing fantasy and reality. Sufferers may be delusional or hallucinatory. The following list contains common traits of psychopaths. While many of these are shared in our previous two categories, remember the important distinguishing factors defining psychosis.

- Exaggerated sense of self worth

- Fleeting or shallow emotions

- A lack of empathy

- Unwillingness to accept responsibility for actions

- Inability to form realistic long-term goals

- Impulsive behavior

- A lack of responsibility

- Inability to control behavior

- Superficially charming and glib

- Being conning and manipulative

Psychopaths tend to mislead and manipulate others through dishonestly and a superficial charm that can come off as glib. Psychopaths may mislead in order to gain advantage or they might be motivated to deceive and abuse merely for their own amusement. Some simply cannot resist these negative impulses. Typically, psychopaths have developed these characteristics over the course of their entire lives. They have incorporated them into an often basically functional routine. Sometimes the traits are even externally reinforced to an extent. As a result, they don't see these characteristics as problematic. In fact, people with high levels of psychopathy often are largely unconcerned with how they are perceived, exhibiting a willingness to demonstrate their fearlessness even if it means they will be overtly perceived as dominating. They also tend not to worry about the consequences of their actions on others. As they tend to have very little empathy, impacts such as these seem irrelevant. They do, in fact, feel that their motivations are of innately greater concerns than those of others. This contributes to a delusional regard of their own motives and actions, as if they served some higher purpose. The delusional nature of psychosis also contributes to the fact that psychotics often believe their own lies. Lying is natural to highly psychotic people, but that does not mean they are always conscious that they are lying. Their detachment from reality can lead them to feel and believe what they are saying even when it is motivated by conscious deception. All of these characteristics naturally contribute to a high correlation of manipulative behavior and diagnoses of psychosis.

People with other psychological conditions or those who are in perfect mental health are perfectly capable of engaging in manipulative behavior under the right circumstances.

Persuasion vs. Manipulation

The line between persuasion and manipulation is so thin that it often gets blurry. Distinguishing these two concepts can often be difficult, especially depending on the circumstances and your own perspective as an individual. Persuasion and manipulation are alike in that in both cases there is someone trying to influence the decisions and behaviors of another. The key distinction between the two is that manipulation is seen to be highly driven by self-interest where one party is willing to go through any length to benefit themselves, including putting others in harm's way. Persuasion on the other is the nicer cousin of manipulation--there is a desire to influence for self-interest but there is often a line drawn to mark boundaries. Persuasion is the more ethical way to go about it, many will argue. When all's said and done, however, the two concepts seem to intertwine especially depending on the techniques used to achieve either of them.

People always have different ideas of what words mean, but to be successful in manipulation and persuasion, you need to know the different ways these terms are understood as well as what we mean when using them in this book. In common speech, persuasion is considered a neutral word; of course, someone can be persuaded to do something that helps the persuader and not themselves, but the word itself does not imply that. Manipulation, on the other hand, tends to mean ill intention of the manipulator.

The ethics of manipulation and persuasion are a topic we have explored throughout these pages, but know that for our purposes, persuasion is changing someone's beliefs, while manipulation is changing someone's actions. This is easy to remember, because NLP involves the neural pathways for both language (belief) and programming (action).

If you want your subject to change their behavior, you have to get them to change their thinking about their behavior. They are a thinking person just like you are, and while they have mental shortcuts that can get in the way (just like they can for you), your subject is entirely capable of talking through their judgment calls with you. In a conversation with you, they can come to re-evaluate their actions, and if you go through the conversation the right way, you will have the opportunity to convince them to change.

When it comes to manipulation, there is a slight difference from persuasion. The difference is that at some points, it is, in fact, the right thing to ask them to change their behavior directly. Now, you don't want to pull this out as your first move. This is something you build up to after a long conversation — after you accomplish steps zero and one, just as you do for persuasion. But the big difference between changing someone's ideas and changing their behaviors is here in step two: more often than not, you should directly tell them what you think they should do differently.

When NLP newcomers learn this at first, they are totally taken aback. They think, how could I possibly be told to tell them directly to change their behavior? But if you think through it a little longer, it makes sense. What is the difference between belief and behavior? Persuasion changes belief by getting close to someone's mind and changing what is in there, and manipulation is getting closer to their mind and changing what is in there, too.

But with manipulation, there is the added hurdle of getting them to follow up on the change in thought. While it is absolutely true that all of our behavior ultimately comes from our mind, our brains are still not simple masters of our actions. Rather, our actions are determined by multiple factors other than simply what our brain tells us to do. The reason you eventually have to ask your subject to change their actions directly is that for new behaviors, a change in thought is just not enough.

Your subject needs voices other than the one in their head, telling them what to do. They have the thought you got into their head through NLP; you are telling them directly, too. But there is still more you have to do.

Social bonds are incredibly important to human beings. If you want to manipulate someone's behavior, unlike when you persuade them into having new thoughts, these thoughts alone are not enough. You telling them what to do is not enough, even once they have recognized you as like them. If you want to change their behavior, next, you have to change the social environment of the person with the undesired behavior.

This is not a catch-all for manipulation, because nothing is. After all, not in every situation will you be able to change the social environment of your subject. If they are not friends or family, but rather a co-worker, this could prove much more challenging. It is only fitting since manipulation is a more difficult and complicated task than persuasion.

But if this is a person whose social environment you have some control over, you have to determine what social factors are leading to undesired behaviors. Is there another family member enabling their drinking or drug use? This is the most prominent example, but all of it is emblematic of the NLP manipulation framework in general.

All of this is to say that when you are not in control of a person's social environment, directly telling them what action they should take is a necessary and challenging part of the process. It is so challenging because there is no way around it, and it is also very easy to do the wrong way.

You have to work hard not to work too hard for them. If they can see how badly you want them to change their behavior, they will want to continue acting the way they do out of spite. Don't give them this opportunity.

Recall how with persuasion, we said never to address objections to your frame. In fact, if at all possible, you don't want to address the frame itself. That's because if you address the frame itself, you are acknowledging the fact that it is not the naturally-occurring reality that you want your subject to see it as. However, with manipulation, the situation is different than it is for persuasion.

With manipulation, you have to respond to objections directly, because you have to tug harder than you do with persuasion. You see, persuasion is a subtler, quieter art than manipulation. This is a direct way of saying that manipulation is loud and aggressive, because it is not.

But you can't be quite as gentle with manipulation. You want them to change their habits, so in order to get your subject to understand the gravity of the situation enough to trigger the behavior change, it is necessary that you are slightly pushier than you are with persuasion. Again: don't be pushy, but you can't be as subtle as you are with persuasion.

Even when you deal with their objections, you are better off preparing for them before they come up. When you are ready for any question or complaint your subject can haul at you, it is a signal to them that you are like them, you see things from their side, and perhaps, you know better. This is Step One yet again. If you demonstrate that you are like them and can reason things out better, they will listen. You are almost ready to get into the techniques of manipulation, but before then, you need to get into the personality of the NLP manipulator.

You might think that you are born with a certain personality, and you can't do anything to change it, but this couldn't be further from the truth. In fact, the kind of personality you should adopt to get people to do what you want is one that anyone can learn.

Why is learning this personality so important? Well, it's important because you need to seem like you are positive about what you are saying. If you seem even a teensy bit unsure in any of your speech or your body language, nobody is going to buy what you are selling. That's why in your body language, dress, facial expression, tone of voice, and words, you need to pull off the personality of someone who knows what they are talking about.

They have the answer to your question; they know what's what. If you can pull off that personality, you basically don't have to do anything else. Personality is everything — don't forget that.

Personality is so important because no matter how unlikely something seems on the surface, if it comes out of the mouth of the right personality, people will believe in it. You have to believe in what you are saying to some extent if you expect to pull this off, so don't think you can playact your way through the whole thing — after all, you are not doing the personality right if you are unsure about the merits of what you are saying. But more important than anything you say is the personality you are displaying while you say it.

Not everyone has this naturally, but it is not nearly as hard to learn as you might think. The right place to start is always your breathing and your posture. You already know what the right posture to take is — stand up straight and without shaking. Now, take deep breaths like for your state control exercises. Just like before, don't breathe loudly. Breathe deeply but not in a way that anyone can tell is unusual.

The third and final thing you have to do is enter the headspace of this unshakeable personality. Everyone has experienced a moment where everything was going right for them, and that is exactly the place you need to go. Revisit that memory as though you were there again right now, and come back as the person you were in that memory.

The world is at your fingertips just like it was back then, especially if you carry this person inside of you. That person is necessary to succeed in manipulating people's behavior in the techniques coming up, so be sure you have your personality ready before reading. You won't be able to pull these off otherwise.

Chapter 10: Characteristics of Manipulators

Use of Language

We have shown how powerful language can be, as a prime tool of persuasion. There is more to the manipulative controller though than mere words. They will use tactics that mislead and unbalance their target's inner thoughts. We now understand that through language, they will:

• Use mistruths to mislead and confuse their target's normal thinking pattern.

• Force their target to make a decision at speed, so they don't have time to analyze and think.

• Talk to their target in an overwhelming manner, making them feel small.

• Criticize their target's judgment so they begin to lose their own self-esteem.

• Raise the tone of their voice and not be afraid to use aggressive body language.

• Ignore their target's needs, they are only interested in getting what they want and at any cost.

Invasion of Personal Space

Most of us set boundaries around ourselves without realizing we are doing so. It is a kind of unspoken rule to protect our own private space, such as not sitting so close that you are touching another person, especially a stranger. A manipulative character cares nothing about overstepping such boundaries. Whether this is because they do not understand, or they do not care is unclear. Initially, they are unlikely to invade their target's personal space. They will seek to build up a good rapport first. This shows that they do understand boundaries because once they gain the confidence of their target, they will then ignore them.

Fodder for Thought

Manipulators tend to be very ego-centric, with limited social skills. Their only concern is for themselves. Everything they do in life will be in relation to how it affects them, not how their actions affect others. Does this mean that they have a psychopathic disorder?

Take empathy for instance. Controlling manipulators are unlikely to ever show empathy. Empathy is a natural human emotion that aids in our survival techniques. A study by Meffert et al. indicates that those with a psychopathic disorder are able to control empathetic emotions (4c). They lack sympathy of any kind because another weakness is simply another tool for them. When they detect any weakness in their target's resolve or personality, they will exploit it. The consequences to their victim are of little importance. The targets weakness's feed the manipulator's strength, making them bolder and often crueler in their actions.

Creating Rivalry

Another tactic of the controlling manipulator is backstabbing. They may tell you how great a person you are to your face, making themselves look good. Behind your back, they are busy spreading malicious gossip and untruths about you. This is a classic trait of a controlling manipulator as it creates a rivalry between people. Then, they can pick sides that will make them look favorable, particularly to their target. It can act as the first stage to getting close to their target. Once bonded, they can start to build up trust, making it easier to manipulate the target in the future. If you recognize a backstabber, keep them at a distance. Their agenda is selfish so it is better not let them into your personal life. There is no point treating them as they treat you, in revenge. It will turn out to be exhausting playing them at their own game. If they know that you are on to them, they may attempt to lure you back with praise, remember that it is false.

Domineering Personality

It is unlikely that a manipulative person will outwardly show any form of weakness. An important part of their facade is to show conviction about their views. They seek to impress, believing they are right about everything. Almost to the point that if they realize they are wrong, they will still argue that they are right. On a one-to-one level, that invariably means that your position is always wrong. As they will chip away at your beliefs, they seek to undermine your sense of self-esteem. Once they have achieved this, then there is no holding them back. They seek to domineer others, often speaking with a condescending tone to belittle their victims. Using ridicule is yet another tool against their target, merely because it will make themselves look better. If you ridicule them back, they will seek to turn the tables, accusing you of being oversensitive to their "joke." The type of joke that the teller is the only one seeing the funny side.

Passive Aggressive Behavior

A common trait of many hard-core manipulators is passive aggressive behavior. Because they prefer to be popular, they do not wish to be seen as doing anything wrong. Not that a manipulator would ever admit to doing anything wrong. They are experts with facial expressions that are meant to dominate and intimidate. This may include; knitting eyebrows, grinding teeth and rolling eyes. It may also include noises such as tutting and grunting sounds. It is a very common behavior for such a character, as there is little anyone else has to say that they will agree upon. For most manipulators, it is their life's ambition to show people up by proving them wrong. This can range from the confrontational look, where they seek to stare their target down. Or, it could be in response to their disagreement on something their target said. They may smirk and shake their head, turn their back, anything to show their strong disapproval. It is all a ploy to make themselves look superior and put others down.

Moody Blues

What of emotional stability of the manipulator? Is it that which makes them behave the way they do? Do they even know what happiness is? The answer to that is a most definite yes, at least to the latter.

Happiness is a tool used initially to help them manipulate, a happy target is more likely to comply. This, in itself, makes the manipulator happy, or at least in a sense of what they consider happiness. But their joyfulness is a perverted model of what most others consider happiness to be. Their happiness is often built on the foundations of another's misery. A misery that they have caused with their cruel manipulations. Equally though, a manipulator is prone to mood swings. Most likely to happen when things are not going to plan. One minute they are euphoric at their latest conquest. Then next they could be completely deflated at their failure to succeed. One thing is certain for those who live with or become a target of this type of domineering character, they will be unhappy all the time.

Intimidation

One aspect of manipulation, often used as a last resort, is intimidation and bullying. When everything else has failed, they begin to use threats to get their own way. Some though may use intimidation from the onset. It may in a source of authority. For example, let's take the role of a manipulative boss. You have requested a day off. They don't want to allow you your request but have no choice, it is your right. This type of person would want their pound of flesh first. They will set goals for you to reach so it will delay or cancel your request, such as moving project deadlines forward. This way they have their little victory over you.

Alternatively, such a manipulator may use the tactic of the silent treatment. Ignoring someone to the point that it becomes obvious you have displeased them. They seek to make you feel the guilty party.

Other more direct intimidating actions may include stance. Using their height or build to tower over you, or standing uncomfortably close. Be careful as they will seek revenge for wrongdoings they perceive done to them. Nothing will go unnoticed under their watchful eye. Everyone is a potential target. But, the weak are more likely to walk into their traps, because they are the ones who are easier to dominate. The vulnerable will have little resistance and are easier to bully and coerce. Many of these traits seem more fitting to men, but women can be cruelly manipulative too.

This is a person who will never back down in an argument. Never admit they are wrong. Never apologize for anything. A manipulator will never show respect but will expect everyone else to show them respect. They love nothing more than to embarrass others. Playing the dumb one is common practice, just to force another person to explain themselves further. At every opportunity, the manipulator will jump in with some sarcastic remark, "hurry up, we're all waiting for your intellectual explanation," or "why has no one else ever heard of this?" Their sole aim is to make the other person look a fool, but without seeming to be the one who made it happen. Oh no, the victim did that to themselves because they are stupid.

Techniques of Manipulation

The approaches we can use to manipulate someone's behaviors are so numerous that they themselves could fill an entire book. Thankfully, this chapter explains the most valuable approaches with more than enough detail for you to start employing them yourself.

Take note of how each method depends on your knowledge of dark psychology and NLP — without them, you can't begin to use them reliably, and that's why this is just one part of manipulation and persuasion. Our first method has been coined as "fear and relief" — in this method, you evoke someone else's fear, and then relieve them by telling them there is still something they can do.

As usual, we want to remind you of the importance of considering ethics with manipulation. If you aren't comfortable doing it, you should consider whether you should be doing it in the first place. Just because something is going to benefit you, doesn't mean it's something you should do.

That said, using fear and relief is not an unethical thing to do in every situation, even though it is not everyone's cup of tea.

The technique of manipulation works just as you think it would — first, you talk with your subject like you always would. You start out with your state control; that way, you are ready for whatever reaction they give to this tactic. Next, you get closer to them. Despite the name, as you can see, fear is not the very first thing you start with. If you literally started with fear, they wouldn't trust you in the first place, and the relief would mean nothing to them. Perhaps the better name for this method would be the peace, fear, and relief method.

Peace is where Step 1 takes place. Match up with their unconscious brain language just like you always do for NLP. After that, you bring in the step of fear. You don't jump scare them, but rather you give them the impression that something bad is going to happen. What you say for this depends on what you are trying to get them to do. Whatever it is, it has to be bad enough that they will be convinced to change what they were already going to do. The key is they have to think it is important enough for them to change their actions.

There is another key part of it too, however. Your subject needs to be relieved very soon after they were made to be scared, because otherwise, they will just associate the fear with you. Your subject associating you with fear will make Step 1 much harder in the future, so it's very important that you don't let this happen. Relieve them as soon as you can, and don't let them think you scared them on purpose. This will preserve their positively-to idea of you, but still, put that fear into their head to get them to change their behavior.

You cannot neglect the thinking side of manipulation. It is still very much necessary, because without it you wouldn't be changing their minds in the first place. To begin with, we have to go back to frames and their structures.

We already talked about the importance of adaptability with frames with persuasion. That is still completely true with manipulation, so keep that in mind. We just don't want to repeat all of it when you just read it, so go back over it again if you need to. But with manipulation, you need to take the structure of framing into greater consideration than you did before.

That's because if you want someone to change their action, rather than thought, it takes much more drastic measures. You need to directly ask them to change their behavior, but you also need to more directly get them to confront their ideas.

What is the structure of a frame? On a basic level, the structure is that of cause and effect. The cause is what is happening in the outside world, and the effect is how it affects the subject. Before you get your subject to change their behavior, they have a certain idea about how their actions affect them and other people.

Your job as an NLP manipulator is to show them how their current framing of cause of effect is wrong. When you change someone's framing, this is called Deframing.is a crucial part of manipulation, because remember, you need to take drastic measures by getting someone to change their behaviors.

If they are thinking the same way they were before when you are done with them, they aren't going to change their behavior — just like there is no chance they are changing their behavior unless someone tells them they should directly. If no one does, they will never even stop to consider the idea that this is something they should do.

Don't forget that manipulation is a matter of both thought and action. While persuasion was all about getting into someone's mind, manipulation is still about that, but it now has an added element of action. And if you want to get someone to change their action, there is a new idea you will have to learn. It is called behavioral tone.

Behavioral tone is a lot like one's emotional intensity, but it is the intensity of one's actions. Don't get the wrong idea, here, because you don't want to scare anyone. But you don't have to scare anyone to come off as a strong person.

Being a strong person is what becoming a confident personality was all about. If you have this kind of personality, everyone will listen to you. But more importantly, for the matter of manipulation, people will do what you say, as well.

If you want people to do what you tell them to do, as the saying goes, actions speak louder than words. People don't think logically in the way that everyone acts as they do. Instead, they are driven by a number of factors. And one thing that will get them to change their ways every time is a strong personality shaking things up in their life.

These chapters are rife with information, and it can probably be overwhelming if you consume them all at once. For this reason, we absolutely recommend coming back to them. But even though it wouldn't cover everything we have been through, we will summarize the basics of manipulation before we move on to mind reading.

Manipulation requires more overt means than persuasion because getting someone to change their behavior is no subtle matter. People's minds are easy to change without their ever knowing, but changing their actions requires changes on multiple fronts, and the mind is only one.

If people, you should try to change their social environment to stop their undesirable behavior. But if that is not possible, you need to emphasize how it is all on them to change their behavior; you need to tell them directly what you think they need to change; finally, you need to use the fear and relief method to make them see what bad things could happen if they do not change.

Now that you are clear on the landscapes and techniques of persuasion and manipulation, it is time to dive into the world of mind reading, psychic resistance, and more.

Signs of Manipulation As It Is Used In Today in the World (Practical Examples)

Manipulation happens in all kinds of relationships in our society. It happens between lovers, between pastors and their following, and politicians manipulate us as well, among many other relationships. In this section, we review the signs of manipulation in different relationships.

Churches

Manipulation in the church can occur in both ways. The people in the church leadership can manipulate their followers and vice versa. It is sad since most of us look at the church as the source of your peace. Most of us go for spiritual nourishment when we feel down from the church. How sad can it be if the church can be the source of your pain? Let us look at how the pastors can manipulate their followers.

1. Lack of open and honest conversations

In some churches, you are not allowed to ask questions. If you find yourself in such a situation, you are met with excuses or dismissal on not getting the information. It is okay when there are concerns not to divulge information that will interfere with the privacy of other members. The leaders should take responsibility for their actions and always be ready to explain to the members why there are certain rules. Church information should be open to its members, and there should be transparency.

2. Leaders never admit their mistakes

We can forgive our pastors for making mistakes. After all, they are human beings, but it is difficult to forgive them when they fail to communicate. Yes, I know what the Bible says about forgiveness, but remember, I am a human being too. When leaders refuse to admit to their mistakes and are always spinning their actions to fit those of a perfect Lamb of God, they create a difficult situation. You should watch out for some recurring defensiveness in your church's leadership. You should also watch out if the church is masking some of its mistakes.

3. They use shame as an influence mechanism

Some churches in our community use shame to influence their members. They will shame their members for giving little money, shame them for missing the service and shame them for their actions. Even with no knowledge of the world, the Bible is clear that to those who belong to Christ, there is no condemnation. Remember, none of those in the church leadership will sit on the judgment seat at the end of the world. Some act as if they have the final say on who will enter the gates of heaven. They will use the carrot and stick theory to manipulate you.

4. They are selective

First of all, you should understand that God created us all equally, and He accepts us the way we are. In some churches, they will restrict you to dress in a certain manner, they will choose people of a certain color, and they will force their members to follow some stipulated rules for them to fellowship in that church. The church should not have superficial lines but should be an all-inclusive place. The church should emulate Christ, who embraced all the rich such as Lazarus and the prostitutes, such as Mary Magdalene. Do not get me wrong; rules and regulations are important to run any organization but rules created to exclude a certain group of people in the wrong. Church leaders should know that they are servants.

Now I do not want you to think that pastors are evil for such actions above. You might find that some are not even aware of these manipulative actions, but others do it intentionally. Flipping the coin, pastors are also prone to manipulation. The church members can do it without the pastors realizing it. All the same, neither of the manipulations is acceptable. Let us look at the other side of the coin and find out how the church members can manipulate their pastors.

Compliments

Compliments are good as they encourage us and make us feel good. Now some members may use compliments to manipulate you. They will seek to influence your decisions in the church's agenda through flattery. You should watch out for such signs, as they are as bad as using criticism to bully another.

Criticisms

Well, you can never avoid criticism, especially if you have a leadership role. During conversations, some members will criticize your actions using their tone and sometimes body language. Always follow the church's rules and regulations and the teachings of the Bible. Be gentle when responding to such scenarios, and you will settle the manner amicably.

Silence

They tell us that silence is the best tool to silence manipulation, but it can also be a sign of manipulation. You find members giving you the silent treatment to control you. The pastor should be aware of this and should not carry the burden but instead should pray for the members.

Prayers

Pastors should take caution with the people they share with their burdens. They should protect themselves and their families from over-exposure. They should find trusted friends to share with their challenges, and even then, they should choose what is important to share and what is not.

Families

Manipulation happens in all kinds of relationships. It can be intentionally used or unintentionally, but in the end, the other party ends up doing something they did not want to do in the first place. In our homes, parents can manipulate their children, and the children can manipulate their parents as well. Children have an early exposure at an early age that they can get what they want through tantrums and when you give in, they get control. Away from the children. Now, what are the signs that teens are manipulating their caregivers?

1. Steamrolling

Teenagers make endless and repetitive requests that are meant to wear out the caregivers to get their way. They will use the 'can I' 'how about now' language all the time. The act like a broken record that keeps playing the same song repeatedly.

2. Lying

Teenagers love to tell little white lies or omitting some parts of the truth to get what they want. They leave out some details if given, would change your affirmation to their request. Most of them also collaborate on the small lies in case the parents communicate; they will have the same information and allow them their request.

3. Retaliation

Most teenagers do some hurtful things to retaliate for not getting their way. They will not clean their room; they will dress inappropriately, they will put on loud music; all these as an attempt to get even with you. It is difficult because you cannot yell at them to stop since they are no longer children, and most caregivers end up giving in to their demands to avoid these hurtful actions.

Caregivers can as well manipulate their children, and it is bad since the children are in their developing age, and it makes their life difficult. Briefly, let us look at the signs that a caregiver is manipulating the child.

- They do not give the child security and affirmation
- They are always critical.
- The caregiver always demands the attention of the child.
- The caregiver makes toxic jokes about the child.
- The caregiver does not allow the child to express their negative emotions
- The caregiver scares the child.

Politics

Politicians engage the emotional system of your brains to get political mileage. They use fear, disgust, and anger and never compassion or hope. Politicians never inspire us to work together for the common good of us all. They use anger, fear, and disgust to manipulate how we vote. They influence how we feel about other candidates and their policies. Most of us are never aware that we are being manipulated.

1. **Informing you that the turn-out will be high**

Politicians will tell you that they turn out will be high to motivate you to go to the polls. If they told you that the turnout would be low, most would not turn out since it depresses the efforts to go out and vote.

2. **Public shaming**

The politicians will never shame you publicly to safeguard their reputation and their votes, but they can use other means to make you feel bad for not voting. You would get ads and letters asking you what your relatives and friends would think of you if you did not vote. It will push you to vote.

3. **Making promises or threats to follow up with you**

It is natural for human beings to do things in the right way when their actions are under observation. In the 2010 US election, some people received a letter to encourage them to vote. Others received the same letter, but with an addition that they will be called to share their voting experience. It brought more voter turnout than the previous general election.

Chapter 11: Hypnosis

Hypnosis can occur with or without the person's knowledge. If a person knows they are being hypnotized, they may be more aware of what is going on, but they are still susceptive to manipulation.

Hypnosis is a technique which alters a person's state of consciousness in order to make them highly suggestible to behaviors which they would not normally exhibit. It has been used historically in everything from parlor shows to intense psychotherapy and is subject to a great deal of skepticism. In the realm of dark psychology, hypnosis could be used to cause the subject to act on another's behalf or otherwise behave in a way abhorrent to their normal state of being. Because people in a state of hypnosis are often hyper-focused on the task they've been given, they are driven to complete that task no matter the consequence.

Hypnosis is used for many different reasons, and it can be used for positive change as well as negative change. Hypnosis has several elements, and they may or may not be present in different iterations of the hypnosis process. It starts with an induction. Remember in cartoons, when they have the illustration of the swirling visual effect, and some head-wrapped mystic is holding a watch with the swirl in front of a person's face? This cartoon depiction is what is known formally as the induction process.

The induction process is when a person is actually trying to change another person's state of consciousness. In order to make the person more suggestible and influence-able, hypnosis uses an actual transformation of the state of consciousness. In order to think about this, you can think about a person who is typical and awake, a person who is paralyzed but otherwise capable, and a person who is in a coma. There are many gradations to the state of consciousness that a person is in. The person who is being hypnotized is not paralyzed, but they are closer to that than normal consciousness. Normal consciousness allows the person to have too much stability and defenses. The state that is induced in hypnosis is one where a person does not have all their defenses in play.

After the induction process has been successfully implemented, then the person can be told what to do or what to think. Since the person who is being hypnotized has their defenses uncovered and weakened, they are able to take instructions without question.

One method that works in NLP as a tool for hypnosis is anchoring. Anchoring is when a hypnotist uses something very familiar to you to bring you to that induction space where you are very suggestible. It might be a nursery rhyme, it might be a name you were called when you were younger, or it might be a song. This works to engage your subconscious, and it tricks you into thinking you are safe and allowed to be engaged in the suggestions.

Another NLP –based method for hypnosis is the NLP Flash. The flash works by switching the reward to punishment, or the punishment to a reward. So, if there is something that you like to do which you are trying to stop doing, like smoking cigarettes, the hypnotist will make you think about a cigarette, and then they will make you experience something very uncomfortable, like an electric shock or some other kind of physical or emotional pain. This is a very dark method and can have very deep implications.

Hypnotism can be a very strong way to persuade someone against their will. It may not be as secretive as the other methods of persuasion, but it can be used without your knowledge.

The next major method of Dark Persuasion is manipulation. Manipulation comes in many forms; what we will talk about here the most is manipulation in interpersonal relationships. Manipulators have many methods, but some of the major ones will be discussed in the following paragraphs.

The first is putting down the other person. The manipulator often will have to be very sneaky about this technique. Obviously, if there is someone who puts you down, you will not like them, and you will start to avoid them. So, the manipulator often starts out as a close friend or a confidant. They build trust in the relationship before diving in. Then, at some point, they will start to disparage the other person in what they do, how they look, or other parts of their personality. The manipulator often knows exactly how much they can push buttons, and they know how far they can go before being recognized as a manipulator. Along with their technique also comes the making the other person feel guilty. The manipulator makes the other person feel like they have wronged them, rather than the truth, which is that they are being tricked. The manipulator will make the person feel like they have some sort of debt to the other so that they enter into a sort of pact where there is inequality. Ultimately, what happens is that the manipulator puts the person down, which makes them feel bad about themselves, and it makes them feel like they don't deserve to stand up for themselves.

Another technique of manipulation is lying. Lying may be one of the more straightforward techniques of the manipulator. They will use excuses and complete fabrications to get other people to behave the way they want to. Lying is something that can start small and morph into a larger problem. The manipulator knows how to keep a person stuck in their web of illusions. Overall, they create a larger illusion of what the "truth" is. They try to create something that appears true to the manipulated person. The lies might have to do with any number of subjects. If the manipulator wants money, they might lie about how poor they are, and make themselves seem broke and desperate. If they want loyalty, they might make up lies about how important the other person is to them. If they want a job, they might lie about their experience in that field and make it sound like they are very successful. If they want sex, they might lie about a whole host of subjects.

Chapter 12: Brain washing

Now that we know where brainwashing started, let's look at the definition of the term. Brainwashing can simply be defined as a process where a person or a group of people make use of some underhand methods to talk someone into changing their will to that of the manipulator. When discussing this topic, it is important to delineate between honest persuasion and brainwashing, as there are several ways that people persuade one another these days, especially in the field of politics.

A very easy way that people persuade others to conform to their will is by stating a few things that could typically induce a yes response from the target. They then use some statement of facts as the icing on the cake. At the end, they state what it is that they want people to do. For example, consider the speech below: "Are you tired of paying exorbitant fares for your child's schooling? What about the rising prices of gas and power supply? Are you concerned about the constant riots and strikes? Well, a good point to recall that the government has mentioned the country is gradually drawing close to recession and that the prices of fuel will continue to rise as they are seeing the greatest drop in the economy since the end of the civil war. If you want the country to change for the better, vote democrats." The truth is that you may not want to agree with the fact that these are brainwashing techniques which may come off as subtle persuasion and that they are techniques in the hands of manipulators.

Some of the common manipulation techniques that you should watch out for include:

Isolation:

When trying to brainwash a person, one of the first things usually done is the isolation of the victim from their family, friends and loved ones. This is to ensure that the victim will not have any other person to talk to besides the manipulator. So, the victim will get all their ideas and information from the manipulator while avoiding any likelihood of a third party stepping in to ask what is going on.

Attack on the victim's self-esteem:

Since the manipulator has successfully isolated the victim, he must look for a way to break his will and self-esteem. They will then use the process to begin to rebuild the victim in whatever image they wish to. The only way a person can be brainwashed is if the person manipulating them is superior to them. This attack on the person's self-esteem would manifest in the form of intimidation, ridicule or mocking the victim.

Mental abuse:

The manipulator will try to brainwash their victim by putting them through a phase of mental torture. They will do this by telling lies to the victim and making them feel embarrassed by telling them the truth in front of other people. They can also bully these victims by badgering them and not leaving room for them to have any form of personal space.

Physical abuse:

Manipulators understand there are many physical techniques that can be used to brainwash the victim. These techniques include depriving the victim of sleep and making sure that they stay cold, hungry or causing bodily harm by exhibiting violent behavior towards them. The manipulator can also make use of some much more subtle ways like increasing the noise levels, making sure that there is a light that is always flickering on and off or raising or lowering the room's temperature.

Playing repetitive music:

According to a study, if a person plays a beat repeatedly, especially a beat that has a range of about 45 to 72 beats each minute, it is possible to introduce an extremely hypnotic state. This is because repetition is much closer to the rhythm that comes from the beat of the heart of a human being. This rhythm, however, can cause an alteration to the consciousness of the person until they reach what is known as the Alpha state, which is where the person becomes 25 times more suggestible than he would ordinarily be when they are in a Beta state.

Allowing the victim to only have contact with other brainwashed people: When the manipulator is brainwashing a person, they ensure that the victim does not encounter any other person/people besides those that are already brainwashed. This is to create room for peer pressure. The truth is that everyone desires to be liked and accepted. This is more prevalent when a person is a new member of a group. In such a case, the person will typically adhere to and promote things that the other members are saying which will secure them a space with their new company.

Us vs. them:

This also has to do with the possibility of being accepted by a group. The manipulator makes the victim feel like there is an "us" and a "them." So, they are offering the victim a chance to choose the group they wish to belong to. This is done to gain absolute loyalty and obedience from the victim.

Love bombing:

This technique has to do with attracting the victim to the group through physical touch and by sharing some intimate thoughts with the victim. Emotional bonding is also used in this technique through a show of excessive affection as well as constant validation.

All the above mentioned are a few ways to brainwash a person. Once a person is brainwashed it is usually very difficult to get them back to normal. They develop more rigid neural pathways than other people and this could be an indication of why it is always very hard for a brainwashed person to double check their situation by rethinking it once they have been brainwashed.

Chapter 13: Preventing Manipulation

Manipulation normally occurs when an individual is used for the benefit of others. It is a situation where the manipulator comes up with an imbalance of power and goes ahead to exploit his victim just to serve their main agendas. Those who are manipulative are the kind of people who will disguise their own desires and interests as yours. They will undertake all they can to make you believe that their own opinions are the objective facts. They will then act as if they are cornered. Manipulators will pretend to offer assistance so that you can improve your attitude, performance, and promise that they will assist you in improving your life in general. That is all that they want you to believe. The hidden truth is that the main aim of these people is to control you, and not control you, as they want you to believe. They are not interested in making your life better, but just to change you. They also want to validate their lives and make sure that you don't outgrow them.

Once you have given these characters back to your life, getting rid of them will not be easy. They will appear to flip flop on issues and act so slippery when you want to hold them accountable. They also tend to promise you help that doesn't seem to be near.

People can be easily manipulated when they opt to put up with behaviors that are passive-aggressive. According to a recent study that was published in the Journal of Social & Personal Relationships, offensive people tend to interfere with the general performance of an individual. The study also noted that ignoring those who are negative could do you more harm than good. When these people are ignored, the research states that their productivity and intelligence is increased. More than 100 participants were examined for this study. The participants were asked to ignore or talk with random people who had been earlier asked to either be offensive or friendly.

The participants were not aware of the kind of people they were going to meet. After interacting for about four minutes, each of the participants was offered a thought exercise that needed them to have a better concentration. The study later noted that those who ignored the negative individuals performed way much better than those who engaged the negative individuals.

The researchers then summarized that ignoring some people in a serious social interaction is one better way of conserving the mental resources of a person. The best strategy is to avoid those who are negative in their speeches and actions. But at times, that can't be enough. A negative person can also be manipulative and sneaky at times. In such situations, you will be forced to apply other strategies.

The truth is that being manipulated is not a good thing. The only possible worse thing than manipulation could just be admitting our dirty little secrets. Each time we realize that we have been manipulated, we not only feel stupid but also ashamed and weak. And all that doesn't stop there. If we continue to fall for the tricks that these people lay on us, they will leave us with an awful feeling about everything around us. Instead of being hurt for another time, the best thing to do could just be not to trust anybody.

Manipulation can only be successful if the target fails to recognize it or just decide to allow it. But regardless of all that, there exists certain things that you can do to recognize that you are under manipulative powers. They can also help you to prevent or stop a possible case of manipulation. Some of the ideas may not be desirable or possible for your situation, but that's just fine because every situation and every person is totally different.

Know all your fundamental rights

One of the single most imperative guidelines, when you are in this similar situation, is to know all your fundamental rights. But that's not all, you should also recognize when any of those rights are being violated. Remember that you are at liberty to stand up for yourself and make sure no single fundamental right is being violated. You should, however, do this carefully and make sure that you do not harm others. Again, you should not forget that you might forfeit these rights if you cause harm to other people. Ensure you are conversant with some of the basic human rights such as:

- The right to be treated with dignity and respect.

- The right to express one's wants, opinions, and feelings.

- The right to give no as an answer and maintain that without any guilty feelings.

- The right to set up one's own standards and priorities.

- The right to take care and safeguard yourself from being emotionally, mentally, or physically threatened.

The mentioned basic rights show the extent to which your boundaries are supposed to reach. We are living in a society where people don't represent any of these rights. The mental manipulators are particularly interested in depriving you of your rights so that they can fully control you and take advantage of you. However, you still have the moral authority and power to state that you are fully in charge of your life and not the manipulator.

Maintain a distance with these people

As noted, one of the surest ways of detecting a manipulator is to check if the individual acts with different faces when in front of various people and situations. Whereas all of us have mastered this art of social differentiation, the mental manipulators are masters when it comes to dwelling in extremes – where they show great humility to one person and rude to the other. They can also feel so aggressive at one point, and totally helpless the next minute. When you see this kind of behavior in people whom you are close to, the best thing to do is to keep a healthy distance. You should also try to avoid engaging with these people until you are really forced to do that. Remember that some of the top causes of chronic psychological manipulation are deep-seated and complex; therefore, saving or changing these people cannot be your job.

Stop Self-Blaming & Personalization

Given that the manipulator's agenda is to know where your weakness is and exploit it, you may even throw the blame game on yourself for not doing your best. In such situations, it is very imperative to reassure yourself that you are not part of the problem. Remember that you are just being manipulated to feel bad about your actions and surrender your rights and power in the end. It is vital to consider the kind of relationship you have with the manipulator as well. These are some of the questions that you should ask yourself:

- Am I getting a respectful treatment?
- Is this relationship 1-way or 2-way?
- Am I satisfied being in this relationship?

The answers to these issues will offer you the most important clues about whether the problem is with the manipulator or with you.

Probe the Manipulators

Mental manipulators will always make demands or requests from you. They do this to make you go the extra mile so that you can meet their needs. At times, it can be very important to put the focus back on the manipulator each time you hear certain solicitations. Ask them some analytical questions to check if they are fully aware of their scheme's inequity. Ask them if their actions appear reasonable to them or if what they want from you is all fair.

When you step out to ask some of these questions, you are simply placing a mirror so the manipulator will be able to view the real nature of his/her ploy. If the manipulator happens to be a master of self-awareness, then he/she will definitely withdraw and back down. Real pathological manipulators, on the other hand, will dismiss the question and insist on having things done their own way. When this takes place, ensure you stand up for your fundamental rights and the manipulators will definitely flee.

Say No in a Firm and Diplomatic Way

Saying no in a firm and diplomatic way is what can be defined as real communication. When it has been articulated in an effective manner, it will give you an opportunity to stand your ground and maintain the best working relationship. It is important to remember that one of your basic human rights is to set your own standards and priorities. It is also within your rights to say no without feeling the guilt, as well as the right to pick your own healthy and happy life.

Set the Consequences

When a mental manipulator persists on violating the boundaries that you have made and is not hearing your "no," you will be forced to deploy the consequences. The ability to be able to point out and assert the consequences is one of the most important skills that you can deploy to resist the efforts of a manipulative person. When they are articulated in an effective manner, consequences will stop the actions of the manipulative person and even compel them to stop the violations and respect instead.

Confront the Bullies in a Safe Way

One fact that is not known to many is that a mental manipulator can turn into a bully when they intimidate and harm others. It is important to note that bullies only prey on those they regard as the weakest, and you can make yourself a target when you remain compliant and passive. However, the fact is that a number of bullies are cowards on the inside. They will often back up when their target starts to stand up for their rights. This is a common practice in office and surroundings, as well as in schoolyards.

Think about the long-term consequences of the actions you undertake

As opposed to just doing what is easiest and fastest, do not forget about the consequences that your actions can have. Remember that psychological manipulators are the best when it comes to making their option the easiest, fastest, and also the least hurtful. They are also best at keeping the people focused on their current feelings. That explains why people do things they later regret. Instead of dealing with a consequence, later on, make sure you choose to do things that you won't be forced to rethink.

Conclusion

Dark psychology is at work in the whole world. You might not like this truth, but you can't modify it.

I hope the knowledge you've gained by reading this will lead you forward, and that your journey will be peopled with the kind of intelligent and lively folks that will make it a thrilling tapestry of experience. Sometimes the destination is fun to think about, but if we miss the journey on the way there, we miss out on the best part. Look up from the path, see who's walking with you and then ask yourself – what did they mean by that hand movement? What does that facial expression mean? How do my own mannerisms mirror theirs? You'll figure out what it all means while you're on your way. Just don't forget to enjoy the journey. It really is the very best part.

I wish you all the best!

-- Caroline Empathy and Power Laws

DARK
PSYCHOLOGY AND
MANIPULATION
IMPROVE YOUR LIFE: THE ULTIMATE GUIDE TO LEARNING THE ART OF PERSUASION, EMOTIONAL INFLUENCE, NLP SECRETS, HYPNOSIS, BODY LANGUAGE, AND MIND CONTROL TECHNIQUES
JOSEPH GRIFFITH

Dark Psychology

and

Manipulation

Improve your Life: The Ultimate Guide to Learning the Art of Persuasion, Emotional Influence, NLP Secrets, Hypnosis, Body Language,

and Mind Control Techniques

© Written by: JOSEPH GRIFFITH

Book Description

Have you been thinking of dark psychology and manipulation? Are you fed up people manipulating you to get what they want? Do you use people? Would you like to master secret techniques to influence people positively?

Well, if this is you, then you have come to the right place.

One thing that is important to bear in mind is that dark psychology refers to the art of manipulating and controlling people's minds. Yes, psychology focuses on how we behave and is central to our thoughts, interactions, and actions. However, dark psychology, on the other hand, is about people using tactics of persuasion, motivation, coercion, and manipulation to get what they want.

Here, you will learn;

- The tenets of dark psychology
- Dark psychology Triad
- Tactics used by everyday people to manipulate others
- Secret techniques of dark persuasion
- How you can positively influence people
- Mind games, hypnotism, and brainwashing

There is so much to learn about the psychological nature of people to prey on others. The truth is that all of humanity has the potential to victimize others. Yes, some try to sublimate this tendency while others choose to act upon their impulses. However, the most important thing for you is to understand your thoughts, perceptions, and feelings that lead to predatory behavior so that you can learn to control yourself and use it for good.

So, what are you still waiting for?

Come with me and let's discover more!

Introduction

You may be wondering what dark psychology is all about and where mind control comes from. In this book, we will discuss what it is and why people can be manipulated and controlled mentally by psychopaths and narcissists. We will also shed some light on what you can do when that happens to you.

One thing that is important to note is that manipulation often happens in families with parents who have narcissistic tendencies. In the case where there is parental alienation, a parent may use their child as a psychological weapon to abuse the other parent. The truth is that mind control, a form of dark psychology, happens in a system where people are – such as churches, families, and workplaces.

The key ingredients of dark psychology are people, narcissistic leaders, lieutenants, scapegoats, and keeping secrets. What is not allowed in this kind of system is having a free spirit or free-thinking mentality. It is such kind of people who are banished from the community of manipulators.

Think about someone that joins a cult, what happens to them? The truth is that cult leaders coerce intelligent people from loving their friends and families in exchange for false promises. People who are manipulated tend to think that the decisions they made belong to them when, in the real sense, they belong to the manipulators.

It is important to note that human social interaction dynamics are powerful. Since time immemorial, people have been manipulated with false doctrines, propaganda, and social pressure. Have you read about Hitler? How did he manage to manipulate an entire country into hating specific groups of people?

It the works of dark psychology!

If you are fighting to rescue yourself from mind control by another person, then read on because you will learn how they do it and how you can rescue yourself from their mind games and undetected mind control.

But how can another manipulate you?

Well, the first thing is that your manipulator will keep you in the dark so that you stay unaware that you are being changed. In other words, they try as much as they can to psychologically lead you to a change of behavior just so that they can satisfy their selfish agendas. Their end goal is to have you do the bidding for them. Think about parental alienation, for instance – the end goal is to hurt the other targeted parent. In other instances, leaders manipulate the masses to satisfy their personal need for control and power – and even fulfillment of their fantasies.

The second trick is that dark psychology purposes to control one's physical and social surroundings. In other words, leaders of mind control offer others ample structure, assignments, and rules to keep others continually on task. The main aim is to ensure that they create a sense of powerlessness in the victims.

How do they achieve this?

They will ensure you are away from your social support network, and with people who are already entrenched in the group. This way, they can easily control your mind so that you lose personal autonomy, confidence, and power. They erode your intuitions, and as your powerlessness increases, your sense of understanding of the world and good judgment diminishes. They attack your worldview, and the outcome of which is cognitive dissonance, and you are not allowed to talk about it whatsoever.

Dark psychology attempts to incorporate a reward system and punishment in the victim's life. In other words, they aim at promoting the manipulator's agenda to undermine the autonomy and individuality of the target. The only time you get positive feedback is when you conform to the beliefs and behaviors of its leaders. Otherwise, you get negative feedback for choosing to hold on to your old beliefs and ways of life.

It aims at creating punishments, rewards, and experiences to promote learning the ideologies of the group and their approved behaviors. In other words, this kind of leadership has a top-down pyramid structure where the leader never loses. What you must bear in mind is that people who are manipulated by users of dark psychological techniques are not valued because of their individuality. Instead, they are used as objects of manipulator's productions, where the leader in the story is the author, director, producer, and playwright of their story.

Read on to learn what dark psychology is and its benefits!

Chapter 1 What is Dark psychology?

"Dark Psychology is the study of the chasm within us all, which only a few enter, and even fewer ever exit. Without a natural predator to cause humans to rally, we prey upon one another."

– Michael Nuccitelli Psy.D.

Several people don't understand what dark psychology is all about. Well, the first thing you must note is that this is a field of study of the human condition about the psychological nature of people to prey on others to manipulate them. The manipulators possess certain deviant drives that are characterized by a lack of purpose. That said, one thing you need to understand is that all of the human race has the potential to manipulate others into doing what they want. Some try to restrain themselves from manipulating others while most act on their impulses.

The main aim of dark psychology is to understand others' feelings, thoughts, and perceptions as well as the subjective systems that contribute to their predatory behaviors. According to dark psychology, the manipulator has a deviant and abusive behavior that causes them to purposively take advantage of others to fulfill their rational and goal-oriented motivation at least 99.9 % of the time. The remainder 0.1% derives its argument from the Adlerian theory and Teleology.

In other words, dark psychology assumes that there is a region within the human mind that allows them to commit atrocious acts without reason. This theory has coined dark singularity.

What is interesting about dark psychology is that it postulates that the entire human race has a reservoir of harm intent towards others. This desire to harm others ranges from minimally obtrusive to pure thoughts of psychopathic behavior characterized by a lack of cohesive rationality – otherwise called the dark continuum.

The mitigating factors that serve as catalysts to dark singularity and where one's actions are said to be heinous and fall under the dark continuum is referred to as dark factor. According to Michael

Nuccitelli, "*Dark Psychology is not just the dark side of our moon, but the dark side of all moons combined.*"

In other words, everything that makes us who we are is related to our dark side. Unfortunately, all cultures, humanity, and faith have this proverbial cancer. From birth to the time you depart – death – there is some side that lurks within each one of us – the evil side. This is the side that is deviant, criminal, and pathological.

"It is the individual who is not interested in his fellow men who has the greatest difficulties in life and provides the greatest injury to others. It is from among such individuals that all human failures spring."

– Alfred Adler

According to dark psychology, some people commit evil acts, not because of money, power, sex, retribution, or other known factors. Instead, they choose to do it because they are horrid – without a goal. In other words, for them, ends do not justify the means. These are the kind of people who injure others for the sake of doing it.

Within each one of us lies this potential!

You and I have the potential to harm others without cause, purpose, or explanation. This potential is considered complex – one that is even hard to define.

According to dark psychology, each human being has a potential of predatory behavior deep within them, a potential that has access to emotional feelings, thoughts, and perceptions. But the most important question is, do you act upon them? Think of a time when you felt like hurting someone not because they wronged you but because you just wanted to. Did you act upon those feelings and thoughts?

If you are honest enough with yourself, then you will realize that you have had such thoughts and feelings of wanting to commit atrocious acts. The only difference is whether or not you acted upon them.

Considering that each one of us considers themselves benevolent, there is a belief that our thoughts and feelings would be non-existent. The truth is that we all have these thoughts but luckily never have a chance to act upon them. That said, others have similar thoughts and feelings and choose to act out of impulse or premeditated. The point is that human behavior related to their evil actions is goal-oriented and purposive.

In short, dark psychology concerns itself with the human part that permits and impels predatory behaviors. Some of the features of this behavioral tendency include; lack of obvious rational motivation, lack of predictability, and universality. It is an extension of evolution. Well, let's look at this tenet of evolution. First, humans evolved from animals and are currently the paradigm of all animal life. The frontal lobe of the brain allows us to become the apex of all creatures. However, being apex creatures does not necessarily mean that our primal instincts to be predators.

"The greater the feeling of inferiority that has been experienced, the more powerful is the urge to conquest and the more violent the emotional agitation."

– Alfred Adler

If you subscribe to this kind of thinking, then you believe that all your behaviors are based on three key instincts – aggression, sex, and instinctual drive to self-sustain. One thing you must bear in mind is that evolution follows the tenets of survival of the fittest and reproduction. In other words, we live in a way to ensure our survival and to procreate. The reason we become aggressive is that we wish to mark our territories and ultimately win the right to reproduce.

It is our power of perception and thought that has contributed to us being apex creatures of practicing brutality. Think of a nature documentary you have recently watched; you will realize that as the lion runs after the antelope, the author ensures that you feel sorrow for the antelope as they are ripped into shreds. While this may be brutal and unfortunate, this model fits the idea of self-preservation. In other words, the lion kills the antelope for food – something they required for survival.

"Defiant individuals will always persecute others, yet will always consider themselves persecuted."

– Alfred Adler

When animals are hunting, they will tend to stalk and kill their prey – mostly young, weak, and female groups. While this kind of behavior is psychopathic, the main reason why they choose this prey is to lower their chances of injury and death. All creatures act in this manner – brutal, violent, and bloody.

However, when we look at human conditions, this tends to change, but a little. Where are often the only creatures on earth who prey upon each other without reason for survival or procreation? They do it for their inexplicable motivations. It is this part of the human psyche that dark psychology addresses as predatory behaviors. The assumption is that there is something intrapsychic that influences human actions – one that is anti-evolutionary. We are the only species that will kill each other for reasons other than food, survival, reproduction, or territory. In other words, we will harm one another with a complete lack of rational reason because there is a part of us that fuels vicious and dark behaviors.

It is this dark side of humanity that is unpredictable in the understanding of who acts on these evil impulses, and even on the lengths, certain people will go with their sense of mercy negated. This includes people who murder, rape, torture, or violate others without cause. It is these actions that dark psychology speaks to as predators seeking out their human prey without a clearly defined purpose. Humans are incredibly dangerous to each other and themselves.

To fully grasp what dark psychology is all about, you must understand the following tenets;

Well, dark psychology is a ***universal part of our human condition***. It is this construct that has exerted influence throughout history. Every creature, society, and person that resides in them maintain this human condition. Even the most benevolent of people know that they have an evil side of them, but the good thing is that they never act upon it – hence lower rates of violent emotional feelings, thoughts, and perceptions.

Dark psychology is a study of ***the human condition about their thoughts, perceptions, and emotional feelings.*** All these are related to the innate human potential to inflict harm on others without cause. Given the fact that all behaviors are goal-oriented, the truth is that as one draws nearer to a black hole of evil, the higher the chances of them having a purpose in motivation.

The severity of dark psychology is ***not deemed less or more heinous through manipulation but plots a wide range of inhumanity***. Let us consider Ted Bundy and Jeffrey Dahmer – they both were severe psychopaths with heinous actions. However, the major difference between the two was that Dahmer committed his atrocious murders for the need for companionship while Ted sadistically caused others pain because of his psychopathic evil. On the rank of the dark continuum, they both rank high, but his desperate need for love can understand Dahmer.

There is a belief that every one of us has the potential for violence. This potential is innate, and a wide range of internal and external factors increase the chance for this to manifest into volatile behaviors. The truth is that these behaviors are predatory, and sometimes, they can function devoid of reason. It is humans who are responsible for the distortion in the predator-prey dynamic. While violence and mayhem may exist in other creatures, humanity is the only species with the potential to harm without purpose.

With a better understanding of causes and triggers of dark psychology, we are in a better position to recognize, diagnose, and lower the risk of dangers inherent in our influence. When we all accept that the potential for evil exists in us, we are better served to lower its chances of erupting. Additionally, when we understand the tenets of dark psychology, we will see how it fits our original evolutionary purpose for the struggle for survival.

Benefits of knowing your dark side

"I guess we're all two people. One daylight, and the one we keep in shadow."

— Bruce Wayne

If you are honest about growth, change, and living your life to the fullest, then you will come across parts of yourself that you will find rather disturbing – and yet you will have to accept. Aside from the bright nature, we know of ourselves, there lies a darker side of our nature – the ugly and frightening part. This is what we refer to in dark psychology as shadow-self.

One thing you must note is that your shadow self is always standing right behind you – just outside your view. When you stand indirect light, you cast a shadow, right. The shadow is the part of yourself that you can't really see. Think about it for a moment, what lengths do you go to just to protect your self-image from unfamiliarity and flattery?

Why is it easier to see another person's shadow but not see your own?

The truth is, when you see another person's shadow, you realize that one can show gifts in one area of life and remain unaware of their evil behaviors in certain areas. Everyone is susceptible to this. Over the years, I have learned that working with my shadow has not only been a challenging but rewarding process too. It is by looking at your darker side that you gain greater creativity, authenticity, personal awakening, and energy. It is this reflective process that contributes to your maturity.

You might be thinking, what is a shadow?

Well, this refers to the dark side of our personality. It is this side that consists of negative emotions and impulses such as greed, rage, desire, selfishness, envy, and striving for power. Your dark side is primarily primitive.

What is it that you deny in yourself? Everything you perceive as evil, inferior, and unacceptable is what forms your shadow. If something is not compatible with your conscious attitude about yourself, this is your dark side. It is your disowned self – parts of yourself you no longer claim to be yours. These parts of ourselves do not go anywhere. Even though we try as much as we can to cast them out, the truth is that we cannot get rid of them. They remain as part of our unconscious.

Realize that you cannot eliminate your darker side. Instead, it stays with you as your darker brother or sister. When we fail to see our darker self, that is when trouble ensues.

So, how is it born?

I want you to imagine a child – it could be yours or someone you know. Each time you look at the child play with others, you see love, kindness, and generosity. But is that all you can see? Well, the truth is, you will also see greed, anger, and selfishness.

Just like them, we possess the light and dark side of ourselves. It is through these emotions that we all are shared humanity. However, as we grow, something else happens – traits linked with goodness are accepted, and those associated with bad are rejected.

Each one of us has basic needs – security, desire to belong, physiological, among others. These needs are either biological or instinctual. Like children, when we express one part of ourselves, you receive negative cues from your surroundings – anger and tantrums. Each time our parents reprimanded us of our outbursts, they sent us to our rooms, right? Our teachers might have shamed us for our lack of dignity in class. Whenever anything like this happened, it threatened one of your basic needs.

The truth is that when this happened, we changed our habits to gratify our needs and learned to adapt to the world around us. In other words, when we are still children, the shadow self is bundled together and swept out of view.

But what happens when you grow up? When you finally know your evil self?

Well, the truth is that when we ignore our shadow self, what we are simply doing is turning it against us. It is this shadow self that represents all the parts of yourself you have disowned. While our shadow self can operate on its own without our awareness – more like it is on autopilot – it causes us to do things we would not do voluntarily, and that is the reason behind regret. You find yourself saying things you wouldn't normally say. Your body language expresses emotions you would consciously not feel. In short, when you ignore your dark side, you end up hurting your relationships – with friends, spouse, or family, among others.

If there is anything I have learned over the years is that whatever qualities you deny in yourself, you will see it in others – a phenomenon referred to as projection. In other words, anything we deny in ourselves, we project it in others. For instance, when someone is rude to you, you get irritated. This is a good bet that you have not owned your rudeness. Well, this does not necessarily mean that the other person is not rude to you. However, if the rudeness was not on your dark side, someone being rude to you would not bother you one bit!

This is a process that does not happen consciously because we are not fully aware of our projections. Instead, our ego uses this mechanism for self-defense – defend its perception of self. Our false identities of "good" stand in the way of us connecting with our dark side. In other words, through projections, we distort reality and create a thick boundary between our perception of self and our behavior in reality. Just as Robert Johnson said, *if we don't work on ourselves, the shadow will always be projected. In other words, it is laid on another just so that we don't take responsibility for it.*

So, what are the benefits of our dark side/shadow?

While our dark side is not something enjoyable to talk about, exploring it offers us an opportunity for growth and development because let's face it – no one likes talking about their flaws, weaknesses, nastiness, selfishness, and hate, among others. Some of the benefits of knowing our dark side include;

Improved relationship

As you gain insight into your darker side and come to terms with the fact that you have this dark half of you, you begin to see things with more clarity. It helps you remain grounded, whole, and human.

The truth is, when you accept the darker side of you, you make it easier for you to accept the darker sides of the people around you. This way, others' behaviors, and actions will not trigger you easily. Instead, it will make it easier for you to communicate with others effectively. As a result, you enjoy improved relationships – with friends, spouse, business partners, and family, among others.

Clearer perception

When you see others and yourself exactly as you are, you view the world around you with a clearer lens. Integrating your shadow self into everyday activities helps you approach your true self, hence offering you a realistic evaluation of who you are. In other words, you will not perceive yourself as being too small; neither will you feel as though you have a high moral ground than others.

Your self-awareness of the dark side goes a long way in helping one assess their surroundings with more accuracy. This will allow you to see others and assess situations with more clarity, understanding, and an expression of compassion.

Enhanced energy and physical health

One thing that is important to bear in mind is that dragging around the baggage of your darker side can be draining and exhausting. It is draining to constantly be working to repress some part of yourself that you don't wish to face in your adult life. When you are fatigued and lethargic, you risk poisoning your unexamined life. Mental suppression has also been shown to contribute to both disease and physical pain.

Knowing and acknowledging your dark side helps liberate the huge amount of energy you were unconsciously investing in protecting yourself. As a result, you experience improved mental, physical, and emotional health. In other words, knowing and accepting your dark side offers one inner strength and a sense of balance so that you are better placed to take on life's challenges.

Psychological integration and maturity

As long as you try to deny your dark shadow or repress certain parts of yourself, unity, and a sense of wholeness becomes elusive. There is no way you can feel whole and balanced when you have a divided mind. However, when you choose to integrate your shadow into what you do, you come one step closer to finding wholeness – and that is what helps you achieve maturity.

Greater creativity

Knowing your dark side helps unlock your untapped creative potential. As Abraham Maslow and Carl Rogers once said, creativeness is a spontaneous occurrence that only people who are mentally healthy have.

So, how then can you engage your dark side so that you have the upper hand at approaching your shadows with ease?

Center yourself

Perhaps this is the most important thing to do before you get into your dark side and yet is seldom mentioned in literature. You might be thinking, "what will happen to me if I discover my dark side when I am not centered?"

Well, it's simple – you will not get a constructive outcome.

One thing you must note is that your shadow self represents various clusters of hidden parts within your psyche. It is only when you are at the center that you will get to know these parts. If one of the parts is blended with you, the process is hijacked, leaving you confused, judgmental, and critical. It will inhibit your ability to integrate your dark self. Before you get to work with your dark side, ensure that you are clear, calm, and neutral. That is what it means to be centered.

Cultivate self-compassion

Before you get to know your dark side, you must cultivate a sense of friendship – unconditional one – with yourself, what is referred to as Maitri in Buddhism. Without friendship and compassion, it will be hard to look at your darkness.

Are you hard on yourself when making decisions?

If so, then realize that it will be challenging to confront your darkness. If you are someone that easily feels guilty and ashamed, you must transmute these emotional feelings into self-acceptance, friendliness, and self-compassion. Start by acknowledging the fact that you are human. Understand that we all have a shadow.

The best way you can cultivate compassion is to start with connecting your heart. Place all your focus on your heart. Take in a deep breath and acknowledge your heart. As you breathe out, simply tell your heart, *"Thank you."*

Cultivate self-awareness

To see your darkness, you must have a self-reflective mindset. In other words, you must have the ability to reflect on your thoughts, actions, and emotions. By practicing mindfulness, you help foster non-judgmental awareness. You center your thoughts and actions in the present moment without necessarily opening the door to the inner critic.

When you have self-awareness and -reflection, you can observe and assess your emotional feelings and choices without criticism.

Be courageously honest

The prerequisites to shadow work are integrity and honesty to yourself. It is easy to think superficially of these qualities, but what you must understand is that true honesty simply refers to the willingness to see unpleasant attributes in your behavior and personality.

Coming to terms with parts of yourself you would rather bury deep inside can be uncomfortable and is probably the reason ego invests lots of energy in repressing them. The ability to see all that and accept them just the way they are can be challenging. If you want to be honest with yourself, look at your behaviors, attitudes, emotions, and dark thoughts – and that requires courage.

The reward of doing this plays a significant role in healing splits in your mind. It also helps unlock untapped potential and a world of new possibilities for your growth and development.

Record your discoveries

It is quite fascinating to see that most of our disowned parts wish to remain out of our view. Just the same way a dream slips out of our mind soon after awakening, the darkness in us can be elusive.

You must keep a journal where you record every discovery about yourself. When you put down your insights and then take time to review them later, you help encode those discovering into awareness.

Chapter 2 Dark psychology Triad

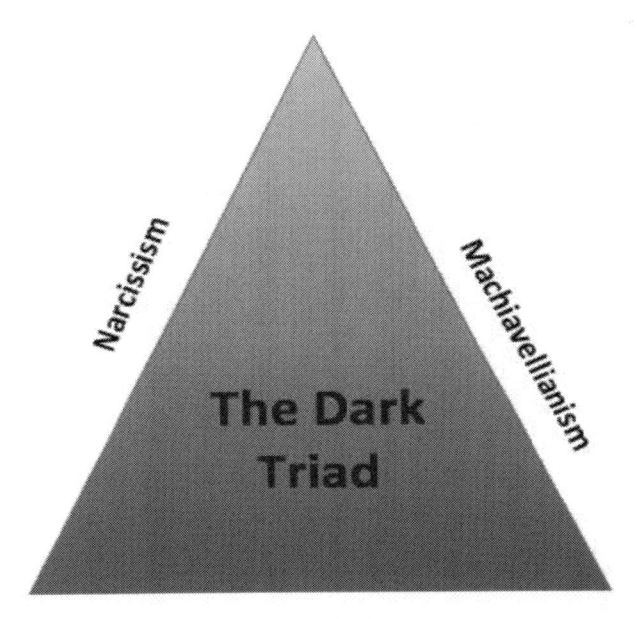

Narcissism

Machiavellianism

The Dark Triad

Psychopathy

So many people argue that the dark triad people are so seductive. Thus, the most critical question we need to ask is why.

The truth is, the Dark triad has three personality traits; narcissism, Machiavellianism, and psychopathy. The term *Narcissism* is derived from the Greek myth of Narcissus - a hunter who fell in love with his reflections when swimming in a pool. In other words, narcissists are people who are not only selfish but also boastful, arrogant, hypersensitive to criticism, and lacks empathy.

Machiavellianism is a word that was coined from the Italian politician and diplomat Niccolo Machiavelli, 16th century. This man earned notoriety when his book *"The Prince"* was interpreted as an endorsement to dark arts – cunning and deceit in diplomacy. Some of the traits associated with this kind of personality include manipulation, duplicity, a lack of morality and emotion, and self-interest.

Psychopathy, on the other hand, includes a lack of remorse and empathy, being volatile and manipulative or others, and showing antisocial behavior. One thing you must note is that there is a difference between psychopathic qualities and being a psychopath, and this lies in the commonly held link with criminal violence.

This indeed is one of the most researched areas in psychology. While this has contributed a great deal to the deeper understanding of the darker side of humanity, how far we differ from each other in the extent to which we constantly exhibit darkness - the darkness in thoughts, emotions, and behaviors in our everyday life, and the question we fail to ask is what lies on the light side of humanity.

The truth is, socially aversive people exist. But what of everyday saints? Don't get me wrong – I am not talking about the person that gives a lot and receives public applauds and awards for their giving just so that they can gain personal success. I am referring to that one person who just by *being*, they shine their light so bright that it radiates in all directions. The one person that is not strategic about their generosity but that one who emits unconditional love – both spontaneously and naturally – because it is who they *truly* are.

According to the study, three distinct features characterize the light triad; Kantianism, humanism, and faith in humanity. Kantianism simply refers to using people as ends to themselves and not just as mere means. Humanism, on the other hand, is valuing the worth and dignity of everyone. Faith in humanity is about believing in the fundamental goodness of human beings.

One thing you need to understand is that the light and dark triads are not opposites of each other. Yes, they are negatively related to each other, but the truth is that the relationship is only moderate, which supports the idea that each person has a little bit of light and darkness in them. While some score high in the dark triad, it is best not to look at them as lesser beings – after all, to have the dark side is to be human.

Instead, it is important to look at them as magnified and unleashed versions of the potential that lies within them.

According to a research study, the dark triad is associated with being younger, male, who is motivated by power, achievement, affiliation, and instrumental sex. They are the kind of people who have self-enhancement values, conspicuous consumption, immature defense styles, selfishness, and perceive creative work and immortality as a path to death transcendence. The dark triad has a negative correlation to such traits as agreeableness, life satisfaction, compassion, a quiet ego, empathy, conscientiousness, and a strong belief that humans are good.

Let us bring this closer home – think of an employee at your workplace who seems to derive pleasure from bothering others or even sabotaging the company. This kind of person does not have a sense of remorse. They tell blatant lies when they are caught doing something unacceptable. These are the kind of people who can be termed as the "Dark Triad." When someone shows evil behavior, it is highly likely that you will see these three traits – narcissism, Machiavellianism, and psychopathy.

Let us dig deeper into each of these features. When do you say that someone is narcissistic, Machiavellianism, or psychopathic?

Well, Narcissism is about having a complete focus on self. It is about believing that you are special and should follow a different set of societal rules than the ones others follow. You are also known for your inability to show empathy. While these kinds of people may show cognitive empathy – empathy only through words – the truth is that empathy lacks in their actions and emotional feelings. When they tell you, "I am sorry ABC happened," what they mean to say is that they don't feel any sadness, remorse, or real feelings to show of it. They tend to do things just so that they can look good and not because they feel like it is the right thing to do.

Machiavellianism is about someone using exploitation and manipulations of others to gain control or to maintain power over others. The thing with Machiavellian people is that they possess a rather cynical perception of what morality is. They think that the reason people follow morals is that they are not smart enough to figure out how to circumvent them. They are so focused on what is in it for them and how to con others just so that they can get the most out of the situation.

When you think of a psychopath, the first thing that comes to mind is selfishness, impulsive behavior, lack of remorse, and breaking the law. While there are people who can't seem to decipher social norms, rules, and regulations, a psychopath knows the difference between right and wrong but does not seem to care at all.

Interestingly, all these three dark triad qualities are genetic. Yes, the surrounding plays a significant role in the development of these personality traits, but the truth is that they are more likely that one inherited them from their genes, making them more predisposed. That said, this does not mean that genetics is destiny. The truth is you can have a genotype for a certain trait, but that does not translate into a phenotype. For instance, you may have a gene for blue and brown eyes, but the phenotype is brown eyes.

Additionally, everyone has certain features of Machiavellianism, narcissism, and psychopathy at some point in their lives. The good thing is that most people can recognize these behaviors and realize that they do not work well in their professional and personal lives.

When you don't have the awareness that these traits are negatively impacting your life and that they are pervasive, only then can it be ruled as a disorder!

It is important to note that these three factors of the Dark Triad produce different outcomes at the workplace and in personal life – depending on how low or high you are in each feature. High Machiavellianism and psychopathy indicate a high likelihood of low performance at the workplace. Yes, a lack of quality in work performance means that you are not achieving a certain baseline, being counterproductive might mean that you are overachieving but in the wrong way.

The truth is, you are using hard tactics, one way or the other when manipulating others – common among Machiavellians and psychopaths. Narcissists, on the other hand, tend to employ soft tactics to exploit others so that they can eventually get what they want. The difference between hard tactics and soft tactics is that hard tactics include threatening others or sabotaging work. Soft tactics, on the contrary, is about giving compliments and gifts to influence people into giving you what you want.

Take a step back into your life and think about these three factors of the Dark triad – are you possibly encouraging one or more of these traits without realizing it? Or are you doing them knowingly just so that you can get what you want?

What can you do to ensure that your dark side does not take control of your light side?

Chapter 3 Manipulation

The art of manipulation is not really about influencing people into doing what you want them to. Instead, it is about getting them to want to do what you want them to do. The most important question here is, "how do you get people to want to do what you want them to do?"

Well, the first trick is to learn their true desires and then reverse engineer it towards the goal you so wish to accomplish. One thing you must bear in mind is that the closer you are to a person, the easier it is for you to manipulate them. If you want to test your manipulation skills, the first person to do this with is your romantic partner.

Think of manipulation as persuasion.

The truth is, you must be willing to persuade people and make them feel like it was their choice all this while. Generally, men seek perfectionism while women see wholeness. You may be thinking, "what does this even mean?" the truth is that men are easily persuaded by mastery and an ego linked to improvement. When you display uncertainty on whether or not he can improve, you are simply taunting his ego in such a gentle way that contributes to progress.

On the other hand, women seek balance in various areas of life – especially relationships with family and friends. Therefore, when you suffocate time, you stir up a burning desire to bring balance. The truth is, we all need balance, sacrifice, and focus in life. According to statistics, women tend to lean more towards balance, while men lead more towards perfectionism.

Amid persuasion tactics, you must not disobey the law of cognitive bias – otherwise referred to as liking and loving tendency. For instance, if Adolf Hitler says that 1+1=2 and Steve Harvey says 1+1=3, even though we hate Hitler so much, we have to accept that he is right and Harvey – loved by many – is wrong. That said, most people will tend to believe Steve Harvey because of association bias. In other words, most people associate him with positive things.

You must care about what others feel and how you make them feel because remember Maya Angelou's saying, *"I've learned that people will forget what you said, people will forget what you did, but people will never forget how you made them feel."*

Interestingly, most people wish to manipulate others over a short duration. What they fail to realize is that the true art of manipulation is in the long game. Realize that patience is a virtue you must exercise when persuading others so that it feels and flows effortlessly. The truth is that this takes time to specifically overcome your mental barriers and get into the right mindset.

Over the years, I have learned that one thing that mentally hurt manipulators is a failure to understand the process and then going with nature. Think about a boulder rolling down the hill – is there someone forcing it down? No! Because it is the force of gravity that is pulling it down. Instead of force against the force of nature, allow it to pull you.

When it rains, the only way we adapt is by putting on a jacket and getting an umbrella. When it is hot, you wear light clothing and shield your eyes with glasses. The point is - try as much as you can not to be delusional and allow yourself to adjust to what is. There are two major ways you can test delusion – doing things in the wrong order still means the wrong thing (also referred to as mis-prioritization.) or setting expectations of the outcome by putting in the wrong input. With people, you must learn their personality type, how they react to different surroundings, and their boundaries.

Here's the point – the mental frameworks are out of the way. One way you are going to get them to do the thing is to lead with a reward. People love it when they feel like it's their choice, and that triggers the release of dopamine – otherwise known as the reward. They want to know how the thing you are telling them to do is going to benefit them.

The trick is not to tell them to do it directly. According to research, at least 90% of the time, people hate being told what to do. The best thing to do is to help them to the same conclusion following their path. The most rewarding thing is them knowing that it was their idea – when, in fact, it was yours. Therefore, you must let them own it. The toughest part is attaching that reward to the thing because if they don't understand how something is of benefit to them, there is a high likelihood that they will never do it.

Once you manage to successfully manipulate others, you must not expose yourself because this goes against the liking and loving tendency, causing people to cut you off – and that is the last thing you want. You must maintain consciousness of how you make them feel and try to persuade for the best and not for evil.

Techniques used by manipulators to gain control

Psychopaths are not villains we watch in movies or read in morality takes – they are real and walk amongst us at home and in offices appearing to us as normal colleagues. According to one study, at least 3-4% of business leaders are psychopaths. The same thing applies to narcissists. Science has shown some evidence that a little bit of narcissism goes a long way in aiding business success.

As you go about your business each day, there is a chance that you will meet a few truly toxic narcissists and psychopaths who will try to manipulate you in one way of the other. You must understand how such people can manipulate others. Here are a few techniques;

Gaslighting

This is a manipulative technique that can be described in various ways. These include three key phrases;

- That did not just happen
- You imagined it
- Are you insane?

Well, gaslighting is one of the most common and insidious manipulative tactics because it aims at distorting and eroding people's sense of reality. In other words, it eats away your ability to trust yourself, inevitably disabling you from seeing the justification in calling out your abuser.

How then can you fight back?

The best thing is for you to ground yourself in your reality. One of the ways you can do this is to take time and write down exactly what happened, talk to a friend, or reiterate your experience to a support system that can help you counter the effects of gas lighters.

Projection

Think about it – have you ever met someone so toxic that claims all the mess that surrounds them is your fault and not theirs?

Well, that tactic is referred to as projection.

Well, the truth is that we all have done this at someone's point in our lives. But the difference between us and narcissists or psychopaths is that they do it a lot. They simply use projection as a defense mechanism to displace the responsibility of their negative behaviors and qualities by ensuring that they attribute all of it to another person.

What is the solution then?

Well, it's simple – try as much as you can not to project your empathy or sense of compassion onto a toxic individual. Also, you mustn't own any of the toxic person's projections. When you project your conscience and value system onto others, this has a potential outcome of being met with more exploitation.

Generalizations

Let us consider an instance where you tell a coworker that they sometimes fail to consider long-term ramifications of their financial decisions. Then they go ahead and tell everyone that you called them "a loose cannon." You realize that this might blow up on you if several conditions come in to play. Your psychopath of a colleague goes to the boss and tells them that you said the deal is a "wreck."

What is going on?

Well, the truth is that your nemesis did not only understand you, but they also had no interest in understanding you.

One thing you must note is that malignant narcissists are not intellectual masterminds. Most of them are intellectually lazy. Instead of taking the time to consider another person's perspective, they simply choose to generalize everything you say by making a blanket statement that does not consider the nuances of your argument. They choose not to consider the different perspectives you paid homage to.

To counter this, you must hold onto your truth and resist the urge to generalize things. Instead, they realize that they are, in fact, a form of black and white illogical thinking.

Moving goalposts

This is a logical fallacy that abusive psychopaths and narcissists use to ensure that they have every reason to be perpetually dissatisfied with you. Even though you offer them all the evidence you need to validate your argument or meet their requests, they will set up another expectation and demand proof.

You must avoid playing such a game. You are the only one that needs to validate and approve yourself. You are enough, and the last thing you want is to let someone make you constantly feel small, deficient, and unworthy.

Changing the subject

When you are discussing something, and someone keeps changing the topic, it sounds innocent enough. However, in the hands of a manipulator, changing the subject is one way to keep off responsibility. A narcissist will not want you to stay on the topic because the last thing they want is you holding them accountable for something. In that case, they will find ways to reroute the discussion to benefit them.

If you are not careful, this sort of thing can go on forever. It can make it impossible to engage in a relevant issue. The best way to counter this is to the user the "broken record technique" when fighting back. In other words, you must keep stating the facts without allowing yourself to yield to distractions.

Each time they redirect the conversation, you must redirect their redirection by saying something along the lines of "That is not what I am talking about – and you know it. Let is stay focused on the real issue here. If you lack interest in this, then you can choose to disengage and spend your time and energy on something a little more constructive."

Name-calling

Each one of us has been called names at some point in our lives. We have been dealing with this long enough, but that does not make it any less destructive. Trust me, this thing might have started from the time you were in kindergarten, but it goes all the way to the presidential politics!

Even if you have encountered bullies since childhood, you mustn't tolerate it. End any interaction that entails name-calling and tell your manipulator that you will not tolerate it. Don't even try to take it all in – as most people do. Realize that the reason they resort to name-calling is that they are deficient and are trying to distract you from what matters.

Smear campaigns

When a toxic person cannot control the way you perceive yourself, they choose to control how others see you. In other words, they resort to playing the Martyr while everyone around you labels you the toxic one. This is a smear campaign that is only preemptive to ensuring that they tarnish your reputation and slander your name.

Realize that at times, true evil geniuses will choose to divide and conquer – by pitting two or more people against one another.

The last thing you want is to allow them to succeed. You must record all forms of harassment and ensure that you don't rise to the bait. Do not allow their evilness to provoke you into stooping to their level and behaving just like them.

Devaluation

Let us consider an instance where you have been newly appointed the unit manager in your organization. Suddenly, one of your colleagues starts aggressively denigrating the former manager who held your position. Have you experienced this kind of manipulation?

If not, then you know the kind of person you need to beware of. Narcissists do this kind of thing all the time. They will devalue your former boss to you (the new boss). They will devalue their ex to their new partner. Eventually, you start to get the same kind of mistreatment as the narcissist's ex-partner or boss. This is not just for those in the professional fields; it also applies to our personal lives.

The very first step to countering this is by raising your awareness of this phenomenon. Realize that the way someone treats or speaks of another is potentially the same way they treat or speak about you in private or in the future. Be cautious!

Aggressive jokers

The issue is not your sense of humor but the hidden intention of that joke. You will hear a covert narcissist make malicious remarks at your expense. These remarks come in the form of jokes so that they get away with saying appalling things to you, maintain their innocent and cool demeanor. When you raise eyebrows at the kind of insensitivity they have, they accuse you of having no sense of humor.

They will try to convince everyone around that they were just making innocent jokes – even when they know damn straight, they were not!

Triangulation

One smart way toxic people manipulate you and distract you from their nastiness is focusing your attention on the supposed threat of another. This is what we refer to as triangulation. In other words, they report back false information about what another person said. To resist this kind of tactic, you must realize that the third-party in all this drama is being manipulated.

The best trick is to reverse that triangulation or gain support from the other person who is not under the influence of the narcissist.

But does manipulation all have to be negative?

Of course not!

The truth is that manipulation can also be used in a good sense. For instance, you can persuade someone to take a vacation or do something that will help them get that promotion they have always worked hard for. These are some of the manipulation techniques you can use to benefit you more;

Using body language to your advantage

It is important to note that how the brain uses physical movements and reactions each day is almost uncontrollable. It is this kind of movement that ca single several people around you to think about what it means. In other words, people can read your body language to try and understand things you couldn't possibly say with words. It is the best way to influence people with more than just words.

According to research, 90% of communication is nonverbal. This simply means that this much of our interactions can just be lost because we sought for promotion with our arms crossed and looking at the floor.

Mastering the art of body language goes a long way in helping one convey the intended message properly. If you take time to read another's body language, you will be in a better position to tell whether they genuinely agree with you, actively engaged in the conversation, or are just taking you for a complete idiot.

When you persistently pick up on the body language of those around you, you stand a chance of improving your abilities as well as identifying opportunities and dead ends in every interaction. Doing things such as gestures, mimicking postures, and movements can help get someone to like you or agree with what you have to say.

Often, we see people nod their heads not because they agree with what is being said, but when they do not agree and can't understand why the person is speaking is even thinking this way. That said, when you nod your head when what you mean to say is you disagree, then you are setting yourself up. When someone is interrogating you, they will pay attention to your body language to determine culpability regularly.

The truth is that we are all animals, and we all behave this way when we are completely stripped of our sophisticated means of communication. The trick is when someone is trying to manipulate you, you can use this subconscious interaction to your gain. For instance, you can speak with your arms open to create a sense of trust. You can also shake hands with your palm facing downwards to communicate dominance and upwards when you want to communicate submissiveness. If you are laughing in a group of people, the very first person you make eye contact with is the person you trust most – use that to your advantage.

Change your perspective

You must cloak the reality of your manipulators with the kind of reality you have created. In other words, to change their points of view, go matrix on their minds. It is all about tact, cunning abilities, and, importantly, being rhetorical.

For instance, you can say something like, "this home is a real fixer-upper – imagine the potential!"

The point is for you to turn half-empty glass on your manipulator's side. The truth is, perspective can make a whole difference in how someone looks at something. Your description can influence the perspective itself. Being rhetoric, in a way, underlies this notion because it encompasses several aspects beyond what was said and how it was said in the first place. It is the content, tone, and appeal to emotion, character, and reason. You can be rhetoric when you want to persuade. You can also use exaggeration when trying to be practical, or a shift of focus where you deem necessary.

The point is for you to put thought into every argument you make – its structure and delivery. It does not matter whether it appeals to the other person's emotion or reason; the point is that you think twice about it. Ask yourself whether you sound like you know what you are talking about – even when you don't have an idea. If you cannot convince someone to stop cutting down trees for environmental reasons, can you do it with a logical argument on how more trees mean more life?

Think outside the box and use that to reframe your perspective on a given situation. This will serve you better and build efficacy of how your argument comes forward. Think about it, when you convince yourself that you had a good night's sleep, you trick the mind into thinking it too. Use the Dunning Kruger effect where smart people underestimate themselves while ignorant people think that they are brilliant.

Leverage your knowledge of others

One thing you must note is that you can depend on others psychological needs and use them as your pressure points. It might come as a need for conformity, acceptance, or inclusion – or it might just be the complete opposite – to stand out and swim against the currents. If you are a risky decision maker, then you might end up making a poor choice. If you are a quiet crowd dweller, there is a chance that you will be discouraged from going after anything that might lead you astray.

What you must bear in mind is that other people's weaknesses are your strengths. All you need is to figure out how you can harness all that to your advantage. Look at these people carefully, study them. Are they overconfident? Can that cause them to stumble? Do you think that they are insecure about something? Can you use that to make a convincing point?

The truth is, each one of us has kryptonite!

The more you study about others' psychological tendencies, way of thinking, and traits, the more you are at an advantage of gaining control over their thoughts. The key here is knowledge. Just like any other point we have made, it is also important that you gain an in-depth understanding and mastery of your pressure points. Your solid defense comes from acknowledging your insecurities and vulnerabilities.

Always bear in mind that their vision is the product of an emotional foundation. That no matter how they try to justify their position, they hold to it for emotional reasons. If you want people to move in your direction, you must discover the emotional value driving their vision – their G-spot. Once you know this sweet spot, only then can you craft an approach that blends their needs with yours so that you all feel successful at the end of the day.

Beware of good timing and opportunity

Think of the jaguar – effective and calculate, right? The biological ability of great timing gives Their ancestral legacy of success and failure. The jaguar knows precisely when to strike, pounce or abort its chase altogether.

My point is, you need to know when to make your moves. From a young age, we have learned that timing is everything – you know when to ask your dad and mom for a gift they should get you on your birthday or Christmas. The most important thing is for you to maintain an awareness of these things and have your eyes out there seeking opportunities round the clock. When someone is preoccupied and tired, that might just be the time to ask them for certain favors. This way, they will put in the energy to refuse or disagree with you.

That said, try not to force opportunities. Instead, it is better if you welcome them with open arms and eyes. If you have been laying low for the right time to throw a pitch at your boss, don't force the conversation too early. You may have to wait for several weeks before you have a good chance, and once you do, don't blow it. When you encounter someone with a proposal, their mood will determine whether the battle has already been won or lost – at least by half.

The truth is, the wonders of psychology are quite endless. With manipulation, you are barely scratching the service. If you don't care to pick up on other people's impulses, expose situations to your advantage. The awareness of body language you exert and that which others send your way will help open your eyes to maximize your exchanges in life.

Chapter 4 Undetected Mind Control

A lot of an individual's communication is not based solely on what they actively try to put out there. A much larger, much more active chunk of our communication is based on what we don't realize that we are putting out in the world. Our bodies can reveal our deepest emotions and feelings without us realizing pretty much, twenty-four seven. This does not happen randomly, of course. The way that our mind communicates without us realizing it is based on two main theories of thought – referred to as the unconscious mind and the limbic brain.

Unconscious Mind

The unconscious mind originates from Freud's Psychoanalytic Theory of Personality. They tend to include feelings of pain, anxiety, or conflict. It is because of these negative feelings and emotions that our unconscious mind stays outside of our conscious awareness. Since, on a subconscious level, we do not want to remember or feel those feelings, we then try to ignore them and push them into our unconscious mind.

Despite this attempt at ignoring and hiding these feelings, our unconscious mind still influences our behavior even though we do not know that it is there. Many individuals compare the unconscious mind to that of an iceberg. The part of the iceberg above the water represents our conscious brain and all of the communication of ideas and feelings that we actively put out into the world.

Our unconscious mind is represented by every part of the iceberg that is below the water and unseen. Within this iceberg analogy, it is important to remember how large an iceberg below the water truly is. This represents just how deep our unconscious mind goes and just how much tends to be hidden below the surface. The amount of information that is hidden just below the surface - within our unconscious mind - is massive. It is like the hidden part of the iceberg in the sense that we have to consider the parts of our body language that connect to our unconscious mind as a huge part of nonverbal communication.

Freud also believed and asserted that our basic instincts and animal urges are contained within the unconscious mind. This includes instincts under actions of life and death as well as sexual instincts. He believed urges such as these were hidden from or kicked out of our present consciousness because our minds view them as unacceptable, irrational, or uncivilized. Freud suggested that individuals often use several different defense mechanisms to stop these hidden urges from rising above the waters into our conscious mind.

Freud also goes on to explain the different ways that the information from the unconscious mind might be brought into conscious awareness. One of the techniques that Freud explained can be used to bring these feelings into awareness is known as free association. Free association is a rather simple and seemingly silly form of psychotherapy. In free association, Freud asked patients to lay back and relax and say to him whatever came to their minds without any sort of filter on it. He wanted them to say anything that they could think of without stopping to think of it is trivial, irrelevant, or embarrassing. Freud then traced the streams of thoughts until he believed that he could uncover the contents of the unconscious mind. He often used this method to try to find repressed childhood traumas or hidden desires.

Freud also believes that dream interpretation could be used to understand the unconscious mind further. Many people think of dreams as a route to the unconscious mind and believe that the information from the unconscious mind could appear randomly in dreams but typically in a disguised format. Because of this, he would often ask patients to keep dream journals and would try to go through and interpret these dreams to try and understand their hidden meanings.

Freud also believes that dreams tended to serve as a form of secret fulfillment of long-coddled wishes. He believes that the fact that these unconscious urges were not expressed in real life means that they could be expressed in the individual's dreams.

The Freudian theory of the unconscious mind did not come across as without controversy. A multitude of researchers have criticized the idea of the unconscious mind and firmly dispute that there isn't an unconscious mind at all. Recently, in the field of cognitive psychology, researchers and psychologists have begun to focus on the automatic and intuitive functions that describe things that were previously being attributed to the unconscious mind. The idea behind this approach is a belief that a series of cognitive functions happen outside of our conscious awareness.

Meanwhile, they do not entirely support the voice conceptualization of the unconscious mind. However, it does offer some evidence that actions that we are not aware of still influence our automatic behaviors. Unlike Freud's psychoanalytic approaches to the unconscious mind, research within the modern field of cognitive psychology is almost exclusively driven by scientific investigation and quantitative data. This idea of the unconscious mind continues to have a great effect on modern psychology and is still used in some modern practices today.

Limbic Brain System

The limbic system within an individual's brain is responsible for a variety of very important brain functions. The biggest responsibility of the limbic system is our instincts for survival and memory access and storage. The limbic system is made up of many different brain structures—two of the biggest and most important parts of the limbic system are the amygdala and the hippocampus. Amygdala is the deciding structure that chooses where each memory should be placed in the brain, while the hippocampus transports that memory to its final location. It is often believed that the amount of emotional response determines the placement that it receives from the person.

The limbic system is also very responsible for hormone levels, body temperature, and motor functions. The limbic brain system is composed of the amygdala, cingulate gyrus, hippocampus, and hypothalamus. These individual structures are very important parts of a person's brain. The limbic system, as a whole, is located on top of the brainstem and underneath the frontal cortex. The limbic system is often connected to survival-based emotions such as fear, anger, and pleasure. The limbic system is also known to influence both the peripheral nervous system and the endocrine system.

The part of the limbic system that is important to this text, in particular, is its connection with memory. Because of the limbic system's perceived importance in the decisions of where memories go and how they are remembered, it is often connected with Freud's ideas of the unconscious mind. Freud's ideas of the unconscious mind are based on the theory that certain memories and feelings are hidden far away from our conscious awareness. It is easy to understand how the limbic system can play a huge part in that, considering that it is the deciding factor of where memories get stored.

You might think, "What does any of this have to do with our body language and understanding the body language of those around us?"

The answer lies in the fact that the unconscious mind is very powerful and controls a huge portion of our true feelings and emotions. By reading body language, we can often unlock these feelings of the unconscious mind without even realizing that they are hidden from the person we are reading. This is a very powerful skill, and it is important to understand the basis behind it. The limbic system and the unconscious mind create this basis for the deeper readings of people.

The Process of Mind Control

A mind controller approaches the victim with the sole intent of cloning themselves, which is making the other person think like them. This is a complicated thing to do, so, to achieve it, one has to possess an inflated ego, lack doubts about themselves, and have a high sense of entitlement. All of us are susceptible to manipulation, and what matters is how much effect the mind control will have on us.

Psychologists studying mind control have found out that the entire process seems to adhere to a common structure. This conclusion was made after a study was conducted on multiple marketing and networking companies which used mind control to persuade clients to purchase their products.

One of the outstanding similarities is that all new members joining the companies underwent a pre-planned training on how to recruit more people and convince potential customers to buy their products. The training sessions are meant to make the employees think like the company wants and use a form of mind twist to convince people.

Let us now look at the mind control process in detail.

Step 1 – Understanding the target

Before anything else, the manipulator will seek to establish a bond or connection with their potential victim. Good intent, or friendship, will be the first step because it makes the victim lower all their social and psychological defenses. Once the controller gains the trust of the target, they now start reading them to devise the most effective method to invade them. The reading aims to tell whether their victim is susceptible to their manipulation. Just like any project manager, they do not like wasting time on a subject they suspect might outsmart them and lead to failure.

Multiple clues are used to scan the victim. They include verbal style, body language, social status, gender, emotional stability, and so on. A person's traits can be used to decode the strength of their defenses.

All this time, the manipulator will be asking themselves questions like, "Are you introvert or extrovert?" "Are you weakly?" "Are you emotional?" "Are you self-confident?"

Humans give a lot of information about themselves when interacting with each other, and this is something that the controller knows all too well. From these signs, they can easily tell if the person is cooperating. They will look at body posture and immediately analyze the victim. Excess blinking might mention that a person is lying. Arms folded across the chest might show a lack of interest or insecurity. Taking large strides while walking might portray fear. As you can see, the body releases so much data at any given time that it is important to be aware of the signs that you are giving out (this will be covered in detail later in this book).

When the attacker has collected enough data from the target, they now understand their interests, strengths, weaknesses, routines, and so on. Using this information, they can decide on an entry point, which will allow for easy and accurate manipulation. They also decide whether the target is worth the effort. If they see one as a favorable target, they move to the next step in the mind control process- unfreezing solid beliefs and values.

Step 2- Unfreezing Solid Beliefs and Values

Each one of us has some beliefs and values engraved deep within. Most of them are the principles that were instilled in us since childhood, and others have been acquired from experiences are we grow older. We rarely let go of them but revise them as we proceed. Most of them are what make up our identities, so we do not like them being interfered with. If, at any point in time, these principles are threatened, contradicted, or questioned, our natural reaction is to defend them through all means possible. However, if a good-enough reason is given to us,

We voluntarily question them ourselves; we undergo a process known as "unfreezing."

Tons of reasons can lead us to unfreeze: a breakup, the death of a loved one, religious interference, getting evicted from our houses, to mention but a few. These situations force us to start seeking answers to complex situations, and this goes as deep as questioning our sole beliefs and values. Take this, for example:

When I was a teenager, we had some family friends who were solid Christians. It so happened that my best friend, who was my exact age, came from this family. His name was Matthew. Matthew used to tell me about the Bible and its teachings, trying to convince me to accept salvation and live according to its teachings.

I remember asking him why he was so insistent on this issue, and he would respond that with salvation, all problems were solvable and that life was much easier and happier. Fast-forward about fifteen years, Matthew's mother was diagnosed with breast cancer. They tried all forms of treatment available at the time, but cancer would grow back. One day, while talking to him about the issue, he looked at me with a pale face and said, "I think what they say about Christianity is not real!"

Unsure about what he had just said, I asked him why he thought so. He responded that they had met tens of spiritual leaders for prayers, but his mother's cancer was only getting worse. What's worse, she would not live for more than a year.

Sad as this story is, it makes us realize that some situations in life might force us to question the strong principles that we grow up with. In this case, my best friend had come to doubt the very same religion that he once felt had automatic solutions to all of life's problems. In the very same manner, a manipulator will dig deep into their victim's life to understand their vulnerabilities and exploit them fully. These people will say anything they think their targets would love to hear. Once the victim swallows the manipulator's comfort, there is a shift in power dynamics, and the target is now ready for the manipulation.

Step 3 – Reprogramming the Mind

The mind control process seeks to separate the target from their initial beliefs and begin reprogramming their mind. The reprogramming is meant to install the manipulator's beliefs and values into the victim's mind. Apart from distancing the initial principles, the controller also tries their best to make them look wrong or bad, or the cause of past mishaps in the victim's life. If the victim absorbs this reprogramming, their defense is lowered to zero. They end up as a robot that is ready to accept any operating system that is offered.

During the reprogramming phase, the attacker will try to ensure the victim has minimal contact with the outside world. They make everyone else to appear insignificant to the victim because this raises their opportunity to deposit their malicious principles into them. This behavior is common in cults, which are mostly crafted to sway their followers from mainstream human life.

Some cults go as far as controlling the food intake of their followers as a way of weakening them. The psychology behind this idea is that a weak person will always turn to the person they feel has the power to protect them or alleviate their suffering. The same happens in relationships, where one partner plays the controlling role, and the victimized one has no choice but to adhere to the other.

You might wonder why some people put up with violent partners, but so far, from reading this book, you must already understand that the problem is deeper than it appears. If you control a person's mind, you can control their lives.

Once the victim has been re-programmed, the manipulator moves into the final phase of the mind control process known as "freezing."

Step 4 – Freezing the New Beliefs and Values

Do you remember the "unfreezing" process we discussed earlier? So, once the victim has been fed with contrasting principles by the offender, the offender applies tactics aimed at cementing the new beliefs into their brains. This is what psychologists call "freezing." The freezing bit is necessary because the controller is aware of the person's new beliefs that might clash with their initial ones. As such, they need to force the victim to choose their malicious principles over their old ones. To do this, they might apply any of the following methods.

One of the methods is using the reward/punishment approach. When the victim acts according to the manipulator's demands, they are rewarded. Hopefully, you see the similarity between the freezing process and dog training. The dog is given treats when it follows the trainer's instructions.

The trainer aims at solidifying the new skill in the dog by rewarding it. In the future, if the dog is instructed to do the same thing, it will not hesitate since it has been made to think that obeying the command is good and attracts a reward. The same applies to mind control; when the victim obeys, they are made to feel that what they did was right and deserves a reward.

Punishments are the second most-applied approach in the freezing process. If the victim deviates from the controller's commands, they are punished. If we go back to the scenario of a cult, they usually have defined punishments for violations of terms.

During the Holocaust, for instance, any Germans who failed to hail Hitler were punished through imprisonment or death. In the same way, any German who was suspected of protecting the Jews was shot. Hitler understood that by punishing anyone who went against his rules, he would force every German to help him attain his objective of ethnic cleansing. The psychological trick used in these situations is that the victim is made to see punishment as justice being served for breaking the rules.

The final method used by mind controllers to solidify their manipulation is to transform their victims into their agents. Better put, once the controller feels that the victim's pseudo personality has materialized, they use them to distribute their worldviews.

Once the controlling process is complete, the victim starts living like the attacker without realizing it. Depending on the nature of the manipulation, the victim might also be used to recruit more victims into the oppressor's way of thinking and living. This is especially true in the context of marketing and networking, which we shall discuss under the topic of deception.

All this explains why a wife is likely to be violent towards the kids if the husband is violent. The kids are also likely to be violent towards each other or their friends. The process of mind control is slow, but once it solidifies, it can result in devastating effects.

The relationship between mind control and emotional influence

The interplay between mind control and emotional influence is clear. Mind control is general in that the oppressor controls the victim's freedom of choice and actions. When it comes to emotional influence, the attack is more specific as it focuses on the feelings. All the same, the consequences of both interferences are that they eventually snatch independence from the victim and place them at the oppressor's mercy. Therefore, we can conclude that emotional influence and mind controls are the same; only that one is specific while the other is broader.

Types of Mind Control

Just to reiterate, mind control is an umbrella term that houses different forms of control. In short, different types of controls might be cast at the victim. The oppressor determines the choice of control. In the definitions of the types of mind control, you will see clear pillars, as we have discussed in this chapter. There are five major forms of mind control studied under dark psychology.

They include:

Hypnosis: The process of malicious interaction where the controller used mind tricks to make the victim accept their recommendations or change the way they react to their surroundings.

Manipulation: A type of social influence through which a person can influence another's perception or behavior using underhanded tactics.

Deception: The Process of propagating beliefs in things and events using partial or complete lies.

Persuasion: A form of control that aims at influencing the beliefs, attitudes, motivations, and behaviors of the victim.

Brainwashing: The process of wittingly convincing a person to abandon beliefs they have held for a long time and to manipulate them to take up new ones.

Since this is a vast topic that we cannot cover in a single book, we shall focus on only two of these types of mind control: manipulation and deception. In the following chapters, you will get to understand what is deception and manipulation as well as the techniques used in furthering them. As you get insight into the way these forms of mind control work, you will also learn how to spot manipulators and overcome their endeavors.

One of the driving forces is that out of the five types of mind control, deception, and manipulation are the ones that can be applied in everyday scenarios. These scenarios can range from relationships to normal conversations, advertisements, and religious beliefs. You need to acknowledge that mind control does not have to force a person to change major aspects of their lives, such as personality.

Control can be used in minimal scenarios, such as being persuaded to buy a pair of shoes at the local store or to vote for someone who would ideally not be your favorite candidate.

Also, these two forms of mind control can be applied by the people that are closest to you. Therefore, it is important to understand the most basic level where you can get manipulated and keep yourself safe. If this has convinced you, though I promise it is not mind control, let us move ahead and discuss deception.

Chapter 5 Hypnotism

"Brains aren't designed to get results; they go in directions. If you know how the brain works, you can set your directions. If you don't, then someone else will."

-Richard Bandler

Hypnosis is pretty easy to understand if you know how it works. Of course, it takes practice to master hypnotizing others; however, simply understanding how it works is very useful in being able to observe dark psychology and manipulation in practice.

Hypnosis tends to be misunderstood as a parlor trick that requires someone to be asleep or in a nearly asleep state to become hypnotized. Then, when they are under the spell of hypnosis, they can be made to cluck like a chicken or bark like a dog or repeat any number of embarrassing phrases for a cheap laugh. Hypnosis happens every day because all hypnosis means is that someone has entered into an altered state or a trance state.

We enter trance states every day. All it takes to enter a trance state is to affix your attention on one thing so intently that some or all of your peripheral awareness can be shut out. Most people, for instance, enter a hypnotic state every day at work or zoning out while on the subway.

Hypnosis can be a potent tool for getting people to compromise their critical faculties, and it ties into what we have been talking about so far in terms of polarization and eliciting the desired response from someone.

Stages of Hypnosis

Stage 1: Absorb Attention

The first step into altering someone's conscious state (hypnosis) is grabbing hold of their full attention. Believe it or not, there are verbal and non-verbal forms of this first stage of hypnosis. Take, for example, the situation mentioned above in which a person can be so zoned in at work that everything around them sort of just fades away.

This is a prime example of the way that our psychological states are changed when we are intently focused on something and of non-verbal hypnosis.

Of course, gaining someone's complete attention can be a bit easier if you are using words. People tend to cling more completely to someone's words when they are describing images or telling a story. It is a lot like how some people prefer visual learning over textual learning. The human mind can follow along better when pictures and mental images are involved because their visual sense is engaged.

You can practice this first stage of attention absorption in everyday speech. Go out with a friend or coworker and see how much more they pay attention to you when you say you have a story for them. Tell them a story, either true or made up, and be sure to include a lot of details. Paint the picture with your words, use a lot of adjectives to describe the scene. The more senses you can engage, the better. Give their mind and imagination something to engage with.

When you have them wrapped up in your story, you have successfully absorbed their attention which will lead you into the 2nd stage of hypnosis:

Stage 2: Bypass the Critical Faculty

The conscious mind is a rather limited entity. It takes in the data that is thrown at you every day, and it processes it rationally. The unconscious mind, on the other hand, is a lot more whimsical. It does not get bogged down with matters of reality. Consider, for example, that your unconscious mind is active when you dream. You may have never seen a purple, flying turtle in real life, but your unconscious mind is free to consider such things as completely real and viable.

The conscious mind deals with what is feasible. In hypnosis, this is what is known as the critical faculty. Think of the critical faculty as a guardian at the gate to the subconscious mind. The critical faculty is what alerts your mind to things that are impossible, unreasonable, and unlikely. If you are attempting to hypnotize someone, the critical faculty is the enemy of hypnosis. The point of hypnosis is transferring a person's mind from a fully conscious state to an unconscious or at least an altered state, and the critical faculties make it impossible for this switch to occur, so it must be bypassed.

Bypassing the critical faculties can be achieved by first absorbing the full attention of a person using simple techniques such as maintaining intent eye-contact with the subject and speaking a little slower and in a low tone than you normal.

Speaking in a hypnotic tone can go a long way in inciting a trance state and bypassing the critical faculty. If you are hypnotizing someone, you want to watch out for signs that your subject is in a trance state. Most importantly, do not give any hypnotic suggestions until you are certain you are past the critical faculty, and your subject is in a trance state. Otherwise, your suggestion will be rejected by the critical faculty.

Step 3: Activate an Unconscious Response

Activating an unconscious response does not have to be as extreme as getting a person to cluck like a chicken. It can be as subtle as evoking a laugh or making someone clap their hands to their mouth in shock. An unconscious response is an action carried out that a person is not aware of or is only aware of after the action has been made. In other words, it is a response that has not been regulated by the conscious mind.

Eliciting an unconscious response is very easy when a person has entered a hypnotic state. Look for dilation of the pupils, a change in breathing rate, or flushing of the skin. These are all signs that your subject has let their critical faculty guard down and have been ushered into a hypnotic state.

Once you observe this, try eliciting an unconscious response; maybe describe in vivid detail a delectable steak dinner so that their stomachs growl in hunger or a swarm of bugs overtaking someone's body so that their skin crawls with goosebumps.

Stage 4: Lead to Your Desired Outcome

This is the point where you, the hypnotist, can lead the subject towards the desired outcome through hypnotic suggestion or associated metaphors. This stage of hypnotism is all about speaking directly to the unconscious mind and taking advantage of the altered state to either help the person or to lead them to a conclusion, outcome, or decision that is favorable for you.

One example of this stage is called priming. Say, for example, that you want to go swimming and you want the subject to go swimming with you. Try telling them a story involving cool, cascading, and refreshing water overcoming oppressive heat. This could lead to a post-hypnotic reaction that has been geared towards your desired outcome.

Pattern Interrupts & Rapid Induction Techniques

The concept of pattern interrupts very simply. Consider each word individually: the first word in the phrase being "pattern." A pattern can be anything you do mindlessly or habitually. Getting up in the morning, brushing your teeth and taking a shower is likely something you do every day that you don't even really think about. This is an example of a pattern. A pattern can also be called a routine. Getting in your car and driving to work can be considered a routine.

Now consider the second word in the phrase: "interrupt." An interrupt in this context is anything that breaks your normal routines or patterns. Interrupts are conscious efforts to change the way you do things, the way you think or the way you act.

The major difference between the two words – the two concepts of "pattern" and "interrupt" – is that one involves an unconscious or passive state of mind, and the other involves a very conscious and active state of mind.

Pattern interrupts are often used in behavioral psychology and NLP to help people break harmful habits and routines in their lives. Routines often give us a sense of drive and purpose. Still, they can be detrimental when we get so used to them that we switch off our brains while doing them, thereby becoming vulnerable to hypnotic suggestion and manipulation.

The average human has about 50,000 thoughts per day, but the majority of these are repeat thoughts. Pattern interrupts are very effective ways to induce new thoughts, which helps the brain develop their ability to think critically. It is the difference between letting your brain atrophy and exercising it.

To get back to basics, consider pattern interrupts a way to alter yours or someone else's mental state from a conscious to an unconscious mode. This is precisely why patterns can be used for hypnosis and NLP.

In particular, the pattern can be very useful for rapid hypnotic induction or getting someone into a hypnotic state very quickly. This may be because of a slight disconnect in a person's mind when a pattern interrupt is used on them. The switch from passive to active brain function isn't seamless. There is a lapse in which the unconscious and conscious mind meld for a brief time, and it is in this time that a person enters a hypnotic state and is susceptible to suggestion.

Consider it a state of confusion that a person enters for a brief time when one of their patterns or thought processes is abruptly interrupted. Confusion tactics are very common and potent methods of rapid hypnotic induction.

Remember the example of polarization we went over in the first chapter? Pattern interrupts and confusion are akin to polarization in the sense that both are used to get someone into a frame of mind where their reactions can be predicted and manipulated.

Getting someone riled up about a certain subject is similar to putting someone into a confused state where their routine has been suddenly broken. It is in this state that a skilled hypnotist can implant unconscious suggestions and therefore predict a certain outcome.

Pattern interrupt techniques have become very popular in hypnosis and manipulation because they are fairly simple to carry out, and they can be done in virtually any setting and sometimes without the person even realizing it. It happens in an instant and garners the desired results in an instant, which is why it has become such an oft used tool to hypnotize and manipulate people.

The most popular method of pattern interrupts hypnotic induction is the handshake technique. In this technique, the hypnotist will go in for the very mundane act of shaking someone's hand. At the last second, before the hand's touch, one person abruptly disengages from the handshake and grabs the other person by the wrist.

Getting up and getting ready for work is a routine that could take hours, and shaking someone's hand only takes a few seconds, but they are both patterns and they can both be broken, and when they are, the mind enters an altered state.

This altered state is the goal of pattern interrupts and why they are such a powerful tool for inducing hypnotic trances.

Using Pattern Interrupt to Induce Hypnosis

Going back again to a concept discussed in the previous chapter, attention absorbing is akin to pattern interrupts for inducing hypnosis. Pattern interrupts are just another means of grabbing someone's full attention, and it can be argued that hypnosis is nothing but getting someone to be fully present in the moment.

The goal of the hypnotist is not to knock someone out or make someone unconscious. It is to heighten their sense of consciousness through full attention absorption. The reason that pattern interrupts are so useful for commanding the entirety of an individual's attention (therefore leaving them vulnerable to hypnotic suggestion) is that when someone's train of thought is instantly broken, the mind is frantically looking for a logical explanation for the interrupt.

It can be as easy as interrupting someone mid-sentence. Let's say you get your friend telling you a story about a run-in they had at a grocery store or a confrontation they had with someone that bumped into them on the street. Try interrupting them in the middle of the story with an unrelated phrase, "I have always wondered what makes the moon so silvery."

Your friend was fully engaged in his or her story, and they may have even been in auto-pilot if it was a story they have told multiple times before. When you interrupted them with your statement about the moon, you broke their thought process. Now, you have their undivided attention.

This leaves them in a vulnerable state of hypnotic suggestion because they are now hanging on your every word in a desperate attempt to get answers. And where will these answers come from? You, of course. It is at this very moment that hypnotists can implant their hypnotic suggestions that can have nothing to do with what the person was talking or thinking about.

This works because when the brain is engaged in a pattern, it is fully engaged in carrying out the pattern to its logical conclusion. When the pattern is skillfully broken, the brain immediately recoils and either is looking for a new pattern or trying to fulfill the old pattern.

Imagine a person walking through a winding corridor and imagine that you can turn the lights out in the corridor and make it completely dark. When you turn the lights out, the person can't see a thing and has no reliable way to navigate this winding corridor. They are looking to turn the lights back on and be on their way again. Then, you turn the lights back on, and they can see.

The vulnerable state of a person is when they are in the dark in search of light. They are similar to what the brain experiences when its thought process is disrupted. It is looking to turn the lights back on so that it can get back on track with the pattern.

Now let's say you don't turn the lights on until you have noticed that the person traversing this corridor has completely turned themselves around in a frantic search for a light switch. They do not notice that they are now facing the opposite direction that they were walking in and start walking in the wrong direction.

This is essentially the concept of implanting a hypnotic suggestion when you have successfully broken the mental pattern of an individual. You get their minds going in a different direction than it was before, just like you confused the person in the corridor with darkness to the point that they start walking the wrong way. The path the person was walking was the pattern, and the darkness in this example is representative of the pattern interrupt.

This is how a skilled hypnotist can control the way a person speaks after they have been inducted with a pattern interrupt.

Hypnotists use pattern interruption to get the mind going in a certain direction. Let's say, for example, your spouse asks you, "Can you hand me the frying pan?" and you answer "Yes" but don't hand it to them. You have simply broken the path their mind was headed, and they are wondering about the unusual response to a mundane question.

You have your spouse's undivided attention now and suppose you continue by saying, "Settle. You don't have to fry anything for what we are eating tonight."

The first word in that phrase, "settle," was a hypnotic command similar to the cliché "sleep" or "relax," and it set the tone for the rest of the hypnotic suggestion. This is just one of the hundreds of ways that a hypnotist can induce a hypnotic state through pattern interrupts.

Not only can pattern interrupts be deployed virtually anywhere and in any situation, but they can be used for psychological manipulation. You have probably been the subject or at least seen a psychological manipulation in action using pattern interrupts. They occur all the time without anyone realizing it.

There is an extremely simple way to manipulate people that pretty much anyone can do, but even this base tactic is an example of successful psychological manipulation through pattern interruption. Picture if you will, a situation in which your spouse is deep in thought about what to make for dinner. You want chicken, but you have no idea what your spouse is imagining making. Suddenly showing her a coupon in the paper or a particularly enticing video online for the chicken recipe can break their concentration on whatever type of food they were thinking of cooking and gets a new train of thought going on chicken. You have successfully used a pattern interrupt to manipulate the situation and heightened your chances of having chicken for dinner.

The other technique here is overload, which aims at manipulating a person's thought process or emotions pushing them past a threshold of tolerance. The way you can push a person past this threshold is by feeding them images or vivid explanation of something and going way over the top with it. Once the imagery becomes too much, the person cannot complete whatever pattern they were on.

Let us consider an instance where you have a friend who doesn't like Asparagus. Imagine telling your friend about this awesome dinner you had – which had featured Asparagus. You give details of smell, texture, taste, and the feel of the Asparagus in your mouth as your teeth shredded through the thick greenery and the roughage of the vegetable. Your friend will be trying to block the imagery, but once it gets to be too much for them, they will be pushed beyond their tolerance threshold and be unable to ignore this new path that their thoughts are taking. Imagine that you were so descriptive of the Asparagus that your friend has lost their appetite or even become queasy. This is yet another example of psychological manipulation through pattern interruption.

Another very simple method for psychological manipulation through pattern interrupt is confusion. Confusion is a tactic that is commonly used in hypnotherapy because it has a way of disarming an individual. It is used to help people overcome irrational fears or to allow them to alter things about their character, like becoming more assertive or more vocal.

Confusion can be used to get the person's mind off the anxiety, anger, fear, or whatever emotion they have associated with a certain concept. Fear of flying is commonly mentioned in hypnotherapist offices. One tactic that is commonly used to help clients get over their fears is by getting them to think intently about the act of flying. What is it about flying that makes them fearful? What makes them have a vision in their minds of the worst possible scenario?. Maybe a fiery plane crash. When they start to envision these things, their mind gets going on a pattern of fear and anxiety as they imagine their worst nightmares coming true.

The hypnotist will interrupt their thought process with a very confusing string of words like, "If a person answers a question with a question, wouldn't that be an answer to the initial question or would the question be a question unto itself and therefore need to answer to the question?"

This confusing diction will completely break the distressing thoughts of plane crashes in the client's mind and replace it with a puzzle that is light and, at the very least, not life-endangering.

This sows a seed in the client's mind and, when done successfully, realigns the association that the client makes when they think about flying. Instead of fear and anxiety, the thought of flying is associated with a sense of ease coming from the pattern interrupt - a confusing question that broke the pattern of fearful thoughts.

Not only is the client disarmed, and some of the stings of the concept of flying has been taken away, but a good hypnotist will have completely replaced what the client associates with flying from fear to ease.

Hypnotherapists can also use the overload tactic of pattern interrupt for the benefit of their clients. For example, weight loss is another common problem that patients come to hypnotherapists with. The therapist will then use an image or sensory overload to turn the client off of a certain fatty food that they have a hard time resisting. They can use an abundance of imagery related to potato chips, for example, to push the client past their threshold of tolerance so that they associate potato chips with an unpleasant experience and therefore become more and more opposed to them.

How to Use Pattern Interrupts for Influence

Pattern interrupts are powerful tools for influence as well because they can send a person's mind into a malleable state that you can use to your advantage or for the benefit of the individual. For instance, let's say that you want to get a dog, but your spouse or roommate is afraid of dogs and don't want to have one in the house.

By trivializing the logic by which a person associates a certain fear or emotion, you force the person to question the validity of the association. This is called the spin-out technique of pattern interrupt because it sends the person's way of thinking about a certain association into a spin. The person will then realize regarding their fear of dogs or abandon their line of reasoning altogether as you have set them on a new pattern through the spin-out interrupt.

Everything we have discussed in this chapter can be used to get a person into a hypnotic trance. The pattern interrupt method for inducing trance is an easy way to achieve a mild hypnotic state, but even these mild states can be a fertile field for hypnotic suggestion.

Make no mistake about it: getting a person off of their initial train of thought and onto another is a form of hypnosis and psychological manipulation. It may seem simple, but just like an instrument, it is easy to pick up but very difficult to master.

Once you have practiced and become adept at using the pattern interrupt method for inducing hypnotic trances, you are going to need to know what to do once you have a person in a trance, which is what we will be going over in the following chapters.

Chapter 6 Dark Persuasion

Persuasion is used around us all of the time. If you have ever watched an advertisement on TV or online, or seen a billboard, you are used to a form of persuasion. But here, we are going to look at persuasion on a more local level rather than looking at the ways that big businesses are going to try and persuade you to look at their products and make a purchase. This is something that we all recognize, so it isn't a trick or dark manipulation. We are going to take a look at some of the ways that a manipulator and others close to us can use the power of persuasion to get what they want, without us even realizing it.

Elements of persuasion

Like other types of control, some components are to be observed when it comes to persuasion. These components assist to precisely identify which persuasion makes it clearer. The ability to convince others is one salient feature that distinguishes persuasion from all other themes of dark psychology. In most cases, the victim is allowed to make choices at will. Eventually, the persuasion tactics lead them to change their will to that of the persuader. The topic can choose the manner they want to believe, whether or not they want to buy a product, or whether they believe the proof behind the persuasion is powerful enough to alter their minds. There are a few components in the persuasion that assist to further describe what is while giving us a deeper understanding of this enigmatic theme.

The first element of this theme is that persuasion is often symbolic. This means persuasion utilizes words, sounds, and images to get the message across to the target victim. The logic behind this is quite simple. For one individual to be able to persuade another into acting in a particular way, they will need to show them why they should act in a said way and not vice versa. This is best achieved by using word sounds or various images you can use sentences to start a debate or argument to prove your point. Pictures are a great way to show the evidence needed to persuade someone to go one way or the other. Some nonverbal signs are possible, but they are not as effective as using words and images

The second key is that persuasion will be used deliberately to affect how others act or think. This one is quite obvious; you don't use persuasion to get them to change if you don't deliberately try to affect others. To get the topic to believe the same way they do, the persuader will attempt distinct strategies. This could be as easy as having a discussion with them or presenting proof supporting their point of perspective. On the other hand, to change the mind of the subject, it could involve much more and include more deceptive forms.

The distinctive thing about persuasion is that it enables some type of free will for the topic. In this way, the topic is permitted to create its own decision. For the most part, they don't have to go for it, no matter how hard somebody tries to persuade them of something. The subject might hear about the best car to buy a thousand commercials, but if they don't like that brand or don't need a new vehicle at that time, they won't go out and buy it.

Think about it for a moment - if the subject is against abortion, how many people will come out and say how great abortion is, it's not likely that the subject will change their minds. This enables much more freedom of choice than is found in the other types of mind control, which could explain why, when questioned, many individuals do not see this as a kind of mind control. Persuasion is a type of mind control that can take place in many respects. While brainwashing, hypnosis and manipulation must happen face-to-face, and in some instances in full isolation, persuasion may happen otherwise.

Subliminal persuasion

The word "subliminal" means underneath our consciousness. Subliminal persuasion means an advertising message that is displayed below the threshold of awareness or consumer awareness to persuade, persuade, or help people change their minds without making them aware of what is going on. This is about affecting individuals with more than words. Some of the subliminal methods of persuasion impact our stimuli with smell, eyesight, sound, touch, and taste. There are mainly three subliminal methods of persuasion to affect anyone.

They include;

- Building a relationship-building relationship makes the other person feel comfortable. This will open up the other individual more. This can be accomplished through a healthy observation strength that matches their mood or state. This helps create confidence
- Power of discussion–the power of a powerful, convincing person is much connected to an advertiser's conversion. The correct words and inflections help you to be openly straightforward.
- Suggestive power-Associating useful and desirable stuff in discussion or interaction enables an individual to become more open to fresh thoughts.

Basic Persuasion techniques

Some techniques can be utilized to make persuasion more successful. All victims are usually presented with different forms of persuasion daily. A food manufacturing plant will work on getting their victims to purchase a new product. At the same time, a movie company will focus on persuading their victims to watch their latest movie projects. Three main techniques of persuasion have been prevalent since the birth of this theme.

Create a need

This is one of the techniques that are often deployed by the manipulator to be able to get the victim to change their way of thinking. This creates a need or rather appeals to a need that is already pre-existing within the victim. If it is executed in a skilled way, the victim will be eating out of the persuaders palm in no time. This means the manipulator will need to tap into the fundamental needs of its victims, like the need for self-actualization.

Food, for example, is usually something that we as humans need to survive, and prolonged lack will pause as a big problem.

If the agent can convince the subject that their store is the best, or if they can get more food or shelter by switching their beliefs, there is a higher chance of success.

Utilizing illustrative and words

The choice of words one chooses to use comes a long way in the success of using persuasion. There are many ways in which you can phrase sentences when talking about one thing. Saying the right words in the right way is what will make all the difference when attempting to use persuasion.

Tricks used by mass media and advertising

The media use two main methods which they use to persuade the masses. First is through the use of images, as well as the use of sounds.

Images

Our sighs and visual processing areas of the brain are very powerful. Just think about it for a minute, have you ever thought of a person without ending up picturing how they look? It is because of this that makes imagery and visual manipulation a preferred method by the media. Companies will often include split-second images of their product or individual inserted into an advertisement that seems quite innocent on the face value. This usually a form of subliminal persuasion. These split-second images that are usually assumed for the most part usually end up taking some form of control of the victim, which persuades them to purchase that particular service.

Sound

Sound is yet another trick that is used by media in the persuasion of unsuspecting victims. Some people usually underestimate the powers that exist within the sound. But answer me this, how many times have you heard a song somewhere only to have it loops through your mind continuously? Songs usually influence us even though we are not aware of it despite knowing you are listening to it. This is what the media tend to exploit in their quest for persuasion of the masses.

There will often be several phrases skillfully hidden, and repeated in an advertisement song that will most likely convince you to be inclined to prefer one company over the other. An example of this is seen at

McDonald's. The melody 'I love it 'is often repeated in a manner that persuades the victims to constantly purchase their meals.

Dark Persuasion Techniques to Be on the Lookout For

After taking a look at the different types of persuasion and what they all mean, you may be able to see why dark persuasion is such a bad thing and can be harmful to the victim. Being able to recognize the different techniques that the manipulator may use can make it easier to understand when it is being used on you.

So, how exactly is a dark persuader able to use this idea to carry out their wishes? There are a few different types of tactics that a dark manipulator is going to use, but some of the most common options include:

The Long Con

The first method that we are going to look at is the Long Con. This method is kind of slow and drawn out, but it can be effective because it takes so long, and it is hard to recognize or even pinpoint when something went wrong. One of the main reasons that some people can resist persuasion is because they feel that the other person is pressuring them, and this can make them back off. If they feel that there is a lack of rapport or trust with the person who is trying to persuade them, they will steer clear as well. The Long Con is so effective because they can overcome these main problems and give the persuader exactly what they want.

The Long Con is going to involve the dark persuader to take their time, working to earn the trust of their victim. They are going to take some time to befriend the victim and make sure that their victim trusts and likes them. This is going to be achieved by the persuader with artificial rapport building, which sometimes seems excessive, and other techniques that will help to increase the comfort levels between the persuader and their victim.

As soon as the persuader sees the victim is psychologically prepared, then they start their attempts. It starts in slow successions of convincing the individual; then, the victim manages to do as the persuader wants. This is going to serve the persuader in two ways. First, the victim starts to become used to persuasion by that persuader. The second is that the victim is going to start making that mental association between a positive outcome and the persuasion.

The Long Con is going to take a long period to complete because the persuader doesn't want to make it too obvious what they are doing. For instance, a recently widowed lady is deemed vulnerable because of her age and from grief. After her loss, a man starts to befriend her. This man maybe someone she knows from church or even a relative. He starts to spend more time with her, showing immense kindness and patience, and it doesn't take too long for her guard to drop when he comes around.

Then this man starts to carry out some smaller acts of positive persuasion that we talked about before. He may advise her of a better bank account to use or a better way to reduce any monthly bills. The victim appreciates these efforts and helps them get from their persuader and takes their advice.

Over some time, the man then tries to use some dark persuasion. He may try to persuade her to let him invest some of her money. She obliges because of the positive persuasion that was used in the past. Of course, the man is going to work to take everything he can get from her. If the manipulator is skilled enough, she may feel that he tried to help her, but the money is lost because he just ran into some bad luck with the investment. This is how far dark persuasion can go.

Graduality

Often when we hear about acts of dark persuasion, it seems impossible and unbelievable. What they fail to realize is that this dark persuasion isn't ever going to be a big or a sudden request that comes out of nowhere. Dark persuasion is more like a staircase. The dark persuader is never going to ask the victim to do something big and dramatic the first time they meet. Instead, they will have the victim take one step at a time.

When the manipulator has the target only go one step at a time, the whole process seems like less of a big deal. Before the victim knows it, they have already gone a long way down, and the persuader isn't likely to let them leave or come back up again.

Let's take an example of how this process is going to look in real life. Let's say that there is a criminal who wanted to make it so that someone else committed the crimes for them. Gang bosses, cult leaders, and even Charles Manson did this same thing.

This criminal wouldn't dream of beginning the process by asking their victim to murder for them. This would send out a red flag, and no one in their right minds would willingly go out and kill for someone they barely know. Instead, the criminal would start by having the victim do something small, like a petty crime, or simply hiding a weapon for them. Something that isn't that big of a deal for the victim, at least in comparison.

Over time, the acts that the manipulator can persuade their victim to do will become more severe. And since they did the smaller crimes, the persuader passes such actions to the victim (blackmailing). Before the victim knows it, they are going to feel like they are in too deep. They will then be persuaded to carry out some of the most shocking crimes. And often, by this point, they will do it because they feel like they have no other choice.

Dark persuaders are going to be experts at using this graduality to help increase the severity of their persuasion over time. They know that no victim would be willing to jump the canyon or do the big crime or misdeed right away. So, the persuader works to build a bridge to get there. By the time the victim sees how far in they are, it is too late to turn back.

Masking the True Intentions

There are different methods that a persuader can use dark psychology to get the things that they want. Disguising their true desires is very important for them to be successful. The best persuaders can use this approach in a variety of ways, but the method they choose is often going to depend on the victim and the situation.

One principle that is used by a persuader is the idea that many people are going to have a difficult time refusing two requests when they happen in a row. Let's say that the persuader wants to get $200 from the victim, but they do not intend to repay the money. To start, the persuader may begin by saying that they need a loan for the amount of $1000. They may go into some details about the consequences to themselves if the persuader doesn't come up with that kind of money sometime soon.

The victim may feel some kind of guilt or compassion to the persuader, and they want to help. But $1000 is a lot of money, more than the victim can lend. From here, the persuader lowers their request from $1000 to $200. Of course, there is some kind of emotional reason for needing the money, and the victim feels like it is impossible to refuse this second request. They want to help out the persuader, and they feel bad for not giving in to the initial request when they were asked. In the end, the persuader gets the $200 they originally wanted, and the victim is not going to know what has taken place.

Another type of technique that the persuader can use is known as reverse psychology. This can also help to mask true intentions during the persuasion. Some people have a personality that is known as a boomerang. This means that they will refuse to go in the direction that they are thrown and instead will veer off into different directions.

If the persuader knows someone more of a boomerang type, then they can identify a key weakness of that person. For example, let's say that a persuader has a friend who is attempting to win over some girl they like. The persuader knows that the friend will use and then hurt that girl. The girl is currently torn between a malicious friend and an innocent third party. The persuader may try to steer the girl in the direction of the guy who is a good choice, knowing that she is going to go against this and end up going with the harmful friend.

Leading Questions

Another method of dark persuasion that can be used is known as leading questions. If you have ever had an encounter with a skilled salesman, verbal persuasion can be impactful when it is deployed in careful and calibrated ways. One of the most powerful techniques that can be used verbally is leading questions.

These leading questions are intended to trigger a specific response out of the victim. The persuader may ask the target something like, "how bad do you think those people are?" This question is going to imply that the people the persuader is asking about are bad to some extent. They could have chosen to ask a non-leading question, such as "how do you feel about those people?"

Dark persuaders are masters at using leading questions in a way that is hard to catch. If the victim ever begins to feel that they are being led, then they are going to resist, and it is hard to lead them or persuade them. If a persuader ever senses that their victim starts to catch what is happening, they will quit using that one and switch over to another one. They may come back to that tactic, but only when the victim has quieted down a bit and is more influenceable again.

The Law of State Transference

The state is a concept that is going to take a look at the general mood someone is in. If someone is aligned with their deeds, words, and thoughts, then this is an example of a strong and harmonious state. The law of state transference is going to involve the concept of someone who holds the balance of power in a situation and can then transfer their emotional state onto the other person they are interacting with. This can be a very powerful tool for the dark persuader to use against their victim.

Initially, the influencer is going to force their state to match the state that their target naturally has. If the target is sad, and they talk slowly, the influencer is going to make their state follow this format. The point of this is to create a deep rapport with the target.

After we get to this state match, the influencer is then going to alter their state subtly and see if they have some compliance for the victim. Perhaps they will choose to speed up their voice to see if the victim will speed up as well. Once the victim starts to show these signs of compliance, then this is an indication that the influencer is at the hook point.

When this hook point is reached - however long it takes - the influencer will change their state to that of their victim. This could be an emotional state that the influencer wants. It could be positive, angry, happy, or indignant. It often depends on what the persuader wants to help reach their goals. This technique is an important one for a dark persuader because it is going to show the impact of subconscious cues on the failure or the success of any type of persuasion.

Chapter 7 Tips to read and Analyze people

Take a moment to imagine a time when the sight of someone sent a chill down your spine. You may not have known why, but you were simply uncomfortable around the person that you were facing. Despite your best attempts to identify the reasoning behind your problem, you found that there was no particular reason that you could discern. The only thing you knew was that you were the only thing afraid of the person in front of you and had no idea how to overcome them.

There was a very good reason for this guttural reaction—your instincts were telling you that something about the other person was not right. You didn't need to know specifics, and all that mattered to you was that your reactions were accurate. This is because all these guttural reactions must do keep you alive. So long as that is managed, your instincts did their job.

When you first look at someone, your unconscious mind goes through all sorts of information to come up with what it assumes is a valid reading of the person. Of course, this all happens beneath your conscious awareness. This means that you are entirely unaware of it as it happens, and yet, you can respond to it without effort. Of course, reacting without second thoughts is a useful trait in a survival setting. You are not trying to rationalize what and why when in a survival setting. You simply react on impulse without wasting valuable time that could be the difference between life and death.

However, if you are not in a life-and-death situation, do you want to be acting on impulse? Will your impulses help you discern whether the person at the interview is lying or simply uncomfortable about something? Or to determine how your partner is feeling during an argument?

There are limitless reasons that being able to rationally understand what is going on in someone else's mind is critical, even if you already have a decent gut reaction. Ultimately, when you can analyze someone calmly and consciously be aware of why you are uncomfortable or what is putting you on-edge, you are better prepared to cope with the problem at hand. This is because you can act rationally. You can strategize on how to better react in the most conducive manner that will allow you to succeed in the situation.

This means that in the modern world, when things are very rarely life or death situations, making an effort to switch to responding rationally and consciously is almost always the best bet. You will be able to tell when someone is setting off your alarm bells because they seem threatening, or because they seem deceptive. You will be able to find out what the problem is to respond appropriately.

Why Analyze People

Analyzing people is something that is utilized by several people in different capacities. The most basic reason you may decide that you wish to analyze someone is to simply understand them. When you have an in-built technique of understanding others, you will discover that having a cognitive instead of an emotional connection is critical to establishing a true connection with someone else's mind.

Consider for a moment that you are trying to land a deal with a very important client. You know that the deal is critical if you hope to keep your job and possibly even get a promotion, but you also know that it is going to be a difficult task to manage. If you can read someone else, you can effectively allow yourself the ability to truly know what is going on in their mind.

Think about it—you will be able to tell if the client is uncomfortable and respond accordingly. You will be able to tell if the client is being deceptive or withholding something—and respond accordingly. You can tell if the client is uninterested, feeling threatened, or even just annoyed with your attempts to sway him or her, and you can then find out how to reply.

When you can understand the mindset of someone else, you can self-regulate. You can fine-tune your behaviors to guarantee that you will be persuasive. You can make sure that your client feels comfortable by being able to adjust your behavior to find out what was causing the discomfort in the first place.

Beyond just being able to self-regulate, being able to read other people is critical in several other situations as well. If you can read someone else, you can protect yourself from any threats that may arise. If you can read someone else, you can simply understand their position better. You can find out how to persuade or manipulate the other person. You can get people to do things that they would otherwise avoid.

Ultimately, being able to analyze other people has so many critical benefits that it is worthwhile to be able to do so. Developing this skill set means that you will be more in touch with the feelings of those around you, allowing you to assert that you have a higher emotional intelligence simply because you come to understand what emotions look like. You will be able to identify your own emotions through self-reflection and to learn to pay attention to your body movements. The ability to analyze people can be invaluable in almost any setting.

How to Analyze People

Though it may sound intimidating, learning to analyze other people is not nearly as difficult as it may initially seem. There are no complicated rules that you need to memorize or any skills that you need to learn—all you have to do is learn the pattern of behaviors and what they mean. This is because once you know the behaviors, you can usually start to piece together the intent behind the behaviors.

You can begin to find out exactly what it is that someone's eyes narrowing means and then begin to identify it with the context of several other actions or behaviors as well. You can find out what is intended when someone's speech and their body language do not match up. Body language rarely lies when people are unaware of how it works, so you can often turn to it for crucial information if you are interacting with other people.

The reason this works to understand people is because it is commonly accepted that there is a cycle between thoughts, feelings, and behaviors. Your thoughts create feelings, and the feelings you have automatically influence your behaviors, as you can see through body language.

Most of the time, this is an entirely unconscious cycle. You are unaware of it happening. However, several schools of therapy have chosen to identify and utilize this cycle, such as cognitive-behavioral psychology. When you can recognize that this cycle exists, you can take advantage of it—you can begin to utilize your understanding of the cycle to follow it in reverse.

Effectively, you will be looking at behaviors that people display and then tracing them back to the feelings behind them. This is why body language is so important to understand. When you can understand what is going on with someone's behavior, you can understand their feelings. When you understand their feelings, you can begin to find out the underlying thoughts that they have. This is about the closest thing to mind reading that you can ever truly attain.

To analyze other people, you have a simple process to get through— you must first find out the neutral baseline of behavior. This is the default behavior of the person. You must then begin to look for deviations in that neutral behavior. From there, you try to put together clusters of behaviors to find out what is going on in the mid of someone else, and then you analyze. This process is not difficult, and if you can learn how to do so, while also learning how to interpret the various types of body language, you will find that understanding other people could never be easier.

Establish a neutral baseline behavior set

The most important aspect of being able to analyze someone else is through learning how to identify their baseline behavior. If you can do this, you can effectively allow yourself to identify how that person behaves in a neutral setting. Effectively, you will learn what that person's quirks may be.

For example, someone who happens to be reserved or particularly timid is likely to show several common signs of discomfort, even by default. They may cross their arms to shield their body, or stand defensively and refuse to make eye contact. As you will learn later through reading, this is a common body language that is regularly exhibited by those who are lying and do not know how to cover their tracks. However, the timid person is probably not lying if their behavior by default involves crossing arms and refusing to make eye contact.

Because people's baseline personality types and quirks vary so drastically from person to person, this becomes a critical first step, and you must make it a point to never skip it. Otherwise, you would assume that any shy person must be trying to deceive you. Getting that picture of baseline personality and nonverbal communication quirks are crucial.

Identify deviations from neutral behaviors

Once your baseline has been established, you can begin to identify any deviations from it. This means that you can find out which of the behaviors that you are seeing do not match up with what you have come to expect via your initial observations. This stage can occur during all sorts of interactions. You may ask a question and then observe to see what the response will be to determine whether that person is answering truthfully. You can probe and look for signs of discomfort. You can effectively test to see how convincing you are being when you are trying to persuade someone to do something.

Identify clusters of deviations

Of course, just identifying those individual deviations is not always enough. You must also make it a point to recognize clusters of the deviations to get the true picture. When you master the art of reading body language, you will see that much of human body language can be interpreted in different ways depending on the context. Often, you need to get that context from looking at other behaviors that are occurring in conjunction with the behaviors you are analyzing. For example, there are several behaviors in deception that could have several meanings. Still, as soon as they occur together, you can usually infer that there is some level of deception occurring, which means that you need to proceed with caution.

Analyze

Finally, as you identify those clusters of deviations from the original, neutral behavioral baseline, you can start to find out what they mean. You can start to trace it back to find out whether or not the person is honest or how they are feeling. When you begin to analyze, that is when you truly get the real snapshot of the thoughts inside the person's mind. You will be able to piece together whether the person has a problem in certain settings based upon seeing general repeated responses. You will be able to tell what is intimidating to them, or what seems to consistently motivate them to keep working toward their goals. In going through this stage, you can start to find out exactly what is needed to influence or manipulate them, if you should choose to do so.

When to Analyze People

Analyzing people is one of those skills that can be used in almost any context. You can use it at work, in personal relationships, in politics, religion, and even just in day-to-day life. Because of this versatility, you may find that you are constantly analyzing people, and that is okay. Remember, your unconscious mind already makes snapshot judgments about other people and their intentions, so you were already analyzing people, to begin with. Now, you are simply making an effort to ensure that those analyses are made in your conscious mind so you can be aware of them.

Now, let's take a look at several different compelling situations in which being able to consciously analyze someone is a critical skill to know:

In parenting: When you can analyze other people, you can begin to use those skills toward your children. Now, you may be thinking that a child's mind is not sophisticated enough to get a reliable read on, but remember, the child's feelings are usually entirely genuine. In essence, they have their feelings that they have, and though the reason behind those feelings may be less than compelling to you as a parent, that does not in any way dismiss the feelings. By being able to recognize the child's emotions, you can begin to understand what is going on in your child's mind, and that will allow you to parent calmly and more effectively.

In relationships: When you live with someone else, it can be incredibly easy to step on someone else's toes without realizing it. Of course, constantly stepping on the toes of someone else is likely to lead to some degree of resentment if it is never addressed. Yet, some people have a hard time discussing when they are uncomfortable or miserable. This is where being able to analyze someone else comes in—you will be able to tell what your partner's base emotions are when you interact, allowing you to play the role of support.

In the workplace: Especially if you interact with other people, you need to be able to analyze other people. You will be able to see how your coworkers view you, allowing you to change your behaviors to get the company image that you desire. Beyond just that, you may also work in a field that requires you to be able to get goodreads on someone in the first place.

Perhaps you are a doctor—you may need to be able to tell how someone is feeling and whether they are honest with you, to begin with. Maybe you are a lawyer, and you need to be able to analyze the integrity of your client and of those that you are cross-examining. Maybe you are a salesperson who needs to be able to tell if you are compelling in your attempt to close.

In public: When you are interacting with people in public, you need to be able to protect yourself. When you can read other people, you can find out whether you are safe or whether someone is threatening or suspicious. This means that you can prepare yourself no matter what the situation is to ensure that you are always ready to respond.

In an interview, you may find that read an interviewer's body language can give you a clue on when to change tactics or move on to something else. You will be able to tell how you are being taken simply by watching for body language and other nonverbal cues.

When watching presentations: When you are watching a presentation, speech, or address, you may fall into the habit of simply taking everything at face value. After all, why would anyone ever make it a point to tell you something that is not true? This is because you are falling for one of the principles of persuasion—an appeal to authority.

In other words, you deem the person speaking authority and therefore deem them to be trustworthy. Instead, make an effort to see the other party as what they truly are by learning to read their body language. You can tell if the politician on television is uncomfortable or lying simply by learning to analyze their behaviors.

In arguments: When you are arguing with someone else, usually, emotions are running high on both ends. No one is thinking clearly, and things that were not meant can be said. However, when you can analyze people, you can start to find out when someone else is getting emotional to disengage altogether. You will be able to identify the signs that you should disengage and try again later to ensure that you are not stepping on toes or making things worse.

In self-reflection: When you can analyze other people, you can start to analyze yourself as well. This means that you can stop and look at your body language to sort of check-in with yourself and find out what is going on in your mind. Sometimes, it can be difficult to identify exactly how you are feeling, but this is the perfect way to do so in a pinch. If you can stop and self-reflect, you can identify your emotions.

In self-regulation: Identifying your emotions then lends itself to the ability to self-regulate. When you are, for example, in a heated argument and feel yourself tensing up and getting annoyed, you may be able to key into the fact that you are getting annoyed and respond accordingly. Conversely, when you can analyze other people, you can look at them and see how they are feeling. This means that if you can see that you are intimidating or making someone uncomfortable, you can make the necessary changes to your actions.

How to defend from manipulators

We are true, human. It's precise because of this that we get to dwell on the view of others in everything we do. We always want and love validation from others so we can subconsciously decide whether or not we will be depressed. In this millennial age, the norm has been just bragging about their wealth in social media.

Many of these boasting are often the reality. In the end, this leads to a loose connection with reality. This kind of self-deception can dig deep into the human spicy, and one day a victim of this may wake up and realize that only in her servants does her perfect world exist. Depression will follow suit tightly.

The first step towards protecting yourself against persuasion and manipulation is to confront the scenario and to take the position of disrupting any illusions. You won't be able to go through your lives usually. You must be careful that you regulate your own decisions. Then choose consciously to see stuff for what they are. This agreement, which seems too good to be true, could be. The other thing you should do is trust your instincts certainly.

Sometimes you have been told a lie most competently that you can believe. But at a specific instinctive rate, you can feel an imbalance between what should, what is, and then what is projected on you. There might be no physical sign that something is wrong, but you think that something is wrong.

The next significant thing when you ask questions is to hear the answers. This can sound unbelievable because you're going to listen to the responses. The reality is that we can deceive ourselves by choosing the responses we receive. We say that we look, but we only care about the reactions that we want to hear and not the answers that we receive.

You may have broken your illusions, but some of you still hold on to the comfort of those illusions. You would not hear the real answers to your questions because of the pain of dealing with the scenario. Actual hearing needs a certain feeling of detachment, but not reality this time around.

You must get rid of your feelings. Your detachment from our emotions would lead you to the next step in processing the new data logically. It can make situations more complicated than they have to behave irrationally. It makes it so hard for your exit strategy to allow all feelings to cool down and spring.

The irrational part of you may want to let everything go hell when you face reality. Your justified anger can encourage you to take short-term measures to calm your feelings. But you may come to regret these actions in the long term. I'm not saying that you should deny your emotions; I'm not saying that you do not act on these emotions. First, deal with the situations and later deal with your emotions.

Act Fast

It's lovely that you have got to grips with the truth of things. But it is so much more to defend ourselves against these dark, manipulative strategies. While you try to protect yourself against the claws of these manipulators, it is often intense and exciting at first. This intensity of these feelings can slowly lead to negation.

The longer you take any action, the quicker the denial will begin, and if it occurs, there is a strong likelihood that you may fall back and end up being trapped on the same internet. You can avoid this by taking action as soon as you know someone is attempting to manipulate you. This can be done in the most natural way possible, as when informing a close friend about some facts of the specific scenario, all the events that will eventually lead you to liberty can be so started.

You should understand that after choosing to behave, the fabric is made of sturdier material than glass. The illusion can work its way back to your core by using fragmented parts of your feelings to solve it. When a liar is caught in a lie, it may try to hire others to implement that lying if they think they no longer hold you.

A disappointing partner with whom you broke stuff lately would attempt to use the other shared links in your lives to change your mind. You are going to need both your logic and instincts if you want to get out of this unscathed. While the reality is that when you find that you have always been lied to, you get emotionally scarred, so you are still left untouched by the scenario.

However, priority should be provided to follow the path that enables you to go to this toxic condition without further harm. You're mentally all over the location. Rage, rage, hurt, and disappointment are the tip of the iceberg. But you must logically believe. Keep your head above the water and warn yourself.

Get Assistance Quickly

When you are trapped in the manipulations of others, confusion is one of the feelings you would encounter. This enables you to obscure your rational thinking and makes you feel helpless. You could even question the truth of what you're currently facing. If you continue to have those doubts, it will lead to denial.

You will likely want to say that you have the whole scenario wrong. You misunderstood specific stuff and came to the incorrect conclusion. Such thinking would lead back to the weapons of the manipulator. Resist the desire to accept a second opinion. In a health crisis, people go to another physician to get a second view. This clears any doubts concerning your diagnosis and a confirmation of what the best course of therapy is for you.

Similarly, receiving an opinion from another person can assist you in discerning reality and your next steps. Just remember, it's better to go to someone who's proven to be interested in your best many times. The next step is to confront the perpetrator if you have the assistance that you need. I recommend you choose the scene or place for this.

Select a location that provides you the upper hand. That would involve some cautious planning on your part. If the offender exists in the cyber world, especially if the person has victimized you, you must engage the police and the authorities concerned. Do some of your research to find out the truth. After you face the offender and take the measures you need to get out of the scenario, the healing method must begin rapidly. The extent and severity you have been harmed, manipulated or abused do not matter. You must go through it and wait for your wounds to heal instead of ruminating about the past.

Time would offer you sufficient distance from your experience, but it would seldom be healing for emotional scars if you learned something about this book. If you don't do anything, an unhealthy scab might form over the wound that makes you vulnerable, if not more than you have experienced. Speak to a consultant, take part in the treatment, and actively facilitate the healing process, regardless of what you choose. It will not occur overnight, but you are sure you get nearer each day and every phase of your treatment.

Have Confidence in Your Instincts

While your brain interprets signals based on facts, logic, and experience, it operates in the opposite direction by filtering data through an emotional filter. The only thing that takes vibrations is your intestine that cannot pick up either the heart or the brain. If you can groom up to the stage where you acknowledge your inner voice and are trained to do so, you will reduce your likelihood of becoming seduced by individuals who try to manipulate you. It's difficult to acknowledge this voice at first.

The reason this happens is that we have allowed doubt, self-discrimination, and our inner critic to take over. This voice or instinct relies on your survival. So, trust that your brain cells will still be able to process stuff in your immediate area when it starts.

Some individuals call it intuition, some call it instinct, and they do the same, particularly when it comes to relationships. You must acknowledge that starting to trust your instincts may not always make logical sense. If you've ever been doing something and felt like you were suddenly watched, then you understand what I mean.

You have no eyes at the rear of your head, nobody else in the space, but you have the small shiver running down the back of your neck, and you're looking at the "sudden understanding." That is what I am talking about. I am talking about that.

The first step in connecting with your instinct is to decode your mind with your voices. You can do this with meditation. Forget about chatting, she said. Concentrate on your middle. You're the voice that you understand. Next, be attentive to your ideas. Don't just throw away your head's eclectic monologue. Instead, go with the stream of thoughts.

Why do you believe in somebody somehow? How do you feel so deeply, even though you knew each other for only a few days? What's your nagging feeling about this other individual? You become more sensitive to your intuition as you explore your ideas and know when your instincts start and respond to them.

You might have to learn to stop and believe if you are the individual who, at present, wants to make stimulating choices. This break provides you the chance to reflect and assess your options. The next part is hard, and many people couldn't follow it. You can't sail or navigate this step, unfortunately. You need to be open to the concept of self-confidence and of trusting others to believe in your instinct.

Your lack of confidence would only make you paranoid, and when you're paranoid, it's not your instincts that kick. It's your fear. Every molehill tends to transform fear into a mountain. You have to let go of your concern, embrace trust, and make your fresh relationships lead. You can hear the voice better without the roadblocks of fear in your mind. Finally, your priorities must be reassessed.

You may not see the past if your mind is at the forefront of money and material property. Any contact you have with individuals would be viewed as individuals who try to use you, and it will quickly become truth if you live so often. You understand how you draw what you believe into your lives. If you always think about material wealth, you will only attract individuals like yourself.

Look at your interactions with this new view with this guide; the old, the new, and the outlook. Don't enter into a partnership you expect to play. Be accessible to them, whether it is a company relationship, a romantic relationship, or even a regular knowledge. You can receive the correct feedback from your intuition. Do not think this, too, that if you encounter suspects, your gut will tell you to go in the opposite direction.

Chapter 8 One last word

There is so much to learn about the psychological nature of people to prey on others. The truth is that all of humanity has the potential to victimize others. Yes, some try to sublimate this tendency while others choose to act upon their impulses. However, the most important thing for you is to understand your thoughts, perceptions, and feelings that lead to predatory behavior so that you can learn to control yourself and use it for good.

One thing that is important to note is that manipulation often happens in families with parents who have narcissistic tendencies. In the case where there is parental alienation, a parent may use their child as a psychological weapon to abuse the other parent. The truth is that mind control, a form of dark psychology, happens in a system where people are – such as churches, families, and workplaces.

The key ingredients of dark psychology are people, narcissistic leaders, lieutenants, scapegoats, and keeping secrets. What is not allowed in this kind of system is having a free spirit or free-thinking mentality. It is such kind of people who are banished from the community of manipulators.

According to dark psychology, some people commit evil acts, not because of money, power, sex, retribution, or other known factors. Instead, they choose to do it because they are horrid – without a goal. In other words, for them, ends do not justify the means. These are the kind of people who injure others for the sake of doing it. Within each one of us lies this potential!

You and I have the potential to harm others without cause, purpose, or explanation. This potential is considered complex – one that is even hard to define.

One thing you must note is that your shadow self is always standing right behind you – just outside your view. When you stand indirect light, you cast a shadow, right. The shadow is the part of yourself that you can't really see. Think about it for a moment, what lengths do you go to just to protect your self-image from unfamiliarity and flattery?

The truth is, when you see another person's shadow, you realize that one can show gifts in one area of life and remain unaware of their evil behaviors in certain areas. Everyone is susceptible to this. Over the years, I have learned that working with my shadow has not only been a challenging but rewarding process too. It is by looking at your darker side that you gain greater creativity, authenticity, personal awakening, and energy. It is this subjective process that contributes to your maturity.

Realize that you cannot eliminate your darker side. Instead, it stays with you as your darker brother or sister. When we fail to see our darker self, that is when trouble ensues.

While our shadow self can operate on its own without our awareness – more like it is on autopilot – it causes us to do things we would not do voluntarily, and that is the reason behind regret. You find yourself saying things you wouldn't normally say. Your body language expresses emotions you would consciously not feel. In short, when you ignore your dark side, you end up hurting your relationships – with friends, spouse, or family, among others.

When you see others and yourself exactly as you are, you view the world around you with a clearer lens. Integrating your shadow self into everyday activities helps you approach your true self, hence offering you a realistic evaluation of who you are. In other words, you will not perceive yourself as being too small; neither will you feel as though you have a high moral ground than others.

The reward of doing this plays a significant role in healing splits in your mind. It also helps unlock untapped potential and a world of new possibilities for your growth and development. So, what are you still waiting for?

It is time to embrace your dark side so that you allow the light inside you to radiate without fear of hurting others of being all that you are meant to be. Your dark side will help you overcome manipulation so that you can shine brighter!   Good Luck!

© **Written by: JOSEPH GRIFFITH**

How to Influence People

USE THE LAWS OF POWER: ANALYZE AND WIN FRIENDS USING SUBLIMINAL MANIPULATION, PERSUASION, DARK PSYCHOLOGY, HYPNOSIS, NLP SECRETS, BODY LANGUAGE, AND MIND CONTROL TECHNIQUES

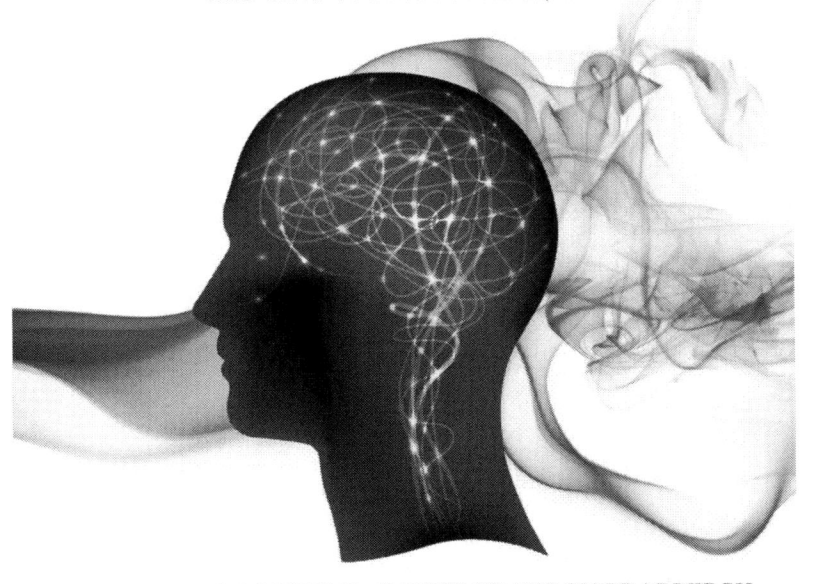

ROBERT DALE GOLEMAN - DANIEL BRANDON BRADBERRY - TRAVIS GREENE CARNEGIE

HOW TO INFLUENCE PEOPLE

Use the Laws of Power:

Analyze and Win Friends Using Subliminal Manipulation, Persuasion, Dark Psychology, Hypnosis, NLP secrets, Body Language, and Mind Control Techniques

© **Written by:** Robert Dale Goleman - Daniel Brandon Bradberry - Travis Greene Carnegie

Introduction

Human behavior has to do with the way humans act and interrelate with each other. It is based on the influence of many factors, like genetic makeup, civilization, and individual principles and attitudes. Human attitude is the answer of people or groups of humans to inner and outer stimuli. It has to do with the selection of each physical act and obvious feeling connected with people, but also with the entire human race. While detailed features of
one's character and nature could be way more reliable, further behaviors are bound to change themselves as one age and develop their personality.

Behavior is not only influenced by factors like age, feelings, perceptions, and attitudes, but they also have to do with our inner world, principles, worldviews, and characteristics. Behavior in social circumstances, another part of human attitude, investigates the paramount importance of social communication and cultural grounds. Other powers contain morals, social setting, authority, influence, and compulsion.

A survey has shown that about 90 percent of the entire human population can be classified into four basic personalities: optimistic, pessimistic, trusting, and envious. Envious people make for 30 percent compared to 20 percent each for the other personalities. Influencing human attitude has been something coveted even in ancient times. Even in ancient societies, it is considered important that someone had the ability to influence others and persuade them about their views and ideas.

The Ancient Greeks and Romans after their thought that it was very important to be able to speak to the public and make them see your point or agree with you. In Athens of the classical years, there were many orators who would teach younger men better public speaking.

Times have changed, but it is always desirable to be an influential person.

A leader, someone who can influence others, change their views on things, and in general, inspire and be more likable. And while most people like the idea of being this person, talking with many of them have let me know that they have no idea how to do it. Some are not even confident about their abilities, while others think that the change they want will never happen.

But the only way for a change to happen is that we actually want and welcome it. And by purchasing this book, you have proven to yourself that you really want it.

Factors Influencing Human Behavior

Before we venture into your new influential skills, let's take a look at the factors which regulate human reaction and behavior.

While every one of us is different, there are a few factors which, in general, are the most important ones for the way things influence us.

The key factors affecting an individual's manner in personal as well as social life are:

- Skills
- Gender
- Racial and cultural background
- Acknowledgment
- Perception
- Behavior

<u>Abilities</u>

Abilities are the qualities either a person is born with or learns from the outer environment.

These can be very important for the life of a said person. These traits are widely classified as:

- Intellectual
- Physical

- Self-awareness

So, these abilities and skills do influence our behavior, but if we want to see how, we have to know what these skills are.

Intellectual abilities - Having an intellectual capacity is being smart, capable of reason, and being good at verbal communication.

Physical skills – Motor skills, stamina, body goals.

Self-awareness abilities - How a person perceives themselves, their abilities, the things they can do, what they want, and what they stand for in life.

It goes without saying that the traits of each person are very important for how they fare later in life and how they influence those around them.

Gender

Past examination shows that men and women are pretty much equal in their work performance and in daily life in general.

Nevertheless, the differences between genders are still underlined by many people in society.

This creates a predicament for women, who are considered prime child caregivers and try to comply with society's view of their role.

Racial and Cultural Background

As a race, we define people who share similar physical traits.

It influences people based on those external features.

Culture, however, has to do with the values, morals, customs, arts, and tastes of people who either share a racial background or belong in the same group, party, organization, or institution.

Race & culture have always influenced society to a great extent.

The ordinary errors such as attributing attitude and stereotyping in accordance with an individual's race & culture fundamentally influence an individual's behavior.

Perception

Perception is how we take in the stimuli from our environment.

We all look in the same way, but we don't see it in the same way.

The same stimuli can produce many reactions to different people.

Perception can take these forms:

Of sound – Decoding the sound signals we get.

Of speech – How do we perceive the sounds and words heard and change them in our head to mean something as far as language is concerned.

Taste – Telling between the different tastes with the signals coming from the taste buds.

Touch – Telling things by feeling them.

Other senses – Balance, pain, sense of time, and many more!

Social – How people perceive the world based on social norms and groups.

Attribution

Attribution is, in other words, how we connect someone's personality, culture, race, gender, and so on and so forth with the actions they do and the way we perceive those.

This framework is based on three criteria:

Agreement – When people would react in a similar way.

Distinctiveness – How easy is this behavior to be correlated with personality traits?

Constancy – How often does the behavior happen? Is it always the same person doing the same things or it's a one-time thing?

Attitude

Attitude is the learned response that guides one's reactions in some situations with similar characteristics.

Now, you have a small idea of what influences you and others when you react to things around you.

Chapter 1 Understanding influence

What is influence?

Influence – a definition: The potential to have an impact on the life, growth or actions of somebody or something or the result itself. "Effective autism interventions in institutions and APS have a more general role to be played in promoting an effective and successful public sector. When they work, these techniques allow organizations more effective, more responsive to the needs and interests of the people and more productive, creative and scalable.

However, it is often regarded as the task of professionals of human resources to solve the problem of jobs and maintenance with disabilities. Nevertheless, they do not have key decision-making positions in many situations. Human resources professionals who actively facilitate jobs of disabilities in their organizations typically do so by using a range of influential skills and strategies, partnering with business sectors and creating corporate support.

Every influence includes an agreement. For influence, we must be able to give meaning to what the person is dedicated to and pursue opportunities to show that importance.

- Influence also includes the resolution of issues, breaking around potential obstacles to successful and lasting outcomes.

- The role of groups of people and teams in an APS (approved practice settings) setting generally involves manipulating them. This is especially the case with teams which can hire persons with disabilities. The higher the importance of hiring disabled persons in your departments, the more the problem becomes standard management rather than an add-on.

- Influence in disability employment invariably involves us in changing perceptions, attitudes and working environments.

- Finally, encouraging people with disabilities to boost their job success is leadership and role modelling–demonstrate how people with disabilities are supported at work to create a positive team that will support you, your own company and eventually the APS.

Influencing is a skill that we all have, and like any skill, it can be developed. Effective development occurs through understanding and appreciating:

- The components of effective influence.

- The context in which you influence.

- The need for you to apply and practise your skill for it to further develop.

In the APS context, effective influencing is supported by three capabilities:

- An ability to respond to and target particular forms of communication.

- An understanding of the psychology of persuasion that sits behind our willingness to be influenced.

- An ability to develop simple influencing strategies and carry them out.

Types of influence

Each experience, communication, emotion, disposition and behavior that you have is able to influence others. Four main types of control occur. There are harmful, optimistic, constructive and life-changing factors. You want to stay away from the first two styles when moving to the second factors. Let's talk about each of them.

Negative influence

The first form is destructive and the most dangerous. Many with this kind of control tend to concentrate on their position, strength or title. They are often self-centered and confident. These are the representatives who have difficulty in getting people to follow them, support them or listen to them. We affect the team or organization poorly or badly; the team produces a negative influence primarily because of the poor results. Do everything you can to stop this kind of effect.

Neutral influence

The actions and attitudes of this kind of influence seem neither to contribute nor to take away what they do. If an individual with such authority were in a group of people, they would not have to do anything to differentiate or be known as a member. They don't lead, help or take over proactively. These are those who have the role or title but do not optimize it so that the company or the organization succeeds. Individuals (employees) often have to guide and inspire themselves to produce results because the boss will not control them.

Note, you will want these first two causes to be minimized. Let's see the kind of influence that you should aspire for.

Positive influence

A person with this sort of influence adds value and allows the individuals with whom you interact happier through the actions and attitudes of that leader. We constantly guide, build and maintain ties with others; all of them are involved in trying to encourage, educate and lead people to better results. We want to make a positive impact on the lives of the people we serve to help them succeed in all areas of their lives. Positive influence requires a high degree of purpose, energy and effort, but all will be and will do better when you lead.

Life-changing influence

This is the pinnacle and most precious kind of influence. Few individuals have this level of influence or touch it. This needs years or decades to live well and confidently so that life improves. Any highlights include Mother Teresa, Oprah Winfrey, John C. Maxwell, and Abraham Lincoln.

The life-changing effect is about influencing someone in a manner where their lives are affected forever because of what you did and said. The positivity of those you impact stays influenced even after you quit the team or organization. It needs to invest your entire life and energy in supporting and encouraging others to achieve and succeed in life and job. It involves establishing your own wishes and needs to add value to others. It's worth the effort because you'll have loyal and dedicated people who are willing to do anything for you.

Chapter 2 Reading Body Language

From our outward appearances to our body developments, the things we don't state will in any case pass on volumes of information. It has been immediate that visual correspondence may account 60% to sixty five percent of all correspondences. Understanding visual correspondence is imperative, anyway it's furthermore fundamental to think to elective prompts like setting. In a few cases, you should investigate the flag as a gaggle rather than have practical experience in one activity.

Non-verbal communication is the implicit segment of correspondence. Our signals, outward appearances and stance, for instance. When we are prepared to "read" these signs, we can utilize it to further our potential benefit for instance. It will encourage you to know the whole message of what someone is making an endeavor to make reference to, and to fortify our consciousness of individuals' responses to what we are stating and do.

We can moreover utilize it to direct our visual correspondence, so we will in general appear to be a great deal of positive, sharing, and congenial.

Being able to communicate well is extremely important when wanting to succeed in the personal and professional world, but it isn't the words you say that scream. It is your body language that does the screaming. Your gestures, posture, eye contact, facial expressions, and tone of voice are your best communication tools. These have the ability to confuse, undermine, offend, build trust, draw others in, or put someone at ease.

There are many times when what someone says and what their body language says is totally different. Non-verbal communication could do five things:

- Substitute – It could be used in place of a verbal message.

- Accent – It could underline or accent your verbal message.

- Complement – It could complement or add to what you are saying verbally.

- Repeat – It could strengthen and repeat your verbal message.

- Contradict – It could go against what you are trying to say verbally to make your listener think that you are lying.

Some regular non-verbal communication signs.

The following are important hints to enable you to figure out how to read non-verbal communication and better understanding the individuals you connect with.

<u>Concentrate the Eyes</u>

When human activity is towards someone, concentrate as to check whether the person in question looks or appearance away. Failure to make direct eye-to-eye connections will demonstrate boredom, impartiality, or maybe misleading – especially once someone appearance away and to the viewpoint. If an individual shows up down, on the contrary hand, it as a rule demonstrates anxiety or acquiescence. Additionally, check for extended students to check whether someone is reacting positively toward you. Understudies stretch as mental element exertion will in general increment, in this manner if someone is focused on someone or one thing they like, their students can precisely expand. Understudy widening will be hard to discover, anyway underneath the right conditions you should be prepared to spot it. An individual's squinting rate can even say a lot concerning what's going on inside. Squinting rate will increment once people are thinking a ton or are pushed. Now and again, swelled flickering rate shows lying – especially once over the span of contacting the face (especially the mouth and eyes). Looking at issue will guide a need for that thing. For instance, if someone looks at the entryway this could demonstrate they need to leave. Looking at an individual will demonstrate a need to address that person. When it includes eye conduct, it furthermore briefs that trying upwards and to the right communicated in language that demonstrates an untruth has been told, while attempting upwards and to one side shows the individual is telling the truth. The clarification for this can be that people search, and to the right ones exploitation, their creative mind to come up with a story, and appearance up and to one side once they are reviewing a genuine memory.

Look at the Face – Body Language Touching Mouth or Smiling

In spite of the fact that people are a ton certainly to deal with their outward appearance, regardless you'll have crucial nonverbal signals if you focus. Give explicit consideration to the mouth once making an endeavor to disentangle nonverbal conduct. A direct grin visual correspondence fascination procedure will be a hearty signal. Grinning is a critical nonverbal prompt to take a gander at for. There are various sorts of grins, together with genuine grins and affectation grins. A genuine grin draws in the whole face, while an imagining grin exclusively utilizes the mouth. A genuine grin proposes that the individual is upbeat and getting a charge out of the corporate of the people around the person in question. Covering the mouth or contacting the lips with the hands or fingers once talking is additionally a marker of lying.

Focus on nearness

Concentrate to let someone stand or sit by you to check whether they read you positively. Standing or sitting in nearness to someone is perhaps one in all the best pointers of affinity. On the contrary hand, if someone backs up or moves away once you move in closer, this may be a proof that the alliance isn't common.

Check whether the other individual is reflecting you

Reflecting includes emulating the contrary individual's visual correspondence. Once interfacing with someone, check to analyze if the individual mirrors your conduct. For instance, in case you're sitting at a table with someone and lay an elbow on the table, hold up ten seconds to analyze if the contrary individual will be proportional. Another regular reflecting motion includes taking a taste of a beverage at a comparable time. If someone imitates your visual correspondence, this can be a terribly reasonable sign that the person is making an endeavor to decide an affinity with you. Endeavor dynamical your body stance and check whether the contrary individual changes theirs similarly.

Watch the head development

The speed at that an individual gestures their head once you are talking demonstrates their understanding – or absence of. Slow hanging shows that the individual is entranced by what you're discourse correspondence and requirements you to keep talking. Fast hanging shows the individual has identified enough and necessities you to end talking or give that person a location to talk. Tilting the zenith sideways all through a communicated in language will be a proof of enthusiasm for what the contrary individual is discourse correspondence. Tilting the apex in reverse will be a proof of doubt or vulnerability. People also brings up with the face at others significance they're captivated by proclivity with the individual.

Take a gander at the other individual's feet

A piece of the body any place people more often than not "release" fundamental nonverbal prompts is the feet. The clarification that individuals coincidentally impart nonverbal messages through their feet is therefore that occasionally they focus on their outward appearances and higher body situating which imperative pieces of information are unveiled by means of the feet.

Watch for hand signals

Like the feet, the hands release fundamental nonverbal prompts once attempting a visual correspondence. This can be a critical tip once reading visual correspondence along these lines focus on the current next half. Watch visual correspondence turns in pockets once standing. Quest for explicit hand signals, similar to the contrary individual placing their hands in their pockets or hand on head. This may show something from apprehension to out and out trickiness. Oblivious educate demonstrated by hand motions can even say a lot. Once making hand signals, an individual can with reason inside the general course of the individual offer a partiality (this nonverbal prompts is indispensable to take a gander at for all through gatherings and once connecting in gatherings). Supporting the apex with the hand by laying an elbow on the table will demonstrate that the individual is tuning in and is keeping the zenith still to center. Supporting the zenith with every elbow on the table. When an individual holds an item between the people in question and along these lines the individual they're collaborating with, this is a boundary that is intended to dam out of the contrary individual. For instance, if two people are talking and one individual holds a stack of paper in front of that person, this can be demonstration of check in nonverbal correspondence.

Inspect the situation of the arms

230

Think about an individual's arms as the door to the body and in this way oneself. If an individual folds their arms while interfacing with you, it's occasionally observed as a guarded, impediment signal. Crossed arms can even demonstrate nervousness, weakness, or a shut personality. Whenever crossed arms are throughout a genuine grin and generally speaking loosened up stance, at that point it will demonstrate all is guaranteed, loosened up edge. When someone puts their hands on their hips it's for the most part they need to apply strength and is utilized by men a great deal than women.

Body parts

<u>Lower Body</u>

The arms share a lot of information. The hands share a lot more, but legs give us the exclamation point and can tell us exactly what someone is thinking. The legs could tell you if a person is open and comfortable. They could also who dominance or where they want to go.

Legs Touching

When a person is standing, they will only be able to touch their bottom or thighs. This can be done seductively, or they could slap their legs as if they are saying "Let's go." It might also indicate irritation. This is when you have to pay attention to the context of the conversation. This is very important.

Pointing Feet

Look at the direction of a person's feet to see where their attention is. Their feet will always point toward what is on their mind or what they are concentrating on. Everyone has a lead foot and it all depends on their dominant hand. If a person is talking that we are interested in is talking, our lead foot will be pointing toward them. But, if they want to leave the situation, you will notice their foot pointing toward an exit or the way they want to go. If a person is sitting during the conversation, look at where their feet are pointing to see what they are truly interested in.

Smarty Pants

This is a position where someone tries to make themselves look bigger. They will usually be seated with their legs splayed open and leaning back. They might even spread their arms out and lock them behind their head. This is normally used by people who feel dominant, superior, or confident.

Shy Tangle

This is usually something that women do more than men. Anyone who begins to feel shy or timid will sometimes entangle their legs by crossing them under and over to try to block out bad emotions and to make themselves look smaller. There is another shy leg twirl that people will do when they are standing. The actual act of this movement is crossing one leg over the other and hooking that foot behind their knee as if they are trying to scratch an itch.

Upper Body

Upper body language can show signs of defensiveness since the arms could easily be used as a shield. Upper body language could involve the chest. Let's look at some upper body language.

Leaning

If someone leans forward, it will move them closer to another person. There are two possible meaning to this. First, it will tell you that they are interested in something, which could just be what you are talking about. But, this movement could also show romantic interest. Second, leaning forward could invade a person's personal space; hence, this shows them as a threat. This is often an aggressive display. This is done unconsciously by powerful people.

The Superman

This is commonly used by bodybuilders, models, and it was made popular by Superman. This could have various, meanings depending on how a person uses it. Within the animal world, animals will try to make themselves look bigger when they feel threatened. If you look at a house cat when they get spooked, they will stretch their legs and their fur stands on end. Humans also have this, even if it isn't as noticeable. This is why we get goosebumps. Because we can't make ourselves look bigger, we have to come up with arm gestures like putting our hands on our waist. This shows us that a person is getting ready to act assertively.

This is normal for athletes to do before a game or a wife who is nagging their spouse. A guy who is flirting with a girl will use this to look assertive. This is what we call a readiness gesture.

The Chest in Profile

If a person stands sideways or at a 45-degree angle, they are trying to accentuate their chest. They might also thrust out their chest, more on this in a minute. Women do this posture to show off their breasts and men will do this to show off their profile.

Outward Thrust Chest

If someone pushes their chest out, they are trying to draw attention to this part of their body. This could also be used as a romantic display. Women understand that men have been programmed to be aroused by breasts. If you see a woman pushing her chest out, she might be inviting intimate relations. Men will thrust out their chest to show off their chest and possibly trying to hide their gut. The difference is that men will do this to women and other men.

Hands

Human hands have 27 bones, and they are a very expressive part of the body. This gives us a lot of capabilities to handle our environment.

Reading palms isn't about just looking at the lines on the hands. After a person's face, the hands are the best source for body language. Hand gestures are different across cultures and one hand gesture might be innocent in one, country, but very offensive in another.

Hand signals may be small, but they show what our subconscious is thinking. A gesture might be exaggerated and done using both hands to show a point

Control

If a person is holding their hand with their palms facing down, they might be figuratively holding onto or restraining another person. This could be an authoritative action that is telling you to stop now. It might be a request asking you to calm down. This will be apparent if someone places their dominant hand on top of a handshake. If they are leaning on their desk with their palms flat, this shows dominance.

If their palms face outward toward another person, they might be trying to fend them off or push them away. They might be saying "stop, don't come closer."

If they are pointing their finger or their entire hand, they might be telling someone to leave now.

Greeting

Our hands get used a lot to greet other people. The most common way is with a handshake. Opening up the palm shows they don't have any weapons. These get used when saluting, waving, or greeting others.

During this time, we get to touch another person and it might send various signals.

Dominance can be shown by shaking hands and placing the other hand on top. How long and how strong they shake the hand will tell you that they are deciding on when to stop the handshake.

Affection could be shown with the duration and speed of the handshake, smiles, and touching with the other hand. The similarity between this one and the dominant one could lead to a situation when a dominant person will try to pretend they are just being friendly.

Submission gets shows by placing their palms up. Floppy handshakes that are clammy along with a quick withdrawal also show submission.

Most handshakes use vertical palms that will show equality. They will be firm but won't crush and for the right amount of time so both parties know when they should let go.

Waving is a great way to greet people and could be performed from a long distance.

Salutes are normally done by the military, where a certain style is prescribed.

Holding

A person who has cupped hands shows they can hold something gently. They show delicacy or holding something fragile. Hands that grip will show desire, possessiveness, or ownership. The tighter the fist, the stronger they are feeling a specific emotion.

If someone is holding their hands, they are trying to comfort themselves. They could be trying to restrain, themselves so they will let somebody else talk. It could be used if they are angry and it is stopping them from attacking. If they are wringing their hands, they are feeling extremely nervous.

Holding their hands behind their back will show they are confident because they are opening up their front. They may hide their hands to conceal their tension. If one hand is gripping the other arm, the tighter and higher the grip, the tenser they are.

Two hands might show various desires. If one hand is forming a fist but the other is holding it back, this might show that they would like to punch somebody.

If someone is lying, they will try to control their hands. If they are holding them still, you might want to be a bit suspicious. Remember that these are just indicators and you should look for other signals.

If someone looks like they are holding onto an object like a pen or cup, this shows they are trying to comfort themselves. If a person is holding a cup, but they are holding it very close and it looks like they are "hugging" the cup, they are hugging themselves. Holding onto any item with both hands shows they have closed themselves off from others.

Items might be used as a distraction to release nervous energy like holding a pen but they are clicking it off and on, doodling, or messing with it. If their hands are clenched together in front of them but they are relaxed, and their thumbs are resting on each other it might be showing pleasure.

Shaping

Our hands are able to cut our words into the air to emphasize the things we say and their meaning. We are trying to create visualization.

If a man is trying to describe the fish he caught during his fishing trip, he might try to show the shape by indicating it with his hands. He might also carve out a certain shape that he wants his ideal mate to be. Other gestures might be cruder when they hold specific body parts and move sexually.

Face

People's facial expression could help us figure out if we trust or believe what they are saying. The most trustworthy expression will have a slight smile and a raised eyebrow. This expression will sow friendliness and confidence.

We make judgments about how intelligent somebody is by their facial expressions. People who have narrow faces with a prominent nose were thought to be extremely intelligent. People who smile and have joyous expressions could be thought of as being intelligent rather than someone who looks angry.

Mouth

Mouth movements and expressions are needed when trying to read body language. Chewing on their lower lip might indicate a person who is feeling fearful, insecure, or worrying.

If they cover their mouth, this might show that they are trying to be polite if they are yawning or coughing. It might be an attempt to cover up disapproval. Smiling is the best signal, but smiles can be interpreted in many ways. Smiles can be genuine, or they might be used to show cynicism, sarcasm, or false happiness.

Watch out for the following:

- Their lips are pursed.
- If a person tightens their lips might be a sign of distaste, disapproval, or distrust.
- They bite their lip.
- People will bite their kip if they are feeling anxious, worried, or stressed.
- They cover their mouth.
- If a person tries to hide a reaction, they might cover their mouth to hide a smile or smirk.
- Their mouth is turned up or down.

Changes in the mouth that are subtle might be a sign of how the person is feeling. If their mouth is turned up a little bit, they might be feeling happy or optimistic. If their mouth is turned down, they could be feeling sadness, disapproval, or grimacing.

Negative Emotions

The silent signals that you show might harm your business without you even knowing it. We have over 250,000 facial signals and 700,000 body signals. Having poor body language could damage your relationships by sending other person signals that you can't be trusted. They might turn off, alienate, or offend other people.

You have to keep your body language in check and this takes a lot of effort. Most of the time, you may not know that you are doing it and you might be hurting your business and yourself.

To help you manage your signals, there are several body languages and speech mistakes that you can learn to prevent. Here are some mistakes you have to avoid:

Not Enough Response

If you are talking with someone, you need to make sure you listen to them. This means you have to smile, nod, and make eye contact. Even if two people don't agree with what each other are saying, you need to let them know that you have heard what they said. This is showing them respect. If you don't do this, you will leave a bad impression.

Using the Word "But"

Constantly using the word "but" while you are talking can cause many problems. Most of the time, this will sound like you are just trying to make us some excuses or you don't care about what they are saying. You might say: "I am sorry that your product didn't get you on time, but you know how the weather is." This statement doesn't show you are sorry. You are placing the blame on the weather instead of addressing the real problem.

Personal Space

Invading another person's personal space can have detrimental results. One good example men always seem to invade a woman's personal space whether they know it or not. This could cause some harassment lawsuits. The best space to keep between you and others is about one and a half feet. Never treat another person's space as if it were your own.

Talking Too Fast

Blinking fast or talking too quickly shows nervousness and distrust. Try to pause between each sentence and let others finish their sentence before your interrupt. Eye contact is very important. If you have a hard time looking people in the eye, look in the center of their forehead. It looks like eye contact without all those uncomfortable feelings.

Not Listening

It doesn't matter what you do for a living, you are going to have to talk with people some time or other. The main thing that will make or break any relationship is not listening. Listening could impact your relationship with employees, suppliers, performance, and sales better than other forms of communications.

Slumping

If a person slumps in their seat, they show that they don't have any energy or confidence. It is important to show passion and let others know that you believe in yourself. If you are hunched over or slumping, you are sending the wrong message. If your posture is strong, you are going to feel energetic and it will be a win for all people involved.

Checking Your Phone

If you are in a public gathering, put away your phone. Everybody is addicted to their phones now, and this is extremely rude. Try engaging with others and stop checking your phone every few minutes. If you have an emergency, that's fine. It is easier to make connections with others if you don't have things distracting you.

Face is Scrunched-Up

You might not realize that your face is scrunched-up or that your brow is furrowed. This can make others think you are intimidating or hostile. You can discourage others from being open or it might make them get defensive. You can verbally assure them that you understand and support what they are saying.

Not Making Eye Contact

I used to work with someone who would immediately stare into space anytime somebody talked to them. They claimed it was easier for them to focus on what others were saying if they didn't look at who was talking. People might use different communication types but always make eye contact. Even if you can keep moderate eye contact, it will communicate confidence, interest, and will put everybody at ease.

Not Smiling

Do you know that smiling can make you feel happy? People like to believe the opposite. If you can keep a nice smile on your face, you will feel more confident and people will want to work with you. If you realize you want to make a face, turn that face into a smile.

Glancing Around

Everybody has encountered someone who will constantly look around while they are talking to you. It probably makes you think that they are trying to find someone else to talk to. Don't be this person. Everyone you talk to needs to be treated with respect.

Handshake Too Weak or Strong

Handshakes are normally the first impression that someone gets from you. If your handshake is too weak, it will show you aren't professional and it might be new to them. If your handshake is too strong, it might warn them that you are being too aggressive. Try to find a happy medium so that you will make a good impression.

When you observe other people carefully, you can pick up on their emotion by their Non-verbal signals. These indicators are not a guarantee. Contextual clues might be used, in addition to what they are saying and what is happening around you at the time.

Chapter 3 How to Analyze Those around You

Your capacity to analyze people might determine whether you will succeed or fail. Human beings are social animals. We almost always need the input of other human beings to achieve our important life goals.

Human conduct, the potential, and communicated limit in regard to physical, mental, and social movements during the periods of human life.

People, as other creature's species, have an average life course that comprise of progressive periods of development, every one of which is described by an unmistakable arrangement of physical, physiological, and social highlights. These stages are pre-birth life, outset, youth, youthfulness, and adulthood (counting seniority). Human improvement, or formative brain science, is a field of concentrate that endeavors to portray and clarify the adjustments in human psychological, enthusiastic, and social abilities and working over the whole life expectancy, from the hatchling to seniority.

Most logical research on human advancement has focused on the period from birth through early immaturity, attributable to both the rate and greatness of the mental changes saw during those stages and to the way that they come full circle in the ideal mental working of early adulthood. An essential inspiration of numerous specialists in the field has been to decide how the coming full circle mental capacities of adulthood were come to during the former stages.

But what happens if we take on people that are unfit for their roles? We suffer defeat. Thus, it is of utmost importance to be able to analyze people. The following are some benefits of analyzing people.

It helps you know your allies

Whether you like it or not, the entire world will not take a liking to you. Some people will be for you, and other people will be against you. To maximize your chances of success, you must work with people who like you while ignoring those who dislike you. Your capability to analyze people will help you single out who are in favor of you. Considering that people can be pretty complex, your capability to understand their true persona cannot be overstated. For instance, if you're pursuing a career that involves serving the public, you will find yourself surrounded by all sorts of people. Clearly, not all of those people wish you well. Nevertheless, in the same breath, not all of them are against you. In such a situation, you have to exercise a lot of care, lest you end up working with your enemy who will eventually bring you down. If you tell your secrets to the enemy, he will run out there and spill it all. If you get close enough to the enemy, he might sow bad thoughts into your mind, which will see you taking the wrong direction. All of these can be avoided by sharpening your capability to tell good people apart from bad people. Of course, this is not a skill you can develop overnight. You have to practice repeatedly until you are good at spotting the fake ones.

It helps avoid conflict

In most cases, conflict arises because of a disparity in expectations. In a relationship, if the man expects one thing from his mate, and his wish is never met, it can cause him grief. And the vice versa is true. These are the kind of scenarios that cause conflict in a relationship. If the man had taken the time to understand what their partner is really like, they would not be shocked later time, when their partner behaved a certain way. Thus, it is important to understand the person that you're getting into a relationship with, for this will minimize your fights. Analyzing a person helps you understand their triggers. You get an opportunity to decide whether you want to involve yourself with them. If you're looking for a life partner, there are some things that you cannot compromise on, and so, you must analyze potential candidates to find out whether they possess these characteristics. If you ignore this step, you are at the risk of having a tumultuous marriage. Understanding what other people's personalities are like is a form of educating yourself on how to act or not act in front of these people. When you learn that someone is not into corny jokes, you will stop yourself from acting in a corny way, and in the same breath, when you realize that someone has a very fun attitude, you will try not to be a bore.

It allows you to appreciate diversity

Human beings are incredibly diverse. And this is a good thing. You cannot really understand this diversity until you pay attention to other people. Someone who comes from Asia might exhibit certain personality traits that differ from the average American. This is not a chance to bash the Asian for being different from you, but rather, it is an opportunity to appreciate the uniqueness of the Asian. People who bash others for being different from them are simply narrow-minded. Analyzing people gives you the power to recognize and accept our differences. It makes you a more cultured person. If you travel to other parts of the world, you will easily fit in because you have a mindset of adjusting. On the other hand, someone who is opposed recognition and appreciation of diversity will find himself at loggerheads with people who are unlike him.

It helps you fine-tune your goals

We don't live in a vacuum. The actions, words, and behaviors of other people will affect us. Every person has an idol that they look up to. Your idol is the person that you would want to trade lives with. Apart from giving you hope; your role model gives you an opportunity to study various qualities, you will require in that line of work. For instance, if you want to become a journalist, you must know that it is not just about having language skills, but you must improve your personality, so that more people will not only be comfortable around you, enough to open up and let out their secrets. When you take on the practice of keenly observing other people, you are in a position to determine which career path suits your qualities.

It helps you understand the motivations of people

At the end of the day, there's a motive behind every action, but these motives are not always obvious. Some people will instantly reveal who they are, but there are people who will try to downplay their real image. But if you're a good observer, you can always tell what is going on. By taking your time to analyze people, you are in a much better position to understand what their goals are. Having this knowledge helps you take self-preserving decisions. Manipulative people are known for acting or speaking in a way that won't betray their manipulative agenda. Unless you are extra careful in your analysis of their persona, you might miss their motive, and become another one of their victims.

It helps you understand a person's strengths

Every human being has both weaknesses and strengths. The reason some of us become successful is that we capitalize on our strengths. Failure to capitalize on our strengths can make us feel disillusioned about life. The skill of identifying our strengths is important in identifying other people's strengths. Thus, when you are looking for someone to work with, you will be in a position to identify their strengths and weaknesses, which will make your team of high quality.

It helps in predicting behavior

Your capability to analyze personalities is vital in predicting how various people will act under different circumstances. Life is not one smooth ride. There are many challenges encountered on the road. In addition, for the most part, success depends on how we handle challenges. Being able to analyze various personalities empowers you to understand how people will react to challenges. For instance, if you notice that someone has the markings of a violent personality, or has anger issues, you might want to skip on that person because their violent nature will become soon apparent.

So why measure conduct specifically?

1. It can change.

Character is fixed and far-fetched to change, so it endeavors sense to center our endeavors at the point where changes can be made: our conduct. Since conduct is inside our locus of control, confirmed criticism on conduct offers a constructive lead for self-improvement, indicating where and how we can adjust to address the issues of a specific circumstance or occupation job.

2. It tends to be watched.

Character is what's within; conduct is the thing that turns out, and it influences – and is influenced by – everyone around us. Estimating conduct enables us to concentrate on the words and activities which shape our collaborations with others. Ostensibly, we aren't specialists on another person's character – we don't have the foggiest idea about what's happening "off camera" – yet we can remark on what we can see before us.

By giving and getting input on practices inside a group, we move to a majority rule, evidential procedure. We can authenticate – or can't help contradicting – each other, and give proof of the practices being referred to from our understanding. This can depersonalize troublesome discussions and remove the warmth from clashes which may somehow or another drop into slanderous assaults. It can likewise give a noteworthy learning opportunity – your onlookers may reveal qualities you didn't have any acquaintance with you had.

3. it's situational.

Our conduct propensities impact the sorts of work we may be the most appropriate to, and whom we work best with. A few people carry on diversely at work than they do at home, regardless of the fundamental character is one and the equivalent. Estimating conduct in a specific setting enables talk to concentrate on the working environment, while all the more wide-extending estimations may sloppy the waters.

4. it's down to earth.

Belbin isn't a mark to apply or a container to place somebody in, it's a language intended to help individuals better see one another. When individuals comprehend the Team Roles and the essential idea driving them, this language can be utilized as a shorthand to depict how various types of work may be drawn nearer or what kind of commitments are required at a specific gathering.

5. It makes people and groups tick.

Getting qualities and shortcomings makes individuals increasingly drew in, more joyful and progressively gainful at work, advancing a positive workplace and diminishing turnover costs.

6. It tends to be anticipated.

Since we can watch conduct, we can anticipate it as well. Individuals may not generally carry on as we expect in each and every way – as people, we generally have the ability to amaze each other – however extensively, we sink into methods for working, conveying and identifying with others that can be required to continue as before over some undefined time frame. This implies we can utilize conduct styles for enrollment and teambuilding, to recommend whether somebody may be a solid match for a specific activity job or to join a current group.

7. It could easily compare to knowledge in foreseeing achievement.

The most ideal approach to manufacture an extraordinary group isn't to choose people for their smarts or achievements. However, to figure out how they convey and to shape and guide the group with the goal that it pursues effective correspondence designs.

8. It tends to be extrapolated.

Character comes down to the individual – it's their point of view toward the world. By its very nature, conduct is progressively liquid and interconnected with others, so it loans itself normally to assemblage. We can total key Team Role data to plan and assemble groups, or guide the conduct inclinations of two people to look at how well an association may function.

How to Master the Art of the First Impression

Since it possibly takes seconds for somebody to choose in case you're dependable and skillful, and research demonstrates that early introductions are exceptionally hard to change, the weight that accompanies meeting new individuals is reasonably extraordinary.

If you try to extend certainty yet haven't first settled trust, your endeavors would blowback. Nobody needs to wind up regarded however loathed. If somebody you're attempting to impact doesn't confide in you, you're not going to get much of anywhere; indeed, you may even evoke doubt, since you seem to be manipulative.

When you perceive the significance of reliability over capability, you can assume responsibility for the early introductions you make. Here are a few hints to enable you to get that going whenever you meet another person:

1. Let the individual you're meeting talk first.

Give them a chance to lead the pack in the discussion, and you can generally pose great inquiries to help this along. Taking the floor immediately indicates the strength, and that won't enable you to assemble trust. Trust and warmth are made when individuals feel comprehended, and they should do a ton of sharing for that to occur.

2. Utilize positive non-verbal communication.

Getting to be mindful of your motions, articulations, and manner of speaking and making certain they're sure will attract individuals to you like ants to an excursion. Utilizing an eager tone, uncrossing your arms, keeping in touch, and inclining towards the speaker are generally types of positive non-verbal communication, which can have a significant effect.

3. Set away your telephone.

It's difficult to assemble trust and screen your telephone simultaneously. Nothing turns individuals off like a mid-discussion instant message or even a snappy look at your telephone. When you focus on a discussion, center all your vitality around the discussion. You will find that discussions are progressively pleasant and compelling when you submerge yourself in them.

4. Set aside a few minutes for casual banter.

It may sound minor, however research demonstrates that beginning gatherings with only five minutes of casual chitchat improves results. Many trust manufacturers, for example, casual chitchat, can appear to be an exercise in futility to individuals who don't comprehend their motivation.

5. Practice undivided attention.

Undivided attention means focusing on what the other individual is stating, instead of arranging what you're going to state straightaway. Posing quick inquiries is an incredible method to show that you're truly focusing. In case you're not checking for comprehension or posing a testing inquiry, you shouldn't talk. Not exclusively does pondering what you're going to state next remove your consideration from the speaker, commandeering the discussion demonstrates that you think you have something increasingly essential to state. This implies you shouldn't bounce in with answers for the speaker's issues. It's human instinct to need to help individuals, yet what a great deal of us don't understand is that when we hop in with counsel or an answer, we're closing the other individual down and crushing trust.

6. Get your work done.

Individuals adore it when you know things about them that they didn't need to share. Not frightening stuff, however straightforward certainties that you set aside the effort to gain from their LinkedIn page or organization site. While this may not work for chance experiences, it's vital when a first gathering is prepared of time, for example, a prospective employee meet-up or a conference with a potential customer. Discover as much as you can pretty much every one of the individuals you're meeting, their organization, their organization's essential difficulties, etc. This exhibits ability and dependability by featuring your drive and duty.

The truth of the matter is, if you can identify with any of those, however you don't reliably look to improve your kin reading abilities, you're subverting your profession and your pay. It's that basic. The abilities required to read individuals are extremely straightforward and incredibly viable. In any case, there are numerous misconceptions and misapplications of the aptitudes, the two of which can bring you not exactly wanted outcomes.

Chapter 4 Understanding the people and world around us

Sensation and Perception

Sensation and perception play an essential role in how we translate and interpret what goes around our world. While they may look similar, they have a different purpose. For sensation, it refers to the process of sensing our environment via taste, touch, sound, and smell. This information is then sent to our brains unprocessed, then perception takes over, which is interpreting the sensations and then bring meaning to everything we have around is. Describing the two will allow us to see the role they play in psychology and how senses work together with how they are being interpreted. Let's start with the sensation first.

By definition, the sensation is identified as the process whereby our senses compile information and transfer it to the brain. Sensing of information includes room temperature, a distant train, the brightness of the light, the smelling of perfume, and when we hear the conversation. There are some other senses we aren't capable of. For example, we aren't capable of noticing radio waves, microscopic parasite walking in our body, x-rays, and radio waves. And we are only being made to sense what we are capable of. Why?

The answer is in the following threshold ;.

1. Absolute Threshold. This is a point where our senses notice something. That is the softest sound and the slightest touch. Whatever goes below this, isn't notified.

2. Difference Threshold. When we sense a stimulus, we have to identify if the stimulus us changing, But how? The difference threshold handles that. It is the amount of change that is needed to determine that a change has occurred.

3. Signal Detection. This is an act to detect what we want to focus on and ignore every other thing. For example, if you have to focus on something in a crowded room with several people talking.

4. Sensory Adaptation. This is concerned with a stimulus that has remained unaltered for a time when this happens; we want to notice it. Take for instance, when you are you sense a perfume, but after a while, you've stopped seeing, why? They remain unchanged, it has become less sensitive, and you adapted to.

That's for sensation, let's check into perception.

Perception means the interpretation of what we take in via our senses. This makes us unique from animals and even from other persons.

It was being figured out that to translate what the brain receives through senses; the brain organizes the information gotten into the specific group to disallow unwarranted repetition.

Retaining Constant Perceptual Constancy

It wouldn't make sense if each time an object is altered. We have to process it completely, and fortunately, it doesn't happen that way too. Humans can maintain constancy in the ability to perceive. That, in turn, make perception constancy to be defined as the ability to see things different yet we wouldn't have to reinterpret the object's properties.

Now we can sum it up that sensation is identified as the input about the physical world that is established by our sensory receptors, and perception is recognized as the process whereby mind organizes, interprets, and selects sensation. So, if we sense something and there is not interpretation, definitely, there is no point sensing it. How is this applicable in real life? In life, there is both positive and negative perceptions, which can influence one's success. And what's the key?

Always work on your mind as a garden, weeding out negative perception every day and leaving the flower, the plant to stay. The more you allow negative thoughts to retain, the more negative perception you will have. Therefore, it is essential you change the way you view your life. You have to work harder so you can experience the change. Just keep staying grateful for what you possess. What method, always list out five positive things that work out in your favor every day. You will be expanding your positive perception ability. Our understanding of the world around involves learning. But what is learning and how does it connect with conditioning. Read on to get the answers.

Learning and Conditioning

Our nervous system is also involved in the learning process. But how is it defined, and what are other concepts? Learning, by definition, is an adaptive function by which our nervous system alters concerning stimuli in the environment, thereby bringing a change in our behavioral responses and allowing us to function in our environment.

Initially, the process is established in the nervous system in a bit to respond to environmental stimuli. As a result, neural pathways can be strengthened, activated, even pruned, and all these can bring about a change in our behavioral responses.

When it comes to reflexes and instincts, they are innate behaviors. That is, they occur naturally and wouldn't demand to learn. However, learning, in turn, is an alteration in behavior that results from experience. In the field of behavioral psychology, it involves mainly on measurable behaviors that are learned; instead, if working hard to understand internal states like emotions and attitudes.

But in learning, there are three fundamental aspects, they are classical conditioning, operant conditioning, and observational learning. The first two, classical and operant conditioning, forms if associative learning, their associations are developed between events that happen together. Whereas the third one, observational learning, is learning by observing others. Let's get into details about the three types of learning.

Classical Conditioning.

Classical conditioning defined as the process whereby we learn to relate stimuli and events that regularly happen together. As a result, we then learn to anticipate what will happen next. Take, for example; some experts have trained animals like to associate the sound of an object to the presence of food. For instance, Ivan was able to condition his dog to identify the relationship between the sounds of a bell with the presence of the meal. This was achieved because each time; the dog hears the sound of the bell, what comes to mind is that it's time for lunch. So in a sense, that scene makes the dog anticipate the meal.

Operant Conditioning.

This is defined as the learning process in which behaviors are reinforced or punished, thereby strengthening a response. So, any act that is backed up with pleasant consequences is more likely to be repeated, whereas actions that are followed by unpleasant experiences are less likely to be repeated. So it merely means that either punishments or rewards can impact behavior.

Observational Learning.

This type of learning occurs when a person observes the behavior of others and imitate those behaviors. For example, it is common for children to learn or imitate adults, so if there is a right attitude that you needed to emulate, applying observational learning to be the best way to achieve it.

It is being used both in the therapeutic and advertising industry. In the commercial industry, they often feature attractive models. Thus, they apply the principles of associative learning.

Attention

In the world of cognitive psychology, attention is a concept that is being studied, and it refers to how we actively process particular information in our environment. Most times, many sensations are going on around us; they demand attention. Unfortunately, our attentional resources aren't limitless; it has boundaries. Therefore, we need to find out how we can experience all these sensations and still lay focus on just one particular thing, and how can we employ the scarce resources at our disposal to make sense of the world around us.

As defined by psychologist experts, attention is defined as taking possessing by the mind, in bright and vivid form out of what may appear to be numerous simultaneously possible objects or lines of thought. Or it could be defined as the withdrawal of some things to deal or pay closer attention to others.

Attention isn't about focusing attention on one particular thing; it also includes ignoring a great deal of fighting for information and stimuli. Attention makes it possible to tune out information, perception, sensation that aren't in correlation with the moment and then focus energy in the information that is vital.

Additionally, the attentional system offers the ability to focus on something specific in our environment while we send our incoherent details. In some situations, our attention might be centered on a particular thing which will cause us to ignore other things. That is, when we lay focus on something in the environment, we at times miss the several things that are right in front of us. And that is why most times in a room, you will be so engrossed that you won't notice that someone is approaching you or has walked inside the toilet.

But to understand more in-depth how attention works, and how it influences your perception, you have in mind these few points out that are highlighted.

Attention is Limited.

Researchers have found that what influences our ability to stay on a given task include how interested we are in the stimulus and the number of distractions that surround us. Attention is limited when it comes to capacity and duration. So multitasking doesn't work well, because our attention is limited.

Attention is Selective.

Since it is understood that attention is limited. We need to be selective about what we decide to focus on. We need to be selective in what we attend to. This stage is so fast that we hardly remember that we've neglected what happens in our environment.

Attention is a Fundamental Part of The Cognitive System.

Attention is even present at birth. This occurs when orienting reflexes help to determine which events in our environment need to be attended to. And right from that stage, the orienting reflex continues to be of immeasurable benefits to us throughout our life span.

Understanding this fact about attention enrich our productivity, it stops us from spending more energy on multitasking, instead of focusing on one thing at a time, which will enhance positive thinking and lead to success eventually.

Intelligence

Intelligence is an aspect that is often talk about in psychology, yet, there isn't one specific standard to define what intelligence is. Some have maintained that intelligence is single, others say that it is a general ability, while some still insist that intelligence covers a wide range of aptitudes, talents, and skills. Regardless of the opinions that are being held today, there is consensus agreement about intelligence. They are:

1. Learning. The ability to acquire, retain, and apply knowledge- these are vital parts of learning.

2. Identify Problems. To put knowledge to use, the likely problems have to be identified and be cared for.

3. Solve Problem. The output of learning is taking the knowledge and use it to solve the recognized problem.

Intelligence includes various mental abilities like planning, reasoning, logic, and problem-solving.

Also, isn't something we can hear or see or even taste? But we can peer into the result of intelligence. However, a big question cones that are there a way to increase one's intelligence? Fortunately, the answer is yes. Psychologists who figured cognitive training and pharmacological intervention, so the approach to aid the improvement of the brain.

There are incredible ways to improve one's intelligence;

1. Exercise. Regular. If you want to improve your intelligence, you have to exercise your brain and body. Like a muscle that requires training, your brain does need too. When you use, you are energizing your body, and this can lead to a wave of energy to your brain.

Exercise aids you in concentrating better and making learning more accessible. Therefore, the more you use your brain positively, the more skilled and a great thinker you become. Your ability to focus will be enhanced when you exercise your brain.

2. Meditation. What meditation accomplishes is neuroplasticity. As soon as this I'd launched, the brain can make physiological changes for the better. Additionally, meditation enhances gray and white brain matter. Their functions differ. For example, gray matter is responsible for processing information, while white matter enhances communication skills.

3. Watch Less of no Television. I know this might be a sad fact, but more relaxed you admit, the better. When you watch television, you think less, and thus you aren't putting your mental power into use. So, if you crave for relaxation, read a book or play a crossword puzzle game.

4. Reading Challenging Selections. Reading improves one's ability to understand and encourage critical thinking. Thus, select more books among the ones that offer aptitude.

Examples of these books include newspapers, classic novel, multi-content periodicals and when you come in contact with new words, check them up in your dictionary or ask an expert who knows and can explain explicitly about the topic.

5. Rest Well. Psychologists hold the widespread belief that ensuring adequate sleep will enhance smartness. It helps one feel revitalized if one gets to bed early and have quality 8 hours rest, waking up will be immersed with productivity and use your brain to the optimal level.

6. Write. You need not be an expert, pick up something you have either seen or read. Doing this will enhance visual simulation and kinesthetic. Also, practice writing with your nondominant hand to improve both side simulation.

7. Play Video Games. Invest quality times to play new games. Seek for Ines that gives you the ability that will enforce quick thinking abilities. Just like scientists recommend, game Tetras.

8. Invest in Cryptology. Logic puzzle enhances brain intelligence and functioning. The puzzle entails a message written in codes for solving. When continuously played, you will strengthen your simulation ability and relaxing.

State of Consciousness

The separate awareness of your unique sensations, environment, feelings, memories, and thoughts are what consciousness is all about. Consciousness in an individual is always changing. Take, for instance, it is very likely that when you were reading this book, you were focused, but at a point, your consciousness shifted to something you had earlier done with a coworker. It might not stop there, but move to change dramatically from one moment to the next one, but all in all, your experience of it seems effortless.

As you may have realized, it is not all forms of awareness that are similar. Thus, there are several states of human consciousness as well as a variety of things that are capable of impacting states of awareness.

Has it ever occured to you that every morning, you always feel energetic, question hypnosis, and even try explaining your dreams? All these are several concepts of how consciousness works. All these briefly mentioned are related to human consciousness, which can be influenced in several ways.

Body Clocks.

Many start their day with full energy, but by midday, it's down. For some, they try to be energetic in the morning with no result, but amazingly, they pick up in the evening. This daily fluctuation of energy levels is identified as circadian rhythm or body's clock. They have a significant impact on consciousness and other psychological states.

Sleep and Consciousness.

There are stages of sleep, namely NREM (non-rapid eye movement)

Stage 1, which is the beginning of the sleep cycle, and it is a relatively light stage of sleep. This stage is considered a transition period that exists between wakefulness and sleep.

In stage 2, when a person sleeps, people become less aware of their surroundings, their body temperature drops, and breathing and heart rate become more constant. This stage lasts for an approximate period of 20 minutes. In the stage, folks spend 50% of their total sleep in this stage.

In phase 3, the muscle relaxes, blood pressure, and breathing rate drops and deepest sleep happen. In the stage, some experience sleepwalking and tends to occur during sleep. REM(-rapid eye movement) stage, which is the final part is the stage where the brain becomes more active, the body becomes relaxed and immobilized, dreams happen, and eyes move rapidly.

Dreams and Consciousness.

Dream entail any images, thoughts, and emotions that are experienced during sleep. It can be either vivid and be filled with unclear and confusing imagery. In summary, you can see the dream as the touchstones of your characters.

Hypnosis and consciousness.

The study of hypnosis has been used in several fields, like pain management and weight loss. Many have found hypnosis to be an efficient therapeutic tool. For some, when hypnotized they record that they feel a sense of detachment while for some, they attain a high level of relaxation. And for some, they think that their action occurs outside their conscious volition. And for some, they might be fully aware of carrying out conversations while under hypnosis. But still, hypnosis is used in reducing pain during childbirth, control of pain during a dental procedure, treatment of rheumatoid arthritis.

Drugs, And Consciousness.

Psychoactive drugs are used in treating chronic medical conditions. They can pose serious problems and bring about an effect on human consciousness.

Someone who used a psychoactive plant would have his mental state have a higher risk of poisoning. This is because the person taking the substances has no control over the strength of the plant's psychoactive substance.

Accessing these drugs can be detrimental to your health and affect your general well-being.

Chapter 5: Steps to Increase Your Influence

Influencing without authority for project managers is a critical task. Maintaining the cats requires a combination of strong management of projects and communication skills. You can master the most complex projects by combining that with influencing levers. There are five forms without authority to impact.

Expertise

Expertise is an important element. Technical knowledge is important as various roles function together in a project. When you operate in a cross-industry unit, the business experience can be crucial. Use your expertise to support your suggestions and requests. One definition of a project manager would be the constraints of a timetable to support a deadline.

Information

When exchanged, knowledge is the most effective. Influence others by daily, clear and concise sharing of information that you learn. As a project manager, you have priorities and plans. Roles and responsibilities can be complicated in diverse working groups. The news is a two-way street. Don't forget to collect it and express what you learn now. Knowledge of stakeholders is key information that project teams need to bear in mind about the main project sponsor.

Resources

The correct tools are a crucial factor for the success of the project. The distinction between success and failure can be the imaginative use of capital. Impact the program by providing examples. Influence capabilities by identifying the main results expected and recording the skills required to achieve results. Influence citizens by managing the pressure of employment and goal problems.

Relationships

Know regarding people and build deeper relationships. This helps you to learn what you can do. Prepare responses and behaviors for criticisms rather than shocks. You should apply for periodic rewards across deep, long-standing partnerships. Finally, there is also a sense of camaraderie that helps people to solve challenges together.

Attitude

The actions or how you perceive people is one of the most significant influencing factors. Be honest and direct–you have long been accepting a crack in your honesty. Don't waste people's time-be prepared and organized. Knowledge and pressure interact, but not pain. Your voice tone, your word selection, and your recognition of difficult situations can be your strongest influence.

Authority

A statement on jurisdiction. Jurisdiction. Authority is definitely the most obvious way of influencing people. You will set their course and goals if you control capital directly. There are a time and a place to use the influence of someone else. For instance, if you cannot overcome major resource dependencies, call the bosses. Yet, you did not try to fix it personally afterward.

Appreciate People

Gratitude is another huge influencer/leader/role model quality. Efficient leaders know the power of simple appreciation for channelizing people in the right direction. A simple gesture like thanking people, appreciating the effort they put into a project or publicly praising their skills goes a long way in inspiring their loyalty towards you.

Always choose to recognize the work or efforts of others and focus on lifting them as glowing role models for others. Few things boost a person's morale than being presented as a sparkling example. This does not just make the person feel wonderful but also helps you reinforce what's the right thing to do. Everyone wants to be appreciated and valued, and will, therefore, be motivated to do things as they should be done.

Another tip that can make you an endearing leader is the ability to help people save face in a potentially embarrassing or awkward situation. The person will feel indebted to you for life. They will feel a deep sense of gratitude that you helped them out of a tricky situation which in turn inspires unwavering loyalty.

You can help deflect focus from the person's blunder. For instance, if someone says something they shouldn't have said erroneously or accidentally, quickly change the topic before anyone notices or pretend nothing huge happened.

Show Abundant Passion And Enthusiasm

Have the proverbial fire in your belly for whatever you do. This makes you an irresistible influencer. People can tell the difference when leaders/role models do something just for the heck of it and when they are truly operating with endless reserves of passion. Seeing you demonstrate the right amount of passion and commitment towards a project/cause lights others up too. This, in turn, grows your influence. It attracts others to work with you in your undying quest.

Stay Consistent

Consistency and commitment is a huge influence catalyst. It accelerates your influence in a positive direction by revealing how dependable your actions. People who are reliable, steadfast and dependable earn greater respect and obedience than those people who constantly change their actions based on what suits them.

Keep your actions and words consistent. Stay consistent with the rules you make. Be consistent in your attitude, policies and leadership pattern. Above everything, stay consistent with your efforts for fulfilling your/the team's goals. People who don't give up are able to attract plenty of followers. Consistent folks are seen as reliable and are the preferred ones to be trusted with brand-new projects, initiatives, and responsibilities.

Find Solutions

Solution providers are always more sought after than problem diggers. Your influencer invariably increases if you possess a solution-oriented mindset. People flock to leaders/role models who have a more solution-focused mindset and are capable of coming up with ingenious solutions to the most convoluted problems.

Folks who use lateral thinking, constructively problem-solving skills, and path-breaking solutions are often people magnets. They become instantly dependable and likable for their innovative thinking and positive approach.

Chapter 6: Sources of influence

1. Personal Motivation

It can be difficult to change behavior, especially if the employees ' personal motivation is weak. The nurses can see that the nursing report takes too much time. You may need to develop new motivations to manipulate actions to alter this equation. Most infants are aware that highly coordinated discharge planning is a new focus today. How can this be if it does not include all workers and is not up to date? The bedside rounding can be refurbished as both an opportunity to improve patient contact and to recognize discharge preparation needs. Missing these requirements can have very great human implications and should be worried, as most nurses are committed and compassionate practitioners.

2. Personal Ability

Often we believe that when we are going to change our actions, it is just a lack of motivation. This may not be the case everywhere. In reality, successful influencers over-invest in encouraging others to improve their ability and make the transition more possible. While reporting to a new nurse may be comfortable, adding the patient and family to the audience can alter this dynamic. Providing standardized reporting platforms in this new forum can greatly enhance the feeling of competence of the nurse. These situations could include any kind of solutions and concerns that the patient and family might have.

3. Harness Peer Pressure

Peer pressure will provide tremendous influence on change behavior. There are opinion leaders in any specific nursing environment. It is important to include opinion leaders in the change process. Opinion leaders can be pioneers of progress or, if disengaged, can sabotage creative attempts.

4. Find Strength in Numbers

Influence is available in quantities. If you make a change such as a bedside study, your workers do not automatically need to purchase 100% at the outset. You need a critical mass of dedicated nurses, but on every tour, you need enough social capital to influence change.

5. Design Rewards and Demand Accountability

What is measured is often said to be rewarded. If the above critical activity in the bedside report was included in the annual performance review, the interest of the nursing staff would be attracted easily. The problem today, with much success evaluation methods is that they are too common and do not include such behavioral standards.

6. Change the Environment

If we look at behavioral factors, we rarely think about environmental control as a cause of impact. Sometimes simple changes may affect behavior in a unit setting. In the example of the bedside report, what if there was no place for staff to sit and report in a nursing facility or unit? What if the tape report had no tape recorders? What if we guarantee that a nurse only served in the same geographical area where the patients were clustered? What if we allowed and encouraged our nurses to sit down and report in the patient's room when they needed to? What if we asked our workers for suggestions on how we could adjust the layout of our space to improve their ability to monitor the bedside?

It is not an easy process to promote change. Effective influencers realize that the more eager you are to set the stage for progress, the more effective you become. No one size fits for the shift. This requires multiple points of control and performance must be reassessed over time.

Chapter 7: The Art of Influence and Persuasion?

Being influential and persuasive is a skill that you can actually develop. With the right tips and knowledge, you can master the art of influence and persuasion and apply it is in various aspects of your life. If you are an entrepreneur or someone who's daily routine needs to convince others to see things based on your own perspectives and get them to agree with you, then mastering persuasion is an advantage. You need to hone this type of personality from the time you have chosen your own career.

With excellent persuasion skills, it will be easier for you to present your new ideas to the public. You can persuade the correct partners to be part of your network, create and present solutions to the right people, convince potential investors to fund your ideas, and convince customers to buy from you.

The good news is that you can have this skill. Here are just some ways for you to master the art of persuasion:

Practice repetition

Repetition is an effective way for you to get the attention of people. A lot of people, especially entrepreneurs, make the wrong assumption that their passion in their chosen field is enough to help them clearly send their message to the right audience and stand out from the crowd. This is a wrong assumption because with the excessive amount of information that the public can access from various sources, it would be difficult for you to stand out. In fact, the majority of the public today already created filters as a means of ignoring unsolicited inputs.

You can combat this by ensuring that you practice repetition. Note that you will most likely convince the public that your message is worthy to be heard if they see and hear it many times – both in verbal and written form. The good news is that with this repetition, you can also imbibe the skill of persuasion into your own personality, especially because it aids you in mastering it.

Use imagination

Another way to master the art of persuasion is to use your own and your target audience's imagination. For instance, you can say things like "can you imagine how happy you'll feel by buying this product?". This will give your audience the opportunity to pain a clear picture of what he/she can expect to receive if he agrees on what you are saying or take what you are offering. Let him/her imagine the pleasure of following what you are suggesting, and the pain that he/she will most likely feel if he/she does not.

Try to obtain a yes early

If you are an entrepreneur, for instance, then try to persuade your target audience to agree with you, even in just trivial matters. It could be as simple as the weather, whether the color of an object is blue, politics, etc. Keep in mind that getting someone to like you is one of the most important aspects of persuasion. It would be possible for you to reach that goal if the person you are dealing with agrees with you.

If you are still a beginner in the art of persuasion, then try to let your target audience clearly see the actual value of what you're offering. You should also clearly indicate what they will be missing if they decide not to have it. Take advantage of the power of leading questions, like "do you want to", "have you been wanting to", etc.

The questions should be leading enough that they will have a difficult time saying no to. You need to customize the questions to ensure that they suit the type of conversation you're having with your audience to persuade them to agree with you at the earliest possible time.

Build your confidence

You can't expect to master the art of persuasion if you're not confident. Your audience should see how confident you are with what you're saying. How can you expect someone to believe in what you're saying if you, yourself, have doubts about it? No matter how competent you are, if your target audience does not sense your confidence, then you'll most likely lose the fight and be left unable to convince them.

When it comes to building your persuasion skills, note that you can develop your confidence by fully understanding how important it is to facilitate a need. Keep in mind that many people need your help and you hold the answers to a certain problem they are facing. Believe that what you're offering or saying is important and can provide a solution to a problem – that is regardless of the field you're in – whether you're in web design, foods, etc.

Keep in mind that someone will always find your products, services and solutions helpful. Believing that you have something that is of great value to someone can significantly increase your confidence, thereby making it easier for you to convince/persuade someone.

Improve your listening skills

The ability to listen to someone intently – whether it's your customers, friends, colleagues, starting entrepreneurs, small business owners, or industry experts – contributes a lot to successfully persuading someone. Through intent listening, you will learn a lot more about the field you're in. Try to listen more than speak. Note that the time you spent not speaking are frequently the most vital moments since the other party will most likely feel that you are genuinely valuing his time.

Listening is also known to be one of the keys to being persuasive. In a study conducted in a business school in Columbia, for instance, researchers discovered that a lot of workers value listening skills too much that this lead to the successful implementation of persuasion. With the set of experiments and tests they conducted, they were able to find out that one's ability to persuade or influence has a huge relationship to the timing he chooses to be verbal when doing the act. Remember that even if you do not speak and just merely listen, you can still persuade others using body language and cues.

Learn how to integrate connection in all your persuasion endeavors

Regardless of whom you are trying to influence/persuade, forging a connection is crucial. Keep in mind that as humans, there is a great likelihood for them to respond positively if you use emotional appeals by connecting to them. The great philosopher, Aristotle, for instance, discovered that it is greatly possible for humans to be influenced if one uses a mix of credible, logically argumentative and emotional appeals. Using emotional appeals more also increases the number of people who can be persuaded.

If you are an entrepreneur who needs to persuade people most of the time, then you can also use and mirror that concept to your advantage. A wise tip is to connect to them in a more emotional level by matching your voice inflections, physical cues and charisma. This is a huge help in building an emotional connection, thereby allowing the person you're talking to realize that you also have similarities. This will eventually forge a bond of trust.

Learn how to give praises

You also need to learn the art of giving praise when it comes to developing your persuasion skills. If you just focus on shooting people with your ideas without even listening to them or making them feel that you also value them, they will feel like they are insignificant. This will cause them to focus on mending their hurt egos, instead of listening intently to what you have today. The good news is that you can be more likable to them if you start to offer them praise. Find something good about the person you're talking to and praise him.

Once he finds you likable through the praises that you give, it will be easier for you to persuade him to listen to you and agree with your idea. Praising someone can make him feel like he is attaining his personal achievement. He will then like you more and he will start thinking that you will be of great help to him when it comes to reaching his full potential.

Just make sure that you're careful when offering praises, though. Avoid resorting to using empty praises. Doing so will only damage your efforts.

Chapter 8: Powerful Verbal and Nonverbal Cues

Verbal communication encompasses both spoken and written words. Words are a form of communication that humans have used to exchange their thoughts and messages, especially when they are not in a face to face setting. This is the most frequent form of communication used, and it is one that we have come to rely on the most.

One example of verbal communication involves public speaking, where communication is conducted and carried out verbally to the groups of audiences. Other examples of verbal communication include your everyday conversations with your friends, family members, co-workers, clients, even random strangers you happen to meet as you go about your day. Verbal communication, in short, happens every day and it has become so routine we do it almost without actively thinking about it anymore.

As opposed to nonverbal communication which requires active thought. This form of communication has no words or sounds to rely on. Nothing but what you see with your eyes and what you make of it. When we use gestures, body movements, and facial expressions to convey our intent that is a form of nonverbal communication.

What both forms of communication have is that they matter. They're equally important contributors to the overall communication process. You might even say that nonverbal communication is more important. The first impression you make on anyone is nonverbal. Even before the first hello and handshake. Take job interviews, for example. It cannot be stressed enough just how important it is to make a good first impression. Making a good first impression is absolutely critical is during a job interview. From the minute you walk into the room, you are communicating with your potential employer through your nonverbal mannerisms. Your posture, facial expression, gestures that you make are going to be the clues that your employer is looking for when they assess you.

This same approach applies to other situations too, like meeting clients or conducting business meetings. The impression that you leave people with can be a big deciding factor in determining the outcome of your success. Saying all the right words, but with the wrong body language, is not going to get you the desired results that you seek.

Analyzing People via Their Verbal Statements

Our analysis and observation skills would be incomplete and inefficient if we ignore the significance of verbal statements. Verbal statements hold a myriad of keys into the doorways of our personalities, intentions, and emotions.

You can glean a lot from the words that you hear. Analyzing people through their verbal statements requires less effort and astuteness than that of nonverbal behaviors. We will take an in-depth look at how our words reveal our intentions, emotions, and personalities. I will include common speech clues you will come across in your daily interactions with those around you. Let's delve into this significant aspect of communication.

Understanding the Relationship between Words, Behavior, and Personality

Everything you do (nonverbal) or say (verbal) speaks volumes about your personality. When you become adept at analyzing people, you will realize there's a synergy between our actions, thoughts, and beliefs, and that each aligns to provide a full picture about whom we are. The words you use, even though it seems insignificant when compared to body language, can actually tell a great deal about your desires, strengths, insecurities, and emotions.

How Words Reveal Your Personality

"Hey! Did you get taller overnight?" At first glance, this statement looks like friendly banter, and it reveals no negative vibe. Now, if you look at the statement from another perception, you will realize that it gives us an opportunity to glimpse the mind of the speaker. In this context, the speaker cares a lot about the height difference. How did we know that?

If you think about snakes all day because you are scared of them, then you might easily confuse a skink for a snake.

In other words, we notice the things we care about. When you observe the friendly banter, you will realize that the person may be concerned about his personal height. This concern helped him to notice the height difference of his friend.

This statement could also stem from the speaker's insecurity about his own height. Remember, when it comes to analyzing verbal statements, you need to take into consideration various factors at play, and this includes watching body language too. In totality, both aspects of communication—verbal and nonverbal—are incomplete without the other.

Before we proceed, let's have a quick look at how you can analyze people through jokes.

Learn to Unclothe the Veil around Jokes

Two teenagers went to a restaurant. When the waiter came around to take their orders, one of the kids jokingly replied, "I want anything that costs a million dollars." To a casual observer, it is a normal and bland banter. To an astute observer, this kid is worried about money. Perhaps his family might be passing through some kind of financial crisis, or his parents and loved ones might have taught him the importance of money.

There's always a hidden message in every joke. Therefore, learning to analyze these jokes will give you a glimpse into the speaker's deepest desires and personality. You should know that the words people use have a deep meaning, irrespective of how well-crafted the words are. A person might tell a joke to you without realizing he is revealing much more about his intentions. That is why it's easy to analyze those who make hurtful jokes to demean you.

Stories Are Powerful

It is easy to recognize a biased story, either verbally or in written form. You can effectively glimpse into the storyteller's psyche by listening to him or by reading his work. Here's an example for us to dissect:

From subject A's point of view: Last night, I was walking down a lonely street with my friends, and a large and muscular dark man appeared out of the neighboring bush and seemed to come toward us to attack. But he changed his mind in the last second and walked past us.

From subject B's point of view: Late in the evening, I was taking a stroll when I misplaced my keys in the nearby bush. It was already getting dark when I noticed I didn't have my keys on me. Time wasn't on my side since I needed to get home quickly to prepare for my date, so I searched and searched through the shrubs until I felt the keys. I jumped out onto the street in excitement and started running home. In my excitement, I nearly bumped into a group of frightened teenagers.

Both stories gave us different perceptive about the incident. The first point of view was from a teenager who didn't see the look of excitement on man's face. Rather, he emphasized the words huge, large, and dark. So why did he place emphasis on the physical attributes of the man who jumped out of the bush? Well, it's because that's the part that concerns him the most. He was scared because of the man's sudden appearance and physical size, and that had a huge impact on the story. We have a full and clearer picture when you take a look at the other man's point of view, and that is the power of perception in stories.

So when someone tells you a story, I want you to dissect the story and take note of the emphasized points of the story. By doing this, you will know how to analyze people effectively.

Common Word Clues You Need to Know

Words are like doorways to the mind. Words are often used to analyze people's thought processes, and the closest you can get to understanding someone's thoughts depends on your ability to decipher and listen to the words he speaks. Words that reveal a person's thoughts are referred to as word clues.

These word clues increase your chances of analyzing and predicting people's behavioral patterns via the words they speak or write. Word clues alone can't determine a person's personality, but they do provide us with an insight into an individual's behavioral characteristics and thought process. You can draw your hypotheses from the word clues and make a conclusion by taking notice of the other aspect of communication.

An Insight into How the Brain Process Words

There's something we have all come to agree on: the human brain is very efficient. We only use verbs and nouns when we think.

For instance, "I walked" or "I jumped." Adjectives, adverbs, and other parts of speech are added during the latter phase of converting thoughts into written language or spoken words. The words that we add at this stage provide an insight into who we are and what we are thinking.

The basic and simple sentence consists of only a subject and a verb. For example, the verbal statement "I walked" consists of only the pronoun I (subject) and the object that is the verb walked. Any other word added to this basic sentence only modifies the action of the verb or the quality of the noun. These deliberate additions or modifications provide an insight into the behavioral characteristics and personality of the writer or speaker.

Word clues help us to make behavioral guesses or develop hypotheses regarding the personality of others. Take a look at the verbal statement "I quickly walked." The word clue in this sentence is quickly since it serves as a modification of the verb walked. This word clue infused a sense of urgency in the statement, but it did not give us a reason. An individual can "quickly walk" because of the urgency of an appointment.

People who utilize this phrase are regarded as meticulous. Meticulous people are reliable and abhor being late for an appointment since they respect societal norms and want to live up to expectations. This set of individuals will also make good employees since they don't want to disappoint their employees.

Conversely, you can also quickly walk when in a dark and lonely area with a bad reputation. Bad weather could also be the reason that you quickly walk.

In summary, people might make use of the word clue quickly walk for a variety of reasons. It's important to always read verbal statements in relation to the circumstances surrounding the speaker or writer.

Types of Nonverbal Communication

1. Outward appearances

Outward appearances are answerable for an immense extent of nonverbal correspondence. Think about how much data can be passed on with a grin or a scowl. The expression on an individual's face is regularly the main thing we see, even before we hear what they need to state.

2. Motions

Purposeful developments and sign is a significant method to impart importance without words. Basic motions incorporate waving, indicating, and utilizing fingers to show numeric sums. Different motions are subjective and identified with culture.

In court settings, legal advisors have been known to use diverse nonverbal sign to endeavor to influence legal hearer sentiments. A lawyer may look at his watch to propose that the contradicting attorney's contention is monotonous or may even feign exacerbation at the declaration offered by observers trying to undermine their reliability. This nonverbal sign is viewed as being so ground-breaking and powerful that a few judges' even spot restrains on what sort of nonverbal practices are permitted in the court.

3. Paralinguistic

Paralinguistic alludes to vocal correspondence that is isolated from the real language. This incorporates factors, for example, manner of speaking, commotion, affectation, and pitch. Consider the amazing impact that manner of speaking can have on the importance of a sentence. When said in a solid manner of speaking, audience members may translate endorsement and excitement. Similar words said in a reluctant manner of speaking may pass on the objection and an absence of intrigue.

Consider all various ways that basically changing your manner of speaking may change the significance of a sentence. A companion may ask you how you are getting along, and you may react with the standard "I'm fine," yet how you really state those words may uncover a huge measure of how you are truly feeling. A virus manner of speaking may propose that you are not fine, however you don't wish to examine it. A brilliant, cheerful manner of speaking will uncover that you are really doing very well. A grave, sad tone would demonstrate that you are something contrary to fine and that maybe your companion ought to ask further.

4. Non-verbal communication and Posture

Stance and development can likewise pass on a lot of data. Research on non-verbal communication has developed essentially since the 1970's, however well-known media have concentrated on the over-translation of protective stances, arm-intersection, and leg-crossing, particularly subsequent to distributing Julius Fast's book Body Language.

While these nonverbal practices can show emotions and demeanor, look into proposes that non-verbal communication is unquestionably more unobtrusive and less conclusive than recently accepted.

5. Proxemics

Individuals frequently allude to their requirement for "individual space," which is likewise a significant kind of nonverbal correspondence. The measure of separation we need and the measure of room we see as having a place with us is impacted by various variables including social standards, social desires, situational factors, character attributes, and level of nature. For instance, the measure of individual space required when having an easygoing discussion with someone else as a rule differs between 18 crawls to four feet. Then again, the individual separation required when addressing a horde of individuals is around 10 to 12 feet.

6. Eye Stare

The eyes assume a significant job in the nonverbal correspondence and such things as looking, gazing and flickering are significant nonverbal practices. At the point when individuals experience individuals or things that they like, the pace of flickering increments and understudies expand. Taking a gander at someone else can demonstrate a scope of feelings including threatening vibe, intrigue, and fascination.

Individuals likewise use eye stare as a way to decide whether somebody is being straightforward. Typical, watchful gaze contact is frequently taken as a sign that an individual is coming clean and is dependable. Tricky eyes and a failure to keep in touch, then again, is regularly observed as a marker that somebody is lying or being tricky.

7. Haptics

Imparting through touch is another significant nonverbal conduct. There has been a generous measure of research on the significance of touch in the earliest stages and early youth.

Ladies will in general use contact to pass on care, concern, and nurture. Men, then again, are bound to utilize the contact to declare power or command over others.

8. Appearance

Our decision of shading, garments, hairdos, and different elements influencing appearance are additionally viewed as a method for nonverbal communication. Appearance can likewise change physiological responses, decisions, and understandings. Simply think about all the unpretentious decisions you rapidly make about somebody dependent on their appearance. These initial introductions are significant, which is the reason specialists recommend that activity searchers dress suitably for interviews with potential businesses.

9. Relics

Items and pictures are likewise apparatuses that can be utilized to convey nonverbally. On an online gathering, for instance, you may choose a symbol to speak to your character on the web and to impart data about what your identity is and the things you like. Individuals regularly invest a lot of energy building up a specific picture and encircle themselves with articles intended to pass on data about the things that are essential to them. Outfits, for instance, can be utilized to transmit an enormous measure of data about an individual. A fighter will wear exhausts, a police officer will wear a uniform, and a specialist will wear a white sterile jacket. At a simple look, these outfits tell individuals what an individual accomplishes professionally.

Chapter 9: Facial Expressions

Emotions are caused by other factors beyond facial expressions. For instance, emotions are largely a function of the human system of beliefs and stored information. In other terms, you feel angry when you score less than average marks because the current system equates that to not being smart enough. And the stored information reminds you that you risk repeating the test or not securing a plum employment position, and this entire matter makes you feel hopeless, upset, and stressed.

There is a possibility that if the belief system did not deem less than average as a failure and the stored information shows a positive outlook for such a score that you will feel happy or excited by the score.

Additionally, twitching your mouth randomly; either way indicates that one is deliberately not listening or degrading the importance of the message. The facial gesture is realized by closing the lips and randomly twitching the mouth to either the right or left akin to swirling the mouth with mouthwash. The facial expression is also to indicate outright disdain to the speaker or the message. The facial expression is considered a rude way of expressing disgust with the speaker or the message and should be avoided at all costs.

Where one shuts their lips tightly, then it indicates the individual is feeling angry but does not wish to show the anger. Shutting the lips tightly may also indicate that the person is feeling unease but struggling to concentrate at all costs. The source of the discomfort could be the immediate neighbors, the message, or the speaker. Through this gesture, the individual is indicating he or she simply wants the speaker to conclude the speech because not all people are enjoying the message.

When one is angry or strongly disapproves of what the speaker is saying, then the person will grimace. A grimace indicates that the person is feeling disgusted by what is being said. In movies or during live interviews, you probably so the interviewee grimaces when an issue or a person that the person feels is disgusting is mentioned. Showing a grimace indicates one harbors a strong dislike for the message or the speaker. A person that is feeling uncomfortable due to sitting on a hard chair, a poorly ventilated room, or sitting next to a hostile neighbor may also show a grimace, which is not necessarily related to the message.

If one is happy, then one is likely to have a less tense face and a smile. Positive news and positive emotions are manifested as a smile or a less tense facial look. On the other hand, if one is processing negative emotions, then the face of the person is likely to be tensed up due to exerting pressure on the body muscles. A genuine smile like when one is happy is wider than an average curve and is temporary. A prolonged smile that is very wide suggests the individual is smirking at the message or the speaker. A prolonged smile may also suggest the individual is faking the emotion.

By the same measure, a frozen face may indicate intense fear. For instance, you have seen terrified faces when attending a health awareness forum on sexually transmitted diseases or some medical condition that terrified the audience. In this setting, the face of the audience will appear as if it has been paused. The eyes and the mouth may remain stationary as the speaker presents the scary aspects of the medical condition. It appears negative emotions may slow down the normal conscious and unconscious movement of the muscles of the face.

If you are a teacher or trainer, then you encounter facial expressions from your students frequently. Assuming that you are a teacher, then you have noticed facial expressions indicating shock, uneasiness, and disapproval when you announce tests or indicate that the scores are out.

From these facial expressions, you will concur that the students feel uncomfortable, uncertain, and worried. The students will show lines of wrinkles, look down, eyes wide open and mouths agape when sudden and uncomfortable news is announced. Even though the students may indicate they are prepared for the test, their facial expressions suggest otherwise.

Like all forms of communication, effective reading of facial expressions will happen where the target person is unaware that you are reading even though they understand that their facial expressions are integral to the overall communication. In other terms, when one becomes aware he or she is being studied, then the person will act in an expected manner or simply freeze the expected reaction. It is akin to realizing that someone is feeling you.

Since the underlying emotion affects the facial expression that one shows. As indicated, the body language overrides verbal communication, which helps reveal the true status of an individual. One possible argument of the body language triumphing over verbal communication could be because the body prioritizes its physiological needs over other needs. The physiological needs are critical to the survivability of an individual.

Over centuries the human body could have been programmed to increase survivability rate by prioritizing physiological needs. Body language largely indicates the physiological state of an individual, which is meant to help the individual and others respect the true physiological status of the person.

Chapter 10: Distance in Communication

Focusing on the United States, there are four types of distances that people use to communicate on a face-to-face basis. These distances are intimate, personal distance, social distance, and public distance. Starting with the intimate distance, it is used for highly confidential exchanges as zero to two feet of space between two individuals marks this zone. An example of intimate distance includes two people hugging, standing side-by-side, or holding hands. Individuals intimate distance share a unique level of comfort with one another. If one is not comfortable with someone approaching them in the intimate zone, he/she will experience a significant deal of social discomfort.

Firstly, personal distance is used for talking with family as well as close acquaintances. The personal distance can range from two to four feet. Akin to intimate distance, if a stranger walks into the personal zone, the one is likely to feel uneasy being in such proximity with the stranger.

Secondly, there is the social distance used in business exchanges or when meeting new people and interacting with groups of people. Compared to the other distances, social distance has a larger range in the range that it can incorporate. Its range is four to twelve feet, and it depends on the context. It is used among students, acquaintances, or co-workers. As expected, most participants in the social distance do not show physical contact with one another. Generally, people are likely to be very specific concerning the degree of social distance that is preferred, as some require more physical distance compared to others. In most cases, the individual will adjust backward or forward to get the appropriate social distance necessary for social interactions.

Thirdly, we have public distance, which is twelve or more feet between individuals. An example of public distance is where two people sit on a bench in a public park. In most cases, the two people on a bench in a public park will sit at the farthest ends of each other to preserve the public space. Each of the earlier types of proximity will significantly influence an individual's perception of what is the appropriate type of distance in specific contexts. One of the factors that contribute to individual perceptions of how proxemics should be used is culture. Individuals from different cultures show different viewpoints on what the appropriate persona; space should be.

Fourthly, there is the concept of territoriality where individuals tend to feel like they own and should control their personal areas. We are inclined to defend our personal space. When someone invades this personal space, then the individual will react negatively as it is an invasion of territory without express permission. At one point, you asked a stranger to keep some distance from you because you felt uncomfortable with the person standing close to you. Sometimes standing next to a person may also denote that you are creepy and may be intending to harm the person.

If one is talking to someone, the person violates your personal space, and you allow it, then it signals that you are okay to intimate ideas. Intimate ideas in this context include highly personal issues that one can talk with another person. For instance, if you walk and sit close and in contact with a woman watching television and she approves your behavior, then it is indicative that she is likely to allow you to have a personal talk that may be intimate in nature. Such discussion may include your health challenges or mental health and not necessarily sexual issues. For this reason, one should carefully weigh the need to invade the personal distance.

Regarding children, violating personal distance will make them freeze due to feeling uncomfortable. If a teacher sits next to a student or stands next to a student, then the student is likely to feel uneasy and nervous. However, they are instances where the invasion of personal space is allowed and seen as necessary. For instance, during interviews or when being examined by a doctor, invasion of private space by the person with an advantage is allowed. The panel during an interview may move or ask you to move closer, which may violate your personal space. A doctor may also stand closer to you, invading your personal space, but this is necessary due to the professional demand for their service.

As such, when one avoids personal distance, and the individual is expected to be within this space, then the individual may be feeling less confident or feeling ashamed. For instance, if a child has done something embarrassing, he or she is likely to sit or stand far from the parent during a conversation. For this reason, it appears that one should feel confident, assured, and appreciated to approach and remain in personal space when needed.

Additionally, staying in personal space during intense emotions may portray one as resilient, understanding, and bold. Think of two lovers or sibling quarreling, but each remains in the established personal space. The message that is being communicated is that the individual is confident that he or she can handle the intense emotions from the other person. For most people, they only allow their lover to stay in their personal distance when feeling upset because they trust that the person can handle the known behavior of the affected person. Since being in personal space places a person within physical striking range, most people will only allow trusted and familiar individuals into their personal space.

Equally, important is that invasion of personal space is justified because it is a part of professional demands. Think of a new teacher that is trying to help a student solve a mathematical equation. In this aspect, the teacher is a stranger because he or she is new to the school. By sitting or standing close to, the student, the teacher is invading the personal space, but the established norms in this context allow the student not to feel unease. For emphasis, this case is not unique as it aligns with stated expectations that people will welcome known or unfamiliar people in their personal space only if they trust them and, in this case, the student feels safe with any teacher. For this reason, the operationalization of distance in communication is mediated and moderated by established culture.

In most cases, one can start with public distance before allowing the interaction to happen in personal or social space. For instance, as a student during tournaments, you could have initiated nonverbal communication with the student from the other college before suddenly feeling connected to the individual and allowing him or her to move into personal space as a potential girlfriend or boyfriend. At first, the target person saw you as a stranger but allowed you to make nonverbal communication within the public space. When the person felt the need to connect more with you and have given you the benefit of the doubt, the person allowed you to move through public distance and social distance to enter their personal space.

For instance, a lot can be learned from studying distance and space in communication. Being allowed into the social and personal distances implies that the person trusts that you will not harm them emotionally and physically. For the intimate distance, being allowed into this distance implies that the person trusts you so much and is confident that you can never harm them and that you share a lot. For instance, a mother holding her baby close enough to her signals that the baby is feeling assured of security and protection. When two lovers move, closer until their faces are almost touching suggests trust and confidence that the other person feels safe and protected.

Relatedly, if arguing with your child or lover and the individual moves farther from you physically, then it suggests that the person no longer feels safe with you being within their personal distance. Issues that can cause someone to expand the distance between you and them include the risk of violence from you and emotional issues. If you occasionally act violently, then chances are, your lover or children will expand the personal distance to social distance because this is where they feel safe due to your personality and character. It then appears that your prior behavior will also affect the distance during communication.

Nevertheless, they are other issues that cause individuals to extend the distance of interaction, and these include having a medical condition or having hygiene issues. For instance, if you are sweaty, then chances are that the other person may prefer to extend the distance of communication between you and them. Having oral hygiene issues may also make the other person move far away from you because the smell turns them off. For this reason, interpreting the distance between communicators should also include hygiene and health-related issues that impact this distance.

For instance, some medical conditions can make people maintain some distance from you or be closer to you physically. For instance, some conditions may attract uneasiness, and this includes epilepsy. People with epilepsy get seizures, and this can make people feel unease being closer to them because they inadvertently fall. On the other hand, having hearing issues or sore throat may make people move closer to you physically to facilitate effective communication. However, these are exceptions when analyzing space and distance as forms of nonverbal communication, but they should be taken into account where necessary.

In some cases, it is welcome to invade personal distance merely by the circumstances. For instance, when attending a match in a full packed stadium or sitting to watch a movie in a movie theater, one will have his personal invaded due to the sitting arrangements. In this context, one may feel uneasy with this arrangement, but he or she has little control over the situation. While we value and seek to protect personal spaces, some situations make us allowing the invasion of this space because it is beyond control.

Chapter 11: Dark psychology and manipulation

Dark Manipulation, otherwise known as psychological manipulation, is a form of social influence that aims to change how someone behaves or perceives others through indirect, deceptive, and/or underhanded tactics. The manipulator uses these tactics to advance their interests at another's expense. The methods that they use can be viewed as devious and exploitative.

Now, social influence is not always dark and negative. It depends on the manipulator's agenda and how they use their tactics.

What kind of outcome do they want to have? For instance, people have often used interventions, with emotional manipulation, to help their loved ones change from their bad habits or behaviors. When social influence is harmless, the person has a right to choose what they are being offered or reject it. They are not forced into making a certain decision. If this is not the case, then it is dark manipulation, and the person is using their interests as an advantage to gain something from the other person.

Some things that motivate manipulators are:

1. The need to feel in control due to a feeling of powerlessness in their lives.

2. The need to feel a sense of power or authority over others and to lift their self-esteem.

3. The need to fulfill a sense of boredom. Often manipulators consider hurting others as a type of game.

4. Sometimes the manipulator is not consciously aware of what they are doing. They often feel like their emotions are invalid, and they forecast those emotions onto others, i.e., trying to justify their fear of commitment.

5. Having a hidden agenda that can be criminal. This can include financial manipulation that is often used on the elderly or unprotected wealthy who have often been targeted to obtain their financial assets.

There are three, things that the manipulator must be aware of and know:

- How to conceal their aggressive intentions and behaviors and how to be sweet and pleasant to get what you want, i.e., buttering someone up.

- Know their victims' vulnerabilities. This will allow the manipulator to know what tactics would be more effective.

- Having no moral qualms about being ruthless, as well as not caring if you hurt the victim in some ways. The end is justifying the means, as the saying goes.

The Dark Triad

Personality Vulnerabilities

Manipulation predators or dark manipulators use many techniques to control their victims. They look for certain types of people with certain types of personalities. Those types of personalities that are often prey to manipulators are those with low or no self-esteem, those who are easy to please, those with low or no self-confidence, who have no sense of assertiveness, and are very naïve.

Let's explain these personality traits in more detail:

- Those who are naïve find it virtually impossible to accept the fact that particular people in their lives can be cunning, devious, and ruthless. They will constantly deny that they are being victimized.

- Those who are over-conscientious give the manipulator the benefit of the doubt, even if they know in the back of their mind, they are right. They are hoping they are not and take the blame.

- Those who have low self-confidence start to doubt themselves and what they are experiencing, they are not assertive, and they easily defensive because they don't want to make waves.

- Those who are emotionally dependent have a submissive and dependent personality. When the victim is more emotionally dependent, the manipulator has an easier time exploiting and manipulating them.

- Those who over-intellectualize want to believe the manipulator and try to understand their reason for harming others, especially the victim themselves.

Those who tend to use others to their own advantage fall under the "Dark Triad'. As defined earlier in this book, it is "a set of traits that include the tendency to seek admiration and special treatment (otherwise known as narcissism), to be callous and insensitive (psychopathy) and to manipulate others .Studies have indicated that the triad consists of a lot of undesirable behaviors, such as aggressiveness, impulsivity, and sexual opportunism.

When people show signs of these characteristics, they are trying to get away with using others to get what they want. Each one of these personality traits can make life difficult for people, but all of these traits combined can be dangerous to anyone's mental health. Those who have any one of these personality traits show some of these behaviors: seeking out multiple sex partners, acting out aggressively to get what they want, having high or low self-esteem, and not viewing themselves highly. Most of these traits are shown by men.

Knowing more about the dark triad will help you protect yourself from those who wish to manipulate you and use you to their advantage. Research has been done to analyze the differences between all three personality traits within the triad. They have found that all three malevolent personalities "act aggressively out of self-interest and lack empathy and remorse. They're skilled at manipulation, exploit, and deceive others, though their motivations and tactics vary. They violate social norms and moral values and lie, deceive, cheat, steal, and bully.

However, psychopathy and Machiavellianism are more related because of their malicious behavior. Those who fall under the narcissist umbrella are very defensive and are surprisingly fragile.

Their arrogance and ego are just a cover for their feelings of inadequacy. Men are prone to psychopathic traits and behavior due to biological factors (testosterone), as well as social norms.

It is important to note those people who have one of these three personality disorders are not trustworthy, are selfish, are not straightforward, are not kind, or modest, and they do not comply or compromise; which are all qualities that are not good for any type of relationship. If you know someone that enumerates any of the dark triad traits, you might want to see if you are a victim of these techniques.

Manipulation Techniques

Lying is one of the very first techniques that manipulators use. It is a technique that pathological liars or psychopaths use when they want to confuse their victims. If they are constantly lying to them, their victims will often be unaware of the truth. Those who use this tactic have no moral or ethical apprehension about it.

Telling half-truths or only telling part of a story is another tactic that can be used to manipulate someone. People like this will often keep things to themselves because it puts the victim at a disadvantage. They can get what they want by waiting to tell them the rest of the story until their needs are met.

Being around someone who has frequent mood swings can often make a person vulnerable to their manipulations. Not knowing what mood that person will be in, whether they will be happy, sad, or angry can be a very useful tactic for the manipulator. It keeps the victim off balance and easy to manipulate because they will often do what the manipulator wants to keep them in a good mood.

Another tactic that is often used by narcissists is known as love bombing. This doesn't necessarily mean that you have to be in a relationship but can be used in friendship, as well. Those that use this tactic will charm the victim to death and have them believe that this is the best relationship or friendship that has ever happened to them. They will use the victim for what they want, and then when they are done, they drop them and the victim has no idea what happened.

A tactic that can be used in extreme cases by the manipulator is that of punishment. This makes the victim feel guilty of something they did wrong, even if they didn't do anything at all. Some punishments that they can inflict on their victims are consistent nagging, shouting, mental abuse, giving them the silent treatment, and even as bad as physical violence.

Denial is often a tactic that is used when a manipulator feels pushed in a corner, and they feel like they will be exposed for the fake that they are. In this instance, they will manipulate the victim into believing that they are doing the very thing the manipulator is being accused of.

Spinning the truth is a tactic often used by politicians. It is used to twist the facts to suit their needs or wants. Sociopaths use this technique to disguise their bad behavior and justify it to their victims.

Minimizing is when a manipulator will play down their behavior and/or actions. They move the blame onto the victim for overreacting when their actions are harmful, and the person has a valid reason for feeling the way they do.

It is often interesting when the manipulator pretends to become the victim. They do this to gain sympathy or compassion from their real victims. They do this so that their victims feel a sense of responsibility to help and end their suffering, especially if they feel that they are the cause of that person's suffering.

Another way that the manipulator can move the blame onto the victim is by targeting the victim and accusing them of wrongdoing. The victim will then start to defend themselves, while the manipulator hides their manipulation away from the victim. This can be dangerous because the victim is so focused on defending themselves that they forget to notice what is right in front of them.

Using the positive reinforcement tactic tricks the victim into thinking that they are getting something for helping the manipulator get what they want. This can be through purchasing them expensive presents, praising them, giving them money, constantly apologizing for their behavior, giving them lots of attention and all-around buttering them up.

There are times when a person knows where they stand with someone. However, in any type of relationship, the manipulator might keep moving the goal just to confuse their victim because they thought that everyone was still on the same page.

Another manipulation tactic that manipulators like to use is known as diversion. This tactic is commonly used to divert a certain conversation away from what the manipulator is doing. The new topic is created to get the victim to lose focus on what the manipulator is doing or trying to do.

Sarcasm is a tactic that can be used to lower the self-esteem and confidence of a victim through embarrassment. The manipulator will use sarcasm – usually saying something about the victim- in front of other people. This gives the manipulator power over the victim because they just made them feel very small.

Guilt trips are another tactic that a manipulator will use against their victim. In this instance, they will often tell their victims that they don't care about them or love them; they will indicate that they are selfish and that their life is easy. It keeps the victim confused and anxious because they want to please the manipulator by letting them know that they care about them and will do anything for them.

Another way that a manipulator will move the blame is to play the innocent card when the victim accuses them of their tactics. They will act shocked or show confusion at the accusation. The act of being surprised is convincing to the victim, and it makes them question their judgment and if what they are feeling is wrong.

A dangerous tactic that a manipulator can use is that of extreme aggression. Rage and aggression are used to force the victim to submit. The anger and rage are a tactic that scares the victim to stop talking about the conversation. They pretty much want to help keep the manipulator's anger in check.

Isolation is another dangerous tactic used by manipulators. It is a control mechanism that is used by manipulators to keep their victims from their family, friends, and loved ones who can expose the manipulator for who they really are. The manipulator might know that their victim can be manipulated, but their friends and family can see right through them, and they are not done using their victim yet.

And, one of the last tactics that manipulators, such as psychopaths and sociopaths use is that of fake love and empathy. These types of people do not know how to love others besides themselves and have a hard time loving others and showing empathy towards others.

How to Use Dark Psychology to Manipulate Others

People around us may use dark psychology tactics every day to manipulate, influence, persuade and intimidate us to take advantage and get what they want. As you get to know that dark psychology includes the science and art of mind control and manipulation. Whereas psychology is different from dark psychology as it is the study of human behavior and our actions, interactions and thoughts are centered with them. Some people get confused and don't know the difference between psychology and dark psychology. However, if you want to manipulate others, you need to know how to use dark psychology.

Here are a different kind of people who know the tactics of manipulating others-

a) Manipulation is an art and you need to know the tactics to meet your needs first, even at someone else's expense. Though these kinds of people are known to be self-centered, and they are good when it comes to manipulating and intimidating others. These people are not bothered with the outcomes but they have an agenda of self before others, no matter what.

b) People who are good public speakers use dark psychological and persuasion tactics to maximize the emotional state of the listeners which leads to an increase in the sale of their product (whatever they were selling to the audience). These people also know the moment and time of taking advantage of the emotional turbulence of other people.

c) Some people meet clinical diagnosis, as they are true sociopaths. However, these people usually are intellectual, alluring but alongside they are impulsive. Just because these people do not have much ability to feel remorse and lack of emotionality, they build a superficial relationship and take advantage of innocent people by using dark tactics. They are not concerned about anyone's feelings and are least bothered with what others might do once the innocents know about their true face.

d) People in politics (usual politicians) use dark tactics to persuade people that they will do the needful and perform the activities in favor of the common people just to get a vote and to become the ruling party.

e) Some lawyers or attorneys focus solely on winning their case regardless of knowing the truth and even after knowing the truth, using dark manipulating tactics to get the outcome of what they want to win the case. They are not bothered about justice but are only concerned about their reputation and self-esteem.

f) People in corporate offices who are in a higher position and deployed as the companies regional head use dark psychological tactics to get compliance, higher performance, or greater efforts from their subordinates. They are not cared about 'what their subordinates deserve' or 'is their salary justified as per the work they are performing within the organization'.

g) People who are involved in the sales department are usually well aware of many of these dark influencing tactics to persuade and convince other people to buy whatever they are selling. They could even disguise the customers, as they are only concerned with selling their product and earning a profit.

Now that you got to know about different types of people who may deceit you by using these dark tricks, here are the different dark psychological tactics to manipulate the people and make them do what you want them to do-

1) If you want to sell your product and wish to manipulate your customers to make them surely buy your product, you can use a decoy option. You can use it as the third option. For example, if you are facing a troublesome situation to sell the more expensive of two products, by adding the third option you can make the expensive product more captivating and appealing. You need to make sure that

decoy option should be the same price for the more expensive option but assuring that it is less effective. It is a good strategy to increase the sale and entice more customers towards your expensive product.

2) To win an argument, speak quickly so that the opponent has no other option left but to agree with you. If you speak faster, it will give the other person the less time to process what you are saying and they will agree with you. While you should do the opposite in case when the other person agrees with you, speaking slowly is better as it will give them the time to evaluate and analyze what you are saying.

3) You can copy the body language of people whom you want to manipulate. Imitating their body actions shall impress them and will make you closer to them and they may start liking you. If you subtly imitate the way the other person is talking, sitting, and walking, they would probably not notice that you are copying them and it may get them to do as per your wants.

4) Scaring the other people to make them give you what you want and need is one of the dark psychological tactics to manipulate people. Anxious people often respond positively to requests afterward as they may be occupied thinking about the danger they are surrounded with. It would make them feel scared and would do as your saying. Additionally, sometimes, even if you will not say anything they will understand what you need and do what you would have spoken them to do for you.

5) To get people to behave ethically with you, you need to display an image of the eyes. It means you should create your image as a person who watches, notice and observe the other person by posting a picture of eyes nearby. The other people could never take you like a side option and will return all borrowed items on time.

6) Tweak such an environment for the people, so that they would act less selfishly. For example, if you were bargaining in a coffee shop, needless to say, you would be less aggressive as compared to what you would be in a conference room. Usually, people tend to act less selfish when neutral items surround them, whereas if work-related objects occupy them, they incline towards more aggression and selfishness.

7) Try to keep your point complicated and do not make it is straightforward for the people to understand in a first move. To comply with people with your request, confuse them. For example- instead of keeping a price tag of your product for 4 dollars, make it 400 pennies, so that people would first analyze how much dollars would 400 pennies make and if they bargain they will do that in pennies rather than in dollars. Or they may just think that the price given is a deal to go for.

8) If you help someone to achieve their goals or sort their problems out, the other person tends to return your favor, as they would feel obliged by what you have done for them. This way when the time comes, you may manipulate the other person and is one of the tactics.

9) Try to ask a question when one is mentally drained and exhausted.

10) Always make the other person focus on their gaining not losing. Moreover, declare the price of your product at last after telling all the features and benefits of your product. For instance, if you are selling your car in 1000 dollars, always let the other person know about its features, specifications, and benefits first. Then declare its price. The benefits will entice the customer towards the car, and then the price shall not be a constraint.

11) Do not use verbs; try to use more nouns to change the behavior of the other person towards you. If you use nouns, it will reinforce the identity of the person for whom you may be using it. It will also indicate a specific group which shall be eloquent.

How to Deal with Manipulation

Though manipulation does not cause any harm or put the subject in any immediate danger, it is designed to deceive and change the attitude, reasoning, and understanding of the intended subject regarding a particular situation or topic and is good to protect yourself and your loved ones against it.

Social influence, such as a teenager inducted into a culture or a society to interact with different people either at home or at work, is admirable. Any social influence that regards the privilege and right of individuals to decide, without been intimidated, is usually seen as something that is helpful.

Then again, social influence is despised when people beguile others to maneuver their way against other people's will. The impact can be very destructive and generally looked down upon as very weak in nature.

As soon as the victim of this seduction doesn't provide the thing that their seducer wants, the seducer is going to leave. So, if the victim starts to feel that they are being used and withholds sex from the seducer, the seducer will simply leave the relationship and move on to their next victim.

The seducer has no worries about the other partner in the relationship. A true seducer is only going to see the other person as a tool, something that helps the seducer get the pleasure that they want. As soon as that tool stops doing the job that it's supposed to, the seducer will move on to find a new person to do the work for them.

A dark seducer may move quickly between one relationship to the next, or they may even stay in a relationship for a long time. It all depends on the situation and how long the seducer is able to keep the victim under their control. Some victims stand up for themselves pretty quickly. The longer the victim is under the control of the dark seducer, the harder it is for them to leave.

This doesn't mean that the dark seducer has learned how to love their victim. It simply means that the dark seducer has become used to the way that things are, and they will use their powers and their mind controls techniques to keep the victim right where they are.

It is important for you to be aware of dark seduction. While some men may choose to use some ideas of dark seduction to help them gain some confidence, avoid some issues with their fear of rejection, and make it easier for them to meet women, there are many that will use these techniques because they don't really care about the other person at all. They have specific goals that they want to reach in the relationship, and they will get there, no matter who gets hurt in the process.

If you do end up getting into one of these relationships, it can be devastating. The dark manipulator is really skilled at using dark seduction techniques to get what they want. They will find a victim who is vulnerable, and they will present the right solution that the victim needs at that time. For example, they may find a victim who just got out of a major relationship, and they will step in to feel the need for that victim not to be lonely any longer.

The seducer is going to be charming, fun, and the perfect person for that victim. The victim may feel like they have found their soul mate, but the seducer is just there to get what they want out of the relationship. Sure it may last for some time, but as soon as the victim is no longer meeting the needs of the seducer, the seducer will be gone.

This will leave the victim hurt and broken. They may have overly trusted the seducer (because the seducer is skilled at reading the victim and knew exactly what to do and say to gain that trust and get what they want), and now they are broken. They may go through depression and anxiety and even have trouble trusting others in the future.

Because of all these negatives that come with dark seduction, it is important to watch out for the signs. If you run into dark seduction with a narcissist or with a psychopath, it is even more important to watch for the signs. These individuals are not there to care about what the other person wants. They simply look out for themselves, they feel that they deserve what they want, and they don't have the capacity to care about how it is going to harm the other person.

Due to the way that the relationship was started, including the romance, attraction, the mutual feeling that you found a soul mate (all created by the seducer to get what they want) when things start to take a lot of wrong turns, it is likely to be too late for you, the victim, to walk away. This can be especially true if you went into that particular picture without a good idea of what you wanted in the relationship. Without this clear picture, you would not have the determination to walk away from that relationship when it didn't meet your expectations.

This is why you must always make sure that you know what you want to get out of the relationship before one begins. This will help you be prepared if the relationship becomes something else because you will be able to see when it is going away from your chosen course. You will give yourself a chance to see it for what it is before you damage your self-worth so much where you will stay in that relationship and accept the bad treatment.

This can be hard. Many times we feel that we need a relationship like we are not worth anything unless we are in a relationship with someone else. Then, when we are not in a relationship, we are going to feel like something is missing, and we jump into the first relationship that comes available. This is where the issues will start.

Before you jump into the next relationship, it is important to take some time to soul search. Remember there is nothing wrong with not being in a relationship all the time. Taking some time for yourself and really exploring where you are at that time in your life, and what you would like to happen in your next relationship can make a difference.

This gives you a good idea of what kind of relationship you want to be in. You won't just jump into the next relationship because you are needy or because you worry about being alone. You will have specific goals in mind, and if you feel the relationship isn't going in the right direction, you will be able to step out before the dark seducer gets too deep and tries to take control over you.

The first thing that you should do here is to start with some deep thinking and even some soul-searching and decide on the details of the relationship that you are looking to enjoy at that time in your life. Describe what you want out of the other person in this partnership. Describe how you want to feel in this relationship. Set out some clear boundaries and then make sure that you understand why you have these boundaries.

Chapter 12 Tips and Tricks for Reading and Analyzing People

Now that we have had a chance to look at speed reading, and what it is all about, it is time to pay attention to some ways that we are able to use speed reading to help us pick out of the right target, work with the target in the proper manner, and ensure that we are going to be able to pick the right technique to use on them.

Speed reading isn't necessarily as hard to do as it may seem. We will often speed read those around us without even noticing. If you have ever ignored or stayed away from someone because you felt the anger and frustration from them, and you didn't want to get into it with them, then this is an example of how you used speed reading to see how that person was doing, and then protect yourself by avoiding them.

As a manipulator though, you need to take this up a notch. Your goal is to catch on to some things that may be hidden, the things that the target and others around you don't necessarily want to share, but they end up doing so through their emotions, their actions, and your own intuition. This is how you really start to know your target and can make it easier to manipulate them. Some tips, and techniques that you can focus on when it comes to speed reading your target, as well as speed reading some other people around you in all situations include:

Listen to What your Intuition is Telling You

Your intuition is going to be super important when it comes to working with a target. Sometimes you will find someone who may seem like the perfect target, but there is something about them that sends your intuition through the roof and you don't feel comfortable with it. It is much better to wait for the right target and listen to your intuition than to jump in and end up with too much work and trouble in the process.

Often our intuition is going to sense things and know things before our conscious mind is able to catch up. And if we learn how to follow it and listen to the warning that it is giving to us, we are going to see that some action is not the best for us to take. It may seem a bit silly and like we are missing out on a lot of opportunities out there, but in reality, it could save us a lot of work and effort in the process.

Now, your intuition can also come into play to help you avoid getting manipulated. Just because you are using dark manipulation and dark psychology does not mean that someone else is not trying to do the same thing to you or that you are immune to some effects. Assuming this is going to land you in a lot of issues and can make it difficult to get the results that you want with your own manipulation. How are you supposed to manipulate someone else and get them to do what you want if someone is already working on and manipulating you at the same time?

Listening to your intuition will not only help you to speed read another person and pick out of the right target to use for your needs but will ensure that no one else is going to take advantage of you. You will be able to sense when someone else is trying to use these tactics on you, especially when you are using them at the same time. So, listen to that intuition so that you can keep yourself safe in the process as well.

The final thing that we are going to take a look at here is the idea of the emotional energy from the target. This emotional energy is going to tell you a lot about that person and can help you to understand what they are feeling and how they are going to act. When someone is happier and upbeat, this usually means they have had a good day or some good news, and they are more likely to want to help you out and do a favor. But when they are down and not feeling the best it is likely that they will be more closed off and harder to work with to get to do what you want.

Now, someone in a different mood may not react in the same manner. They may not want to open up, if they are in a bad mood, they will think the world is out to get them and will be more frustrated when you do ask for a favor. Or they will get sad and want to close up to you. If you ask this kind of person for a favor or try to manipulate them, it is going to end up badly for you. The target is going to get upset, will refuse you, and it could end the relationship and the bond that you are trying to create.

This doesn't mean that you have to give up hope. But it helps you to stop and think about whether this is the right time to ask or favor or try to manipulate your target. But that doesn't mean that they won't be ready to manipulate later on. It simply means that you need to do some work first.

This may not open the door for your work right now, but it will later. The target is going to be thankful that you took the time to help them feel better about the situation, and they are going to remember that you made them laugh, made their day better, and helped them to get out of a sour mood. And later, when they are in a better mood and you need some help, they will be more willing to help you out without any issues along the way.

Speed reading people is a unique thing that you can add into your psychology plan and it could really take some of your manipulations to the next level. This method is going to ensure that you really know the person you want to target and will make it easier for you to find the right target, figure out how to manipulate them, and even learn when the right time to start some manipulations is.

Step by Step Tips for Reading Others

1. Create a drawing board for your mind

Human and behavior are so close like a living man is to his breath. However, you should expect so many diverse ways of practices from them. You could be on a public bus, and someone suddenly clears his throat. This means so many things, depending on the situation at the ground in the bus or an occurrence that just ending in the van. When this happens, you give yourself a guessable opinion of what that could mean, and that's the origin of understanding people.

Another person might scratch his beards, which most times might mean disapproval or a non-challenge attitude towards the discussion at hand. So, taking proper notice at everything around us goes a long way in understanding when people cross their legs, or suddenly squints or strokes their necks. People do these things and behave each time for different reasons, which indicate anger, nervousness, deception, or disapproval at times. Funny enough, a particular signal might mean a thousand things, so you would ask, how do I get the exact meaning? It's never far-fetched; all you need do is get a mental picture of the situation at hand. This way, the baseline or background check you've created between your opinion and the signal would match.

2. Check for consistencies

Paying close attention to the mental picture you've created in your mind and someone's words or gestures is a sure way to hit it right. How do I mean? You should always endeavor to update you about any sudden changes between the initial background check you've created for that person in question and what he now does. Inconsistency is the father for a foul play, so you should take note of this. Let me explain for a while, the head producer of your company has always been coming early to the workplace and leaving immediately after the close of the day's business.

Suddenly, you noticed that he has started going late all of a sudden, to you, what do you think is happening? This further takes you to other questions that what might have happened? Studying consistencies gives you a light to the status quo and when it finally changes form. You would notice his recent change in behavior is due to something you do not know, which you must confirm, and that forms the basis of knowing more. It also creates the ground onto which you question further, asking more questions into knowing the exact cause of such inconsistency.

3. Take note of gestures earlier

Remember, actions don't just occur, but with a corresponding meaning it stands to hold. Of course, there are possibilities of having a combination of gestures all at once, and you wonder what that means again. No big deal just take notice earlier and refer back to your background check and its relevance in the newly discovered gestures that just joined the old one. Studying someone's personality critically is a clear indication to relate to them without reservations, and it includes getting to know how the person in question handles risks, ego, challenges, fatigue, etc.

For example, if your head producer after leaving the workplace so early still gives another particular strange signal, don't you think you should watch his back? You would discover that when you probe people like that, he gives you another great message, and that's how the chain goes on and on. Just take note of precaution and better caution to deal with the situation.

4. Make a proper comparison

Its fine to notice the change in people's behaviors, but it's more beautiful to know what has changed and why it changed. You may have been studying someone for a while now due to his different way of acting than usual, but you need to get close. Make your observations key to ensure how recurrent the action takes place, the venue it takes place, and with whom it takes place. This art of studying gives you a clearer picture of who the person is, who he has been, and the thin line between the two.

Inquiring is the firsthand theory in bringing assumptions into better understanding, so it's essential to make a proper comparison so, you could act faster as you should. Does the person act differently when money is involved? Does the person relate well after confronting him with your observations? These, and many more questions would come to fore, and you begin to have a direction.

5. Identify the voice strength and walking posture

Due to the pressure associated with guilt, the most influential person isn't the one with a faint voice. The power of a voice determines if the person in question is at fault or not. However, you should know a loud sound is different from a confident and a strong one. So always take note of the sure voice in the crowd when issues arise, or you need to read people's minds through verbal communication. For example: In the case of the head producer, take note of his walking posture and how he does his head. With this, there is a high possibility of analyzing people that way successfully because his head down might mean he lacks the confidence to face his guilt.

Conclusion

The ability to influence others is a very helpful function. Influencers share a common collection of behaviors that ensure consistent performance. To influence their decisions, it is important to build a strong relationship with your peers.

Influencers find out the advantages of an idea and place a scenario or condition around it so that it has a considerable impact on the person—brand influencers themselves. Influencers aren't just advertisers, let's face the fact that they are one of the major businessmen and don't just create forums, as they have their websites. You don't just compete and sell because you could start your own business. They're just selling their titles. When you support another business or corporation, it's like you've watched the brand or organization's name.

Influencers explore other means of manipulating other and high levels of suppleness. For example, an influencer anticipates achieving a certain number of followers by the end of September, but the outcomes are far too far or have not reached the intended goal so that the influencer searches for and seeks to maximize his followers. Remember that a superbly agile influencer can always manipulate a scenario.

Robert Dale Goleman - Daniel Brandon Bradberry - Travis Greene Carnegie

EMOTIONAL INTELLIGENCE 2.0

TO LIVE A BETTER LIFE, FIND SUCCESS AT WORK AND CREATE HAPPIER RELATIONSHIPS, IMPROVE YOUR SOCIAL SKILLS, EMOTIONAL AGILITY, AND LEARN TO MANAGE AND INFLUENCE PEOPLE

JOSEPH GRIFFITH

Emotional Intelligence 2.0

*To live a better life, success at work and happier relationships.
Improve your social skills, emotional agility, manage and influence people*

© **Written by: JOSEPH GRIFFITH**

Book Description

Do you feel like you have been stuck in the same place for so long without making progress? Do you feel as though the decisions you have been making lately are all over the place? Do you wish to build stronger relationships, succeed at work and in school? Do you wish to achieve your career and personal growth?

Do you consider yourself emotional intelligence?

If not, then rest assured that you have come to the right place!

One thing that is important to bear in mind is that Emotional Intelligence plays a significant role in helping you recognize, manage, and understand your emotions and how they influence that of others. It is through emotional intelligence that you can fuel your performance – whether in your personal life, at home, or in the workplace.

Think of a place where your confidence, optimism, empathy, self-control, and social skills all work hand in hand to accelerate success in all areas of your life. Don't you want that?
In this book, you will learn;

- What Emotional Intelligence is
- The keys to Emotional intelligence
- How you can identify your emotions and those of others
- How to use your feelings to guide your thinking and reasoning
- Understanding how feelings change and develop with the unfolding of events
- Managing to open your arms to the data of feelings and using that in making informed choices for successSo, what are you still waiting for?

It is time to sharpen your intuitions and position yourself for success and a better life.

Come with me!

Introduction

You probably have heard of Emotional intelligence at home, school, or in the workplace. This concept continues to grow in popularity, especially in a brain-dead world where people strive to achieve success but don't know how to tap into their emotional feelings to realize their goals.

You may be thinking, "Why is emotional intelligence growing in importance among peers in an evolving workplace or overall life?"

One thing that is important to bear in mind is that emotional intelligence is not a trend! It is here to stay. According to reports and statistics compiled by major companies across the world, it is evident that people with emotional intelligence undoubtedly affect their bottom line. For instance, if an employee has a high level of emotional intelligence, they will not only be productive and generate revenue for the company, but also realize their personal and career goals.

Look around you – are there people you know – whether at home or the workplace – with high emotional intelligence? Do you know people who are really good listeners? Irrespective of the circumstances, they can communicate well. It is almost like they know exactly what to say when to say it and how to say it so that others are not offended. These people are caring, considerate, and can find solutions for problems. When you approach them for guidance, they leave you feeling optimistic and more hopeful in life.

You probably know other people who have mastered the art of managing their emotions. Instead of getting angry when provoked by a stressful situation, they choose to look at the problem from a different perspective to find a solution calmly. These people are excellent decision-makers and have mastered the art of listening to their gut feeling. Irrespective of their strengths, they have the willingness to look at themselves with an honest eye. They take criticism positively and use it to improve their performance.

It is such kind of people that we wish that we can be like them.

What sets them apart is nothing other than a high degree of emotional intelligence. You can have that too. You can learn how to manage your emotions in every situation while ensuring that you take care of the emotional needs of the people around you.

You may be thinking, "I can never be like this. I don't have what it takes to be like these people."

Well, I am here to tell you that you can be just like these people. As you begin to accept emotional intelligence into every area of your life, you will begin to see an improvement in your technical abilities, interrelationships, and overall success. It is through emotional intelligence that you can fuel your performance. It impacts your confidence, optimism, self-control, empathy, and social skills so that you can understand and manage your emotions and accelerate success in every area of your life.

It does not matter what your profession is, whether you work for a small or large organization, whether you are a senior or junior in your company. What matters is that realizing how effective you are at controlling your emotional energies is the beginning of a successful adventure. Yes, emotional intelligence may not be something taught and tested in our educational curriculum, but the truth is that it is really important.

The good news is that it is something you and I can learn, hence the reason why we have compiled a book with all the tips that will help you improve your emotional intelligence skills and implement them in everyday life. Our clients have given us positive feedback on how these skills have not only helped them advance in life, but also helped them motivate and inspire others to be better.

In short, emotional intelligence is what helps you identify your emotions, manage them effectively, and constructively react to others' emotions. When you understand how those emotions shape your thoughts and actions, you gain better control of your behavior and establish a new skill set that will help you to effectively manage your emotions. When you are emotionally conscious, you position yourself for growth and a deeper understanding of who you truly are. This way, you can communicate better with the people around you and strengthen your relationships.

To get you started, you must discover the foundation of your emotional intelligence. The best way to do that is to;

Practice observing your feelings

Take a look at your life – the chances are that you will notice how hectic and busy your lifestyle is. It is this kind of life that makes it easy for you to lose touch with yourself and your emotional feelings. You must try to reconnect with your feelings by setting a timer for various points throughout the day. As soon as the timer goes off, you stop what you are doing, stand on your two feet, and take in a deep breath. Then bring your thoughts to what you are feeling in that moment, where the emotions are coming from, and where you feel the sensation in your body and what it feels like. Realize that the more you practice this, the more you make it your second nature.

Pay attention to how you act

As you practice self-awareness, you must pay attention to how you act and carry yourself in different situations. When you experience a certain emotion, observe what actions are like and how they affect your daily activities. Soon, you will realize that managing your emotional feelings comes easily, and your reactions become more conscious.

Question your opinion

We all live in a hyper-connected world that makes it easy to fall into a "bubble of opinions." In other words, you find yourself in a state of existence where your opinions are reinforced by others all the time. The last thing you want is for your voice to be completely lost because you are always flowing with the whims of life and what others decide for you.

You must take time to assess both sides of the story and bring your views forward with confidence. It does not matter what people think of you and your opinions. What matters the most is that you are willing to get your opinions challenged even when you feel that you are right. This way, you gain a better understanding of others and become more receptive to their ideas.

Be responsible for your emotional feelings

The first thing about responsibility is accepting the fact that your emotions and actions come from you. It does not matter what the situation or circumstances are like because no one tells you to react the way you do. No one tells you to feel what you feel. When you accept the responsibility of your feelings and actions, you begin to impact your life positively.

Celebrate the positives in your life

The key to emotional intelligence is to celebrate and reflect on all the positives in your life. No one has a perfect life – we all go through ups and downs. It does not matter whether you have more positives or negatives in your life. The trick to celebrate every win – whether small or big. When you embrace the positives in your life, you allow yourself to develop more resilience and increase your chances of enjoying fulfilling relationships so that you can successfully move past adversity.

Don't ignore the negatives

Just because you have chosen to embrace and celebrate the positives in your life does not mean that you ignore the negatives. You must take time to reflect on all the negative feelings you might have, just as you would the positive feelings. This will help you understand the root cause of these negative feelings so that you can master how to control them and become an all-rounded individual.

Breathe

No matter what life throws your way, you must not forget to take time to just breathe. Taking time to take deep breaths will not only help you master how to manage your emotions but also help you avoid outbursts. Just walk out the door and wash your face with cold water, take a walk, or just take in the fresh air – anything to calm your nerves. This goes a long way in helping you get a hold of what is happening so that you can effectively respond to the situation.

That said, emotional intelligence is a lifetime process! It is not something you develop overnight. The truth is that to grow your emotional intelligence; you have to train your mind to accept continual improvements along the way – so that you can be better with each passing day.

Chapter 1 What is emotional intelligence, and why is it important?

Most people don't know what emotional intelligence is, even if it is something we should have in our lives. Well, emotional intelligence simply refers to the ability to identify our emotional feelings and manage them, and that of the people around us.

Emotional intelligence generally involves three key skills;

- Emotional awareness – the ability to identify your emotional feelings and name them
- Ability to harness our emotional feelings and apply them into problem-solving, thinking and reasoning
- Ability to manage our emotional feelings, which includes regulating them where necessary and helping the people around us to do the same

Unlike the general intelligence that has a psychometric test or scale, emotional intelligence does not have one. This is the reason several people think of emotional intelligence not as an actual construct but instead as an interpersonal skill. However, despite all the criticism, emotional intelligence is sometimes referred to the as emotional quotient.

Today, several companies have included emotional intelligence tests into their application and interview processes mainly because they think a high emotional intelligence makes one a good coworker or leader.

While there are research studies that have demonstrated a link between emotional intelligence and job performance, there are others that show no correlation. The lack of a scientifically valid scale to measure emotional intelligence makes is challenging for one to accurately measure or predict one's emotional intelligence, whether at home or in the workplace.

So, what does it mean to be emotionally intelligent?

Well, someone who is emotionally intelligent is one who is highly conscious of their emotional states, whether negative – sad, frustrated – or positive – happy and subtle. If you can identify your emotional feelings and manage them effectively irrespective of the situation you are in, then the chances are that you have emotional intelligence. For you to be termed emotionally intelligent, you must demonstrate that you are tuned to the emotions others are experiencing. When you can sense and understand what other people are going through, you become a better friend, parent, partner, or leader. And the good thing is that you can hone these skills easily with the tips we will give you in this book.

That said, when emotional intelligence was first introduced to the masses, it played a role in uniquely filling the missing link: people with average IQ outperform those with a high IQ. It is because of this anomaly that a massive wrench was thrown into what most people assumed that IQ was the only source of success.

Now, lots of research studies point to emotional intelligence as a central factor in differentiating between high performers and the rest of the pack. This correlation is so strong that over 90% of the top performers are said to have high emotional intelligence.

In other words, emotional intelligence is the intangible thing each one of us has and influences how we behave, handle social complexities, and make decisions to achieve success.

Despite the significance EQ has on our lives, the truth is that its intangible nature makes it hard for us to know how much of it we have and what it is that we can do to improve it if we lack it.

So, how then can you tell when you have emotional intelligence?

Robust emotional vocabulary

We all experience emotional feelings of different kinds, but the truth is that we don't handle them the same way. There are only a few people who can accurately identify their emotions as they happen. Research demonstrates that at least 36% of people can identify their emotions as soon as they occur. This is such a huge problem because it means a large number of individuals are unable to label their emotional feelings – hence contributing to misunderstanding. This explains why people end up making irrational decisions and counterproductive behaviors.

When you have a high EQ, you will not only master your emotions but also understand them and use a vast vocabulary of feelings to do that. While there are times when someone says that they feel "bad," the truth is that emotional intelligence allows one to specifically pinpoint their emotions as either irritable, downtrodden, frustrated, or anxious. In other words, when your word choice is specific, you gain a deeper insight into precisely what you are feeling, its origin, and what you must do to overcome them.

Curiosity about people

It does not matter whether you are an introvert or an extrovert because if you are emotionally intelligent, you will demonstrate curiosity about the people around you. It is through this kind of curiosity that you can demonstrate empathy – a significant gateway to a high EQ. The more you show someone that you care about them and what they are experiencing, the more you will be curious about them.

You embrace change

If you are emotionally intelligent, then you have the flexibility and ability to constantly adapt to change. You will know that fear of change is the reason why you will remain paralyzed and is a major threat to your happiness and success in life. You must look for the change that is lurking around you and then form a plan of action in case these changes happen.

You know your strengths and weaknesses

When you are emotionally intelligent, you will not only understand emotions but also know what you are good at and what you are terrible at. You will know who and what pushes your buttons within your surroundings so that you can position yourself better to achieve success. Having a high emotional intelligence simply means that you can lean on your strengths and leverage them to realize your potential while raising your awareness of your weak points so that they don't hold you back from reaching your fullest potential.

You are a good judge of character

Did you know that much of emotional intelligence build down to social awareness? This is simply your ability to read people, know what they are all about, and gain a deeper insight into what they are going through. With time, this skill goes a long way in helping you become an exceptional judge of character so that others don't become a mystery to you. It allows you to know what makes them tick, understand the things that motivate them, and the things they try to hide beneath the surface.

You are hard to offend

Having a strong grasp of who you make it hard for others to get under your skin. If you are emotionally intelligent, you simply are self-confident and have an open mind – the two factors that help you develop a pretty thick skin. The truth is, you can even poke fun on yourself or let other people make jokes about you because you can draw a mental line between humor and degradation.

Letting go of mistakes

If you are emotionally intelligent, then you know better than to ruminate on your past mistakes. You can distance yourself from your undoing without necessarily forgetting them. When you keep your mistakes at a safe distance but handy enough to refer to them when the need arises, you position yourself to future challenges and achieve success.

Well, no one said that this was going to be a walk in the park. The truth is that to walk this tightrope between remembering and ruminating, you must have a refined self-awareness. When you ruminate on your past mistakes, you set yourself up for anxiety and becoming gun shy. On the other hand, forgetting all about your past mistakes makes it easy for you to repeat them again in the future.

The key to balancing these is to learn how to transform your failures into nuggets of improvement. This way, you create a tendency to bounce back up each time you fall.

Don't hold grudges

Did you know that when you hold on to grudges, you activate negative emotions as a stress response? Well, each time you think about an unpleasant past event, the body sets into a fight-or-flight mode as a way of surviving. This forces you to get up to either fight or run away for the hills whenever you are faced with a threat.

The truth is, when the threat is imminent, this reaction is essential for your survival. However, when the threat is something that lies in ancient history, holding on to it will only wreak havoc on your body and negatively affect your health with time. According to research studies at Emory University, findings demonstrate that holding on to grudges tends to elevate our blood pressure and heart disease.

In short, when you hold onto a grudge, you are choosing to hold on to stress. And if you are emotionally intelligent, then you know to keep off this tendency at all costs. When you let go of a grudge, it is not a sign of weakness. Instead, it makes you feel better and sets you up for improved health and overall wellbeing.

Neutralizes toxic people

Dealing with difficult people is not only frustrating but also energy draining. With high emotional intelligence, you are in a better position to control your interactions with toxic people by ensuring that you can keep your emotions in check. When you must confront a toxic person, you know the importance of approaching them rationally.

In other words, you can identify your emotions and ensure that your anger of frustrations does not get the best of you into fueling chaos.

You also know that the other person has a standpoint and that if you can listen to where they are coming from, you all agree on it common ground and find a lasting solution. Even when things are completely derailing, people with high emotional intelligence can take toxic people with a grain of salt to ensure that they don't let themselves be brought down.

Don't seek perfection

Emotionally intelligent people don't set perfection as a target because they know well that perfection does not exist. The truth is, we are all human, and that fact alone makes us fallible. When you make perfection a goal, then the truth is that you are setting yourself up for a nagging feeling of failure that only makes you want to give up or lower your efforts.

In other words, you end up spending much of your time complaining about your failures and what it is that you could have done differently instead of moving forward. Emotional intelligence allows you to view failure as a lesson to improve yourself without forgetting to celebrate every small achievement you have accomplished so that you can stay motivated to accomplish more in your future.

You disconnect

When you can take regular breaks off the grid, this indicates high emotional intelligence. This is mainly because taking time off to reflect on yourself is one of the best ways to keep off stress and ensure that you have things under control so that you can live in the moment. Making yourself available 24/7 sets you up for constant baggage of stressors.

You must force yourself to go offline from time to time to just breathe and do nothing! When you turn off your gadgets and just focus on yourself, you allow your mind and body to take a break. According to research, taking a break from technology – something as simple as reading emails – can lower stress levels. Through technology, we can constantly communicate and expect that you are available round the clock. This makes it difficult for you to enjoy a stress-free moment away from the busyness in everyday life. When you take breaks, you allow yourself to have a change in your train of thought and relax without worrying about when you will have work drop onto your phone.

Limit caffeine intake

When you are constantly taking caffeine, you trigger the release of adrenaline – a source of the fight-or-flight response. It is this mechanism that makes it easy for on to sidestep rational thinking in favor of something fast for their survival.

Well, one thing you must understand is that this kind of survival mechanism is brilliant if a bear is chasing you. However, this is not something you need when responding to a court of emails. Taking too much caffeine throughout the day keeps your body in a hyper-aroused state of stress constantly such that your emotions begin to overrun your actions. With high emotional intelligence, you know that caffeine is not good for you and avoid allowing it to get the best of you.

Get enough sleep

It is hard to overemphasize the importance of sleep to boosting your emotional intelligence and helping you manage your stress levels. Getting enough sleep every day plays a significant role in ensuring that you give the brain the time it needs to recharge, shuffle through the day's memories, storing them, and discarding anything that is not good for you. This ensures that once you get up, your brain is not only alert but ready to get set go!

People with high emotional intelligence understand that their self-control, memory, and attention are reduced when they are sleep-deprived. Therefore, ensure that you make sleep your top priority, henceforth!

Stop negative self-talk in its tracks

Are you allowing negative self-talk to hold you back from reaching your fullest potential? One thing you must bear in mind is that when you ruminate on negative thoughts, you give away your power to them. The trick is whenever you have negative thoughts come to your mind, ask yourself whether they are facts or not.

When you feel as though something always happens or never happens, realize that this is the brain's way of perceiving a threat. Emotionally intelligent people can separate their thoughts from facts so that they can escape the cycle of negativity, gain a new outlook of life, and push forward with optimism and positivity.

Won't allow anyone limits your joy

Do you let other people's opinions deprive your sense of pleasure and satisfaction? If you do, then you must realize that you are no longer the master of your happiness. Being emotionally intelligent means that whenever you feel good about something you have done, you will not let anyone's opinions or remarks take that good feeling away from you.

Yes, it may be hard to switch off your reactions to what they say or think of you. However, you don't have to compare yourself to them. The trick is to take their opinion with a grain of salt. This way, no matter what others think, do or say about you, you allow your self-worth to rise from within you and take control of your thought process and actions.

That said, unlike IQ, you must note that emotional intelligence is malleable. As you train your mind to repeatedly practice new, emotionally intelligent behaviors, this promotes the growth of new pathways that make them into habits. Your brain will start reinforcing the use of these behaviors, their connection to the old and destructive behaviors to die off. Before you know it, you start responding to your environment with emotional intelligence without thinking about it.

Importance of emotional intelligence

There are several benefits that emotional intelligence has to offer – most of which we will discuss in detail in the coming chapters. That said, emotional intelligence plays a key role in leading us on the path to a fulfilled and happy life. This is mainly by offering us a framework through which we can apply standards of intelligence to our emotional responses and understanding these responses to ensure that they are logically consistent with our belief systems.

With the ever-changing workplaces and the body of research, we must master the art of emotional intelligence so that we can work with others cohesively as a team, respond and adapt to change effectively, and manage stress so that we can pursue our business objectives successfully. When you work on improving your emotional intelligence, you set yourself up for personal happiness, professional success, and overall well being.

Chapter 2 The Four Attributes of Emotional Intelligence

Self-management

You may be wondering what self-management has to do with your emotional intelligence. Well, one thing that is important to bear in mind is that self-management involves using what you know about your feelings so that you can manage them in such a way that they can generate positive interactions with the people around you. You want your emotions to motivate you in all situations. When you acknowledge that you have negative emotions, you position yourself to be in control of your actions.

Think about it for a moment – if you are a manager at your workplace, do you think people would want to work with you if you don't have control over yourself and the way you react to situations? Trust me; no one wants to work – much less interact – with someone whose actions are informed by their prevailing mood. Achieving results by bullying and shouting at others is something of the past. It is something that has no place in the modern world where people are aware of their rights, and employment tribunals are there to ensure that workers are treated ways inhumanely.

I am not saying that self-management means that you can never be angry. We all go through situations that get on our nerves sometimes, and it is perfectly reasonable to be angry. However, the key to being emotionally intelligent is ensuring that you are in control of your feelings and can channel them into problem resolution.

Some people have a strong tendency to overstate the negative aspects of a given situation in their minds. If you are one of them, you must apply the reflective cycle in such situations so that you can have a realistic view of what is happening and what you can do to yield the desired outcome.

To engage your emotional intelligence, you must use your feelings in such a way that you can make constructive decisions about your actions. When you get stressed, it is easy to lose control of your emotions. It is easy to lose the ability to act appropriately and thoughtfully. To put this into perspective, take a minute to think back to a time when you were stressed and overwhelmed. Was it easy to think with clarity? Did you make rational decisions at that moment?

Probably, not!

When you are stressed out and overwhelmed, the ability to think clearly and to assess your emotions accurately tends to be compromised. The truth is, emotions are bits and pieces of information that tell you about yourself and the people around you. However, in the face of stress and threat, they seem to take us out of our comfort zones, and we easily lose control of our abilities and ourselves.

Self-management ensures that you not only manage stress but also stay emotionally present in every situation so that your emotions don't override your thoughts and self-control. It allows you to make informed choices that ensure that you stay on top of the situation, control impulsive emotions, actions, and healthily manage them. It allows you to take the initiative, commit to the things that matter most in your life, follow through on these commitments, and adapt to changing circumstances.

Three steps of self-management

Step 1 Identify what you are feeling

Most of the time, when you miss a meeting, missed a deliverable, have an easiness about your spouse, or long-term sentiments that something is wrong within your surroundings, it is important that you identify that emotion. Is it anger, sadness, anxiety, or frustration? Whatever your starting point is, you must learn how to exercise your self-awareness before you do something about it.

Step 2 Determine the underlying cause

This is often a very challenging step because you need to assess, reflect, and honestly find out the root cause of your emotional feelings. Are you resentful of your boss because they told you that you missed the targets? Is it your spouse you suspect is having an affair and is making you feel sad, disappointed, or frustrated? Find the root cause of your emotions.

Step 3 Act

Once you know what emotions you are feeling and where they are coming from, the next thing is for you to act. There is always something you can do to break out of the cycle of negative emotions. It can be something as simple as recognizing the emotions you have are unjustified or misplaced, or that you are directing them at the wrong person.

When you recognize the truth behind your emotional feelings, you gain better control over them so that you can manage them even when you are angry or stressed out. Don't get me wrong – I am not saying that you should pretend as if these emotions are non-existent and just dismiss them. No, you must accept that they are there and be willing to manage them.

When you master the art of self-management, you set yourself up to think logically about every situation and determine various ways you can handle them. This way, you diminish the anger and fear you have so that your level of emotional intelligence rises above normal.

One thing you must bear in mind is that your team will always be looking up to you for cues on what the right behaviors are and what is and what is not acceptable. If you demonstrate an inability to control your own emotions, then you are simply telling them that there is no reason to control theirs. It is this lack of self-discipline that encourages people to ape undesirable habits – what Goleman refers to as "emotional hijacking." In other words, you allow your mind to be taken by your primitive emotions hence standing in the way of you making a realistic and objective assessment of the situation.

The truth is that these emotional breakdowns are building up gradually and involuntarily – the symptoms of which are often overlooked. When you are frequently being bullied and feel unsupported, your behavior may eventually result in negative consequences. However, when you make an honest evaluation of your actions and that of the people around you, you will not only identify what the problem is but also find possible solutions to the problem before it gets out of hand.

In other words, the key to developing your emotional intelligence self-management is conducting an honest appraisal of your behaviors. Once you identify a negative form of behavior, you can work on eradicating or controlling it.

Think about it, do you often allow others' moods and attitudes to affect you? Are there times when you or any other member of your family/team has been influenced in this manner?

If so, then it is high time you made a conscious effort of insulating yourself so that you can be objective when assessing the situation. Only a handful of people can have this kind of effect on you, and you must know who they are. It could be because you have a personal relationship with that person that, in a way, is more profound than a usual working relationship. It could be someone you respect, closely identify with, or admire.

The point is that you raise your awareness of the fact that they influence your emotions. Knowing that they exist plays a significant role in minimizing the negative influence their emotions might have on you, embracing who you are so that you can learn why their moods and attitudes affect you. When you have this knowledge, you can make a conscious effort to neutralize these negative emotions.

Tips to improve your self-management skills

- Breathe
- Differentiate between emotions and reason
- Share your goals with someone important in your life – a mentor or a spouse
- Count from one to ten
- Sleep on it
- Talk to someone you trust
- Laugh it out

- Think about it
- Talk to yourself better
- Visualize it
- Get enough sleep
- Get your body language in check
- Workout
- Control what you can and relinquish control over what you can't

What did Steve Jobs do when someone in the audience publicly attacked him during the Apple Developer Conference? Well, returning to his company after a decade of being away, Steve Jobs was publicly attacked by someone, and do you know how he responded? He used some of the self-management tactics we have discussed here.

The first thing was that he paused for a couple of seconds before saying a word. He may or may not have counted to 10, but he paused and took in a deep breath. This allowed him time to compose himself, get a realistic perspective of the situation before he could say anything. He then took a sip of water and said: *"You know, you can please some of the people some of the time, but ..."*

Just doing that allowed his mind to change to a positive mindset. He then took another long pause – possibly to gather his thoughts on what to say next. You can do the same – be aware of your emotions and adequately manage your emotions. It is not about what other people say or think about you that matters; it is how you respond to their thoughts, actions, and words that count!

Self-awareness

Emotional self-awareness is the second element of emotional intelligence. It refers to one's ability to understand their emotions and how they affect their performances. Think about it what you are currently going through, what do you feel about it, why are you feeling that way? How is it helping or hurting what you are trying to achieve?

Self-awareness is also about how others see you and how you can align your self-image with the bigger picture. It is about having a clear sense of your strengths and weaknesses, something that gives you a realistic sense of self-confidence. It is also something that offers you clarity of what your values and purpose so that you become more decisive when you set your course of action. As a leader, you can get candid and authentic, speak with conviction about your vision.

Let us consider the following example where a chief tech officer at a company is bullying their colleagues without knowing it. The thing is that this officer is good at what they do, but they suck at managing others. Often, they would play favorites, tell people what to do, and do not seem to listen to what they have to say. Anyone he doesn't like is shut out. When confronted about their behavior, they quickly deny and blames other people or turns back to you, saying that you are the problem.

What do you think about this tech officer?

Well, they lack emotional self-awareness.

According to research, a boss who is arrogant, stubborn, and a bully is often considered by their subordinates as being incompetent. These character traits have been shown to have a strong correlation with poor financial results, poor management of talent, and a lack of motivation/inspiration to the junior colleagues. Generally, they are a poor team leader.

One study conducted by Korn Ferry Han Group reported that among leaders with several strengths in emotional self-awareness, at least 92% have teams with high energy and performance. In other words, when you are a great leader, you tend to create a positive emotional climate that stirs motivation and extra effort among employees – and this is because of a good emotional self-awareness. On the other hand, leaders with low self-awareness were reported to create at least 78% of a negative work climate.

That said, what you must bear in mind is that emotional self-awareness is not something that you can achieve at one go and be done with it. Instead, it is a trait that you have to keep nurturing every opportunity you get. It is a continual endeavor and a conscious choice you make to be self-aware. The good thing is that the more you practice, the more it gets ingrained in you and becomes natural. In short, being self-aware is simply checking in with your sensory experience regularly to allow a positive shift in behavior.

The very first step to building your emotional intelligence is to raise your awareness about your emotions. What you are currently feeling is often a mirror of what you experienced during your early life. The ability to manage core emotions – such as anger, fear, joy, and sadness – all depend on your consistency and quality of early life's emotional experiences. If your primary caretaker, as a little child, valued and understood your feelings, there is a high likelihood that your emotions are a great asset in your adult life. However, if the vice versa happened, there is a chance that you will try to run away or hide from your emotions.

Take a minute to reflect on the following questions;

- Do you experience emotional feelings that flow and change from one moment to the next?
- Are your emotional feelings accompanied by strong physical sensations – such as chest pains, stomach cramps, or throat blockage?
- Do you experience individual feelings and emotions, and do they show on your facial expressions?
- Can you experience intense feelings strong enough to capture your attention and that of others?
- Do you pay close attention to your emotional feelings, and do they inform your decision-making?

If any of these experiences don't ring a bell, then the chances are that you turned off or tuned down your emotions. If you are going to build your emotional intelligence and become emotionally stable and healthy, it is important that you connect with your core feelings, embrace them, and get comfortable with them. The only way you are going to achieve this is by practicing mindfulness.

In other words, being mindful is choosing to purposely focus your attention on the present moment without judging. When you are mindful of what you are doing at that very moment, it helps you shift your attention and thoughts towards what you are doing at that moment so that you can appreciate the bigger picture. It can calm and focus your mind so that you are more self-aware of your surroundings.

Tips on how to improve your self-awareness

Get out of your comfort zone

You might have heard the saying, "magic happens outside the comfort zone!" Well, that is also true for emotions. If you look around your life, you will notice that there are several instances where you run away from your emotional feelings – and you are not alone. However, one thing you must realize is that this is not a long-term plan. You must allow your feelings to surface and offer the information it carries.

Instead of trying to shove you're emotional away or running from them, you must learn how to guide yourself to it and through it. You cannot ignore what you are feeling because if you do, you are not doing yourself any good because they will only disappear at that moment and resurface later.

Realize that getting out of your comfort zone is not all that bad. If you are going to expand your frontiers, you have to develop the willingness to do things that might make you uncomfortable. Trust me, with practice; you will start enjoying all the fruits of your labor.

Identify your triggers

Think of a trigger as anything – a substance, situation, person, or condition – that makes you emotional and prompts you to act in a certain way. For instance, you may have a manager that feeds on others' energy like a vampire, and that makes you angry. It could be a noisy surrounding with your colleagues gossiping and laughing loudly over the phone when you need to concentrate on some work. It could be a colleague that lacks effective communication or people management skills

Whatever it is, most people typically respond by shutting down. If this is something that happens to you in a place where emotional outbursts are considered a taboo, realize that enclosing those emotional feelings inside will do you no good. This is because your body language will be screaming, and someone keen enough will notice that.

When you learn to identify your triggers, you are setting yourself up for improved emotional intelligence. This is because you begin to learn how to develop the ability to control the outcome of your actions. You will learn how to calm down, take charge of your actions, and keep your presence of spirit. To do that, you must identify the specific cases and begin generalizing from there. When you have a deeper understanding of what pushes your buttons, the situations become more manageable because the emotions you experience will not come as a surprise to you anymore.

It is also important that you go all the way to identifying the root cause of your triggers. In other words, you are finding out exactly why those people or situations get on your nerves. Why do you think a noisy surrounding triggers agitation or irritation? Is it because you are more skilled in reading and writing than you are in listening and talking? Or maybe they hate you have for your manager is because they remind you of a past manager who bullied you at the workplace? When you identify that your reactions are channeled to the wrong person, you might be able to get along with people better.

Don't judge your feelings

Feelings are like waves of the ocean; they come and go. The truth is that they are just what they are – feelings- nothing more nothing less! Trying to label your feelings as either "good" or "bad" or as "positive" or "negative" will only cause you to lose your ability to recognize them and raise your awareness of them. It is human nature to want to judge everything that comes their way and then separate them into two large boxes. The truth is that doing this will only make things counterproductive.

The thing is, everything that you regard as a "bad or negative" feeling will automatically be something you want to avoid at all costs. The truth is that there is some shame that comes with feeling bad or having negative feelings. On the other hand, when you have positive or good feelings, you want them to linger, and you may even see the need to reward yourself for having them. The problem is that you let them run wild, which eventually drains you of your energy.

The thing is, whether the feeling is good or bad, or positive or negative, they carry certain information. You either feel content because you have achieved something, frustrated because the reality is different from what you expected, or sad because you lost something.

However, if you allow your emotions to come and go just as they are – without judgment – then you might just have the opportunity to understand what they are and what the mind is trying to communicate. In other words, your emotions will just run their course and vanish without trying to control you.

Don't make decisions in a bad mood

There are times in life when we feel as though everything else is moving in the wrong direction. Whether you call this bad luck, feeling down, or depression, the truth is that you cannot feel anything right because there is a black veil that clouds your thoughts.

The problem is that once the bad mood takes charge of your brain, it is easy to lose sight of the good things happening in our lives. You start to feel like you hate where you live, where you work, what you do, and the people around you irritate you. Even though you know deep inside that what you think and feel is not true, you can't seem to get rid of these thoughts and emotions.

One thing you must bear in mind is that emotional intelligence, through self-awareness, helps us to take note of the situation and accept it just as it is. And you need to be okay with that knowing that there is little to nothing you can do to change it. The trick is to wait it out – with time; it will just pass. In other words, try to postpone making any life-changing decisions at this point, at least until you are out of this zone!

Don't make decisions in a good mood either

This is the other side of the equilibrium where you don't want to make major decisions just because you are feeling good – happy, ecstatic, or excited about something. Think about it, when you are walking down the streets and meet a salesman, they try to get you excited about what they are selling to the point that you lose control of your mind. This happens such that when they offer you their merchandise, they get you to feel good about having it that you end up paying more for something that is not even worth it.

Don't get me wrong – I am not saying that feeling good is a bad thing. The point is, you must beware of your good moods just as much as you are of bad ones.

Get to the birds-eye view

Have you ever heard someone tell you that you are "above things?" well, this is something applicable to emotional intelligence as well. Take a minute to imagine yourself rise above your personality such that you can watch yourself from above. Think of yourself soaring high like an eagle and then watching yourself from high up there – getting a bigger view of yourself from an observer's eye. How many things do you think you will see and understand about yourself?

While you may not look at yourself from above, the truth is that taking on an observer's view of yourself might just be what you need to understand your behavior. It will allow you to be aware of your thoughts and emotions in every situation you go through in life. You must try injecting yourself with the trigger and reaction so that you can process the whole information and get a new perspective of things. The aim here is to constantly remind yourself of the real emotional feelings underneath all the layers.

Revisit your values and actions accordingly

From where I stand, life is pretty much dynamic. The kind of work we do every day is hard, and our families are very much demanding. Even in the midst of all that, it is important that you set aside time to learn something new, have fun, and be at peace. Engage in activities that give you these things – such as playing sports with your kids, watching your favorite TV series, responding to emails, and making phone calls to friends and family. All these activities are enough to fill your day. However, these things are also the reason why your focus is on the outside when you should look at what lies inside you.

One thing that must bear in mind is that all these things on your to-do list can be overwhelming and draining of all the energy you have left. The trick is to stop and review your values and actions.

Take time to ask yourself whether your career is moving in the right direction if your job requires you to do things you are not comfortable with, if your colleagues treat you right, whether you have enough time for the things that matter most in your life, or if your current path leads you where you would like to be in a couple of years.

All these things are not there to scare you about the present and the future, but instead to help you evaluate your values, trust, responsibilities, and determine whether they are sustainable. The goal is how you wish to change the world and make it a better place for you and your family.

Check yourself

It is important to understand that self-awareness is mostly an internal process and that there are external implications of what happens inside you. This is why you must learn to get in the habit of examining yourself regularly to ensure that everything is okay.

Think about how your face looks like, whether your eyes look swollen, if your makeup is done right, what about your clothes, do they fit well? Are you beginning to wrinkle? Is your working space tidy? Do you assume the right posture when working? Do you communicate with confidence? When walking, do you take long steps?

The trick is to ensure that you are aware of your normal self and alert to the times when you feel stressed. Realize that everything changes, and when you are aware of the things happening in and around you, it becomes easy to pick out stress factors fast enough before they can reach your conscious mind.

Fill your blind spot with feedback

You must remember the windows of knowledge – which simply refers to the intimate parts of you that no one else knows about. Each one of us has three parts. What most of us are aware of are the private and the public parts of ourselves. However, what we fail to recognize is that blind spot – the part that we do not see.

The truth is, your view of self cannot be impartial, but other people can see what you truly are. The question is, are you willing to seek others' help? You must talk to someone you trust – spouse, partner, parent, or friend – to give you feedback about yourself. Ensure that you observe the rule of communication – when you ask for feedback, you should listen more than you talk. You must open your heart to the truth, and instead of trying to get defensive, let the people closest to you tell you their observations truthfully without trying to hold them back.

That said, one of the foundations of emotional intelligence is self-awareness. It is through self-awareness that you can learn how to spot your emotions, the root cause of these emotions, and your reaction to them. With time, you will learn how to master the control of them so that you can use them to serve your mind and its true purpose.

The last thing you want is to go through the motions of life without really paying attention to your emotional feelings. You don't want to completely ignore your feelings or allow them to control you and get the best of you. Realize that emotions are powerful forces that do either work miracles in your life or ruin your life completely. By mastering the art of self-awareness, you can finally take back the control of your life into your hands and steer it in the direction you desire to go.

Social awareness

It is one thing to recognize and understand your emotional feelings. Still, it is quite another to accurately pick up and understand others' emotions and what they are going through. If you are going to improve your emotional intelligence, you must be willing to suspend what you like so that you can practice social awareness. You have to stop talking, running monologues in your head, anticipating another person's answers before they can even utter a word, and trying to create answers when someone is speaking.

In other words, social awareness requires that you shift your focus from self to look outwardly towards others, learn about them, and appreciate them. Social awareness is all about being grounded on our ability to recognize not only others' emotions but also understand them. While we may be tempted to focus only on our emotions, that luxury is not there if you are going to work in an environment where you are not the only one that exists in it.

Realize that when you tune your emotions to other people, you allow yourself to pick up on vital cues to what is happening with them. This way, you can read the room and measure your response to ensure that it is connected to the person you are directing it to.

How can you do that?

Ensure that the lens you are looking through is clear

This simply means that you must be present and willing to give others your undivided attention. You must brace yourself to take up the role of an observer by using your five basic senses and realize that your sixth sense is your emotions.

Note that your emotions are important lenses for the brain and are what helps you interpret the cues from others. Ensure that you are mindful enough not to over project your emotions on others. Instead, use them as spider senses to stay alert and focus on what others are going through.

Watch their body language

While someone may not always find the right words to express their feelings, the truth is that body language says it all. It is constantly communicating. According to research, it is not yet clear how much of the message is interpreted through body language. However, one thing you must understand is that even if there is a disparity between words and body language, you believe the latter, right?

This is why when you are evaluating a person's body language; you must do a head-to-toe assessment. Start with their eyes and let your eyes lock with theirs – are they blinking, shifting, or trying to look away? That might be indicative of deception, sadness, or depression. Look at their face, is their smile forced or authentic? What about their posture – is it upright or slouched? Are their hands fidgeting? All these cues help inform your social awareness when interacting with others.

Listen carefully

Listening is one way of communication. There is no way someone can talk nonstop without really paying attention to what the other has to say – by listening. It is not just about words but also the tone of their voice, the speed at which these words are used, and the spacing between words.

When you are interacting with others, you must learn how to make a conscious effort to stop everything you are doing to just pay attention to what they have to say, how they say, and why they are saying it in the first place. When someone is speaking to you, don't continue answering an email, texting, or doing some other activity. Give them your undivided attention, observe, and listen so that you can accurately pick up every piece of information they are trying to deliver.

That said, social awareness goes a long way in helping us recognize and interpret non-verbal cues other people use when communicating a message to us. It is these cues that help you know what others are feeling, how their emotions are changing every moment, and what is truly important to them.

Note that mindfulness is an ally of emotional and social awareness. To build your social awareness, you must recognize the important role of mindfulness in the social process. The truth is, you will not be able to pick up nonverbal cues when you are trapped inside your head, thinking about things that don't even matter. If you are going to be socially aware, then you must be present at the moment.

While you may pride yourself in your ability to multitask, the truth is that it will cause you to miss subtle emotional shifts happening in other people, which eventually gets in the way of you understanding them. The trick is to set your thoughts aside and then focus on the interaction itself. Follow the flow of the other person's emotional response by realizing that it is a give-and-take process that calls for attention to changing emotional experiences.

By focusing on others, your self-awareness does not have to diminish. When you invest your time and efforts on others, you make it easy to gain a deeper insight into your emotional state, values, and beliefs. If you are uncomfortable hearing others express their views and opinions, you learn something important about yourself.

Relationship management

This is about making your relationships effective, fulfilling, and fruitful. The trick to doing that is by becoming aware of how effectively you can use nonverbal cues when communicating with others. The truth is, it is almost impossible to avoid transmitting nonverbal messages to the people around us concerning your feelings and thoughts.

The muscles on your face – especially those around the eyes, forehead, mouth, and nose – play a significant role in conveying emotions without even using words. They also allow you to read other people's emotions. When you master how to use and interpret these cues, you can significantly improve your relationships.

The other way is by using humor and play to relieve stress. These are natural antidotes to stress, and they can lower the burden so that you can keep things in perspective. Laughter does not only relieve stress, but it also brings the nervous system into balance, calms the body, sharpens the mind, and makes you more empathetic.

Finally, you must learn to see conflicts as opportunities to get closer to others. In every human relationship, conflicts and disagreements are quite inevitable. You cannot possibly have your needs, expectations, and opinions met all the time – and that is not necessarily a bad thing. The truth is, conflict is good, and resolving them healthily and constructively goes a long way in strengthening trust between people. When conflict is not perceived as threatening, it can foster creativity, freedom, and safety of relationships.

Criteria for effective relationship management

Decision

You must make every decision regarding what the best course of action is in a given situation. This is something that should be informed by prior research you do to deepen your understanding of how others feel and why they feel that way.

The truth is that you will have thoughts about varied ways of interacting with others and the different reactions you are likely to get when you say or do something. There is also a chance that you will be aware of the effect this has on you and how to manage it appropriately.

Interaction with others

The way you interact with others should be informed by the research you conduct, and you could write it, or communicate with them face to face or through group discussions.

An outcome

You must realize that what you say or do and how you say it is informed by certain outcomes you desire to achieve. This is what makes relationship management an intentional activity.

Your needs

Your desired outcomes must be guided by particular needs you wish to meet, one at a time.

Chapter 3 Busting myths about Emotional Intelligence

As a human being and a leader, it is kind of difficult to not see the importance of emotional intelligence. It is because of emotional intelligence that I have achieved success both in business and life in general. It is this skill that has helped me see and understand my clients' pain points, stimulate a positive working environment, and improve my relationships both at the workplace and outside.

However, despite emotional intelligence's popularity and usefulness, several myths are surrounding it. It is a real shame having them because it can be a powerful thing you can use to drive success and happiness into your life. Here are some of the misconceptions about emotional intelligence that you need to let go of so that you can make the most of it in your career and life.

Emotional intelligence does not exist

There are people – including psychologists – who believe that there is no such thing as emotional intelligence. The truth is that emotional intelligence is a relatively new concept, and different people have different ways of defining what it is. One thing you must bear in mind is that testing for emotional intelligence is not a scientific thing to do.

Emotional intelligence is real, and it is something that dates back to the '30s and '40s when people were trying to express their interest in this area. Edward Thorndike came up with the term social intelligence and explained how this was a component essential in our lives and in ensuring that we succeed in what we do. Several other people contributed to emotional intelligence until Goleman took it to the next level in 1995.

Even though this took a journalist to spread the concept across to the masses, the truth is that psychologists have been trying to understand this concept for decades. While some believe that this is not something that exists, there are several other experts who strongly believe and demonstrate its existence.

It is all about empathy

Even after decades of writing and speaking to people about the science of emotional intelligence, it is interesting that there are still people who believe in one or more of emotional intelligence myths. What is shocking is that most people think that emotional intelligence is all about empathy.

While empathy is a component of emotional intelligence, the truth is that it is only a slice of the whole ability. It is much more complicated than just being charmingly empathic. It is the capacity of one to recognize their emotional feelings and those of the people around them, how to manage these emotions, and interact effectively with others. It is through emotional intelligence that one learns how to strike a healthy balance between social, emotional, and intelligence competencies.

It is not about awareness but behavioral change

According to researchers, raw knowledge in itself is not about a change in behavior. For instance, we all know that smoking, eating fast foods every day, and lack of physical exercise is bad for our health. Even with this knowledge, people still need to be motivated to change their habits so that they can make choices that support their overall wellbeing. It is about calling people into the right kind of surroundings for the desired outcome to happen.

Just because you are aware of another person's emotional feelings does not mean that you have high emotional intelligence. It is about using the knowledge you have and the motivation to do it and the right environment that supports your actions.

If you are a manager, you can use emotional intelligence to your advantage during the hiring process. While it would not hurt to screen people's levels of emotional intelligence, what is good is to train them and equip them with the right skills to improve their EQ. Henceforth, you can build a culture and surrounding where these skills are put into good use.

Emotional intelligence is equated with other personality traits

There is no way you can equate emotional intelligence to such personality traits as optimism, calmness, agreeableness, motivation, and happiness, among others. Even though these personality traits are very important and help one achieve success in their lives, the truth is that they have very little to do with intelligence. They have very little to do with emotions and absolutely nothing to do with actual emotional intelligence.

Unfortunately, there are trained psychologists who tend to confuse emotional intelligence with character traits. The truth is that these personality traits should be called exactly what they are instead of mixing them up in an assortment named emotional intelligence.

Emotional intelligence predicts success

For decades, people think that those who are most successful in life are emotionally intelligent. While it is easy to see how emotional intelligence influences how a person communicates, leads and negotiates, research demonstrates that we tend to conduct business with the people we choose and like.

Yes, emotional intelligence plays a significant role in one's success, but it is not the only indicator/predictor. Take a look at all the top successful people across the world and assess them one by one – you will be surprised to find that most of them lack even an ounce of emotional intelligence.

What you must understand is that people are very diverse, and there are equally diverse ways one can achieve success, become accomplished leaders, enjoy a successful professional life, and build a brilliant company. Unfortunately for some, emotional intelligence is not part of the equation. According to research published in the journal of Applied Psychology, there is no correlation between emotional intelligence and job performance.

You either have EI, or you don't

Some people believe that emotional intelligence is innate. In other words, they strongly think that it is something you are born with or without. The truth is that emotional intelligence is something that anyone can learn and develop.

Yes, it may not happen overnight, but you can become emotionally intelligent if you continually practice self-awareness, relationship management, social awareness, and self-management. It is through these skills that you can master how to channel your emotions in the right direction and for the right reasons. The best way to start is to become mindful of your words and know your triggers. Trust me; once you step up your empathy skills, you are on your way to achieving emotional intelligence.

You have to give up emotional intelligence to be mentally tough

Over the last couple of years, several people have tried to discuss the importance of mental toughness. This is something that is commonly directed towards people who have served in the army – specifically the Navy Seals and marines.

I have found this advice to be more useful in helping one strengthen their focus and resilience. However, when it comes to emotional intelligence, mentally tough people tend to ignore their emotions and those of the people around them. And this is something that clashes with misconceptions that emotions are a sign of weakness.

If you cannot raise your awareness of your emotional feelings and that of the people around you, there is absolutely no way you can say that you are emotionally intelligent. Rather than trying to be mentally tough, you mustn't allow other people to use your emotions against you. For instance, if you see a high-performing athlete, they might seem that they are in the "zone," but the truth is that they have no idea what is happening around them. They tend to keep a cool head just until the game is over.

Realize that mental toughness is not just about driving stricter timelines. It is about taking a pause just to listen to what lies inside you so that you have a better understanding of yourself and those around you and where they are coming from. It is about having the discipline not to get too immersed in emotions.

There is no dark side to emotional intelligence

Whenever we talk about emotional intelligence, it is always about something positive. However, just like any other force, there is always a light and dark side to everything. A good example of this has a leader who drums-up fear just so that they can satisfy their own selfish needs. In this case, it would be to keep employees in check or just have people vote for them.

When people hone their emotional skills, they increase their likelihood of manipulating others. This is mainly because when you can control your emotional feelings, you tend to mask your true feelings. When you know that other people are experiencing certain emotional feelings, the chances are that you will tug at their heartstrings and motivate them to go against their best interests.

This does not mean that you should start being wary of emotional intelligence. If you have bolstered your emotional intelligence, you will be in a better position to identify when someone else is trying to cover your eyes and cloud your judgment.

It does not influence our decisions

In reality, it is not possible to decide without have an emotional bias. The truth is that every feeling starts with an external stimulus irrespective of what someone said or what the physical events are. From that point, the brain generates an emotional feeling that causes the body to produce responsive hormones. These hormones, in turn, get into the bloodstream to create either a positive or negative feeling.

There is no correlation between emotional intelligence and physical wellbeing

According to research studies, having a higher emotional intelligence is associated with the improved psychological and physical health of an individual. This is something that you and I might consider obvious, right?

Having the ability to notice, understand, and repair our moods goes a long way in ensuring that we make healthier decisions in life. For instance, if you are stressed, you might feel the need to turn to comfort foods, cigarettes, alcohol, or something else just to try and overcome that emotion. Unfortunately, all these things you are turning to are unhealthy vices. The worst thing is that when you ignore these emotional feelings, you start experiencing such symptoms as fatigue, stomach pain, muscle tension, and other potentially life-threatening ailments like heart disease.

Chapter 4 Steps on how to grow Emotional Intelligence

Step 1 Tapping into your emotions

Note your emotional reactions to events throughout the day

It is easy to place your emotional feelings on your experiences throughout the day. One thing you must note is that taking the time to acknowledge how you feel about your experiences is critical to improving your emotional intelligence. Ignoring your feelings means that you are ignoring important information that has a significant impact on your mindset and how you carry yourself. You must choose to focus your attention on your emotional feelings so that you can easily connect them to your experiences.

For instance, if you are at the workplace in a meeting and suddenly a colleague cuts you off when you are still presenting your point. What emotions are you likely to experience? What are you are being praised for the good work you have done, what would you feel?

When you get into the habit of naming your emotions as they happen, you raise your awareness of the surroundings and every experience you go through along with the emotions those experiences stir up. This way, you start to increase your emotional intelligence little by little.

The trick is for you to get in the habit of tapping into your emotions throughout the day. Think about what you are feeling as soon as you get up and before you go to bed, and make it a habit.

Pay attention to your body

Rather than trying to ignore the physical manifestations of your emotional feelings, you must start listening to them. Realize that your mind and body are interconnected with each other, and none can survive without the other. In other words, the body and mind affect each other deeply.

To raise your emotional intelligence, you must learn how to read physical cues and use them as clues to finding out what emotions you are experiencing. For instance, when you are stressed, you might feel like there is a knot in your stomach, a tightening on your chest, or paced breathing. When you are sad, it might feel like getting up with slow and heavy limbs. When you are happy or anxious, you might feel butterflies in your stomach or your heart racing fast.

Observe how your emotions and behavior are connected

Take a minute to reflect on the last time you felt a strong emotion; how did you react?

Often, when we feel strong emotional feelings, we try to mask them so that we don't have to deal with them much less have people realize that we are going through something. Well, emotional intelligence is about tuning into your gut feeling in every situation you experience every other day instead of choosing to react without really taking the time to reflect.

Realize that the more you gain a deeper understanding of what spurs your impulses, the more you increase your emotional intelligence so that you are in a better position to use what you know to change your behavior in the future.

Here are a couple of examples of behaviors and what underlies them;

- Feeling embarrassed or insecure has a likelihood of making you withdraw from others and from engaging in conversation.
- When you are angry, you might realize your voice rise or stomp away angrily
- When you are overwhelmed, you might panic and lose track of what matters the most in your life.

Avoid judging your own emotions

Do you know that every emotional feeling you have is valid – even if it is negative? One thing you must note is that even if your emotions are negative, judging them will only inhibit your ability to feel them fully and hence inability to use them positively.

Think of it this way – every emotion you are feeling carries bits and pieces of information connected to something that is happening around you. Without this information, you will remain in the dark about what the right way to react is. This explains the reason our ability to feel our emotions is a form of intelligence.

Yes, this is not something you will master overnight, but with the practice of letting go of negative emotions, you can effectively connect them to what is happening around you. For instance, if you are bitterly envious, the first thing you need to ask yourself is what that emotion is telling you about the whole situation. It is important that you fully experience every positive emotion, as well. Try to connect your satisfaction or happiness to what is happening in your life so that you can master how to feel them often.

Notice patterns in your emotional history

It is one way to learn about recognizing your feelings, but it is quite the other to connect them to your experiences. When you have a strong emotion, it is important to try and reflect the time when you last felt that way. Try to assess what happened before, during, and after the event.

This will help you see a pattern so that you can exert more control over your behavior. Take note of how you handled the situation before and what the outcome was. This way, you can make a better decision this time to handle the situation differently so that you can get the desired outcome. It is also important that you keep a journal of emotional reactions and how you feel with each passing day so that you can determine whether there is a pattern in the manner in which you react to situations.

Practice deciding how to behave

One thing you must bear in mind is that you can't help what emotions you feel. However, you can choose to stay connected to everything that is happening around you. Without this set of information, you are likely to be left out in the dark about how you can appropriately react. This is why having the ability to feel your emotions is a form of intelligence.

When something unpleasant happens in your life, you must take a moment to feel your emotions. Allow that wave of sadness and anger wash over you. Once that wave is gone, the next thing is for you to decide on what the appropriate course of action should be. Instead of repressing your feelings, you must communicate them or keep trying instead of throwing a towel.

Don't try to escape your emotions. Yes, letting your negative feelings rise to the surface may not be the best thing to do, and you may be tempted to tamp them down by drinking yourself silly, burying your head in movies, or turning on habits that numb your pain. The truth is that when you do this, your EQ will start going down.

Step 2 Connecting with other people

Be open-minded and agreeable

When it comes to emotional intelligence, being open and agreeable go hand in hand. When you have a narrow mind, you are generally saying that you have a low EQ. however, when you allow your mind to be open, you not only gain understanding and reflect on what is happening internally, but it also gets easier to handle conflicts in a self-assured and calm manner. You will simply become socially aware of what others are going through and see possibilities begin to open to you.

One of the best ways you can strengthen your EQ is to listen to debates on radio or Television. Ensure that you consider both sides of the argument and find out what subtleties require your close inspection. When someone fails to react the same way you would, don't try to be angry at them. Instead, consider the reasons they reacted that way and try to see things from their perspective.

Improve your empathy skills

Empathy simply refers to the ability to recognize how others are feeling so that you can share emotions with them. When you are an active listener, you can pay attention to what others are saying so that you get a better sense of what they are feeling. In other words, you are using the situation to make informed choices that will help improve your relationships – and that is a sign of emotional intelligence.

If you want to grow your empathy, you must be willing to put yourself in the other person's shoes. Try to think about how you would react if it were you in the same situation. When you actively imagine what it must be like to experience the same situation, you will not only identify with their hardship but also see ways to help them through support and care.

Whenever you see someone experiencing strong emotions, the first thing you need to ask yourself is how you would react in the same situation. Being truly interested in what the other person is saying or experiencing helps a great deal in ensuring that you react more sensitively. Rather than allowing your thoughts drift from side to side, ask yourself questions and put what they are saying in summary form so that they know that you are in the conversation with them.

Read people's body language

You must read between the lines and pick up what the other persona is truly feeling by focusing on their body language and facial expressions. There are times when people say things when their body language and facial expression is saying a different thing. You must practice being observant so that you can pick up on what is less obvious – because that is where people's emotions lie.

If you are not sure that you can accurately interpret another's body language and facial expressions, try taking a quiz. When they raise their voice, it indicates that they are not only stressed but also angry about the whole situation.

See the effect you have on others

When it comes to emotional intelligence, understanding others' emotions is only half the battle. It is important that you also understand what effect you have on them. When you are around people, do you tend to make them nervous, anxious, angry, or cheerful? When you walk into a room where people are having a discussion, do they get enthusiastic and open up more, or do they retract and end the conversation?

When you put these things into perspective, you will not only identify the patterns you need to change but also see how you can appropriately change to improve the situation. If you are someone who tends to pick fights with loved ones or cause people to close up when you are around them, you might need to consider changing your attitude so that you improve the emotional effect you have on others.

Start by asking your loved ones what they think about your emotionality and where you can improve so that you become a better person. It could be your tone of voice, listening skills, or something else. Whatever it is, you can ask the people you trust to help you recognize the effect you have on others and how they can help you change for the better.

Practice being emotionally honest

When someone tells you that they are "fine" with a scowl on their face, then it means that they are not communicating honestly. The same thing happens; you are the person on the other side of a conversation. One thing you must realize is that for people to read you better. You have to be able to physically open up about your emotions. When you get into an argument, tell people that you are angry, upset, or disappointed in them. When something is making you happy, share that happiness and joy with the people around you.

When you are yourself, you make it easy for other people to get to know you better. People will tend to trust you more when you show them where you are coming from. That said, one thing you must not forget is that there is a line: learn to control your emotions so that you don't hurt the people around you.

Step 3 Putting EQ to Practical Use

See where you have room for improvement

In life, being intellectually capable is very important. However, being emotionally intelligent is an essential need. When you have high emotional intelligence, you are in a better position to seize job opportunities as they present themselves or lead a better relationship. The four core elements of emotional intelligence we have discussed in the previous chapter will help you figure out where in your life, you need improvement. Is it self-awareness, self-management, social awareness, or relationship management? Whatever it is, you can work on improving it and boost your emotional intelligence.

Lower your stress level by raising your EQ

When you hear someone say that they are stressed, what they are simply saying is that they are feeling overwhelmed by a wide range of emotions. Life is filled with difficult situations ranging from relationship breakups to job loss. In between these things are millions of stress triggers that have the potential of making any daily issue a challenge. If you are stressed a lot, it is hard to behave the way you want to. However, when you have a plan in place to help you relieve stress, you stand a chance of improving your emotional intelligence and all aspects surrounding it.

What triggers your stress? What can you do to help alleviate your stress? Create a list of all forms of stress relief from hanging out with friends to taking a walk to enjoy nature – anything to put it into good use. That said, if you feel that your stress levels are getting out of hand, you must consider getting the help you need from a professional therapist. They can give you the tools you need to cope with stress and raise your EQ in the process.

Be more light-hearted at home and work

When you have optimism, it becomes easier to see the beauty in life. It becomes easy to turn your awareness into everyday objects so that you can share your emotional feelings with the people in your life. Trust me; no one wants to sit and spend time with someone who lacks optimism.

When you are optimistic, you draw people to yourself and enjoy all the possibilities these connections have to offer. If you are negative, on the other hand, you will push people away instead of building your resilience. Emotionally intelligent people know how to use their humor and fun to make themselves and the people around them feel happier and safer – and they can use laughter to get through tough situations.

Chapter 5 Emotional Intelligence at school/workplace

Each passing day, each one of us makes emotionally charged decisions. Each time we are planning something, we feel as though our plan A is better than plan B and end up making choices based on our gut instincts or emotions. However, when we understand where these emotions are coming from in the first place, only then will we become attuned to each other – especially when working in a team.

With the increase in globalization, emotional intelligence has found a significant place in our lives because the places where we school or work have become more cross-cultural and global. It is because of globalization that our interactions have become complex along with how we express these emotions.

One thing you must remember is that emotional intelligence in school or at the workplace all boils down to expressing, understanding, and managing good relationships and addressing problems even when you are under intense pressure from above.

Today, the conventional measure of intelligence pays attention to logic and reasoning in such areas as math and reading comprehension. The general idea that this kind of reasoning is what determines our success and productivity at the workplace is persuasive and intuitive as well. This is mainly because it measures our ability to grasp and digest facts in our surroundings.

However, the idea that there is only one form of intelligence has recently been subjected to intense scrutiny. In the classroom, many psychologists have embraced the theory of multiple intelligences. The two major areas that are measured in tests include verbal-linguistic intelligence and logical-math intelligence. But these are only two areas out of nine different bits of intelligence with varied features.

That said, not all these intelligence have found their way into the world of business. For instance, bodily-kinesthetic intelligence is what most dancers, athletes, and other forms of physical labor use. It is through this form of intelligence that minds have been opened to greater possibilities of thinking and achieving success.

On the other hand, the ideas about rational intelligence took root from the enlightenment that happened soon after scientific thoughts were codified for the very first time. The very early facet used by natural philosophers was the idea of rational objectivity, which required that individuals strive to view the world around them not as they desire it to be but as it is. While this idea may seem sound on the surface, the problem is that it often causes people to move away from using their gut feelings and using their emotions in finding solutions to real-life problems. It is important to note that rational intelligence does not only focus on hard facts but also logical reasoning that results from unproductive scenarios of win-lose cases.

In the workplace, today, excelling means striking a balance between interpersonal intelligence and intrapersonal intelligence. The former simply refers to the ability to detect and respond to other people's emotions, moods, desires, and motivations. On the other hand, the latter simply refers to the ability to raise our awareness of self so that we are more aligned with our beliefs, values, and thought processes.

When you combine these concepts, what you get is a good overview of emotional intelligence and how they are related to business leadership. When you don't have the guiding influence of rational intelligence, emotional intelligence ends up being subjective in such a way that it is no longer conducive to business goals. However, if they are harnessed appropriately, it serves as the key to driving internal collaborations and external alliances.

EI is the key to communication in the workplace and school

In its most refined form, emotional intelligence offers empathy, which is important in helping us to fully understand others' perspective even when it contradicts our view of things. According to research, there is evidence that shows women who have high emotional intelligence tend to act in collaborative ways by embracing an inclusive leadership style as compared to men.

It does not matter whether you are a man or woman when you practice emotional intelligence, there are so many more benefits it has to offer at the workplace and to all stakeholders across the industry. This is by;

- Helping leaders to motivate and inspire good works among its employees by understanding others' motivators.
- Bringing more people to the table and helping one avoid pitfalls of group thinking.
- Empowering leaders to not only recognize possibilities but act on opportunities that other people may not be aware of in the first place
- Assisting in conflict identification and resolution in such a fair and even-handed manner
- Producing higher morale and helping other people tap and leverage their professional potential to the fullest.

Just like rational intelligence, emotional intelligence is something you and I can cultivate by exerting effort and willingly taking time to study more. The very first step to developing emotional intelligence is by strengthening your power of introspection. It is about recognizing your emotional feelings, thought processes, and biases so that whenever you are making decisions, they are not only informed but well-rounded. When you exercise emotional intelligence, you must act in confidence, rise above your fears and worries, and be able to question the status quo and bypass knee-jerk reactions.

Emotional intelligence in hiring processes

Even though technical skills are things that can be imparted through training, the truth is that it is more challenging to teach emotional intelligence during the recruitment process at the workplace. While companies can integrate theories of emotional intelligence in their hiring processes and professional development in all spheres, the truth is that it is not easy to achieve that with a 100% accuracy.

For instance, when hiring entry-level employees, you may wish to test for their EQ when you have a group of candidates competing for the same new position or a promotion. Most managers, leaders, and stakeholders identified as having high emotional intelligence and high leadership potential tend to deliver better results as part of their development process.

Even though most roles at the workplace could benefit from emotional intelligence, the truth is that not all roles require highly developed emotional intelligence. The higher one climbs in their career ladder, the more valuable emotional intelligence becomes.

This explains why professionals such as the Human Resource or Public Relations departments benefit a lot from emotional intelligence because they are mostly involved in the hiring process. This is mainly because their emotional development plays a significant role in helping companies maximize their contributions and optimize their investments for future growths and developments.

Emotional intelligence in the globalized economy

Just as the global economy has developed into a system of partnerships, negotiations, and communications, emotional intelligence plays a bigger role in the public sphere. This is why emotional intelligence is strongly correlated to such traits as self-control, perseverance, and increased performance and productivity even under pressure. It is what offers leaders with the emotional fortitude to adjust and adapt to change, deal with setbacks, and achieve goals no matter their skills.

It does not matter how the economy transforms. What matters most is that conventional intelligence will always be the center of success in the global economy. That said, bear in mind that even the most technical of all roles require one to greatly expand their networks with diversified stakeholder portfolios, taking up roles in complex atmospheres, and investing both emotional and mental capital to handle the most unexpected of situations. Both rational and emotional intelligence are here to stay, and it takes brilliant leaders, managers, and students to exhibit both.

Chapter 6 Emotional Intelligence and health

Physical health

According to research, there is evidence that shows emotional intelligence has a significant impact on our physical health directly. Instead of using a traditional aspect of emotional intelligence, you had better use trait meta-mood scale (TMMS), that speak to the core aspect of EQ;

Attention

This refers to the ability to take note and focus our attention on our moods.

Clarity

This simply refers to the ability to clearly understand the nature of your moods.

Repair

This refers to one able to maintain a positive mood; repair negative emotions were necessary to achieve their goals.

When you look at things from this perspective, what you will note is that emotional intelligence can affect human physical health. For instance, you have the power of attention, clarity, and repair; there is a high likelihood that the following scenario holds to you.

First, you might begin to feel easily irritable and cannot seem to put your mind on one thing. After a couple of considerations, you realize that you didn't have your breakfast because you woke up late and had to prepare the kids for school and get ready for work. You realize that all you have had are two cups of coffee since you woke up. What you are feeling essential is hunger pangs. You decide to take a break to go into the breakroom to fix yourself a healthy snack because you can't hold till lunch, which is still 2 hours away.

In the above rudimentary example, the truth is that you paid attention to your mood, identified the reason that underlies it, and exerted your effort into repairing the negative emotions you are feeling before they get out of hand – by coming up with a solution that will address your needs and contribute to your desired outcome.

What do you notice about this example? Well, the truth is that emotional intelligence positively affects one's health.

Several research studies that have been conducted match the elements of emotional stress and behavioral response to heart, hormonal, and enzymatic activity. Some involved research participants are writing about their traumatic emotional events – including recall and assessment. During these sessions, their blood pressure was under evaluation.

Without offering an exhaustive account of the research studies, the results demonstrated that people who accurately perceive their emotional feelings could cope with stressful situations. They also demonstrated the ability to overcome hesitance in seeking medical help, accepting changes in their bodies, and proactively seeking a resolution to achieve better health.

This is something that can be manifested in such habits as an improved diet, overcoming alcohol addiction, and a regular workout regimen. All these behavioral patterns are associated with strong emotional intelligence, increased level of dynamism, accepting personal reality, and being accountable to own wellbeing.

In other words, self-awareness, motivation, and self-management increase your likelihood of enjoying positive health irrespective of how and when they manifest in your life.

Mental health

According to research, mental health conditions are linked to lower levels of emotional intelligence. For instance, someone with Borderline personality disorder (BPD) has been shown to show heightened sensitivity to the expression of emotional feelings. What is interesting is that people with BPD often struggle to label their emotions and what they truly mean. The downside to this is that they cannot seem to control their emotions.

Someone with depression has been shown to have a lower EQ score. These kinds of people tend to demonstrate less sensitivity to changing emotional contexts, hence causing them to get stuck in negativity.

Social anxiety, on the other hand, has been linked with a low EQ as well. Such a person tends to fear what others will think or say about them. They have a high likelihood of perceiving neutral expressions like hostility, which causes them to misinterpret social cues.

The other thing that is important to note is that substance abuse contributes to severe deficits in aspects relating to emotional intelligence. As opposed to the conditions we have already mentioned, drug abuse contributes to impaired emotional perception and regulation.

What is even interesting is that research studies have shown that there is a link between low emotional intelligence and self-destructive habits. In other words, some people use self-harm as a way of regulating their emotions. By improving one's emotional intelligence, you impact their mental health significantly, such that people can have reduced tendencies of aggression and quickly recover from trauma.

This explains the reason why mental health awareness is on the rise and risks reaching proportions that will stretch services. While there have been more studies on mental health, the truth is that no one should doubt the fact that we need more information in this area. Mental health is a condition that can strike anyone at any age, gender, profession, or culture. There are several reasons mental health issues occur, and yet there is no single case that can be considered the same as the other.

That is why we propose emotional intelligence in supporting strategies that help people recover from mental health issues. Don't get me wrong; I am not saying that you should replace therapy and medical attention with emotional intelligence. However, people who are suffering from mental issues on the lower end of the spectrum could benefit a lot from EI.

Through self-awareness, one can identify their strengths and weaknesses and leverage them to their advantage. When you know your weak areas, you can position yourself better to improve so that you can improve your mental balance. Remember that self-awareness is a core component of emotional intelligence and has been tested in a wide range of fields. When someone has mental health issues, raising their awareness of their emotions allows them to recognize their issues before they can get out of hand – prevention is better than cure!

That is why self-awareness is integral to our mental balance. For instance, if you are aware of your emotions and actions and can recognize that there are certain areas you need help in controlling your emotions, you can effectively learn how to manage them. This is because your awareness will shift to your emotional feelings and the strategies you can use to manage them. Instead of taking on more tasks than you can handle, you take on projects you can complete, lower stress levels, and achieve mental balance. Doing this will not only help you get better but will also improve your self-confidence, create positivity, enhance your mindset, facilitate balance and happiness in your life.

There are so many ways you can improve your mental state and boost your emotional intelligence. One of the ways you can achieve this is through the practice of mindfulness. Mindfulness plays a significant role in helping people deal with their current situations. For instance, when you pause to just take in a deep breath, you not only allow your mind to shift to the present moment, but also allow your mind and body to regain balance and more control.

The other way you can achieve mental balance is through meditation. While not everyone will feel comfortable with meditation, the truth is that it is very effective. You don't have to be religious to practice meditation. When you meditate, you offer your mind focus and scope. It needs to deal with emotional imbalance. One thing with mental health is that it is associated with a lack of energy and motivation. However, when you meditate and allow your mind to feed on positive self-talk and affirmations, you not only release all negativity but also allow the mind to see possibilities where the balance was lacking.

Yes, someone with mental health issues might not feel positively changing their thought process. However, small changes here and there go a long way in bringing positivity into their lives. Instead of thinking that they can't do something, they can simply turn that into something positive like "*I've got what it takes to do this.*"

The other trick is to use music, something that has been shown to boost emotional intelligence. It does not only improve one's mood and emotions but also encourages one to use a reflective process, which offers them the opportunity to assess themselves, their emotions, thoughts, and progress.

For you to realize growth, you must learn to motivate yourself to meet both your intrinsic and extrinsic needs – which can be physical, mental, nutritional, physiological or a combination of all. The best way to use motivation is to direct it through the use of process goals effectively. Within mental health facet, one of the key drivers is the use of motivation in creating energy. According to research, when one lacks motivation, they risk having one aspect of mental health. Today, embrace the use of motivation strategies – such as positive self-talk and goal setting – to reverse this trend.

Finally, how many friends do you have? Are these friendships quality? Well, it is one thing to have many friends, but it is quite another to have friends who look out for you and who build you into a better person each day. This is what quality friendship is all about, and is the kind of support mental health cases need. To improve your emotional intelligence, you must look for opportunities to meet new people and build new relationships. While this is something that can be challenging for people with mental health issues, the truth is that positioning oneself within the right time and space makes it possible, when your purpose of building new friendships and growing the existing ones allows one to open up and achieve coherence of trust.

Chapter 7 Emotional Intelligence and relationships

The secret to a lasting relationship is emotional intelligence. This is mainly because emotional intelligence makes people extremely aware of changes happening around them – whether the change is small or big. When you build your emotional intelligence, you simply boost your sensitivity that we all are seeking in our partners. Through active awareness and empathy, you will gain the ability to sense when there is a slight shift in the dynamics of your romance so that you can act accordingly.

Realize that you have the potential to attain the kind of love you have always dreamed of. A relationship where you enjoy deep intimacy, real commitment, mutual kindness, and soulful caring. This is simply because of empathy – out innate ability to share with others our emotional experiences.

However, for anyone to reach this height of intimacy and romance, you need all the skills of high emotional intelligence – sharp emotional awareness, acceptance, a vigilant active social awareness. Your emotional awareness will help you avoid making mistakes by getting lustful or intoxicated in love. Acceptance, on the other hand, goes a long way in helping us experience emotions that have the potential of harming us if left unattended. Finally, the active awareness vigilance is what helps us to appraise our relationship so that we know what is working and what is not.

So, how then can we build emotionally intelligent romantic relationships?

One thing you must realize is that you don't have to choose the wrong lovers and end up in a failed marriage, you don't have to sit and watch romance seep out of your long-term relationship. Look inside your relationship and determine whether there are conflicting needs and wants that might come between you and your partner. The truth is, you deserve a loving and healthy relationship filled with romance. The last thing you want is to resign yourself to boredom or bickering in your love life.

The truth is that you have the potential to attain the kind of love you have always wanted. This does not mean that your emotional intelligence should be at a peak before you can find love. Research shows that most people falling in love helps them stay motivated to educate their hearts. This explains why most of the deeply passionate lovers are in their eighties because they find out that a high emotional intelligence in both partners adds up to romance that never stops growing, does not lose its spark, and always seeks to strengthen them – both individually and collectively.

Here's how you can boost the EQ in your relationship;

Actively seek change in your relationship

Look around you, and all the people you know are in relationships, what you will realize is that none of them likes change. People fear change because they think that it will destroy their romance and attraction to each other. However, the opposite is true. Change helps you realize everything you have been missing.

One thing you must bear in mind is that change does not necessarily have to mean worse. Research shows that things often come out better than ever on the other side of change. Think of your romantic relationship as an organism, that by nature, must change. It is through change that a relationship gets to grow. Your ability to embrace change plays a significant role in helping you gain courage and a sense of optimism.

Take a minute to think about your relationship – what is it that your partner needs most from you? Is it something new? Do you need time to reassess things together? Are there external influences in your life that are demanding some change in your roles in the relationship? Do you consider yourself happier than you used to be?

Without emotional intelligence, these questions are very challenging and scary to answer, and is the reason why several lovers ignore the signals of change until it is out of control.

Look at challenges as opportunities instead of problems

Did you know that courage and optimism are what help people view dilemmas as challenging opportunities rather than problems?

Take a minute to think about how creative you and your partner can be. This is the point where you don't need to blame each other for emotions. In other words, you are not controlled by negative emotional influences. You are simply alert enough not to repeat the mistakes you have made in the past.

With high emotional intelligence, you are free from resignations and ruts so that you start looking at problems as opportunities for growth. You are not scared when the problem arises because you know that you can simply get down and do some brainstorming to solve the problems. You view differences as opportunities for you to meet with each other, get closer so that you can both emerge on the other side of victory stronger together and individually.

Respect all the feelings you have for each other

The truth is that none of us is delighted by the discoveries we make about our partners. However, one thing you must realize is that when it comes to emotions, you must accept them all. Falling in love with someone does not mean that you will never be angry, disappointed, jealous, or hurt.

The truth is that the way you respond to these emotions is all up to you. What matters the most is that you feel them. Several relationships have been ruined by blame, and millions of couples have dismissed their need for deep intimacy because of shame. The truth is that these things are cruel reminders of fear, anxiety, and anger. If you have done what it takes to build your emotional intelligence, you will choose to experience the emotions together so that you can get on with your lives together.

Keep laughter in your love life

Several couples intellectualize their emotions without even realizing it. If you are one of them, you need to realize that acceptance is what you need, and a large part of that comes with lots of laughter. To be accepted in your relationship, you must learn to laugh with each other.

If you are not capable of laughing together, the chances are that you will not be able to stand each other's unique flaws and inevitable stumbles any more than you can tolerate your own. You will not have the ability to embrace surprises; however pleasant they might be. However, when you work on growing your emotional intelligence, you will not only ensure that you constantly improve your relationship but also ensure that you never get trapped by expectations of perfection.

Pay attention to how you feel when your spouse or partner is not around

Fortunately, there are several ways you can use to monitor precisely how your relationship is going. These are the three-gauge means of measuring your wellbeing when trying to figure out how the rest of your life is supposed to be.

The first thing is to ask yourself whether you feel restless or irritable? Do you find yourself dragging through the day after a night of marital bliss? Do you find yourself resenting family and friends even though you are both spending time alone together?

One thing you must realize is that love never feeds from a tunnel vision. Realize that where you coo like doves with your partner does not matter if you lack energy, clarity of mind, and benevolence at all times. Yes, you may enjoy all the sex you have together, but if you lack energy the morning or day after, then something is amiss.

So, how then can you know that the other person is "the one?"

Well, the truth is that when you are first falling in love, you must know that the person you are about to settle down with is "the one." The last thing you want is to make a mistake, get in the wrong marriage and end up in a lifeless union. Here are some of the tips that will help you know;

Listen to your body and not your mind

Unfortunately, most people choose their mate for reasons that have nothing to do with what they feel and instead have to do with what they think. What is more, is that we tend to drive our relationships based on how things should be or have been.

This is where you go wrong!

The truth is that you don't lose at love because you allowed your emotions to run away from you, but because you let your mind run away from you.

You may think that you are in love for so many reasons – such as infatuation, lust, status, security, or social acceptance. You think that you have found true love because your current partner meets your expectations and some image you have created in your head of your dream partner. What you must realize is that unless you know how you feel, your choice is only destined to be wrong!

Whenever you imagine your dream partner, the best thing is to transport that form of mental debate to justify your choice so that you can check it with your body. Take in a deep breath, allow your mind and body to relax, and focus by getting out of your head and into your body. What does your gut feeling tell you? is there a persistent feeling that keeps growing inside, telling that something is wrong? If so, then the chances are that your choice is wrong!

The truth is, if you allow your mental image versus physical sensation to lead you, you will never know what you *truly* want.

Heed the messages from your whole body

When you are in a new relationship, it can be difficult to get clear signals from the rest of your body because they are likely drowned out by all the sexual desires running around. This explains why you need to pay attention to other important and more subtle feelings – migraines, lack of energy, muscle tension, and stomach pains. These feelings could simply mean that your desires are not really what you need.

However, if you find yourself glowing of love, have liveliness, and a spark of energy, this could be the real deal. If it is only lust or infatuation, the chances are that you will feel it in other parts of your life and relationships.

Take a moment to ask yourself the following high emotional intelligence questions;

- Does this relationship energize me and the totality of my life? Has my work life improved? Am I taking better care of myself?
- Is my head and focus straighter? Am I creative and more responsible?
- Does my "in love feelings" go beyond positive feelings of caring about the other person in the relationship? Am I generous, more giving, and empathic towards the people around me more than I was before?

The truth is, if the responses you get from your body are not exactly what you wanted to hear, it is time to push beyond your fears of loss so that you can look at things from a bigger picture perspective. Finding out at this point that you have not found your true love will spare you of all the heartache, pain, and a pile of negative emotional memories you risk experiencing down the line. Consider this a legacy that can keep you from making the same mistake again and ending up in sour love in the future.

Take a chance on reaching out

When you are in a new relationship, there is always that feeling to be on your guard. We tend to automatically put up barriers and walls when it comes to knowing each other deeply. When you leave yourself open and vulnerable at this point in the relationship, you tend to feel scared, when in the real sense, you are trying to find out if the love you feel for the other person is real.

You must become the first person to reach out. This is something that will reveal an intimate secret, demonstrate affection, laugh at yourself when everything seems scary. Think about it – do the other person's reactions fill you with vitality and warmth? If it does, then the chances are that you have found a kindred soul. If not, then you have found someone with low emotional intelligence, and it is time for you to decide how you wish to respond.

What you need to feel loved vs. what you want

If you are going to find someone you truly love, then you must know the difference between what you would like from what you cannot live without. These are some of the exercises that will help you get it right;

Start by selecting at least five features or traits you feel are most important to you in the other partner. Order these character traits in descending order. Some of the traits may be neatness, adventurous, humor, emotionally, open, considerate, smart, affectionate, monetarily successful, well respected, famous, charismatic, spiritual, empowering, nurturing, and conversational, among others.

As you consider each trait, ask yourself whether they make you energetic, calm, and stirs you emotionally. Find out whether these traits make you feel pleasant, unpleasant, or indifferent.

Realize that a desire will be fleeting and superficial, while something you consider a need will automatically register at a deeper level of feelings.

Repeat this exercise over and over again so that you gain a deeper insight into the differences between what you need in love, and what you desire. Ask yourself whether the other person in the relationship thinks that you are in love with meeting these needs.

How to respond to a low EQ partner

One thing you must realize is that we don't all grow our emotional muscles at the same rate. If you have a high emotional intelligence compared to your lover, the most important thing is to learn how to respond to them.

What words do you want your partner to hear? You must take the time to reconsider what words to use. If you are not sure about what exactly you need and the reason you need it, there is a high likelihood that your message will be mixed up.

You must choose a time when you and your partner are not in a hurry to take a walk together, go on a date, or brunch. While at it, ensure that you are intimately into the conversation so that at the end of it, you both can remember the discussion. During the day, send your partner "I feel" text messages concerning your needs. This will help your partner see what is wrong with them for a chance to improve. For instance, you can text them, "I feel like making love every day, but I don't like the smell of garlic and onions. Would you be willing to brush your teeth before we go to bed?"

There is a high likelihood that your partner will respond defensively. If they do, you must repeat their concerns back to them. Repeat the message and pay attention to what they have to say about it. If possible, keep repeating it over and over again until you are satisfied that they heard what you communicated to them.

Chapter 8 The interaction between EQ and Social Intelligence

It is important to note that social intelligence is about developing experience with people and learning from our failures and successes in our surroundings. In most cases, social intelligence is what people commonly refer to as tact, street smart, or common sense.

What you will note about people with high emotional intelligence is that they carry on conversations with different kinds of people and can verbally communicate with the right words – hence referred to as social expressiveness.

Additionally, such people are adept at learning how to conduct a wide range of social roles and responsibilities. They are well versed with informal rules of the game, are excellent listeners, and can thoroughly analyze what makes the people around them tick. They know this by focusing their attention on what the others have to say and their behaviors.

They not only know various ways of conducting a wide range of social roles but also can put their skills into practice so that they are at ease with a wide range of personalities. In other words, they are careful what impression of themselves they create in other people. This is something that not everyone can do because it needs a delicate balance between controlling and managing your self-image before others and ensuring that you are reasonably authentic in letting others see your true self.

That said, one thing you must bear in mind is that social intelligence is more about the future. It came about just so that people could strive to survive and figure out the best way to get along with others, get out of situations, and earn a favorable outcome. It does not matter whether you have paper qualifications in social intelligence. What matters the most is that if you don't know how to apply it in life, you might end up straining or ruining your relationships and lose opportunities.

Yes, there are times when you want to give people feedback so bluntly, but editing your words to convey the message constructively goes a long way in ensuring that you don't end up putting your foot in your mouth. Unlike social intelligence, emotional intelligence is more about the present, hence its close relationship to emotions and feelings. When you read someone's facial expressions, you can easily tell whether they are happy or not. You can tell whether they are nervous, shy, or angry about the situation at hand.

But, what are some of the social competencies of emotional intelligence?

Read on!

Social competencies of EQ

Empathy

When we want someone to see things from another's perspective, the first thing we tell them is *"put yourself in their shoe."* Well, that is what empathy is all about. It is the ability to communicate and lead by understanding another person's views, thoughts, and feelings.

When we improve our empathy, the truth is that we become better versions of ourselves. We strengthen our relationships and make them more meaningful. We strive for success in the workplace. We realize it improved health and overall quality of life.

If you look at the top performers in your company, what you will notice is that 90% of them have high emotional intelligence. This is because the more people understand their thoughts, emotions, and feelings, the better they get at understanding someone else's thoughts, emotions, and feelings. When we become better at listening to others, we become better human beings.

But what happens when you lack empathy?

Well, according to research studies, scientists have linked a lack of empathy to a wide range of societal vices – such as theft, murder, and drug dealing, among others. Think about the prisoners, are they empathic people? Most likely not. Most of these people lack empathy and didn't care to think about what their victims might have been feeling. If they had empathy, there is a high chance that this might have prevented them from engaging in acts that put them in prison in the first place.

One thing you must note is that empathy is the ability to trust other people. The truth is that when your friends feel that you care, you earn their trust. If they trust you, that simply means that they will be willing to take risks with you and become more open with you. The reason why your friends communicate with openness with you is that they have built their trust in you.

In other words, as trust continues to grow, it promotes the sharing of information, thoughts, and feelings. It is this form of sharing that expands the foundation upon which you and the others relate with each other. Think about it for a moment, when your friends talk about their interests and ideas, what do you do as you listen to them?

Simple – you stop what you are doing to give them your undivided attention. With empathy, you can raise your awareness of other people's feelings during the conversation. When someone asks you for help, it is important that you understand what they are not saying in their words but are saying with their body language.

You must bear in mind that a significant portion of communication is often related in non-verbal cues. The truth is that we may not even realize it, but when we communicate with our facial expressions, noise, gestures, among others, empathy allows us to understand what these non-verbal cues mean. When you master what non-verbal cues mean, you become better at understanding how the other person truly feels.

A solid foundation in emotional intelligence begins with a show of empathy!

You can grow your empathy with practice and the use of the right process. It is possible to take empathy to the next level, something that, in turn, boosts our overall emotional intelligence. When you have the right tools, the process of learning about empathy does not necessarily have to be costly or complicated.

Types of Empathy

There are three types of empathy;

Cognitive Empathy

This simply refers to the kind of empathy that helps us know what the other person is feeling and what they might be thinking. It is often referred to as "perspective-taking." This type of empathy is connected to the intellect, thought, and understanding. It goes a long way in helping people negotiate, stay motivated, and understand a wide range of perspectives.

The only pitfall to this is not putting yourself in another person's shoes to feel what they are feeling.

One thing you must bear in mind is that cognitive empathy is all about thought as much as it is about emotions. The truth is that understanding sadness is not the same as feeling sadness.

If you came home upset about losing your job, your partner would respond in this manner. It is the same way a doctor looks at their patients to try and understand their illness. They don't dive into the patient's emotions. In other words, cognitive empathy is about responding to problems with brainpower.

This can be a great asset in situations where you are required to get into the other person's head so that you can interact with their circumstances with tact and understanding. Think of cognitive empathy as mixing apples and oranges. This implies that for you to truly understand what another person is feeling, you have to feel them in some way.

Emotional empathy

This simply refers to the ability to feel physically along with another person as though your emotions are contagious. It is concerned with mirroring neurons in the brain, physical sensations, and feelings. It plays a significant role in helping people close their interpersonal relationships and careers.

The pitfalls to this are the fact that emotional empathy can be overwhelming and even inappropriate in some circumstances.

It helps to think of emotional empathy as sound because it involves directly feeling the other person's emotions. Have you heard of the term empath? Well, this means a person with the ability to take on the emotional and mental state of another person, fully. Unfortunately, this form of response can seem disconnected from the brain and thinking. However, emotional empathy is deeply rooted in the human mirror neurons.

Each one of us has neurons that fire in certain ways whenever we see someone acting in animal-like behavior. It makes you relate to their actions both in the brain and body. This is exactly what emotional empathy does – feel someone else's experiences in reaction to certain situations.

Think about your loved one for a second – they come to you in tears. What do you feel? Well, the truth is that you will tend to feel a pull on your heartstrings. When you connect with someone in this way, you strengthen your intimacy and promote a strong bond between the two of you.

Just like cognitive empathy, emotional empathy has its flip-side, and this happens when you cannot manage your distressing emotions. This often leads to emotional burnout. In other words, when you feel too much of what another person is experiencing, you risk making even very small interactions overwhelming.

Compassionate empathy

This is the kind of empathy in which you not only understand another person's predicament but also feel with them. You are spontaneously touched to help. It is concerned with actions, emotions, and intellect. This plays a significant role in helping you become considerate of the other person fully.

The downside to this kind of empathy is that we are always striving to have it, but we cannot fully have it. In most instances, compassion is necessary. It may be fitting for monetary negotiations, political convincing, among others. It is the first response we give our loved ones, and it strikes a powerful balance between the two parties involved.

It is important to note that the heart and thoughts are not opposing each other. The truth is that they are intricately connected. It is through compassionate empathy that we honor the natural connection we have with others. When your child comes to you in tears, you are driven to understand why they are crying and want to comfort them by sharing in their emotional experiences and helping them heal. It is a lot to handle.

There are times when we feel swayed to one side or the other with more feelings, thoughts, fixing, and wallowing. The thing with compassionate empathy is that it is about taking the middle ground and then using our emotional intelligence to respond appropriately to the situation. It is about thinking what the other person might want – to be held, action to fix their situation or just a listening ear. You do this without necessarily feeling overwhelmed by sadness or the need to fix things.

In other words, compassion gives us that mindful touch to handle even the toughest of situations.

However, one thing you must remember is that empathy is a teeter-totter. In other words, if you go too much into another person's psyche, do you risk losing yours? If you dive too deep in their world, are you risking missing out on an integral part of the human experience? If you feel too much, is it inappropriate? If you feel too little, if it hurtful?

You must understand that not all situations are equivalent, just like not all the types of empathy are the same.

Take a minute to think about a real-life example in your own life where each type of empathy is applicable. I believe that you must have encountered compassionate empathy at some point in your life. Realize that any type of empathy takes practice to gain emotional fitness – just like any other balancing act. Finding a sweet spot where you can empathize effectively is worth the work.

Do it today!

How to improve empathy for a successful life

- Be quiet inside and out
- Watch as well as listen
- Ask yourself what you are feeling
- Test your instincts
- Challenge yourself
- Get feedback
- Explore the heart and not just your head
- Walk-in other people's shoes and examine your biases
- Cultivate your sense of curiosity

Social skills

This is a broad term that refers to the skills we need to handle and influence other people's emotions in an effective manner – in the context of emotional intelligence. While this may sound like manipulation, the truth is that this is as simple as understanding that giving others your smile makes them smile too. Because of your smile, you can make someone feel much better and positive than they were before.

Think of social skills as the last piece of the emotional intelligence puzzle. Once you can understand and manage yourself, only then will you be able to understand other people's emotions and feelings, and influence them.

Some of the most important social skills include;

Communication skills

This is a vital piece of emotional intelligence; you must pay attention to what others have to say and also convey your thoughts and feelings to them in an effective manner.

You may be wondering what makes a good communicator. Well, if you can listen well to the people around you, understand what they said, and seek open and full information sharing, then you are a good communicator. If you are prepared to hear others' problems and not just ready to hear good news alone, then you are a good communicator.

Good communication means dealing with tough situations, setting them straight, and not allowing problems to fester. You must ensure that you register and act in emotional cues in communicating so that the message is right.

Leadership skills

This may sound strange, but one thing you must note is that leadership skills are all part of social skills. Emotional intelligence is a huge part of leadership and not vice versa. What you must note is that leadership skills and emotional intelligence are inextricably linked to each other. As we have mentioned earlier, only people who are tuned into their emotions and that of the people around them have the hope of influence.

One of the key aspects of good leadership is influence, and having the ability to bring others along with you. You may refer to this as charisma, but the truth is that leadership is much more profound than that. In short, it is good emotional intelligence.

To be a good leader, you must have the ability to articulate a vision and enthuse others with it. It does not matter whether you are formal or informal; the trick is to ensure that you offer leadership, support, and guide the performance of the people you work with, hold each person accountable, and lead by example.

Persuasion skills

Persuasion simply refers to the art of enthusing people, winning their hearts to your ideas, and leading them on your proposed course of action. If you look around at people you know are persuasive, you will realize that they not only have to influence but also have the ability to read others' emotional currents in a given circumstance and fine-tune their words so that they appeal to the people around them.

Conflict-management skills

We all know that conflicts can arise at any given time. They seem to appear out of thin air. However, the art of resolving conflicts as soon as they arise is crucial both at home and in the workplace. It all begins by raising our awareness of the importance of diplomacy and tact, and how these can be used to address difficulties in various situations.

Being a good conflict manager means that you have to be willing to bring disagreements out in the open when resolving them. You must ensure that you use information sharing as a way to encourage debates and open discussions, minimize hidden currents, help each party recognize the other's feelings and logical position so that you can obtain a win-win solution.

Chapter 9 Understanding Emotional drain and dealing with them

Life is not easy; we all know that. There are so many ups and downs, mountains and valleys, highs and lows, and you never really know what to expect. There are times when life is even a little tough for us to handle anything at all. It does not matter what the reason might be, but the truth is that it finds a way of kicking us when we are down.

One thing we fail to realize is that when we suffer, we get emotionally and mentally drained. The thing is that the effects of these manifests in ways we can see. Our energy gets sapped to the point that we feel physically exhausted, and what we can do at that point is break down. You must know when life is too much so that you can position yourself to better control and manage your emotions. Here are some of the signs to look out for;

Hopelessness

This is a sign that you are emotionally drained. When you have pushed, fought, and clawed through the storms, all your energy gets sapped, and you begin to ask yourself why you are even bothering when things don't seem to get better. This is the point of hopelessness and is very dangerous. When you get to this point, you risk making your pain and suffering permanent because you have accepted that this is your way of life. If you are at this point, it is high time you seek help.

Crying often

For most people, crying is something they left behind during their teen years. As we grow older, we get to manage and control our emotions better, and we only cry when something big happens in our lives. However, some have been pushed to the limits, and crying has quickly become their way of life – a sad movie makes you cry, someone wrongs you, and that makes you cry, or an old friend seeks forgiveness from you, and they make you cry.

When you are crying easily like this, it indicates that you are emotionally exhausted. In other words, even the smallest emotional push brings you into tears.

Insomnia

Are you experiencing trouble getting sleep? This might have something to do with your emotions. When you are emotionally drained, you risk suffering from insomnia. You may think that just because you are stressed, you will fall asleep easily. However, insomnia occurs often because you are spending most of the time in deep thought, fighting with the demons in your head, and have trouble getting a good night's sleep.

Lack of motivation

When you are emotionally drained, you don't seem to care about striving for anything. You no longer have goals that wake you up in the morning. You are just going through the waves of life, and you let it sway you in whatever direction it likes. You find yourself neglecting your work, health, hygiene, and family.

Detachment

If you have been punched hard by life, it is easy to detach yourself from the rest of the people around you. You have allowed the pain to become part of your life such that you have become numb to it because you have gone through way too much that the reality no longer exists for you.

You must find out what is making you emotionally drained. Is it your partner, family, friends, work, boss? How do you when someone is sucking your energy reserved dry?

- You think about them all the time
- You are physically exhausted
- You find happiness when they leave
- They don't lift you up

- Once you have been together, you feel the need for some downtime
- They demand too much of you
- When they talk, they leave you feeling frustrated than you were before
- You can't seem to say what you mean when you are around them

Things you can do if you are experiencing emotional exhaustion

Exercise

Whenever you are exhausted, exercise is usually the last thing you can think of – after all, working out is a form of physical stress. However, research shows that when we exercise, that can relieve mental stress. It will not only help your mental balance, but also bring changes to the body, heart, spirit, and metabolism. It offers stimulation and a calming effect against depression and stress.

Research has shown that working out can reduce the levels of body stress hormones – like cortisol and adrenaline. Instead, it promotes the release of feel-good hormones called endorphins – natural painkillers and mood elevators – which tightens the muscle.

Breathing exercises

Breathing has been shown to help relieve stress and increase relaxation. When someone is panting fast and has a form of erratic breathing, this is an indicator that they are under duress. However, when you take in slow and deep breaths, it has a calming effect. You must learn how to control your breathing to mimic relaxation.

The best way to breathe is to do it slowly and deeply while focusing your attention on the movement of your diaphragm – up and down. Then hold your breath for at least seconds before you exhale thinking about relaxation for another 5 seconds. Repeat this process for about 15-20 times while ensuring that you do it slowly and deeply.

Meditation

This is a practice that has been shown to help relieve stress and calm the mind. This is by lowering both the heart rate and the blood pressure – physiological signs of stress.

The first thing is for you to choose a place and time when there are no distractions. Then get comfortable by finding the right posture that will promote relaxation. Allow your mind to get into a passive mental state. You must allow your mind to go blank so that thoughts and worries don't get in the way of your relaxation. Watch your thoughts come and go without necessarily passing any judgment.

The trick is to focus your attention on a mental device. You can use simple words of affirmation or mantra so that you repeat them over and over. Alternatively, you can choose to focus your attention on a fixed object within your space. The goal is to ensure that you block out any form of distraction as much as you can. Once you have mastered this, you can dedicate at least 20-30 minutes to meditation every day.

Journaling

If you thought this was just for professional writers, you had better think again. If you ask anyone who has been journaling, they will tell you how much it benefits their mental health by releasing emotional drains.

This is mainly because journaling allows you to write down all your deepest thoughts, emotions, and fears, which is a great way of understanding, managing, and letting go or emotional drains. Research shows that journaling plays a significant role in lowering anxiety, boosting better sleep patterns, improving memory, minimizing depression, and making someone kinder.

One Last word

Indeed, emotional intelligence is one of the most important things one must have in life to ensure success in every situation.

One thing that is important to bear in mind is that emotional intelligence is not a trend! It is here to stay. According to reports and statistics compiled by major companies across the world, it is evident that people with emotional intelligence undoubtedly affect their bottom line. For instance, if an employee has a high level of emotional intelligence, they will not only be productive and generate revenue for the company, but also realize their personal and career goals.

You probably know other people who have mastered the art of managing their emotions. Instead of getting angry when provoked by a stressful situation, they choose to look at the problem from a different perspective to find a solution calmly. These people are excellent decision-makers and have mastered the art of listening to their gut feeling. Irrespective of their strengths, they have the willingness to look at themselves with an honest eye. They take criticism positively and use it to improve their performance.

Well, I am here to tell you that you can be just like these people. As you begin to accept emotional intelligence into every area of your life, you will begin to see an improvement in your technical abilities, interrelationships, and overall success. It is through emotional intelligence that you can fuel your performance. It impacts your confidence, optimism, self-control, empathy, and social skills so that you can understand and manage your emotions and accelerate success in every area of your life.

It does not matter what your profession is, whether you work for a small or large organization, whether you are a senior or junior in your company. What matters is that realizing how effective you are at controlling your emotional energies is the beginning of a successful adventure. Yes, emotional intelligence may not be something taught and tested in our educational curriculum, but the truth is that it is really important.

Take a look at your life – the chances are that you will notice how hectic and busy your lifestyle is. It is this kind of life that makes it easy for you to lose touch with yourself and your emotional feelings. You must try to reconnect with your feelings by setting a timer for various points throughout the day. As soon as the timer goes off, you stop what you are doing, stand on your two feet, and take in a deep breath. Then bring your thoughts to what you are feeling in that moment, where the emotions are coming from, and where you feel the sensation in your body and what it feels like. Realize that the more you practice this, the more you make it your second nature.

The key to emotional intelligence is to celebrate and reflect on all the positives in your life. No one has a perfect life – we all go through ups and downs. It does not matter whether you have more positives or negatives in your life—the trick to celebrate every win – whether small or big. When you embrace the positives in your life, you allow yourself to develop more resilience and increase your chances of enjoying fulfilling relationships so that you can successfully move past adversity.

No matter what life throws your way, you must not forget to take time to just breathe. Taking time to take deep breaths will not only help you master how to manage your emotions but also help you avoid outbursts. Just walk out the door and wash your face with cold water, take a walk, or just take in the fresh air – anything to calm your nerves. This goes a long way in helping you get a hold of what is happening so that you can effectively respond to the situation.

That said, emotional intelligence is a lifetime process! It is not something you develop overnight. The truth is that to grow your emotional intelligence; you have to train your mind to accept continual improvements along the way – so that you can be better with each passing day. So, what are you still waiting for? Start working on improving your emotional intelligence and watch how your life changes for the better.   Best of Luck!

© Written by: JOSEPH GRIFFITH

GASLIGHTING

Recognize Manipulative and How to Avoid the Gaslight Effect. Narcissistic Abuse Recovery, Aggressive Narcissist, Personality disorder, Codependency, Empath, Covert Emotional Manipulation

Jack Mind

GASLIGHTING

Recognize Manipulative and how to avoid the Gaslight Effect.

Narcissistic Abuse Recovery, Aggressive Narcissist, Personality disorder, Codependency, Empath, Covert Emotional Manipulation.

Written by: Jack Mind

Introduction

Gaslighting occurs in personal relationships and professional relationships, and in other cases, gaslighting is used by public figures to change the perceptions of targeted members of the population. Gaslighting is a form of psychological abuse. It can make you start to doubt your ability to perceive reality correctly. It can make you think you didn't see what you thought you saw or hear what you thought you heard; and you start to wonder if you can trust the information you are getting from your five senses. Moreover, this, in turn, will make you begin to think that there must be something wrong with you, and you will begin to doubt your sanity.

It doesn't matter whether it is happening in a personal relationship (parent to child, between romantic partners) or a professional relationship at work or even between members of the same community. Gaslighting creates an abusive situation which can cause serious health problems if the victim continues to be in such a position for a long time.

And no matter whether it occurs in a personal relationship or a working relationship, between a public figure and the members of the public or somewhere else, it is essential to be aware of the signs that you or someone you know might be a victim of gaslighting, as this awareness is the first step to getting out of the damaging situation. The first step to take towards being free from gaslighting is to recognize exactly what gaslighting is. It is often very hard to recognize the signs of gaslighting, because they affect the mind so much that, after a long period of time, the victim doesn't trust their own thoughts.

This book discusses in detail how to distinguish gaslighting behavior from typical behavior by shedding light on the different kinds of gaslighting techniques. It also aims to provide you with information about what to do if you find yourself a victim of such a negative situation.

Gaslighting, which will be defined fully in the following chapters, is a technique used by narcissists to manipulate people. Narcissists are self- centered and arrogant people who lack empathy for others. They live in their own world and believe they are unique and special. Hence, they always seek attention and praise from others.

A narcissist will frequently use gaslighting, as a narcissist's goal is to disorient the victim to gain total control over them. A narcissist achieves this aim by gradually sowing seeds of doubt in the victim's mind, and in the end, the narcissist controls the victim to do their bidding.

In addition to promoting awareness about gaslighting, this book is written with the more precise aim of exposing the extent to which narcissists use gaslighting as a means of manipulation to control and abuse their victims both physically and mentally. They expose the words narcissists say and the actions they take to abuse victims. It is one thing to recognize what gaslighting is, and it is another to know how narcissists use it. It is also a different thing entirely to uncover the effects of gaslighting and guard against them - or better still, avoid the effects in the first place.

Most importantly, they show you how to protect yourself and even remove yourself from the control of a gaslighting narcissist.

Chapter 1. Gaslighting

Gas-lighting is the endeavor of someone else to wind your reality. Narcissists can't and don't assume liability for their conduct. Rather, they look to disgrace and accuse others of evading the awful feelings. This is once in a while referred to as projection.

The problem is, gaslighting is slippery. It plays on our most exceedingly awful feelings of dread, our most restless musings, and our most profound wishes to be comprehended, acknowledged, and loved. At the point when somebody we trust, regard, or love talks with incredible conviction—especially if there's a trace of legitimacy in his words, or if he's hit on one of our "red buttons"—it tends to be difficult not to trust him. Furthermore, when we glorify the gaslighter—when we need to consider him to be the love of our life, a commendable boss, or a brilliant parent—then, we make it more difficult to adhere to our sense of reality. Our gaslighter should be correct; we have to win his endorsement; thus, the gaslighting goes on. Neither of you might know about what's truly occurring. The gaslighter may truly accept each word he lets you know or genuinely feel that he's just sparing you from yourself. Keep in mind: His own needs are driving him. Your gaslighter may appear to be a solid, influential man, or he may have all the earmarks of being an unreliable, fit of rage tossing young man; in any case, he feels frail and feeble. To feel ground-breaking and safe, he needs to demonstrate that he is correct, and he needs to get you to concur with him. Then, you have admired your gaslighter and are edgy for his endorsement, although you may not intentionally understand this. But if there's even a little bit of you that believes you're bad enough without anyone else—if even a little piece of you believes you need your gaslighter's love or endorsement to be fulfilled—at that point, you are powerless to gaslight. What's more, a gaslighter will exploit that helplessness to make you question yourself, again and again.

Gaslighting defies boundaries

When somebody is gaslighting you, they are trying to convince you that your boundaries and perceptions are ridiculous and invalid.

If something they say bothers you because it is abusive or untrue, they will tell you that you are overreacting, or that what you are saying is stupid. They will tell you that it doesn't bother anybody else except you and that you're just being overly sensitive. Even spiritual people are not immune from this, because you might be told that their behavior wouldn't bother you if you were more enlightened. So, in essence, gaslighting and manipulation techniques make you doubt your boundaries or make you drop your boundaries altogether by convincing you that your boundaries are stupid and invalid.

The truth is that your boundaries aren't anybody's business but yours. Nobody gets to determine what boundaries you will have. If something bothers you, then nobody gets to tell you how you feel. When you enforce a boundary, you are not only fighting for the boundary itself, but, more importantly, for your right to set boundaries in the first place. Don't let another person convince you that your boundary isn't big enough for you to take a stand over. It is. Such a way of thinking is really disrespectful.

It's very disrespectful and dishonoring to stand on somebody else's boundary. There is a difference between controlling somebody else by telling them how to behave, and setting a boundary by which you are telling the person not to behave a certain way to you. Reinforcing a boundary means that you are going to have to walk away from someone or from something when they do something wrong to you. Now, realize that it's not about stopping someone from living their life the way they want to live their life, nor is it taking their freedom away from them. It's simply about choosing to engage with or not engage with people who behave in a certain way or who don't respect your boundaries.

Setting up an angry beast

The second form of manipulation is to become an angry beast. This is where somebody tries to become angrier than you when you get angry with them, in order to squash your challenge or rebellion. You might even be just mildly annoyed about something and want to talk to your partner about it, but they explode at you so that you find yourself backing down. You will be so shocked because you were talking about something which was relatively small, and they just turned it into something huge. You will want to back down and not deal with that type of drama. Often, you will be trying to defend your boundaries, and that is what causes the explosion.

This angry beast will come at you with an emotional response that is way out of proportion to the situation or the position that you're trying to defend. You will back down and, often times, you won't even try to stand up for yourself again because you are absolutely not willing to go up against that angry beast. The gaslighter is counting on that.

But when you are defending a proper boundary or setting a boundary, it doesn't really matter what the boundary is all about nor does it really matter whether that person sees it as valid or not. Once you have clearly communicated a boundary and the other person says that he will not accept it, you must follow through on the consequences or you will be intimidated into silence and submission. That is what the angry beast wants.

Hijacking the issue

The next manipulative technique is hijacking the issue. This happens when you raise a topic that challenges someone, and he takes it off on a tangent to distract you so that you will not set that boundary or defend that boundary. For example, let's say it's late at night and your spouse hasn't come home from work. They haven't called and you are really worried because you have no idea where they are or if something has happened to them. They finally come home, and you confront them with how worried you were, and ask them where they were and why they didn't even call you to let you know that they would be late.

Rather than answer your concern and questions, they go off on a tangent about how stressed they are at work and how you're not just getting it. They might start to get angry and accuse you of having no sympathy for them. You then find yourself on the defensive side of the conversation, and even apologize to them. Now you're no longer talking about the original topic – how late they were and why they didn't call – but talking about them, and what's bothering them. In the end, they will avoid answering your question altogether.

They have hijacked the conversation and turned it in a different direction. You will often find yourself sitting them down and apologizing to them, and feeling like you shouldn't bother them with your little concerns.

People who use these manipulation tactics are not doing so in a conscious way. They're not doing this on purpose. So they are not hijacking a conversation on purpose, but they are doing it none the less. They don't intend to work up to being an angry beast, or trample on your boundaries, but they do. They do it to control and manipulate you into always putting them first.

Chapter 2. Understanding the Ins and Outs of Gaslighting

In 1944, a movie called **Gaslight** was released that changed the way people thought about manipulation and its immense power. This movie shows the story of a husband character that manipulates his wife and her life to such an extent that she begins to believe that she has become insane.

In this movie too, just like in my life, the wife, Paula, gets completely caught up with the charms of Gregory, the man who woos and wins her. After a whirlwind romance, they get married, and then the tragedy begins. Gregory begins to show his true personality so subtly that Paula begins to think that everything is alright with her husband and that she is going crazy.

The husband in the film dimmed the gas lights in the house and insisted that the wife imagined that the light was dim. His insistence and manipulation were so powerful that the poor, hapless woman begins to think that she is going crazy. And so, the name gaslighting came to be used for such devious and evil manipulative tactics to deliberately steer people away from their real lives and life experiences.

The movie itself is based on a 1938 play of the same name. The ultimate aim of the villainous husband was, of course, to drive his wife to insanity so that he could put her away in a mental institution and claim her inheritance.

Gaslighting is the name used by psychologists to refer to the tactics used by people with a personality disorder to control and manipulate the lives of other people, either individuals or a group of people. These tactics are so strong and go so deep that the manipulated people tend to doubt and question everything in their own lives; their reality, perceptions, feelings, experiences, and interpretations of these experiences. If someone can have this kind of maniacal control over your life, then there is little doubt that your life and sanity are in danger.

At this juncture, it is important to differentiate gaslighting from those tactics that many people use to annoy and irritate the people around them. Gaslighting tactics have a dark quality that annoying but innocuous behavior of certain people doesn't have. It is imperative that you clearly differentiate between the two so that you don't end up judging everyone you come across wrongly.

But you must know for certain that gaslighting is a very serious problem, and you must learn to discern such behavior and stay as far away from such people as possible. After all, having your reality taken from you can be quite dangerous, and if not managed sensibly can prove disastrous for you and your loved ones.

The difficult thing about understanding gaslighting is that the behavioral signs might start out as something very small and insignificant. For example, the manipulator could correct a small detail in a story or life experience you are narrating. Of course, then his or her correction makes sense, and you accept it wholeheartedly. Slowly, that 'past victory' becomes the focal point and keeps rearing its ugly head in all your interactions with the concerned individual, and before you know it, you become his or her slave completely losing touch with your reality and life.

Deliberately, you will be pushed to such an extent that taking simple daily decisions might become difficult for you. Driven by the seeds of self-doubt sowed by the gaslighter, you could find yourself second-guessing every decision you make. Like I already told you in the introduction chapter, even the clothes I wore became my husband's decision. At some point, the victim is likely to feel that he or she cannot take any decision whatsoever and depends on every little thing on the manipulator.

Furthermore, the aggressor will slowly convince you that his or her behavior is also your fault. The more you apologize for your behavior, the greedier the aggressor's ego becomes, and the person demands an increasing level of apology and supplicating behavior from you.

The aggressor gets so deep into his or her gaslighting attitude that you will find it exceedingly difficult to reach out and seek help from other people in the fear that they will go against your aggressor. When you are completely and irrevocably under the aggressor's control, then the person dumps you and seeks new 'conquests.'

History of Gaslighting

While the term 'gaslighting' was introduced during the early 1940s, the concept of manipulative behavior for controlling people and altering people's imagined realties has been part of human history for a long time. The victims were simply 'diagnosed' with this condition. They simply withered away in a lunatic asylum or some other institution, alone, depressed, and completely neglected.

Can you recall the story of 'The Emperor Clothes?' What happened there? Did the smart salesman drive every observer on the street to believe that the emperor was clothed in the finest of garments when, in reality, he was stark naked? A little, guileless child saved the day for the rest of the people who believed that if they couldn't see the clothes on their emperor, then it was their fault.

In 1981, psychologist Edward Weinshel wrote an article entitled "Some Clinical Consequences of Introjection: Gaslighting," in which he explained the concept in the following way. The manipulator 'externalizes and projects' the image or thought, and the victim 'internalizes and assimilates' the information into his or her psyche unquestioningly. The 'victim' takes in all the faults, mistakes, and irrationality in such relationships.

Why Does Gaslighting Happen?

Simply put, gaslighting is all about having control. This need for control or domination could stem from personality disorders like narcissism, antisocial issues, unresolved childhood trauma, or any other reason.

Gaslighting behavior is usually seen between people involved in power dynamics where one person invariably wields more power than the other person or people in the relationship equation. The victim of gaslighting tactics is typically on a lower rung than the manipulator and is also terrified of losing something in the relationship. The target of the manipulative relationship is likely to be a codependent partner in the relationship.

For example, in a romantic relationship, the wife might feel the compulsion to put up with manipulative behavior because she

WANTS to be in the relationship and/or desires the other things that it brings. Such people are ready to change their perceptions to align with those of the manipulative partner so as to avoid conflicts and to allow things to happen smoothly.

On the other hand, the manipulator continues to be one because he or she is scared of being seen as something less important or significant than desired. Another critical perspective of the gaslighter is that the person may not realize that he or she is behaving in ways that could harm or hurt the 'target.' They could be indulging in gaslighting tactics simply because they were reared like that.

For example, if a person was brought up by parents who believe in the concept of absolute certainty, then this person may not know that other perspectives can exist and that they can be right. Such people could be primed to think that anyone who has a different approach or perspective is wrong. Further, they could believe that people with these 'wrong' notions should be corrected, and thus resort to gaslighting tactics; an approach found commonly in a family and among loved ones.

And then, there are the ones who employ gaslighting to show off their dominance and power with little or no care toward the pain and agony inflicted on the target. Sometimes, the 'dominance and power' could also be a facade for the manipulator's insecurities and fears. Whatever it is, gaslighting is employed to dominate unfairly over other people.

Where Does Gaslighting Happen?

Gaslighting can happen and be experienced by anyone and everyone. For example, you could be a victim of such tactics from your spouse, partner, colleague, or sometimes, even a parent. In fact, gaslighting tactics are not restricted to the personal or professional realm.

Gaslighting strategies are used even in public life, affecting an entire group of people. There are multiple instances in which you can clearly see gaslighting techniques by President Donald Trump and his administration. Most experts agree that politics is a field where spreading lies is taken and accepted to be a stereotypical attitude. However, President Trump seems to have taken it a bit too far.

In the initial days of his office, President Trump - along with his administration staff - are believed to have lied so blatantly that there was a shade of arrogance and utter contempt for the intelligence of the American people. It was like the concerned officials were baiting the common people, telling them to rise up and revolt against the nastiness if you can; this was a clear sign of narcissistic personality disorder.

For instance, the administration lied about the crowd size at the Presidential swearing-in. It was clear that photos from President Obama's swearing-in were manipulated to look like the current one. It was so easy to detect this lie that for some people, it was like a war cry to the media, which was most likely to be discredited by Americans for putting such lies on their websites and publications.

At a personal level, gaslighting tactics are used by manipulative people who want to control the lives of their family members. Think of a physically and emotionally abusive spouse wreaking havoc on his or her partner or the children in the family, and you can easily discern gaslighting behavior.

Where is Gaslighting Typically Seen?

Geographically speaking, gaslighting behavior is not exclusive to any part of the world. Wherever power dynamics are in play and where the need and desire for control over people and resources exist, gaslighting behavior can be witnessed. Multiple studies reveal that this kind of unpleasant and dangerous behavior is prevalent not only in personal relationships but also at the workplace, and even in public life as in the way some politicians and their coterie interact with the common man on the street.

MHR, an HR services provider, conducted a survey in the UK which revealed some shocking numbers. Over 3000 people undertook the survey, and 58% of this group claimed that they had experienced what they believed was gas-lighting behavior at their workplace. About 30% said they did not experience such behavior while 12% said that they didn't know! The disturbing results of this survey poll reveal how widespread gaslighting is in the UK. Some examples of gaslighting behaviors at the workplace include:

- Taking credit for your work

- Mocking you, your behavior or dress style in front of other colleagues

- Setting unreasonable and unrealistic deadlines

- Deliberately withholding information that is crucial for the success of a project you are working on

Most of the elements mentioned above are seemingly insignificant but add up to a lot in retrospect. And moreover, unlike bullying, which is easily discernible, gaslighting behaviors are subtle and are meant to slowly but surely put doubt on your capabilities and value to the organization. Such attitudes cannot be caught until after the damage is done to the target's psyche.

Another US-based report says that 3 out of 4 people in the country are not aware of the term, and this state of ignorance is despite the widespread prevalence of gaslighting behavior in the entertainment and media industries where power-play dynamics are perhaps the strongest.

Nearly 75% of the surveyed people said that they had heard of the term but did not know its meaning. The study revealed that about a third of the female population had termed their romantic partners as 'crazy' or 'insane' in a very serious way. About 25% of the male population had also used these two words to describe their partners.

Therefore, gaslighting behavior is not restricted to any particular geography or industry, and can be witnessed in different countries, cultures, and industries.

Common Gaslighting Situations

Here are some common examples of gaslighting scenarios that could help you understand if and when you are being gaslighted by various perpetrators.

In a home environment - Alice's father, Andrew, is a bitter and angry man who is carrying a lot of negativity right from his childhood. His power play is most evident with Alice, thanks to her dependence on him for a lot of things. Alice's mother is the breadwinner in the family and is away most of the time at work.

Alice spent a lot more time with her father than her mother and had unwittingly built herself into a codependency situation with Andrew. She was highly sensitive to his mood swings and was always worried that some action or behavior of hers would bring on a dark mood in her father.

Whenever her father was in a dark mood, he would lash out at Alice by saying that 'You're worthless,' 'I wonder why you were born,' and quite frequently using foul language too. If Alice tried to argue back with him, he would laugh it off and say, 'Why are you so unnecessarily sensitive?'

Alice had become so accustomed to this situation at home that she did not even think it important enough to speak to her mother about it that was too busy with her work to find time for her daughter. Alice was completely under her father's control and even accepted it as natural. She believed that her father was only helping her toward self-improvement and that there was nothing wrong with him.

Another common situation is when adult children manipulate their old parents. Here is a sample case that you are likely to find in many homes.

In a romantic relationship - In the eyes of most people, Julie's life could be seen as being as ideal. Married for over five years to her first love who is now an adoring husband, financially secure (her husband, John, is an investment banker who rakes in the moolah), and with two beautiful children, Julie might look like there is no dearth of happiness in her life. And yet, she knows what she is going through. Before her marriage, Julie was an artist with some great skills.

After she got married, John did his best to prevent his wife from trying to advance her skills and make a name for herself in the art world. He always found fault with her work and made her feel worthless. Every time she tried to paint something, he would say, 'A lousy artist like you is not going to make it in the art world which is filled with brilliant artists. Your work will never match up to theirs.

Don't waste time and money on this. Instead, just focus on looking after the family.'

Also, he would always bring up a bad experience that she had had during her early artist days. She had created a painting and wanted feedback from a famous artist who was a good friend of her husband's. The man had said that her skills were way below even an average artist and that she should not even try moving forward. Julie's husband never failed to bring up that comment and used it to make her believe that she was fit for nothing more than taking care of the family.

Julie's husband used that one bad experience and feedback to remind her of her worthlessness continually, and repeated practice and such habitual behavior enslaved her to her husband completely. Now, although she lives comfortably, she realizes that her life is actually empty. She wants to break free from her husband's manipulative ways, but he uses their children to strengthen his power over her.

In a workplace scenario - Jolly was a salesgirl in a large cosmetic showroom. After working for five years, she was given a promotion to work in, which not only gave her a higher salary but also opened up career growth prospects. Jolly was very happy with the promotion and started working with her new boss, Penny.

Initially, Jolly found Penny helpful and sweet. Slowly, Penny started passing on insignificant tasks to Jolly, who did them uncomplainingly. However, this did not stop at all and, in fact, increased so much that she had no time and energy to learn anything new at the job. She was just about able to finish all the work assigned by her boss, who kept her at arm's length and discouraged interactions of all kinds except with giving out tasks.

A department meeting was called one day, and Jolly was part of it. Penny addressed the other people and said, 'Meet Jolly, who has been with us for nearly three months now, and she has yet to learn the ropes of the new department. I hope she catches up soon or else we might have to send her back after demoting her.' Jolly turned red with embarrassment and shame at this open and unexpected insult from her boss. And she realized that she had unwittingly become a victim of gaslighting tactics!

Emotional Hot Spots that are targeted

Nearly anyone can be a target to gaslighting tactics considering the subtlety involved in the process. Very few people can really discern the difference between gaslighting and simple annoying behavior. Most often, people will tend to categorize gaslighting behaviors as a mere annoyance and tend to ignore it. Yet, there are certain types of people who become easy targets for gaslighting. Some of them are:

Empaths - Empaths are people who are extremely sensitive to everything that is happening around them. They can quickly, and most often, unwittingly absorb both positive and negative energies from their environment. Such people can be easy targets for gaslighters because it is quite easy to influence them. Just sending negative vibes to empaths can enhance their sensitivity to a gaslighter's needs.

Insecure people - Gaslighters typically target people with significant inferiority complexes. Men and women who feel insecure about themselves are easy targets considering that they are already in a vulnerable condition.

Moreover, insecure people are continuously looking for positive affirmation from others, which is exactly what gaslighters want in the initial stages of any new relationship. Gaslighting tactics start with heaping praise, often when it is not necessary and praises on the victims initially, and once they are trapped, the true color of gaslighters come to the fore.

And yet, it is time to reiterate that some gaslighters are so good at what they do that even the sanest and most sensible people can become their targets. Therefore, it makes sense to be aware of the concept of gaslighting tactics and their multiple negative effects and to be wary of such people.

Chapter 3. How to spot a gaslighter

If there is an attribute that gaslighters appear to have in abundance, it is charm. They are generally likable people that appear to overflow tons of charm, and this may make it difficult to identify them on the surface. There are, however, a few manners of behavior by which they can be identified, and these include:

Withholding: Here the gaslighter retains information on what they know or what is the fact by pretending not to understand their victims. They may begin sentences with phrases like "Are you trying to confound me by?" or "Please, don't accompany this again. Haven't I told you...?" It is a tactic to perplex the victim by making him/her vibe like they are off-base or misconstrued a situation.

Countering: The victim's facts are made to be false as victims are blamed for their 'carelessness' or 'jumbling things up' although the victim's memory is great.

Diverting: In this case, the gaslighter attempts to occupy the victim or make them question themselves by changing the subject of discussion. An example is "I'm certain your crazy sister advised you to screen my calls." Or "None of this is valid, you're making them up to hurt me."

Downplaying facts: When the victim complains about an unsavory situation or communicates a fear, the gaslighter laughs at the issue or downplays its earnestness, making the victim feel like a youngster with a tantrum. You hear phrases like "You're angry because of that?"

Outright denial: The gaslighter will deny guarantees that they made, totally telling the victim that they never said so and that the whole conversation happened in the victim's mind. For example, "I never advised you to keep dinner waiting for me!"

Pathologizing: Especially savage gaslighters may choose to play specialist with your mental health and 'diagnose' you of instability in an offer to conceal their behavior. They can proceed to make claims that you are 'unstable,' 'not all there,' 'spacey,' or 'vengeful' in an offer to unhinge their victims. They may even advise you to book an appointment with a psychiatrist, all the while acting as if they are working for your wellbeing and subsequently making you accept that something is genuinely amiss with you.

Discrediting: A gaslighter will, under the pretense of helping you, spread falsehoods and bits of gossip about you to the people within your circle. They would pretend to be stressed over you and utilize that chance to tell others that you are unstable or have been acting bizarre. They may also turn around to reveal to you that others think you are crazy as a way to drive a wedge among you and the people you would normally go to for help.

Put blames on you: A gaslighter will always find a way to blame you for whatever off-base they do. Attempt to have an important conversation about how they hurt you, and they will turn the discussion upside down that you will start believing that you are the reason for their bad behavior.

Shaming: Another tool the gaslighter utilizes in keeping the victim calm is by unobtrusively shaming them by making victims feel inept about the fact that they have been victimised. You will, at that point, apologize to them for speaking out about a bad behavior you called out when they have convinced you it's all in your head. A husband that has been cheating may turn the tables on you by saying: "I can't trust you would think that I would cheapen our relationship in that manner! If you trust I did this, it means you have been unfaithful to me," he may say.

Use kind words to keep you daydreaming: When you call out a gaslighter, they may amaze you by using kind words that may make you assume that maybe they are not all that bad after all. But if they utilize kind words when faced without changing their behavior or stopping the things that hurt you, they are just manipulative because, after some time, you will start thinking that you are excessively emotional.

Chapter 4. Cognitive Dissonance | How Manipulation Affects You

When a person is being manipulated, cognitive dissonance is a common occurrence. You may be asking yourself what cognitive dissonance actually is, and the thought behind it is actually quite simple. When you get a feeling that is uncomfortable because it goes against your beliefs or your normal way of thinking, it is referred to as cognitive dissonance.

A good example of this would be if you are usually an honest person and you tell a lie. Naturally, this is going to make you feel quite uncomfortable. The contradiction of the behavior you expressed as compared to your normal behaviors is quite different, and the person that does this will experience cognitive dissonance.

In general, people try to be consistent with their thoughts, ideas, attitudes, and behaviors. When these items are challenged, or they go against your level of normalcy, many people will try to change this lack of agreement by doing things like overly explaining their behavior or action. This makes it more comfortable and allows them to move past it.

The first theory behind cognitive dissonance came from a psychologist by the name of Leon Festinger. It centered around the fact that most people will do their best to find internal consistency. Festinger said that we all have an internal need to make sure that our behaviors and our belief systems stay consistent. When they are inconsistent, it leads to internal disharmony, which is something everyone will try and avoid if they can. In fact, people will go to great lengths to find internal balance after experiencing cognitive dissonance.

There are a variety of different factors that will impact the amount of dissonance that a person may experience. One of those factors is how concrete they feel in certain beliefs that they hold. Another factor is how consistent they are in their beliefs throughout the course of time.

Thoughts and mental actions that are very personal, such as your understanding and belief in yourself can cause greater dissonance inside of you than other beliefs.

The higher value something holds in you internally, the greater the dissonance you will experience if you go against that belief. It is normal for people to have thoughts that clash; however, this is something that tends to come and go as most people strive to have consistent thought patterns, behaviors, and beliefs. The more dissonance a person experiences, the more pressure they will also experience to find balance and relieve themselves of uncomfortable feelings.

It's actually pretty amazing how cognitive dissonance can influence a person's actions, thoughts, and behaviors. Cognitive dissonance can be seen in just about every area of life. It is predominant in situations that behaviors conflict with a person's belief system. This is especially true when dealing with the area of self-identity. Let's look at an example of cognitive dissonance so that you have a very clear understanding of what we are talking about here.

- We see cognitive dissonance occur frequently when people are making purchasing decisions. Let's say you are someone that is very conscious of the environment, and you do your very best to make green decisions. One day you go and buy a new car to find out that it is not very eco-friendly. This will cause cognitive dissonance because you care about being friendly to the environment, yet you are driving a car that is not very friendly to the environment. The dissonance can be reduced the number of ways to make the belief and the behavior go together better. You could choose to sell your new vehicle and get one that is going to get better mileage and be friendlier to the environment, or you could choose to cut down on how much you are driving the new car. Some may choose to utilize public transportation or even ride a bike to work. Each one of these is a solution to help resolve the dissonance that is being experienced. They all help bring balance.

There are a variety of ways that people will try to find balance when experiencing dissonance. Minimizing the drawbacks of a decision or action is one way that people do this. A great example is to think about people who smoke, and they may take the time to convince themselves that the risks are being blown out of proportion. This helps their minds to accept the bad habit of smoking and, in turn, alleviate the dissonance hey experience when they smoke and think about it being bad for their health.

Another thing that people will do to get rid of the uncomfortable feelings caused by cognitive dissonance is to look at the beliefs that outweigh the action that was dissonant. This is done by looking for new information to change their old patterns of thinking.

This new information, even if it isn't exactly correct, can allow the uncomfortable feelings to dissipate, leaving the person feeling more balanced and at ease.

People will also try to reduce the significance of the belief that conflicts how they normally feel. An example of this is the person who works in an office building and sits in front of a computer all day. They know that sitting for long periods of time is unhealthy, but it is hard to change it since it is there job to sit in front of that computer. Rather than change their behavior, they will try and justify the action of sitting all day. They do this by telling themselves that the fact that they eat healthily and exercise once in a while will be enough to combat the negative effects of sitting all day. This helps to reduce the uncomfortable dissonance they are experiencing.

The last way that people deal with cognitive dissonance is to change the conflict that is occurring inside. By changing a belief so that it coincides with other beliefs, the dissonance will be alleviated. This change of belief systems is effective when trying to deal with dissonance, but it is also quite difficult. Obviously, if you are trying to change your core values and beliefs to deal with dissonance, it is going to be a challenge.

More often than not, people will find other ways to deal with the cognitive dissonance that does not require them to restructure their entire thought process and beliefs on a particular subject.

It is important to remember that cognitive dissonance can be very disconcerting. When your beliefs and your actions don't match up, it can take a toll on your ability to make decisions that will be beneficial to you. When we notice cognitive dissonance, it should be looked at as an opportunity to grow and learn.

When you are dealing with a gaslighting narcissist, cognitive dissonance can give you a great clue as to what is going on. If you find yourself doing, saying, or agreeing with things that go against your values and beliefs because of what someone else is saying, it is a good sign that you are being manipulated. Our bodies do a great job of helping us understand the experiences that unfold in front of us on a daily basis. You can use cognitive dissonance to your advantage so that you maintain the beliefs and values that ring true to you rather than allow yourself to be influenced by a nefarious manipulator.

Effects of Manipulation

Manipulation can come in a variety of different forms, and unfortunately, there are a variety of different negative effects that come along with it. Whether you are mentally or emotionally manipulated, the effects can be devastating. Sometimes they are short term effects that can be moved passed relatively easily while other times they are long-lasting and can impact your life forever. When you know the effects of manipulation, you are better equipped to handle them, and your life will be able to improve more easily.

Psychological and emotional abuse occurs when people are manipulated, and unfortunately, they are not simple wounds that will heal. In fact, it is likely if you have been abused with manipulation that you will carry the scars for the rest of your life. Seeking help is sometimes the best course of action, depending on the experience that you have had. When it comes to mental manipulation, you may find that you have problems with trust, security, respect, and intimacy, and these are only a few of the issues that you may be facing.

We are going to take the time to look at the short- and long-term effects that occur from mental and emotional manipulation.

The gaslighting tactic, is both mental and emotional abuse. So, if you have or you are dealing with a narcissist who uses gaslighting, it is very likely that you are experiencing some of these effects. Recognizing them can be the first step toward finding improved health and happiness.

The Short-Term Effects of Manipulation:

- If you have been mentally or emotionally manipulated, it can be very difficult to understand what is unfolding. You may feel surprised or confused by events. The feelings of "this can't be so" are very common. You may question why the people closest to you are acting so strange, even if they aren't acting strange at all.

- It is also likely that you will question yourself if you have been through or you are going through this type of abuse. You may wonder if your memory is deceiving you, or you may feel like there is something wrong with you, in general. When everything you do is questioned, this is the result. Gaslighting will cause this effect frequently as you will always be wrong or questioned by the narcissistic party in the relationship.

- If you have experienced mental or emotional manipulation, another short-term effect could be anxiety and hypervigilance.

People become vigilant toward themselves and other people to try and avoid further manipulation. They will avoid behaviors that make things chaotic or ones that may end in outbursts. Anxiety will rule them, and any extra chaos could lead to a break down so, they will avoid any and everything that may cause that.

- Passiveness is another effect that comes from being psychologically and emotionally manipulated. Oftentimes, more emotional pain comes when you take action in a mentally or emotionally abusive relationship, so being passive becomes part of everyday life. It is important to note that being passive can be a hard thing to break, especially during times of emotional stress. Being passive can become a default and a constant presence in day to day life.

- The feeling of guilt or shame is also a common effect of mental and emotional manipulation. When you are constantly being blamed for the negative actions taking place in your life, you start to believe that you are the cause. This can lead to feelings of guilt or shame as you take their bad behavior out on yourself. Obviously, this is only going to make you feel worse, and it is an unfortunate side effect of being with a narcissist or a manipulator.

- Avoiding making eye contact with others is another short-term effect of mental and emotional manipulation. When we don't make eye contact with people, it allows us to feel smaller like you can hide inside of yourself and that you will take up less space. This is a common thing to do when someone is hard on you all the time and makes you feel as if you are insane. We feel that it helps to protect us in some sort of way. Fortunately, this is a side effect that tends to go away rather quickly after we remove the toxic manipulator from our lives and start being around people that genuinely care for us in healthy ways.

- The last short-term effect that we would like to mention is the feeling that you need to walk on eggshells around people. When you live your life with an emotional or mental manipulator around, you will never be able to tell what will upset them next. Due to this fact, you will start to obsess about everything that you are doing. The obsession takes place because you are trying to avoid causing any outbursts, and it can bleed over into other relationships that you may have.

While there is nothing good to be said about being manipulated psychologically or emotionally, we can take some solace in the fact that if we can move away from these abusive relationships, the above issues will likely resolve. There are side effects of these types of abuse that will not go away so easily.

In fact, there are side effects of emotional manipulation that could stick around forever. Seeking professional help to figure out a course of action to help you heal is oftentimes the best place to start. Let's take a look at some of the long-term effects that one may experience if they have suffered or are suffering from mental or emotional manipulation.

The Long-Term Effects of Manipulation:

- One of the 1st and most devastating long-term effects of mental manipulation are the feelings of isolation or complete numbness. Many find that they feel they are no longer a participant of the world but that they have become observers. Things that used to make them happy now don't make them feel anything at all. When someone no longer recognizes their emotions, it leads to a sense of hopelessness. Many fear that they will never be able to accurately feel or experience their emotions again. This long-term effect does not have to last forever. If you are able to get out of the abusive relationship, you can find healing for your damaged emotions.

- Another long-term effect is constantly seeking approval. People that have been emotionally or mentally manipulated are likely going to be exceptionally nice to every person they come into contact with. Additionally, they will go to great lengths to please others. They will likely be extremely focused on their appearance, and they will constantly be striving to accomplish more and more goals. They will do their best to be perfect in every way so that others will approve of them. While some of these things don't seem so bad, keep in mind that it will be to an extreme which is not good.

- People that have suffered the abuse of manipulation are oftentimes left with feelings of resentment. This resentment can be seen in different ways like impatience, frustration, irritability, and placing blame. When you have been treated poorly, it can be extremely difficult to witness anything other than that negative behavior. So, releasing feelings of resentment can be quite difficult, especially if you are going at it on your own.

- Depression is another real threat to those that have experienced or are experiencing manipulation. Depression is something that may never be overcome once it has taken a hold on your life. It takes a lot of work to dig your way out of the effects of depression. When people are depressed, they start to lose faith in those that they care about and that care about them. They feel alone and sad without a sense of purpose within their world. It becomes hard for them to believe in themselves or in anyone else, and this takes a lot of time to heal from.

- Another long-term effect that may be experienced is the excessive judgment of yourself and others. Due to the fact that a narcissistic manipulator will constantly judge you, you will start to judge yourself and others much more critically. Here will be very high standards when it comes to things like appearance and behavior. This can lead to problems within all of your relationships, including your relationship with yourself.

As noted, long term effects can be devastating an impact your life negatively in just about every aspect. There is hope in coming back from these negative effects after you have been able to remove yourself from a manipulative situation. Keep in mind that there is nothing wrong with admitting you need help and seeking it out. You really can find a lot of healing through therapy or groups, which will help you become yourself once again, allowing you to truly start enjoying life.

Chapter 5. How Gaslighting Narcissists operate to make their Victim Think that they are Crazy

So, we mentioned that narcissists have a hand in gaslighting, but what do they do/ they actually are huge manipulators, and they play a major role in changing the reality of others. Here, we'll discuss how they gaslight others, and why narcissists are bad news for many people.

What Is A Narcissist?

A narcissist is, by definition, someone that suffers from narcissistic personality disorder. Those who are narcissists tend to have an overly inflated sense of importance, and a need for admiration and attention in their relationships, and oftentimes don't have empathy for others.

Narcissists only care about themselves. They don't worry about you, or the guy next to you, but instead, they're only in it for their own benefit. However, they actually have an incredibly fragile ego that will shatter and is very vulnerable if they're hit with the smallest amount of criticism.

Narcissists are textbook manipulators, and they're not fun to deal with. This type of personality causes many issues in different areas of life, and you may run into one of these types without even realizing it. Typically, though, those who suffer from narcissistic personality disorder are unhappy in a general sense if they're not given the admiration they want. They may find all of their relationships unfulfilling, and others may not like being around these types of people.

So how does a narcissist come into your life? Well, those that suffer from this love to latch onto those that will hype them up, making them feel like they're special or unique, and in turn enhance their own self-esteem as a result. They may desire an immense amount of admiration and attention and have difficulty taking criticism in the slightest. They oftentimes see all criticism as defeat.

They are incredibly envious of your accomplishments, to the point where they will want to undermine them however, they can. This can be anything from snarky accomplishments regarding your success to underhanded comparing of others.

Narcissists love to use gaslighting too, but we'll get to that in a bit. For now, let's talk about how they will undermine you. If you do something great, they'll try to belittle it, saying that it's not worth it, and you need to do better. Sometimes, if the narcissist is a parent, they'll compare you to your sibling or someone else in the family. They oftentimes will try to belittle anything you do, turning you into a mess in response.

It's not good, and narcissists in general only care about themselves. Of course, many times only a small fraction of people are actual narcissists, but in general, there are more male narcissists than female narcissists, and you oftentimes will run into them when you're dealing with bosses, coworkers, or even people you may be friends with or date.

But, how can these people use gaslighting? Well, they do so in a very crafty manner.

Narcissism and Gaslighting

Narcissists love to use gaslighting. In fact, it's their favorite, most preferred tool of gaslighting. Why is that? Well, it's because it's the perfect way to make you think you're crazy, to completely undermine what you think is right, and to basically tell you that your way of thinking is wrong.

Remember, gaslighting is a very sneaky way of making you feel like your reality is so distorted to the point where the person will question their own sanity or even their memory. Their goal is to make it so that they're right, you're wrong, and that's all they want from this.

The goal is to make you think you're crazy, which we'll get to in a bit. There are other tools narcissist will use, but gaslighting is their bread and butter.

"Oh, I never said that."

"Oh, you're remembering it wrong, clearly you should get yourself checked out."

If you've ever heard those two things before from someone, you're dealing with a Grade A Narcissist.

Gaslighting is used by narcissists because it's how they love to hide the abuse they're inflicting upon you. In essence, gaslighting is lying straight to your face, with one singular goal in mind, to be the ones in control, the center of attention, and you're nothing.

Basically, every time a narcissist gaslights you, they're basically completely ruining what sense of reality you have, making you realize that it's nothing, and they're everything.

They want to break you down slowly but surely. Memory is one of the easiest ways to do this. Why is that? Well, it's because they know that if you can't remember things right, you're not going to be able to trust yourself, distorting your own personal perception and reality that comes with this.

So yes, it does happen like that, and the goal is for you to completely rely on the abuser to tell you what's real so that over time the abuser is the one in control of your life, the one taking the reins here in the game.

The Art of Making Others Crazy

This is something that a lot of narcissists use gaslighting for. Remember, gaslighting is basically refuting anyone's reality, making it so that what they think is right really isn't.

When a narcissist gaslights, they will put down and refute anything that you say. They will do this to make it sound like they're the ones who are right when in reality, it's their own mind games.

It's all a game for a narcissist. They want to make it so that your reality isn't correct. While you might believe that you're right, the narcissist will tell you right away that you aren't. Over time as you continue to be refuted by the narcissist, you start to doubt your own reality. You start to think that you're the bad guy when in reality, it's just your narcissist playing games.

When a narcissist gaslights, they can change the view that you have of people, in general, being good. You might think that people, in general, are good, which they are, but oftentimes, if you have a narcissist in your life, this person will not protect your feelings. Someone you may think is good turns out to be bad, and someone that you thought was bad turns out to be good since that's how the narcissist wants you to think.

A narcissist will use gaslighting for the sole reason of, they know exactly how to manipulate you. You start to doubt your own reality, and over time, you start to wonder if maybe you are crazy. After all, after so often, you may wonder if you're not right in the head. But remember, more often than not, narcissists were the cause of this, and they're the reason why you think this way.

Lots of times narcissists will start by buttering you up, making you feel loved and appreciated since that's what they want you to believe. After a while, they will start to, over time, start to treat you like crap. When you call them out on it, they'll start to mask their true feelings, and you'll be seeing a totally different side.

But the reality is, that mask that they put on is, of course, their mask, and the abusive nature that they've had till now is their true form.

They will tell you what you think is what happened isn't what happened, but that's actually how it is. But of course, in the world of the narcissist, they'll only make you believe what they think is right.

Gaslighting basically takes away everything that you think is correct, which then causes you to follow what they think is the way when in reality, they're manipulating you.

You're basically forced to believe that you're crazy, or if you don't think you're crazy, that the abuser is wrong, but you can't stand up for yourself. They will either manipulate you until you believe you're wrong and they are right or drive you to the point of insanity.

Gaslighters and narcissists love this. Because they know that, once you discount your own personal beliefs enough, you'll start to really think that you are crazy, and slowly start to believe them.

Making People do What the Narcissist Wants

This is done because most of the time, when you start to discount how a narcissist acts, they will immediately gaslight you, saying that it didn't happen this way.

You notice your narcissist abuser is acting gross and mean, and you notice that for example, they're flirting with other girls. They totally are, and you call them out on it, but they will immediately say that isn't the case, tell you that you're crazy, that you're making stuff up, and basically tell you whatever you saw was wrong.

Deep down, you know what the truth is. That the actions you saw were valid, but over time, this person will continuously tell you that you're crazy, that you didn't really hear or say what was said.

You start to doubt your own reality, and you begin to wonder if you remembered everything right. Perhaps you didn't catch the other person flirting with girls. You start to go silent on it. When in reality, your narcissist was totally doing that, didn't come clean, and now this person is seeing girls, and every time you call them out on that, and their own trust and validity, basically tells you that you're insane, and you're wrong.

You stop fighting the narcissist after a while. You notice that every time you fight them there really is no end to it and the fact that you're constantly told that you're crazy every time you do isn't a good thing for you either. So, what do you do from here?

The answer is most people tend to give in to their abusers.

Instead of doing what they feel is right, which is calling out the abuser and recognizing the toxic traits, you start to do exactly what the abuser wants. Because whenever you're gaslight, you start to feel like you're wrong, and that the narcissist is right. You're pretty much duped into believing that the narcissist is the right person, and you're wrong, making your reality practically nothing.

If you let this continue, you're basically feeding the supply of narcissism that the other person craves. You may start to perceive things wrong, and oftentimes, it gets to the point where you swore it was that way, but maybe your stuff is gone, because the narcissist hides it, and then they claim that you're irresponsible, and not worthy of trust. They will then tell you that you're wrong and crazy, and they'll start to make others think that you're crazy.

They will even pit others against you to isolate others. Oftentimes, they'll try to put you against others, so you drop them, and the only person in your life is the narcissist. They'll make up lies, and you can't really trust anyone but the person who is gaslighting you.

When in reality, the one who is gaslighting you is the last person that you should be trusting!

Gaslighters don't really realize just how harmful they are, or maybe they do. They will start to make you question even the most random of strangers. You might start to brush off someone's actions as being harmless, but the gaslighted will call it flirting, and soon, you start to attack anyone who comes at you.

Have you ever seen this? Maybe you've experienced it. Where you will hear about how someone was looking at you the wrong way, you start to grow weary and angry with the other person, and over time, those relationships break down since you think they can't be trusted. When in reality, it's the narcissist who can't be trusted, because they're the one putting you in this direction.

A narcissist will hurt literally everyone in your life, pit you against the friends and family that you have so that you're distracted from what the narcissist is really doing, which is feeding you harmful lies.

It's a messy situation and not something that most of us want to deal with.

So yes, a narcissist will use gaslighting. It's the prime tool of narcissist because they know that they can bend others to the will that they have, making it very easy to manipulate them, and that's why many narcissists will smile at you with a warm, fake smile, and then stab you in the back whenever you turn around, or put your family and friends against you, so the only person you can really rely on, is the narcissist themselves

Chapter 6. The Effects of Gaslighting

Effects of Gaslighting

1. Gaslighting can have catastrophic effects on a person's psychological health; the procedure is gradual, chipping away the person's certainty and self-esteem. They may come to accept they merit the abuse.

2. Gaslighting can also influence a person's social life. The abuser may manipulate them into cutting ties with friends and relatives. The individual might also isolate themselves, believing they are unstable or unlovable.

3. Especially when the person escapes the abusive relationship, the effects of gaslighting can persevere. The person may even now question their discernments and have difficulty making decisions. They are also more reluctant to voice their emotions and feelings, knowing that they are probably going to be invalidated.

4. Gaslighting may lead a person to create mental health concerns. The constant self-uncertainty and disarray can contribute to anxiety. A person's sadness and low self-esteem may lead to despondency. Post-traumatic stress and codependency are common developments.

5. Some survivors may battle to confide in others; they may be on constant guard for additional manipulation. The individual may criticize themselves for not catching the gaslighting earlier. Their refusal to show vulnerability might prompt strain in future relationships.

Recovering from Gaslighting

Gaslighting is a secret form of abuse that blossoms with uncertainty. A person can grow to distrust everything they feel, hear, and recollect. One of the most significant things a survivor can get is validation.

The individuals who have encountered gaslighting may also wish to look for therapy. A therapist is a natural party who can aid in reinforcing one's sense of reality. In therapy, an individual can modify their self-esteem and recover command of their lives. A therapist might also treat any mental health concerns caused by the abuse, for example, PTSD. With time and backing, a person can recoup from gaslighting.

Are You Being Gas lighted?

Gaslighting may not include these experience or feelings, but if you recognize yourself in any of them, give it additional attention.

1. You are constantly re-thinking yourself.
2. You ask yourself, "Am I excessively sensitive?" twelve times each day.
3. You regularly feel confounded and even insane at work.
4. You're continually saying 'sorry' to your mom, father, sweetheart, boss.
5. You wonder now and again if you are a "sufficient" sweetheart/wife/representative/companion/little girl.
6. You can't get why, with so many beneficial things in your life, you aren't more joyful.
7. You purchase garments for yourself, goods for your apartment, or other personal buys in light of your partner, considering what he might want rather than what might cause you to feel incredible.
8. You often rationalize your partner's conduct to loved ones.
9. You end up denying data of loved ones, so you don't need to clarify or rationalize.
10. You realize something is off-base, but you can never fully communicate what it is, even to yourself.
11. You begin lying to maintain a strategic distance from the put-downs and reality turns.
12. You experience difficulty settling on basic decisions.

13. You reconsider before raising blameless subjects of discussion.

14. Before your partner gets back home, you go through a list in your mind to foresee anything you may have fouled up that day.

15. There is a sense that you used to be a different person — increasingly sure, progressively carefree, progressively relaxed.

16. You begin addressing your better half through his secretary so you don't need to reveal to him things you're apprehensive may agitate him.

17. You feel as if you can't do anything right.

18. Your children start attempting to shield you from your partner.

19. You get yourself angry with people you've generally coexisted with previously.

20. You feel sad and dreary.

Gaslighting tends to work in stages

From the start, it might be generally minor—in reality; you may not see it. At the point when your partner blames you for intentionally attempting to undermine you by appearing late to his office party, you attribute it to his nerves or expect you didn't generally mean it or maybe even start to ponder whether you were attempting to undermine him—but then you let it go. Inevitably, however, gaslighting turns into a greater piece of your life, distracting your musings and overpowering your feelings.

Eventually, you're buried in full-scale sorrow, miserable and dismal, unfit even to recollect the person you used to be, with your perspective and your sense of self. You may not continue through every one of the three phases. But for many women, gaslighting goes from terrible to more awful.

Stage 1: Disbelief Stage 1 is portrayed by disbelief; your gaslighter says something over the top—"That person who approached us for bearings was extremely simply attempting to get you into bed!"— And you can't exactly accept your ears. You think you've misjudged, or perhaps he has, or possibly he was simply kidding. The comment appears to be so unusual; you may ignore it. Or on the other hand, maybe you attempt to address the blunder but without a ton of energy. Possibly you even get into since a long time ago, included arguments, but you're still quite sure of your perspective. Although you'd like your gaslighter's endorsement, you don't yet feel frantic for it.

Stage 2: Defense Stage 2 is set apart by the need to safeguard yourself. You scan for proof to refute your gaslighter and contend with him fanatically, frequently in your mind, frantically attempting to win his endorsement.

Stage 3: Depression gaslighting is the most challenging of all: downturn. Now, you are effectively attempting to demonstrate that your gaslighter is correct, because then perhaps you could do things his way and at long last win his endorsement.

Chapter 7. Signs you are Being Manipulated with Gaslighting

The signs of gaslighting can be hard to see, especially for the person that is being manipulated by this tactic. Obviously, the effects of gaslighting are extremely detrimental. So, if you can recognize the signs of it as it is happening, it gives you an advantage and the possibility of getting out of this toxic situation before it completely destroys you and your life.

Oftentimes, people that care about you will recognize the signs before you will be able to. They may try and talk to you about the issues that they are seeing, but you may not be willing to hear them if the effects of gaslighting have already taken hold.

When someone you trust or once felt that you could trust comes to you and expresses their concern over signs of gaslighting, you should spend time reflecting on what they have to say to ensure that you are not a victim of this horrific abuse.

We are going to discuss a variety of different signs that you may witness if you are being gaslighted. Becoming a victim of gaslighting can impact your life negatively in every way. By looking over the following signs, it may become easier to understand what is going on, which can, in turn, give you the clarity and confidence to remove yourself from your current situation.

If you find yourself doubting your own emotions, you may be experiencing the repercussion of gaslighting. Oftentimes people will try to convince themselves that things really aren't so bad. They will assume they are simply too sensitive and that what they are seeing as reality is tragically skewed from actual reality. If you have never had an issue with doubting your feelings, it can be a very good sign of gaslighting tactics.

Alongside doubting, your emotions will come doubting your perceptions of the events that unfold in front of you, as well as doubting your own personal judgment.

Many people that are being manipulated by gaslighting will be afraid to stand up for themselves and express their emotions. This is due to the fact that when they do the gaslighting narcissist makes them feel bad or inferior for doing so. If you find that you are choosing silence over communication, it is a pretty good sign that gaslighting is present in your relationship.

At one point or another, we will all feel vulnerable or insecure. These are normal feelings; however, if you are in a situation of gaslighting, you will feel this way consistently. You may always feel like you need to tiptoe around your partner, family member, or friend to ensure that they don't have a negative outburst. Additionally, you will start to believe that you are the one causing problems for them instead of the reverse.

The gaslighting narcissist will do their best to sever ties between you and the people that you care about. This can leave the victim feeling powerless and completely alone. The narcissist will convince their victim that the people around them don't actually care. In fact, they will try to convince the victim that everyone thinks that they are crazy, unstable, or flat out insane. These kinds of comments make the victim feel trapped. It also causes them to distance themselves from the people that do actually care, which, intern, makes them in even less control than before.

Another sign that you are in the grips of the abuse that comes from a narcissistic gaslighter is feeling that you are crazy or stupid. The narcissist will use a variety of different words and phrases to make you question your own value. This can become extreme to the point that the victim may start repeating these derogatory comments. The sooner you can see the sign of verbal abuse, the sooner you will be able to make the decision to not let it deconstruct your sense of self-worth.

The gaslighting narcissist will do their best to change your perception of yourself. Let's say that you have always thought of yourself as a strong and assertive person, yet all of a sudden, you realize that your behaviors are passive and weak. This extreme change of behavior is a good sign that you are succumbing to gaslighting tactics. When you are grounded in who you really are and what your belief system stands for, it will be harder for the narcissistic gaslighter to get you to be disappointed in yourself. When you can recognize that the viewpoint of your worth has changed, it can give you the motivation to take back control of your own life.

Confusion is one of the narcissistic gaslighter's favorite tools. They will say one thing one day and then do something completely opposite the following day. The result of these types of actions is extreme confusion.

The behaviors of a narcissistic gaslighter will never be consistent. They will always try to keep you on your toes so that you are in a constant state of anxious confusion. This gives them more control. Finding that your partner, family member, or friend is exceptionally inconsistent with their behaviors should clue you in to the fact that you are likely in a toxic relationship with them.

If your friend, partner, or family member teases you or puts you down in a hurtful way too, then minimalize the fact that your feelings are hurt. It is a surefire sign of gaslighting. By telling you that you are too sensitive or that you need to learn how to take a joke, they are brushing your hurt feelings to the side. Someone who truly cares about you, even if teasing, will take the time to acknowledge the fact that they hurt your feelings. If you are constantly being questioned about how sensitive you are, be aware you could be succumbing to the abuse of gaslighting.

Another sign that narcissistic gaslighting is occurring is when you constantly feel that something awful is about to happen. This sense of impending doom starts to manifest early on in gaslighting situations. Many people don't understand why they feel threatened whenever they are around a certain person, but after further investigation and getting away from the narcissist, they understand it completely.

Gut feelings should always be listened to, so if your body is telling you that something is not right between you and another person, you should remove yourself from the situation before things get terribly out of control.

There are always times in our lives that we owe other people apologies; however, when you are in a gaslighting situation, you will spend a plethora of time apologizing to people. You will feel the need to say I'm sorry regardless of if you have done anything wrong or not.

You may really be apologizing for simply being there. When we question who we are and our value. It leads us to apologize profusely. If you notice how much you are saying, I'm sorry is increasing, and the things you are saying sorry for are minimal; you may be in a gaslighting situation.

Second-guessing yourself or constant feelings of inadequacy when you are with your narcissistic partner, family member, or a friend are excellent signs that they are gaslighting you. If no matter what you do, it is never good enough, you should be aware that you may be being manipulated.

When it comes to 2nd guessing yourself, we're not just talking about second-guessing your decisions but second-guessing things like your memories.

You may wonder if you are actually remembering things as they happened because your narcissistic abuser constantly tells you differently. If you have never had a problem recreating and discussing your memories and all of a sudden you are trying to figure out whether or not what you are saying is true you may want to take a closer look at the person you are dealing with instead of looking at yourself.

Another sign that you are succumbing to the powers of gaslighting is functioning under the assumption that everyone you come into contact with is disappointed in you in one way or another. Constant feelings that you are messing things up are daunting and unrealistic; however, it is amazing how many people don't recognize when this is happening. They simply start to apologize for all of the time and assume that no matter what they do, they will make a mess of things, which will lead to others being disappointed in them.

When someone that you are in close contact with makes you feel as if there is something wrong with you, it could also be a sign of gaslighting. We aren't talking about physical ailments; we are talking about feeling as if you have fundamental issues. You may sit and contemplate your sanity and reality. Unless these were problems for you prior to entering into a new relationship, you should definitely pay attention to the sign.

Gaslighting can also make it extremely difficult for you to make decisions. Where you once made solid choices for yourself, you now have a sense of distrust in your judgment. This can make decision making extremely difficult. Instead of making your own choices, many victims will allow their narcissistic abusers to make their decisions for them. The other alternative is not making any decisions at all. Obviously, this could have extremely negative impacts on a person's life.

One other great sign that you may be dealing with a gaslighting situation is when someone you are close to constantly reminds you of your flaws. Sure, a bit of constructive criticism is welcomed in most people's lives; however, when your weaknesses or shortcomings are constantly being pointed out by someone that is supposed to care about you, it is a clear sign that something is wrong. You should never despise who you are because of heinous comments made by a narcissist. So, if you take a step back and look at the people in your life, it will be easy to figure out who genuinely cares about you and who is trying to control you based on the way that they speak to you.

Along the same line, where a gaslighter will tear you down, they will almost never admit or recognize their own flaws. If their flaws are pointed out, it is likely that they will become aggressive.

The gaslighter is almost always on the offensive and ready to attack. This means that they will have an inability to recognize their own inadequacies and they will quickly place the blame on you if you try and point them out. They are excellent at playing the victim. Additionally, misdirection will be used so that they can turn things around and continue to dote on your shortcomings even if they are fictitious.

Another sign that you are being manipulated by a gaslighter is when you start to make excuses for their bad behavior. People will go to great lengths to cover up the abuse that they are facing and dealing with on a daily basis. They tell themselves and everyone else that things are OK or even better than OK. The victim will come up with a variety of excuses as to why their narcissistic counterpart is acting the way that they are. These excuses are not usually accepted by the people questioning the victim; however, the victim will just continue to make excuses rather than admit there is an actual problem.

Recognizing these signs can be a bit difficult when you are involved in a gaslighting situation. When these signs are being pointed out to you by friends, relatives, or other people that care about you, take a moment to stop and really think about what they are saying. Accepting the signs of gaslighting abuse can be difficult, but it is also necessary for preserving your happiness and sense of self-worth.

It is important to note that the longer you are in a relationship with a gaslighting narcissist, the harder it will be to recognize the signs. Spending the time at the beginning of a friendship or a relationship to truly get to know the person and decide whether or not continuing on with them will lead to toxicity can save you from devastating abuse. Remember that people are not always what they seem, so being mindful and present in each moment as it occurs is imperative to keeping yourself safe.

Chapter 8. Things Narcissists Say During Gaslighting.

Stuff Your Gaslighting Abuser Says

If there's one thing I've learned from interacting with people who have had to battle being with a manipulative gaslighter, it's that without fail, the abusers all seem to have certain choice phrases that they all use. It's almost like they all graduated from Gaslight University or something. Here's what your abuser will say:

1. You're only acting this way because you're so insecure.

2. You're too sensitive!

3. Stop being paranoid.

4. It's really not a big deal.

5. I was only kidding!

6. You take things too seriously.

7. You're acting crazy right now.

8. You know you are a little nuts, right?

9. You're just making all that up.

10. Stop being so hysterical!

11. Can you be any more dramatic?

12. You're so ungrateful!

13. That's all in your head.

14. No, that never happened.

15. You're lying. No one believes you. I'm not buying your nonsense.

16. If you had just paid attention.

17. We've already talked about this. Don't you remember?

18. Don't you think you're maybe overreacting?

19. If you had just listened.

20. You keep jumping to the wrong conclusions.

21. You're the only person I've ever had all these issues with.

22. I'm discussing, not arguing.

23. I know exactly what you're thinking.

24. What does it say about you that that's what you think?

25. The only reason I criticize you is that I'm looking out for you.

26. Don't take every single word I say so seriously.

27. You need to get better at communicating.

28. Calm down.

29. You're overthinking this. It's really not that deep.

30. What if you're wrong again, just like the last time?

Think about the context in which you hear these phrases being said to you. Were you talking about sex? Family? Money? Habits one or both of you have? You'll notice that these phrases often pop up when the conversation is centered upon that.

It's a sad truth that, for the most part, the victim is a woman, and a gaslighting narcissist is a man. The reason for this polarization of genders in narcissism is that, often, women have learned to doubt themselves and to apologize whenever there's a problem or disagreement with their significant others. Men, however, are not socialized this way.

Chapter 9. Empowering Ways to Disarm a Narcissist and Take Control

Techniques to handle narcissists

Now comes the difficult part. Deciding what to do with the narcissistic person in your life, and what the best outcome is. This can depend greatly on your individual circumstances as well as the person at hand.

Get away

Typically, extreme narcissists lack normal levels of empathy, don't pull their own weight, and tend to make the people close to them miserable within the space of a few weeks or months. They are unlikely to have a great deal of insight into their damaging behaviors and are unlikely to have an epiphany compelling them to change.

It may be tempting to try and open their eyes to the cause of their problems, help or change them, but this is far more likely to misfire with defensiveness or lead to resentment (depending on how extreme they are).

Relationships you could potentially cut off include not only romantic partners, friends and ex-colleagues, but also family. If you are not legally bound to remain in contact with someone – such as engaged in a business, joint ownership of property, administration of a will, or where a dependent is involved, then you have the potential to cut away if you need to.

Less drastic steps include taking a break or managing the situation. Breaks can help to gain clarity, but it depends upon the relationship at hand, and whether you deem it to be worth saving. If abuse is currently involved in the relationship, an immediate cut-off should be instigated, rather than attempting to make the best of it.

It's important to choose the people you spend time with wisely, because humans tend to adopt the characteristics of those around them. Professor Nicholas Christakis of Yale University explains this in terms of the ripple effect, whereby altruism and meanness ripple through the networks of people, and become magnified. Whatever enters your system - including the actions of your peers, colleagues and family - will affect your personality development and outlook. Surrounding yourself with good people will make you behave in more kind and empathic ways.

Avoid the inner circle

If you need or want to keep a narcissist in your life, it is much safer to do so at a distance, rather than as part of their inner circle - who become privy to their chaotic changes in temperament. Creating justifiable distance (but remaining warm) allows you to be a welcome part of their life without suffering so many falls from grace. They may well start to think of you quite fondly. Get too close, however, and you may become an undervalued part of the furniture, without your own identity or boundaries to respect. In addition, you are giving more opportunities for your words and actions to be misinterpreted as threats or competition, and you are far more likely to have your fingers burned.

Whilst you may have identified the narcissist as a damaging individual, many people (particularly those under their control) will never be able to see the situation clearly. This can feel extremely unfair and unjust to those who can, particularly in family or romantic situations, if they are directly affected by narcissistic control, abuse or manipulation.

It is usually those people who "question" the status quo that the harmful narcissist finds most threatening, and subsequently suffer most acutely at their hands, as the narcissist feels compelled to bring them down to maintain their position. If the narcissist is a family member, particularly a parent, or a partner, this can be particularly damaging, with the victim often trained to unquestioningly agree or go along with the narcissist's opinions, to maintain their love and their favor. Those that follow receive their rewards, whilst those that question, are isolated, ridiculed and ousted, often labelled as a "black sheep," "troublesome" or "combative."

Avoid narcissistic injury

Sometimes, cutting the chord on a narcissistic relationship is not an option. You may feel you should at least try and continue a nonabusive relationship, in which case avoiding "narcissistic injury" is key to avoiding conflict.

In the minds of narcissistic people - both healthy and extreme - they are competent, have unique and special talents, and accomplished. In the case of healthy narcissists, any reasonable threat or challenge to these self-beliefs can be handled carefully, objectively, and in a proportionate way by the individual.

Threats to healthy narcissists don't include other successful or accomplished people - they may be positively competitive, but not derogatory. If a healthy narcissist takes a blow to their self-esteem, negative feelings may be processed without a melt-down or flying into a rage. Extreme narcissists, on the other hand, tend to exist in a world of hypervigilance. Any perceived threat or challenge is likely to be aggressively countered. Failing to do so could result in painful crashes to their self-esteem (narcissistic injury), as their opinion of themselves are overinflated, delicate and variable. This hypervigilance includes people they see as threatening, so it may be beneficial for you to lie low and purposely reduce the traits of your own that may make them feel competitive or badly about themselves.

Avoid exposing them

Exposing the narcissist and getting the "truth" out for all to see can be appealing and feel like the right thing to do. You may think this is the best solution for them, you and anyone else involved - that they will suddenly see clearly and take responsibility for changing their behavior. Forget about being right for a moment and bringing the truth to light.

Pointing out that the narcissist is not as wonderful as they think, can result in a huge backlash, that you then must be around, and may not be able to escape. They are not ever going to agree with you, as they are tied to their elevated identity. Rather than changing their minds, they will be more likely to simply despise you for your opinions.

Admire and listen to them

Being amenable is probably the most passive technique that you can take, but so long as you are not already on the narcissist's "naughty list" can be really effective at pulling you through difficult times, until you reach calmer waters or are able to end the relationship. Clinical psychologist Al Bernstein suggests that remaining quiet and allowing the narcissist to come up with reasons to congratulate themselves is easy, effortless and requires nothing more than listening and looking interested.

Admiring them, their achievements and qualities as much as they do can be a fast route into their "good books." So long as you avoid getting too close, this position in their good books can allow you to maintain a happier status quo with the narcissist still in your life.

Don't reject them

Rejecting a narcissist, whether in reality or in their perception, is likely to make them feel incredibly hurt or angry - as it causes a deep narcissistic injury. A jilted lover may feel a great deal of pain when the source of their affection no longer wants them. So, too, a narcissist feels deeply aggrieved when a source of narcissistic supply - or anyone else for that matter - decides that they are not "good enough."

Extreme narcissists – ever hypervigilant - may feel rejected for reasons that more average people would not. Being too busy or not having a good enough reason to deny their request for your company or collaboration can easily be taken to heart and result in an unexpectedly intense response. It's best to give them a legitimate reason that is beyond your control than to show that you're choosing to reject them. Being too busy to meet or see them is best if your reason is irrefutable, like having to work late to meet a specific deadline, attend an important wedding, or are booked onto a vacation or trip elsewhere.

Avoid showing weakness

If you show a narcissist what it is that makes you vulnerable, or what it is that you really want, they may at some point use it against you when they want to manipulate you. Narcissists will frequently learn what it is that you want most from them, and set about denying it so that you are in a constant state of "need". If a narcissistic mother does this, she may control her children through their neediness for her love. The same goes for a romantic partner. They'll ration your supply of what you enjoy most from them to keep you controllable and pliable.

If they know your greatest concerns or fears they may leverage these to manipulate you. They may even use you as a distraction from their own inner turmoil when they are experiencing crashing self-esteem, by needling you on your points of weakness, to make themselves feel strong again.

For example, an NPD manager suffering a meltdown of anxiety after a disastrous sales pitch may proceed to milk his staff for reassurance on his performance, whilst then moving the conversation on to subjects that he knows are extremely personal and emotional for them - transferring his fears to them and feeling better himself.

By not conceding any weaknesses to a narcissist and always taking a diplomatic "I know I'll be happy either way" approach, their power will bring you down whilst raising themselves higher is lost. This may take on the appearance of a game of cat and mouse, until eventually the narcissist must concede that you are not "easily pinned" or risk exposing themselves and being seen as a pessimistic and negative person.

Give them an "out"

You can give them the opportunity to stop playing manipulative games by offering them an "out" such as: "You're being uncharacteristically pessimistic today. You're usually such an optimist! Is there anything wrong?" and in doing so call them to return to their "higher state of glory" without continuing their attack. Subconsciously, they may even be aware that you successfully navigated their manipulation and decide to give you a wider berth in future, or that they need to keep you on the side.

If the attack is particularly vicious or nasty, avoiding emotions but maintaining a cool, calm and empathic approach can work well to bring them back around. Whether you believe it or not, providing them with a defense that effectively excuses their behavior will be much appreciated - as it helps them to avoid a crushing sense of shame and subsequent denial loops, and simply feel that they are understood and forgiven. You may even be surprised to find that this approach results in a voluntary concession and what may seem like the beginnings or a more responsible approach, but this is not something that should be anticipated or expected.

Don't expect fairness

Extreme narcissists are likely to be far more concerned with getting what they want, than ensuring that everyone is treated fairly. Reward their behavior rather than their words so that they only get what they want, when you get what you want too.

Extending credit or accepting promises from an extreme narcissist is a dangerous leap of faith that may not be rewarded. Lack of follow through is just as likely to occur because the narcissist forgets their agreements - their attention being consumed with themselves and their own concerns rather than remembering their obligations.

They want to look good

Understanding what a narcissist wants means that so long as you avoid triggering narcissistic injury, they may be able to be worked with. You may even be able to maneuver them, if you start to think like them.

Extreme narcissists really want to look good. If you can align what they want with what you want, you may be able to achieve great successes together. Alternatively, you may simply be able to manage and placate them to make your life easier or until you are able to leave the relationship.

Understand their narcissistic supply

Narcissists need people to gain narcissistic supply. You might compare that a healthier person needs others for mutual love and support, but as we proceed higher up the extreme narcissism scale, the need becomes more one-directional and desperate in nature, to prevent painful relapses to a place of low self-esteem. So, what exactly do they want from you?

Highly narcissistic people often prioritize relationships and career choices based on how much praise or attention they can receive. Many narcissistic people hamper their own development (or never develop a range of interests in the first place), by making choices for praise and success over other forms of enjoyment. If they have chosen you as a part of their life, it may be that you provide a high level of narcissistic supply.

If you have not been chosen voluntarily, you may find that your relationship quality depends on how readily you give narcissistic supply, or whether you question or criticize them.

Taking responsibility for not damaging their wellbeing - whilst protecting your own - is as important for them as it is for anyone else. You would not feel great about filling the liquor cabinet in the home of an alcoholic, nor should you feel great about pedaling exorbitant approval and attention onto this already dependent individual. Moderate and considerate amounts to avoid attack or denigration is enough for you to get by.

An audience

Narcissists often want an audience. They may spend a great deal of time talking about themselves. This serves their need to feel special (since they are always the subject of the discussion). They also get to let other people know how much they have accomplished in life. And the result of this is that they get lots of praise from other people.

Status

Presuming they don't feel threatened by people of high status, they may want to associate with them in order to feel superior to others. If you think you classify as "high status", this may be what they are using you for. In this case - check your own score for narcissism. It is not unknown for narcissists to flock together and form superficial friendships and relationships to "show off" to others and highlight how special they both are, such as in a "trophy" partner / wealthy-partner relationship. Alternatively, they may want company from someone who is lower than they are to compare to themselves to, for a similar sense of superiority.

Some may choose a mix of friends - a bunch of successful equals to go out and "show off" with, and one or two best friends to feel superior to, to impress and revel in their attention.

Sex

It may be that the extreme narcissist does not engage in sexual relationships for the emotional value it has; but for sex, and sex alone.

They may revel in their ability to seduce, in their sexual performance, or in a sense of higher status or dominance within the sexual dynamic.

Love

Narcissistic people like to feel that there is someone who loves them and wants to be with them. Depending on how they view themselves, this may result in higher levels of infidelity or cheating. If a narcissist defines themselves as "good" or "moral" then cheating itself (or engaging in any generally scorned upon activities) could result in crushing shame and self-loathing, making it less likely to happen. On the other hand, if the narcissist is reluctant to see their partner as an equal, the likelihood of cheating increases.

Avoid flooding them with supply

If you are concerned about providing a narcissist with supply, keeping them in line can be aligned more with what they don't want. Being all about appearances, narcissists feel more shame than guilt. They really don't want to look bad.

Asking them to consider their reputation may make them think far more carefully than asking them to consider other people's feelings. If they think their actions will be perceived badly by others, they are far less likely to act. This can be achieved by asking them what people would think about what they did or asking probing questions to trigger them into having an alternative idea themselves.

Chapter 10. Ways to Stop a Gaslighter in Their Tracks

If you've read up to this point, then chances are you're probably thinking of a long list of people that have just got to be narcissists or gaslighters in your life. However, as a caution: Not everyone is a narcissist just because you have a little tiff here and there. Also, keep in mind that you might be recollecting past events through the narcissistic glasses, and so everyone might seem to be that way.

With that said, if you've asked yourself the questions listed in this book, and have observed for yourself that you really are dealing with a gaslighter, how do you deal with them? Let's get into that.

Putting an End to Gaslighting

Pay attention to the pattern. One of the major reasons gaslighting is so effective is that, for the most part, the target is completely ignorant of what's happening. The minute you move from ignorance to complete awareness, you will have successfully taken back some of your power. You will find it easier to shrug off the narcissist when they start playing games again.

Keep in mind that the gaslighter might never change, no matter what you do. Sometimes, the only way there can be any change is with the help of a professional. Gaslighting is all that the manipulator knows how to do, so you cannot expect them to give that up in favor of logic or reason. There is no other better coping mechanism that they know. This is not to say that they should not be held accountable for their actions. I'm just making sure you now not to hold on to the hope that they will change. They could, but don't hope for it. Accept that they're wired the way they are, and only professional therapy can help them become better people.

Remember that gaslighting behavior is not necessarily about you. It all really comes down to the fact that the gaslighter needs to feel like they're in charge. They need that rush of power. At their core, the gaslighter is riddled with insecurity. The only way they know how to get rid of that feeling is to make others feel less than they are, or at least give themselves the illusion that they are better than everyone else. Keep this in mind, and you will not bother internalizing anything they say or do anymore. You will be in a better position to manage the relationship you have with them or to end it altogether.

Create a support system that you can rely on. Dealing with a gaslighter on your own is no walk in the park. It helps to have other people that you can talk to, who will validate your perception of reality as well as your sense of self-worth. If you've noticed that ever since you got involved with the narcissist, you've somehow been cut off from the people that matter to you, then now is the time to reach out to them. Do not buy into the narcissist's lies about how no one else can love you the way they do. That is simply not true! Commit to spending time with your friends and family. Make appointments, if you must. Treat these appointments with as much commitment as you would a business meeting. The less isolated you are, the less of a hold the gaslighter can have on you.

Spend a long time thinking about whether you want to keep investing in the relationship. This is crucial, especially since having to deal with the gaslighter's shenanigans eats away at your peace of mind, self-worth - and even your health. Is the gaslighter your manager, or your boss? Then take proactive steps to find another job, making it a non-negotiable agreement with yourself that you're moving to a different, better job. If the gaslighter is your lover and you'd like the relationship to continue, then keep in mind that you'll both be needing some therapy, and you will have to make that a non-negotiable aspect of your relationship if you decide to stay.

Start to build your self-esteem back up. Having been with a gaslighter for too long, it's easy to forget just how awesome you are! You need to take some time to remind yourself of everything about you that is amazing, no matter what the gaslighter has said to make you think otherwise. You might need to begin journaling so that at times when you are low or starting to buy into the insidious lies they have packed your head with, you can reopen that, and remind yourself of your awesomeness. Don't just write about the great things about you. Write about times when you felt the most alive, the most joyful. As you do this, you will naturally find yourself craving those times again, and taking action to liberate yourself and your mind.

Be open to getting professional help. It's difficult being the victim of gaslighting. Your self-esteem, sense of self, and sanity will have taken a beating. You might find that you're slow to make decisions, constantly unsure of yourself, and always wondering if you're good enough. You might even be suffering from depression or anxiety. If you find that you're overwhelmed by feelings of helplessness, uncertainty, hopelessness, and apathy, then chances are you need to seek the help of a professional psychotherapist right away, so that you can rebuild yourself after the devastating damage caused to you by the gaslighter

Change Is Possible

There it is. The answer you've been hoping for, waiting for with bated breath: it's possible for people to change, no matter what personality disorder they have been diagnosed with. Think of these diagnoses as a shorthand way of describing certain people. You can never use one word to totally encapsulate a person's life. When words like extrovert, introvert, or narcissist get bandied about, they seem to imply a permanence to the individual's personality. That's not always the case.

It helps to consider that these disorders are not necessarily descriptions of who people are in summary. It would be more accurate to think of these labels as the perfect descriptions for behavioral and/or inter-relational patterns, and nothing more. The same applies to narcissistic personalities.

Born of Vulnerability

A lot of researchers are of the opinion that Narcissistic Personality Disorder is a result of growing up in conditions where it's not safe to be vulnerable. The narcissist as a child had to accept that it was a sign of imperfection to be vulnerable, and that showing any vulnerability meant that they had no worth at all. This theory is the reason there's often a connection made between insecure attachment styles and narcissism, meaning the narcissist is driven to control all their relationships because they are afraid to be in a position where they need to depend on someone else.

The narcissist is adept at keeping people from knowing who they really are. They will refuse to acknowledge their vulnerabilities or opt to suppress them or project them onto others so that they can keep crafting the person they want to be in relation to others. For the narcissist to change, they must be willing to be vulnerable. This means leaving themselves wide open to emotions that they have suppressed and denied over the years. The trouble with narcissists is not that they are unable to change, it's that they are *unwilling to* because it would mean that the identity of the person they have struggled to craft will be blown to bits. In a narcissist's mind, all the relationships which they have failed at simply offer more reason why they should remain the way they are.

Understand that the narcissist defines themselves by how others perceive them. A narcissist can't be a narcissist if they don't have anyone to put on a show for. They need to be the center of attention, and so they love to have the spotlight of attention from those who bother to stick around them. Over time, of course, their performance starts to get old. The narcissist knows this and is constantly running scared that others will realize there's really nothing to them. This is one of the reasons the narcissist refuses to change, as they are more certain than ever that the fix is not to come clean and be vulnerable but to put on a more flamboyant show and pile on some more makeup to conceal all their flaws.

When the Narcissist Finds True, Secure Love

When the narcissist happens to find someone who cares about them and is not just sticking around for the flash, they're still deathly afraid that this person will think they're not worth it. The fear they feel is a subconscious one that they are not aware of, but it is very real. This is what fuels the narcissist to do things like shift blame and guilt onto their partner or act all grandiose.

When their antics are exposed to the light of day, and everyone sees them for what they are, they get angry because they've slipped up and alienated everyone who mattered to them. Rather than change their ways, this causes them to double down on who they are. They become even more narcissistic than ever before, ironically leading to the abandonment and rejection that they're so afraid of.

Breaking the Cycle

To help the narcissist, there's nothing else to do but break that vicious cycle. As gently as you can, you need to throw a wrench in the works whenever they try to control you, create distance between you, blame you, or defend themselves. This means letting them know in no uncertain terms that you're willing to have them in your life, but not on those terms. What terms, then? You should show them that they can join you in the sort of intimacy where they can be loved for who they really are, flaws and all. They only need to be willing to let that happen.

The point to take away from all of this is that narcissism is simply one way of relating to others, and you can always change the way you relate with people. It's not going to be easy for narcissists to let themselves get so vulnerable as to allow intimacy, but it is possible.

The Narcissist to who wants to Change

If you happen to know someone who's a narcissist but has expressed the willingness to do better, then you can let them read the book. Here is a list of things the narcissist will need to do to become a better person. This is addressed to the narcissist, not the victim.

Learn to recognize and respect boundaries. When you do, you'll find that you stop losing relationships, and improve them. You must understand where you end, and another begins. You need to understand that other people have their own beliefs, thoughts, and emotions, and they can be completely different from yours while remaining valid. To help you understand boundaries better:

- Listen twice as much as you speak.

- Use other people's names when you write to them, and when you speak to them, too.

- Get curious about the people around you. Ask questions to learn what matters to them and what's new in their lives. Don't be inappropriate in your asking.

- Be mindful of encroaching into other people's personal space and time. Always ask permission first before you do.

- Rather than issue orders, ask open questions. Don't ask leading questions. Don't assume you know better than others.

- When others make a choice that is different from yours, respect it. You won't always get what you want, and that's okay.

Be genuine, always, in all ways. You will find it more refreshing than lying, pretending, and manipulating others. How can you be more genuine?

- Keep your word. If you know you won't keep a promise, don't make it.

- Did you make a promise you can't follow through on? Then own it.

- Don't say or do things that will make others feel like they've been cheated.

Observe yourself often so you can grow in mindfulness. The more you observe, the better you can see how you cause problems in your relationships and push people away. Assume that there's the usual you, and then there's your higher self who observes you from a higher point of view. Here's how to be more mindful:

- Ask your higher or observer self whether whatever you're about to say or do will have good or bad consequences.

- Ask your observer self if your actions and words are all about you showing off, or about you building a great relationship with others.

- Feel like you just did or said something off? Ask your observer self how it would feel if someone said or did that to you. Then apologize and make amends quickly.

Be willing to seek professional help. This will help you along your journey to becoming a more rounded individual, faster. You don't have to struggle with this on your own. You need the guidance of a psychotherapist. You need to be willing to be honest if you're going to make permanent, lasting change. It's going to be so worth it in the end because you will finally discover your authentic self, and your relationships will be better for it.

Do forgive yourself. This is the only way to get the healing you need. It's also the only way that you can be more comfortable with being vulnerable. An added plus is you'll finally be able to flex those empathy muscles. It might be hard to forgive yourself, and you may find yourself crippled with remorse sometimes. Just be kind to yourself in moments like this. You only did the best you knew to do so that you could cope. It's not your fault that you weren't allowed to be your true self when you were growing up. Focus on the fact that now, you can do better. Now, you can rediscover yourself.

Be okay with being human. You won't be perfect. You never were. You have flaws, but that's okay! Learn to be comfortable in your own skin. This is the way to allow rich, beneficial, loving relationships in your life; this is how you grow. You simply need to be fine with who you are. Be okay with being true to yourself, even if it means being vulnerable.

It's going to take you some time. Be patient. You will find yourself. You will also learn that the thing you feared the most is not real. The people who love you don't up and leave just because of imperfection or five. After all, we're all flawed in our own way.

The Trouble with Emotional Abuse

The trouble with emotional abuse is that because it leaves no scars, you can see, it often gets dismissed, or is almost impossible to spot when it happens. Make no mistake: the damage from emotional abuse is very real, and it can last a long, long time.

When you're psychologically abused, the other person is saying and doing things to make you think whatever they want. Generally, the goal is to make you confused, disillusioned, and totally dependent on them for your sense of self-worth and identity. It is an incredibly hurtful, despicable thing to do to another person, and can lead to very real mental health issues like depression, Post-Traumatic Stress Disorder, and anxiety.

Unmasking Emotional Abuse

There are a lot of myths about emotional abuse, which do a very good job of camouflaging it so that it's hard to detect. Let's rip the mask off, so you can have an easier time figuring out whether you or someone you care about is being abused.

Myth #1: Emotional abuse is always accompanied by physical abuse. It isn't. There can be emotional abuse with no physical abuse; this often flies under the radar.

Myth #2: Emotional abuse is nowhere near as damaging as physical abuse. This is just pure falsehood. If it hurts, then it hurts. It is not a productive argument to say that one form of abuse hurts more than another. Abuse is not okay. If you're being abused, then you deserve better, and you need all the help you can get.

Myth #3: Emotional abuse only affects women. Abuse can happen to both women and men. There is no exception. Also, it happens in other contexts besides relationships, such as at work, and with friends as well.

What to Do If You're Being Abused

If you're emotionally abused, then you're constantly criticized for everything you say and do. You're blamed all the time, even for things that could never be your fault. You're made to feel ashamed. Your gaslighter constantly threatens to hurt you physically or to do something they know you don't want them to. You feel like you have zero control over your life, as the abuser takes all your power away, sometimes even going as far as controlling your finances so that you have no choice but to stay with them and do whatever they want.

If you recognize yourself in the paragraph above, then you need to do something. You need to reach out and ask for help. There is no shame in that. As a matter of fact, asking for help is one of the bravest things you can possibly do, especially when you're in a situation where you have been completely worn down and out by the abuser.

Talk to anyone you can about what you're going through. Confide in them, and not only will you have someone on your side, but you will also be able to occupy your time by hanging out with others besides your abuser. Work on getting more and more people you can talk to who will back you up.

Have a safety plan in place. While there's not necessarily physical abuse going on along with the emotional abuse, it's still important to be safe. This means you need to think up plans for how you can escape from the relationship whenever you are finally ready to up and leave the abuser.

Don't Make Excuses for the Abuse

A lot of the time, people will fall back on mental disorders in order to justify when they do what they do. They don't talk about it like they want to make genuine change. It's just a copout for them to keep treating you the way that they always have.

It's not uncommon for the person abusing you to try to make light of the situation or try to blame you for a reason they're acting the way they do. It can seem like your significant other doesn't know when they do what they do or are completely incapable of realizing the implications of their actions. However, this is just more smoke and mirrors on their part. They know what they're doing. The whole point behind being seemingly unaware is to make you feel even less sure of yourself. Next thing you know, you start wondering if you're not overly dramatic or delusional! I want you to know that your abusive partner is very aware of how they're hurting you, and they always are in control of how they act disorder or no. Want proof?

They will decide when to abuse you, and how far they will push it. A perfect example is when they threaten to hit you but don't. Or when they abuse you in ways that you can never really tell others, because there's no proof, and it can seem like you're making something out of nothing.

They only ever abuse you, not others. If they truly had no control over their actions, wouldn't they abuse everyone in their lives? But they don't, do they? That's because they can control themselves. If it were that they suffered from a disorder, then everyone in their life would get the same treatment, and not just you.

They escalate their terrible behavior. When it's a matter of having a disorder, there can be changes in the person's state of mind. Even then, though, there is a consistency in the way that they behave. However, you may have noticed your abuser will sometimes choose not to abuse you for a while. Other times, they will steadily ramp up the abuse as your relationship goes on. This is more proof that they really can decide to be different or better.

You need to keep in mind that regardless of whether the gaslighter has an actual mental health problem, you are not the one to be held accountable for how they treat you! It's possible to be diagnosed with a disorder and still choose not to act out in controlling, manipulative ways. They will simply need to acknowledge their issues and be open and willing to seek the help that they need. Please, always remember that you're not the reason they act the way they do, and therefore you're not the cure they need. They must own their actions, and they alone can take the first step they need, to change themselves.

Chapter 11. A Match Made in Hell: Narcissists And Empaths

There is one specific union which is never going to end well. We are of course talking about the match between a narcissist and an empath. The reason is that both are at totally opposite ends of the empathy spectrum, and as a result, they clash constantly.

This chapter is going to explore why narcissists and empaths are a terrible match, but we're also going to discuss the fact that this is a match which happens more often than you would think.

First things first, we need to explore what an empath is, to really understand why this union is one to avoid at all costs.

What is an Empath?

There is a difference between someone who is an empath and someone who possesses empathy. A person who has empathy can understand the feelings of others and put themselves in their shoes. This is most people, but everyone varies with the degree of empathy they have. Someone can be a highly sensitive person, e.g. have a high amount of empath, but that still doesn't make them an empath.

An empath is someone who is extremely sensitive to the emotions of others, to the point where they take them on as their own. For example, an empath may be standing next to someone in the line for the bus, and that person may be feeling angry about something that has happened that morning. As a result, the empath will begin to feel angry, but they have no reason to feel angry themselves. They're picking up on the vibrations and emotions of the other person and exhibiting that emotion as their own.

Empaths are not rare, and many people have this tendency in their lives. Whilst it is considered a gift, the person who has it may not consider it so! Life can become very overwhelming for people who are so sensitive to emotions around them, and many empaths find large groups to be very draining. As a result, they will either avoid large gatherings or will leave quite early.

An empath also has to find ways to manage their "gift" in order to stop it taking over their lives.

In addition to being sensitive to emotions, empaths are also drawn to people who are in need. Empaths are very pure and positive people, and they like to help others who may be going through a hard time or maybe suffering in some way but not vocalizing it. The problem occurs when an empath cannot draw a line between their own emotions and the emotions of another person, and they find it extremely difficult to walk away from those in their life, simply because they can feel their pain and their general emotions.

The main traits of an empath are:

- Usually introverted but can be extroverted too,
- Like their own space and time alone,
- Can become overwhelmed in large groups,
- Highly sensitive,
- Very intuitive,
- Can easily become overwhelmed when in a relationship and needs to learn how to step back a little and take their own space whenever needed,
- Often give too much of themselves, as they normally have big hearts,
- Their senses are highly attuned,
- They often need to be around nature to feel calm.

Aside from absorbing the emotions of others like a sponge, one of the biggest risks of having this empathic gift is the fact that empaths are a huge target for narcissists and other "energy vampires". An energy vampire is someone who is very negative or someone who is very manipulative and finds it easy to literally suck the life out of an empath, who is willing to give to the point of exhaustion. To protect themselves against such people, empaths need to have plenty of time and space to themselves.

Why Are Narcissists And Empaths Drawn to Each Other?

Now we know what an empath is, why are empaths and narcissists a common coupling?

There is an attraction on both sides here. Firstly, the empaths recognize the struggle of the narcissist, e.g. their lack of confidence and their underlying struggles. The empath can feel this but they also have a nurturing side which makes them want to make things better. Of course, we know that nobody can make a narcissist better, but the empath wants to try.

In addition, narcissists are, as we know, extremely charming and can trick people into thinking they're a wonderful person, when underneath they may have other intentions. Because an empath always wants to see the best in people, they have a tendency for falling for the charm. You would think that their intuition would allow them to see past this smokescreen, but the narcissist is an expert at deception and often manages to slip beneath the radar.

The reason a narcissist is attracted to an empath is because of their opposite nature. Remember, narcissists, don't have empathy like a non-narcissistic person. An empath is totally the opposite and has empathy by the bucket-load. This intrigues the narcissist, but they can also see that this may be a person who can easily be manipulated. As a result, the narcissist makes a bee-line for the empath, showing their full charm armory.

Whilst every relationship is different, the chances are that a union between a narcissist and an empath will follow a very common path. The narcissist will charm the empath completely, and the empath will fall completely underneath their spell. The narcissist will then begin their gaslighting techniques as the empath begins to show their confidence and tries to have their own life outside of the relationship.

The empath struggles to understand why the narcissist is causing them distress because they look for the best in everyone. As a result, the narcissist uses tactics to make the empath question their own thoughts and feelings, which is confusing because they're already overwhelmed with emotions, due to their empathic nature.

Empaths feel everything very deeply, so when the narcissist hurts the empath, they will feel it ten times amplified. This causes a rollercoaster relationship to begin, with ups and downs, crazy highs and crashing lows. The highs and lows are addictive, and the endless gaslighting and charm offensive make them stay.

A relationship between a narcissist and empath is very similar to a relationship between a narcissist and a regular person, however, the difference is the depth of feelings that an empath experiences. As a result, they will have highs and lows which exhaust them, and when this occurs in conjunction with all the other emotions they're picking up on a day to day basis, the effect can be extremely damaging.

Is There a Future For This Relationship?

Put simply, no. There is less chance of this relationship surviving compared to any other narcissistic-affected relationship. The emotional highs and lows, along with the dependency which the empath will develop toward the narcissist will make the relationship impossible to survive.

The empath will have a very hard time leaving the narcissist, and it will probably take several attempts to actually go through with it. Despite that, it is hoped that the empath eventually finds the strength to walk away.

This type of relationship has no future. The narcissist will drain every last drop of positive out of the empath and leave them completely overwhelmed, emotionally confused, and they will question their sanity to the point of exhaustion.

Of course, the empath will desperately want to "fix" the narcissist and they will try time and time again to do it. In the end, however, they will realize that it's just not possible and they will give up and move on - at least, that is the hope.

How an Empath Can be Severely Emotionally Damaged by a Narcissist

A narcissist will use the empath's emotional sensitivity against them. This is a weak point in the eyes of the narcissist, and something they don't really understand themselves. Being able to feel everything so deeply is so intoxicating to the narcissist, so exotic and different, that they want to explore it and find out more about it. They then realize that this is an "in", something they can use alongside their gaslighting tactics, and it works very successfully.

An empath is generally a very pure and good person. They try to help and they try to see the good in others, but their emotional sensitivity is their undoing in this situation. They also try time and time again to right the situation, to make the narcissist see the error of their ways, to show them that they understand and want to help, but remember, the narcissist sees no error in their ways. In the eyes of the narcissist, they're not the one to blame, the empath is. By blaming the empath, they are damaging their self-esteem and their self-worth to a very severe degree.

The constant bombardment of gaslighting, making the empath feel like they're literally going crazy, will work completely against the overwhelming feeling of experiencing emotions outside of their own head. As a result, the empath may suffer an emotional breakdown, due to complete exhaustion.

An empath will struggle severely with a relationship touched by narcissism because it is something they simply cannot understand themselves. Both sides are totally at odds - the narcissist doesn't understand the emotional sensitivity of the empath and the empathy they show with almost everything they do. The empath doesn't understand the narcissist's total lack of empathy and how they can be so cold and unforgiving, yet so charming and giving when they want to turn on the act. The empath may know that something isn't right, they may want to walk away, but their need to see the good in everyone keeps them where they shouldn't be.

Put simply, an empath could suffer mental health damage by staying in a relationship with a narcissist, and that will take professional help to right and overcome. They will struggle with building lasting, trusting relationships in the future, and they may also turn against their emotional sensitivity and empathy, and see it as a hindrance, rather than a positive trait or a gift.

A narcissist has the power to destroy an empath.

Points to Take From This Chapter

In this chapter, we have explored the damaging relationship between a narcissist and an empath. You might not have known much about empaths before this chapter, but now the hope is that you understand much more.

Perhaps you're an empath, or you're very emotionally sensitive yourself. In that case, you need to be very wary of anyone in your life who might be exploring your sensitivity. A narcissist will see an empath as easy pickings, a real target, and someone who is easy to manipulate. To be able to turn the tables, you need to identify the signs, and you also need to develop the strength to walk away.

The main points to take from this chapter are:

- An empath is someone who is very emotionally sensitive and can take on the emotions of others as their own;

- Empaths are usually introverted, quiet, kind people, who try to see the best in everyone;

- Empaths can also become overwhelmed by emotions very easily, and they feel everything very deeply;

- Narcissists are attracted to empaths because they are curious about their empathy, but also because they may see them as an easy target;

- Empaths are attracted to narcissists because they want to help, but also because they're a target for the charm offensive which often comes at the start of a relationship;

- A relationship with a narcissist may be enough to cause an empath to have an emotional breakdown or burn out reaction if the manipulation is severe enough;

- The empath will feel the hurt and pain of the treatment by a narcissist very deeply, but will still want to do their best to help their partner;

- Empaths are likely to need a lot of help and support when walking away from a narcissistic partner and may heed professional help in order to allow them to develop loving and trusting relationships in the future.

Chapter 12 – How to stop being manipulated by a gaslighter

Gaslighting has become a hot topic today because it is a harmful manipulation tool either an emotional, psychological manipulation thing that is happening to many people than we even realize. So before now, we have really talked about what gas-lighting is and how do you know that you have been a victim of gaslighting and the tactics that gaslighters use.

As stated before, gaslighting is a subtle way of somebody avoiding responsibility after that person has done something bad. In extreme cases, it is a way to emotionally abused or gain power over somebody in harmful ways. If you haven't read the chapter that talks about the signs of gaslighting or how to know if you are being gaslighted, then go and do that now because if you haven't done that, then you won't really understand what this chapter is saying. It won't make sense if you don't recognize what gaslighting is and if you don't realize that it is happening to you. So we are going to talk about some ways to deal with gaslighting.

Clarify yourself

And the first thing is to clarify to yourself how you know you're being gaslighted and then write it down. Write down the specific things that is done or said to you that make you know that you are being gaslighted. Write down specific examples as they come up and write down the things that this person is making you feel crazy, question yourself on, make you feel like you are losing it and making you question your own sanity. Those people use certain tasks to Gaslight you. It is leaking and it's up to and if you're not aware of what the person is doing, you might not even realize that it is happening to you.

Do some ground exercise

The next one it's for you to start doing some grounding exercises and just take time to be quiet and be still with yourself so that you can start connecting with yourself again. You might take some time to do some deep breathing. Whatever those grounding and meditating exercise is do it to start connecting with yourself again, because gaslighting makes you doubt and question yourself. It makes you. Believing yourself.

It makes you feel like you can trust yourself again. So you need to start taking time to connect with yourself, again, you need to take the time to start tuning into your inner wisdom and tune to your ability to believe and trust yourself. Because that has been taken away from you, if you haven't gaslighted for a long time at some point in your life, you really need to reconnect with yourself so that you can start to realize that you are being manipulated. You need to be able to trust yourself and see that this person is meant to mess with you and to throw you off. So, you need to get things backgrounded by taking the time to connect with yourself in your thoughts, your beliefs, your perceptions and really ground yourself in that stuff.

Decide whether you want to continue the relationship

The next one is if it is someone that is currently in your life that is any plating you this week, and if it is becoming a big issue, then you might need to decide whether you want to continue the relationship. So you really need to decide if you need to distance yourself from this person or discontinue the relationship altogether. This is a very serious thing when you are being made to feel small weak or made to feel insignificant, stupid, crazy, insane, then you really need to take it seriously and decide if it is worth it to continue in that relationship. Even though there are certain times that these people will be caring, loving, and wonderful and allow you to have a great moment with them. But other times, they try to make you feel small, stupid or crazy, so you really need to listen to yourself and really decide if it is worth it. Decide if that person is worthy of staying in your life since that is how they are treating you and making you feel low and taking away from you your ability to feel confident in yourself.

Reach out to a trusted loved one or friend

The next thing to do is to reach out to somebody like a friend or a trusted loved one and tell that person because; chances are if you have been a victim of gaslighting for a long period. And it has really ever affected your sense of self-worth and ability to trust yourself; then you need to do some healing that is not just going to go away. You really need to dig into it because things like that will start to impact your core believes. It will start to manipulate your self-worth, so you need that intervention to be able to heal from it and be able to move forward from the wounds, the pains, the hurt, and the damage that this might have caused you. So this is something that you really need to take seriously.

Take a Stand

The last one is to take a stand and not let yourself continue to be a victim. Once you recognize that the gaslighting is happening, then you want to be able to see what the person is doing. You need to stand up to them and say something like I see what you doing and I'm not going to fall for it. No matter how hard they try to convince you, and no matter which Tactics they're using, try to stand up to them and say that that's not what happened, you are lying, you are making this stuff up. Try to take a stand and take your power back instead of being a victim or allowing yourself to get manipulated or even abused in this harmful way.

If you're doing some of these things and implementing some of these strategies, then it will help you to be able to regain your personal sense of clarity, and then you will start to trust yourself again. You will be able to connect with yourself and even to believe in yourself, and you will be able to trust your senses, your memories, your perceptions, and your version and your interpretation of reality, and you will be able to put a stop to people that are playing the mind games with you.

Having healthy boundaries is very good in any area of your life especially when it comes to Gaslight. You need to put in those boundaries, say no way, this is not going to happen to me, and no way am I going to fall for this. I'm not going to let you treat me this way. Having healthy boundaries is Crucial.

Dealing with the Narcissist

Now that you've realized that there is a narcissist in your life, what should you do?

Take a step back and analyze the situation.

Determine how bad the situation is. Try to understand the narcissist's background and his degree of his narcissism. Note or recall what drives him to narcissistic rage. Recall how he tries to punish you. Be aware of the tactics that he uses. Do all these objectively. Being carried away by emotions, shouting or crying will only feed the narcissist. The narcissist has already painstakingly set up a strong image or reputation and you might not come across as credible when you tell others, so you have to do your homework.

Accept that the narcissist will not change.

Hoping that you will be able to knock some sense into the narcissist or that you could explain and things to enlighten him will not work. As far as the narcissist is concerned, he has done no wrong.

Seek help.

Find people – friends, counselors, religious leaders, or parents- any one you can confide in and who can give advice and emotional support. They can also give feedback from a neutral viewpoint.

Set boundaries.

Write down which boundaries the narcissist cannot trespass and a consequence if they do. Writing things down before talking to the narcissist will help you speak without sounding emotional.

Be realistic.

Know the narcissist's limitations and work within those limits. It will only be emotionally draining and a waste of time to expect more from the narcissist than he is capable. Do not expect him to learn to care because he can't.

Remember that your value as a person does not depend on the narcissist.

Don't punish yourself for getting into a relationship with him. Instead, focus on rebuilding your self-esteem, meeting your own needs and pursuing your interests.

Speak to them in a way that will make them aware of how they will benefit.

Instead of voicing you needs, pleading, crying or yelling; learn to rephrase your statements by emphasizing what the narcissist will gain from it. You have learn to appeal to their selfishness. This is a good way to survive in situations when you cannot leave.

Bring up your ideas to the narcissistic boss when there are witnesses. By having others around to hear your idea, he will find it difficult to claim credit for it.

Find proof of or document any kind of abuse.

Make use of technology- CCTV or video recordings, for example- to document instances of abuse. Find witnesses to back you up.

Do not fall for the narcissist's tactics again.

Refresh yourself on his tactics and be on your guard against falling for them again. The narcissist may try to use pity, projection or hoovering. This time, be wiser. It may take practice, as you may have become used to being the "Echo" or codependent. Being aware will help you to resist.

Leave.

The best way to deal with the narcissist is not to. For the sake of you emotional and physical well-being, not to mention your sanity, it would be best to leave. If you do leave, expect various tactics from the narcissist to either make your life miserable or to get you (actually his supply) back. You will also undergo a period of distress, akin to mourning when you leave. Seek help and support to get through this stage. Do not be hard on yourself for having allowed yourself to be deceived by the narcissist. Your experience will make you stronger, wiser and, in time, ready for a healthy relationship. In the meantime, focus on your own interests and rebuilding your self-esteem.

Chapter 13- Narcissistic Personality Disorder

A narcissistic personality disorder is a disease that affects approximately 1% of the population with a higher incidence of males than females. It is characterized by excessive arrogance, lack of empathy and a great need for admiration. The main marker of a narcissistic personality is grandiosity. They are interested in power, prestige, and vanity and believe that they deserve special treatment.

Narcissistic personality disorder should not be confused with a person with high self-esteem. A person with high self-esteem can be humble, while a narcissist cannot. They are selfish, overconfident, and ignore the feelings and needs of others. Also, the disorder has a negative impact on a person's life. In general, one may be dissatisfied with one's life and be disappointed when others do not admire it and are not given the special attitude or care it needs. All vital areas are affected (work, personal, social ...), but one is not able to realize that their behavior negatively affects their relationships. People do not feel comfortable with a narcissistic person and they will feel dissatisfied with their work, their social life, etc.

Symptoms and characteristics of narcissistic personality disorder

Some Of the Symptoms and Characteristics of a Narcissistic Personality These are:

- Concern for fantasies, successes ...
- Faith, which is of great importance, only feels understood and connected to people who believe they have high status.
- They need and require continuous admiration.
- Exaggeration of your achievements and abilities.
- Feel for rights or privileges.
- To envy others and have too much conviction that others envy.

- Think and talk most of the time in yourself.
- Suggest unrealistic goals.
- The expectations of others to provide special services.
- I believe that no one can question their motives and demands.
- Take advantage of others to get what they want without the hassle.
- Arrogance, arrogance.
- Easily rejected and injured.
- Strong desire.
- Responding to criticism with shame, indignation, and humiliation.

Narcissistic personality disorder: causes

There is no definite cause for narcissistic personality disorder, but researchers agree that there are environmental and genetic factors that play a role in the development of the disease.

Some of the genetic factors show that people with a narcissistic personality have less gray matter in the left insula, the part of the brain associated with empathy, emotional regulation, compassion, and cognitive functioning.

The healthy development of man shapes many of the narcissistic personality traits. Researchers believe that the onset of the disorder can occur when there is a conflict in interpersonal development. Some examples of contextual factors that may change the developmental stages of "normal" include:

- Learn manipulative behavior from parents or friends.
- To be overly praised for appropriate behavior and overly criticized for inappropriate behavior.

- You suffer from childhood abuse.
- Incompatible parental care.
- Being very pampered by parents, friends, family ...
- To be too delightful without realistic feedback.
- Receive many compliments from parents or others about their appearance or abilities.

Narcissistic personality disorder: treatment

Psychotherapy

Psychotherapy is one of the keys to approaching the treatment of narcissistic personality. It is usually used to help a person connect with other people more adaptively and gain a better understanding of their own and others' emotions.

If a person has a narcissistic personality, you may not have heard of the diagnosis. Studies show that they usually do not receive treatment, and if they receive it, progress is slow because it is based on personality traits that have formed over the years. Therefore, it takes years of psychotherapy to make changes. The changes aim to take responsibility for their actions and to learn ways to connect more appropriately. This includes:

- You are accepting and maintaining relationships with classmates and family.
- They tolerate criticism and failure.
- Understand and regulate feelings.
- Minimize the desire to achieve unrealistic goals.

Initially, group therapy was thought to be inappropriate because group therapy requires empathy, patience, and the ability to relate to and "connect" with others, something in which a person with narcissistic personality disorder presents with deficits. However, studies show that long-term group therapy can benefit them by providing a safe context where they can talk about their boundaries, receive and give feedback, and raise awareness of themselves and their problems.

Of cognitive-behavioral therapy, in particular, the scheme-focused treatment produces excellent results. It focuses on restoring narcissistic schemas and strategies to deal with them while confronting narcissistic cognitive styles (perfectionism ...).

treatment

There is no specific treatment for this disease, but sometimes these people may experience depression or anxiety, and psychotropic medications can be helpful. People with a narcissistic personality can abuse drugs or alcohol, so treating addictive problems can be something useful in this disorder.

Criteria for Narcissistic Personality Disorder

1. The exaggerated notion of personal importance not based on reality.

An inflated view of oneself is one of the main ways narcissists give themselves permission to dominate and control others. Narcissists believe that their priorities, interests, opinions, and beliefs have more value and are more important than anyone else's. Not all narcissists show the world their grandeur; some appear to be very humble or even shy to the outside world, but when they are in intimacy, this will dominate their coexistence.

2. The concern with fantasies of success, wealth, power, beauty, and love above normal.

Narcissists often have a fantasy-filled life and are rarely satisfied with the ordinary, however satisfying or beautiful it may be. This preoccupation with fantasy prevents the narcissistic personality from leading a real and stable life. They feed desires for wealth, fame, power, or status obsessively.

3. The belief that you are a special and unique individual, and can only be committed to or understood by special people.

This idea is an integral part of a survival mechanism that helps them cope with the world. They often define themselves by what they consider their special qualities and inform us of those qualities as soon as we know them.

4. The intense need for admiration.

Love me, watch me, pay attention to me. Narcissists tend to magnify and be their reference.

5. Feeling of worthiness.

Normal rules, regulations, and patterns of behavior infuriate narcissists, who think they are so unique that they do not have to obey reasonable expectations or respect appropriate limits. They may be equally plagued by hard work, illness, or injury. On the other hand, the rules that are imposed by them on others must always be respected.

6. The tendency to exploit others without feeling guilt or remorse.

Depending on the other characteristics of his personality, the narcissist may induce us to do all his work for him or, for example, take our money, allow us to pay his bills, receive gifts without ever giving, charge more for services and pay less, leave waiting for hours around the corner in the rain, without considering that this behavior is disrespectful. Your sense of worthiness makes these behaviors normal, preventing them from feeling guilty or remorseful.

7. Lack of significant empathy.

The narcissist has very little ability to put himself in someone else's shoes. Your pain, your problems, and your point of view dominate the universe. Perhaps nothing more reflects the narcissist's behavior than the inability to understand and identify with the experience of others. This is particularly true when the person who needs understanding is someone the narcissist is exploring, that is, his current target (loving, working, family, or friend).

8. The tendency to be envious or to imagine oneself the envy of others.

The narcissist has difficulty adjusting to a world in which other people seem to have "more" or "better" things. Narcissists often fail to recognize that they are envious and turn sentiment into contempt.

9. Arrogance

Narcissists often have a snobby attitude toward people they think are not up to their "high" standard of intelligence, competence, accomplishment, values, morals, or lifestyle. Believing that the other is inferior helps them reinforce and inflate their conviction of superiority. Criticizing and diminishing others make them feel good about themselves. They are often homophobic, racist, prejudiced of all kinds simply because they think they are superior to a specific group.

Characteristics of narcissistic personality disorder

1. The excessive vision of the self, rather than a solid self-confidence, reflects an excessive concern for supposed excellence.

2. Active and competitive when looking for status, since their personal value is measured according to the status they have

3. If others do not recognize that status, they think they deserve, and they feel intolerable mistreated, get angry, become defensive, or depressed. If they are not known as superiors, their belief of inferiority and lack of importance is activated.

4. He is, therefore, hypersensitive and experiences very intense feelings in response to the criticisms of others.

5. They need, at all costs, the recognition of people whom they consider essential.

6. They do not tolerate discomfort or negative affection. They reject the vital circumstances that require a certain sacrifice and tolerance towards others such as marriage, and he thinks that he does not have to make concessions and yield to the other.

7. If limits are placed or criticized they become very unpleasant and defensive.

8. They show a very demanding and insensitive appearance, show little interest in emotionally supporting the other. They are very difficult to influence and are characterized by being great exploiters.

9. When others react to their exploitation and get angry with him, the narcissist thinks that what happens to him is that they are jealous of him.

10. Carefree of the feelings of others, very self-centered. When they have a conversation with others, they can give the feeling of unique personal interest. Although they can be warm in a first interaction, they immediately show arrogance, hurtful comments towards each other or insensitive actions.

11. They often envy the successes of others and discredit the people they see as competitors. Spend a lot of time comparing yourself to others

12. The worth of others lies in the ability of others to admire him. The narcissist likes people who offer him devotion.

13. He feels very comfortable giving orders because he believes he is the only one who is in possession of the truth. The others seem mediocre, compared to him; they are only mere apprentices or aspirants to be like him.

14. In the face of an argument, they can misrepresent the conversations to make others feel guilty. In order to justify the bad treatment that it gives to others, they look for more or less solvent reasons that excuse their lack of consideration towards others, placing themselves in the best possible situation.

15. Their apparent loquacity facilitates access to others but those friendships lack the intimacy component. Finally, they are perceived as boring conversationalists.

16. Behind its facade, there is a great feeling of incapacity, incompetence, and lack of pleasure in any achievement. Everything they do is aimed at sustaining their fragile self-esteem.

17. The difference between self-esteem and narcissism is according to Bushman and Baumeister (1998): "High self-esteem means thinking well of oneself, while narcissism implies passionately wanting to think well of oneself." So for the narcissist, self-esteem is the result of external success, what they do not trust is their personal worth.

18. They take great care of their image and their manners since they continuously sit in a shop window. You can demand the same from nearby people, influencing them to behave in a model way and if you don't get it, criticize and ridicule them thinking that it is "for your own good". But if the people around them fulfill their wishes, the narcissist can feel their shadow, so he criticizes them in the same way.

19. Since the image is everything, the situations in which it may be exposed to others or to the possible criticism of these poses a great threat.

20. For your person to look, they exaggerate their merits and minimize those of others.

21. They dismiss emotions such as sadness or anxiety because they think that feeling something like this is "weak." They do not like to talk about their problems or their negative emotions for fear of being seen as a fragile person. They do not like to feel vulnerable since it is a symptom of inferiority. He prefers to offer an image of imperturbability.

22. They have big unrealistic dreams of job success, economic and looking for ideal romantic love. They also have great fantasies of power.

23. They give great importance to material possessions and in general in everything that implies recognition by others.

24. He presumes to lead a different type of life and this is how he can be involved in insecure businesses, risky sports, lots of sexual conquests, repeated plastic surgery. Whenever there is the possibility of standing out from others, it will.

25. You experience lasting feelings of boredom, of meaninglessness in your lives, of worthlessness, of emptiness, you feel impoverished from an emotional point of view and you crave deeper emotional experiences.

26. It has a sense of corruptible morals and ethics, has changing values and interests, and belittles unusual and conventional valuesand norms. You can show sexual behavior that includes promiscuity, lack of inhibition and marital infidelities.

Chapter 14- Toxic Relationships Recovery

How to Reduce Conflicts in Relationships

Being in touch with your feelings and emotions can be an important way to protect yourself from future abuse. We are doomed to repeat history if we choose not to learn from it. It can be necessary to take a long hard look at your own needs to determine if you are capable of having these needs met within your current relationship. Self-reflection requires honesty. Honesty can be painful, but it is through this pain that we are able to complete a metamorphosis.

This tactic of manipulation can keep victims glued to an abuser's side. Self-love can be a powerful wedge, allowing the abused partner to become the comfort that they're so desperately seeking from the abuser. No matter the outcome, staying or leaving, we must learn to care for ourselves. A person who doesn't value themselves will accept demeaning and degrading behavior because they feel as though they deserve it.

You deserve to be happy. Your situation may feel absolutely hopeless, but I can promise you that you have it within yourself to make any decision you need to in the interest of self-preservation. Admitting to yourself that you're in an abusive relationship can feel a bit like taking a step toward the edge of a cliff that drops into oblivion, an unknown abyss. You know that you are comfortable in this misery, but this isn't happiness.

Taking these next steps takes courage.

Forgiveness

This isn't forgiveness for abuse; that will come later. This is an honest look at the relationship. It is imperative to understand that, as a victim of abuse, you participated in this situation. There is something inside that has been ashamed and afraid to take any ownership of this hardship. Listen, you have wounds that you will need to heal.

There are reasons that you gravitated toward an abusive partner, and that is something that will need to be addressed one day. For now, forgiveness.

You are worthy of attention, love, and kindness. Begin to manifest these things by caring for yourself. Understand that you had a hand in this dynamic and forgive yourself. This is the first step toward trusting yourself again. There are so many ways to process the guilt that we feel in these situations, and you can choose what works for you. Reflection is enough for some, but others find it helpful to write yourself a letter.

Invest in Yourself

Abusive relationships have the potential to rob us of our confidence. Narcissistic partners want you to feel as though you are silly and irrelevant, and your goals do not matter. It is much easier to lord over another person if their spirit is broken. Loving one's self can be the most difficult thing in the world when it feels like everything is against you. Any normal human being dropped in a situation such as this is miserable and dejected.

Make a plan to begin gluing the shattered pieces of yourself back together. This sounds like a huge and abstract undertaking, but it doesn't have to be.

Learning to love yourself again can be as familiar as coming home to an old friend. We are going to take it step by step.

Human beings are uniquely cognizant, which affords us a measure of control over our own lives that the rest of the animal kingdom is missing. Situations (like abusive relationships) can force us into a fishbowl and take away this control. It can be so easy to overlook that we can be exactly what we want to be. We can make it so easy to love ourselves by becoming our own hero. Be the sort of person that you would love and admire.

Make a list of the qualities and values that you want to embody. List goals and milestones that you want to achieve. It can help if you close your eyes and picture a person that you really admire; this person can be a role model or someone that you have completely made up. What makes this person so admirable to you? Independence? Bravery? Fashion sense? There is nothing too silly. You are authoring the next changes that will occur in your own life. This list may have as many entries as you need. The following is an example to use as a template, should you become stumped:

Who I want to Be:

- Creative

- Funny

- Brave

This list is a way for you to take back your self-image from your abusive partner's hands. It is your job to decide who you want to be. You decide what you value, your hair color, your goals, and the way that you handle conflict. You don't have to see yourself through the eyes of someone who is incentivized to keep you down.

Now that you have created your list, break it down entry by entry. This is going to be a map to achieving your goals. Working on your list will give you a project to focus on when the days become dark, and it is a fast-track way to relearn self-love. Creating these lists also inches us closer and closer to self-reliance. Each individual goal from your list is now a new list, with steps that you can take to achieve these things. Example:

Creative:

- Research different creative mediums.

- Buy the sketchbook or supplies needed to begin learning new skills.

- Use art to express anger or sadness.

<u>Experiment with other methods.</u>

There is no goal or quality that cannot be broken down in this way. Take the pen back from your partner and begin writing your own story again. Stimulate these healthy conversations with yourself, because this communication is going to be necessary moving forward.

Find an Outlet

In order to protect yourself from bottling up the words of an abusive partner, it can be important to find an outlet to use for self-expression. Journaling could be a great way to document the abuse and rise above it. There is a lot of unreleased tension in victims of abuse. Stress and anxiety have become a staple of everyday life. Any moment might bring another fight.

Vent your anger or sadness through a journal or other artistic medium. Allow your mind to rant and rave about the things that you are feeling. Having a way to relieve some of the pressure can be vital in abuse cases. It can also be helpful to find an interest to focus on and is a great way to learn a new skill.

Research

In the same way that you bought this book, begin obsessively consuming material about narcissists, codependents, or abuse. There is a certain mystery to the way that our brains work in these situations. Sometimes we can be unsure of our own actions and motivations. In order to heal, it is necessary to understand.

Demystifying abuse will allow you to pull back the veil shrouding the abuser. The only way that you are going to believe that your partner has something wrong is if you are faced with the facts over and over again. Learn the patterns of abuse and clinical definitions.

Absorbing articles, videos, books, and other literature on the subject will also allow you to predict your partner's next moves. The abusive partner may seem erratic and unpredictable, but there are reasons behind every behavior. Every name that you have ever been called out of malice.

Both narcissists and codependents require validation in the same way. This validation is achieved through manipulation and sometimes name-calling and random fights. A narcissist can seem loving one moment and vile the next, but this is just another part of their process.

Learn everything that you can while you are trapped in this situation. Anticipate the attack and allow the words to roll right off of your skin.

When you understand the motivation, then the fights stop seeming so personal.

Exercise

Eating and living in a sedentary way is often related to depression and stress. Take back your wellbeing by taking care of your body. This will help improve the way that you feel physically and your self-esteem. Exercise will also help fight all the negative emotions with the brain chemicals that it produces. Exercising for just thirty minutes a day can drastically allow you to change the way that you see yourself. Abuse will slowly and deviously steal away your confidence and happiness.

Exercise is recommended by doctors to treat both anxiety and depression. Endorphins are released that encourage an overall calm that can combat feelings of negativity brought on by your surroundings. The movement can also induce a meditative state that allows you to forget about the troubles that await you when you return home.

Challenge Your Comfort Zone

When your life feels stale, prison-like, and depressing, it can be difficult to spring back to life. Challenging yourself to escape this comfort zone is hard, but it can also be a very rewarding experience. There are so many volunteer organizations that would love to have assistance. Social activities of this nature may also allow you to find new friends and reestablish a support system.

Your partner will object to these ventures, especially if they are narcissistic. It can be a good idea to shrug off their watchful eye and do some activities that you are interested in. If you are concerned that they will be angry when they find you, remember that they are angry (for sport) constantly anyway. There is no winning, so you might as well take care of your own needs.

Self-soothing

Break free of the abusive trauma bond by becoming the person that you turn to for your own comfort. Do not allow your partner to take away the pain of a fresh fight by becoming a different person right in front of you. Learn tactics to calm yourself down, as this talent has the potential to save you from the bondage of an abusive relationship.

When you need to calm yourself, use cozy blankets in a quiet room. Read a book until your body feels less stressed. Listen to relaxing music or play a podcast to drift along on the tone of a stranger's voice. Sometimes it can even be helpful to just allow yourself to feel the anger and sadness and then go about your day.

Baths are a wonderful way to calm down. Candles can also be helpful. Learn about the things that work to relax you and reach for those the next time you are upset. Abusive partners will dangle comfort over your head so that you bend to their will. Behaviors like this make a narcissist feel powerful. Learn to be your own hero and your own light in the dark.

Praise Yourself

If you are dating a narcissist, then your self-image has been ripped to shreds. The narcissist is doing this for their own gain. Their view of you has nothing to do with who you actually are. Begin to shake off all that negative and toxic commentary and challenge yourself to replace it with words of encouragement. There are so many areas where you excel. You have so many brilliant ideas. You are so resilient.

Next time your partner is calling you names or mocking you, pretend that they are doing these things to a friend.

You would tell that person that the abuser was all wrong and that they are worthy of love. Treat yourself with the same respect.

Stop the Comparison

Comparing yourself to others can add another layer of toxicity on an already toxic sandwich. Your relationship isn't good right now, and there is no need to hold yourself up to someone who has it together at the moment. You are learning some of the most important lessons of your life, and it is already difficult.

Spending too much time on social media can damage your confidence further. Avoid the things that do not make you feel good. Your journey is completely different from those around you. You are dealing with a situation that many people would not be strong enough to make it through.

Time for Yourself

In order to maintain your sanity in the chaos around you, it is necessary for you to spend time doing the things that you love. Music, swimming, hiking, or dancing would all be great examples of activities that allow for escape and relaxation.

It is imperative that you keep your relationship from defining your life.

Your partner may object to you spending time without them around because they would rather you not have the chance to calm down. For your own sanity, do whatever you need to do to go out on your own without your partner. There need to be boundaries set that your partner will not cross.

Activities that allow for reflection can also be a good idea. Meditation and yoga will help to solidify your overall mental health. Learning to keep your center in the face of chaos can be a useful skill to have in these situations.

Therapy

It is not always easy to get to a therapist when you are in an abusive relationship. A professional is going to be the best way to seek help for yourself. Therapy will also allow you to reclaim your sanity and stolen self-esteem. A professional will be able to offer you guidance tailored to your specific situation.

Talking to a professional is the quickest and most effective way to address your mental state and the condition of your relationship.

The therapist will be able to help you see your situation in an objective way. This can also help to restore your self-worth.

Is There Anything to Save?

Use these same eyes to look at your partner. Make a list of qualities that you require in a mate or in a relationship. Things that are important to your overall happiness and wellbeing. Do you want independence within your relationship? Do you want a partner who doesn't lash out in anger?

Objectively, if you are making no excuses for anyone else's behavior, can your partner be the person that you need them to be? Have you been looking at this relationship in rose-colored glasses? Do not allow fleeting moments of kindness to obscure mountains of bad behavior.

Codependency is a deeply rooted behavior that can take lots of effort to change. To save a relationship that is plagued with codependency, both partners must be willing to take steps to change their behavior. Therapy is likely going to be necessary because personal accountability is lacking from the side of the controlling partner. You know your partner better than anyone else, and it is going to take so much honesty to be able to move forward in a way that benefits both parties.

Empathy is the deciding factor. Has your partner ever done anything for you without expecting repayment? Do you believe that your partner is attached to you, or the things that you are able to do for them? These questions are also dependent on the level of control that your partner is exerting upon, because if abuse is involved beyond manipulation, then you need to leave.

If you are involved with a partner that you suspect is a narcissist, things will not change. Empathy is necessary for the relationship to evolve into something that isn't harmful toward both parties. There are extenuating circumstances (such as shared children) that force some victims to continue relationships with narcissist partners. Extensive therapy is needed to keep the abusive partner in check, and these situations involve the victim forgoing a healthy romantic relationship.

Unless children are involved (and usually even if children are involved), the most sensible course of action is to go. Narcissists panic when they have been threatened with being alone. They will not move on until they have found someone that they consider to better. These individuals will pretend that they are going to change their behavior to save the relationship; they may even believe this.

The fact of the matter is that narcissism is a slow poison. Most psychologists that this disorder is incurable and will be a detriment to anyone close to the abuser.

A narcissist will promise change. Their behavior will get better for a few weeks or maybe even a month. They may even want to save the partnership. It isn't possible for these partners to act in opposition to their nature for very long, and their nature is to serve themselves through the oppression of those closest to them. If you are in the blast-zone, then you are always at risk.

How to Know When it's Time to Go

For those in narcissistic relationships, this research is likely a sign that the end is drawing near. You have probably made up your mind already when it comes to the dissolution of your relationship. Most readers of this book are either retroactively reading about their experience or are entering the miserable stage of limbo right before the trigger is pulled. A stage of stagnation where you are left wondering if you will ever find the courage to say the words.

If you are teetering on the edge of singledom, listening to your own body can be a clue to your deeper desires.

Do you still enjoy spending time with your partner? Do you dread being in the same room with your significant other? What does your body tell you about time spent together?

If there is any physical violence in your relationship, the time to go is now or the soonest that you can safely escape. When you are caught in a cycle of abuse, it can be best to make up your mind and wait silently for an opportunity to run. The best thing that you can do for your future is to guard your safety now. Leaving is a provocation and should be done swiftly and quietly. Have people in your life on standby, ready to assist you with your escape when you give the word.

Readers who are involved in codependent relationships must assure that their partner is willing and capable of change. If the offending party is comfortable with the dynamic of the partnership, this is a strong indication that nothing will change. Never feel guilty for taking steps to ensure your own happiness. You are not responsible for the feelings of others. Threats and further attempts at manipulation are a good sign that you are making the right choice.

Those who leave partners who have controlled and belittled them throughout the relationship have this deeply ingrained view that they are unworthy of love. Victims believe that if they leave such a situation, no one else would want them.

Their hobbies, interests, values, and looks have been torn apart for so long that it can be hard for them to see themselves as worthy.

The fights are always manipulated to seem as though the victim is deserving of the abuse. The victim made a tiny mistake, so the abuser is justified in exploding. No matter what the victim does, it will never be enough to stop the flood. If you have found yourself asking your partner to stop criticizing your every move, you may be one of these victims. Do you believe that you have been treated like a partner should be treated? If the answer is no, then it is time to formulate a plan.

Conclusion

Gaslighting is a kind of psychological mistreatment. Somebody who is gaslighting will attempt to make a victim question their impression of the real world. The gaslighter may persuade the victim into believing that their recollections aren't right or that they are blowing up over nothing. The abuser may then present their own contemplations and emotions as "the genuine truth." Gaslighters/narcissists can cause a lot of injuries.

On the off chance that you are involved with a gaslighter/narcissist, it might have damaged you in ways that you aren't truly aware of yet. Contemplate how the gaslighter/narcissist might be affecting your perspective on yourself and your general surroundings. Just as being able to speak your feelings helps you connect with them—and with the energy to stand up for yourself—so does expressing your feelings in a different way.

Gaslighting is the favorite tool of a narcissist, and a narcissist will seek to keep you under control by gradually eroding every bit of your sanity. Doubting your own senses is in no way healthy for you, and you have to be aware of how narcissists operate to avoid the mess of dealing with them in your future relationships.

Millions and millions of people around the world are finding their real voice against gaslighting and are now enlightening more people about the damaging effects of gaslighting. It is no understatement when I repeat that countless people have fallen victim to this form of abuse at one point or the other in their lives.

The good news is there are countless survivors who have fought their way through depression and other devastating effects of gaslighting and are now living healthy lives. I believe that with the proper management techniques, any victim can get over the emotional abuse and mental manipulation to go on and lead a productive and fulfilling life.

My thoughts are with you, and you can find strength in the fact that you can make it through the trying times. Use that strength to carry yourself through until you find your true self again.

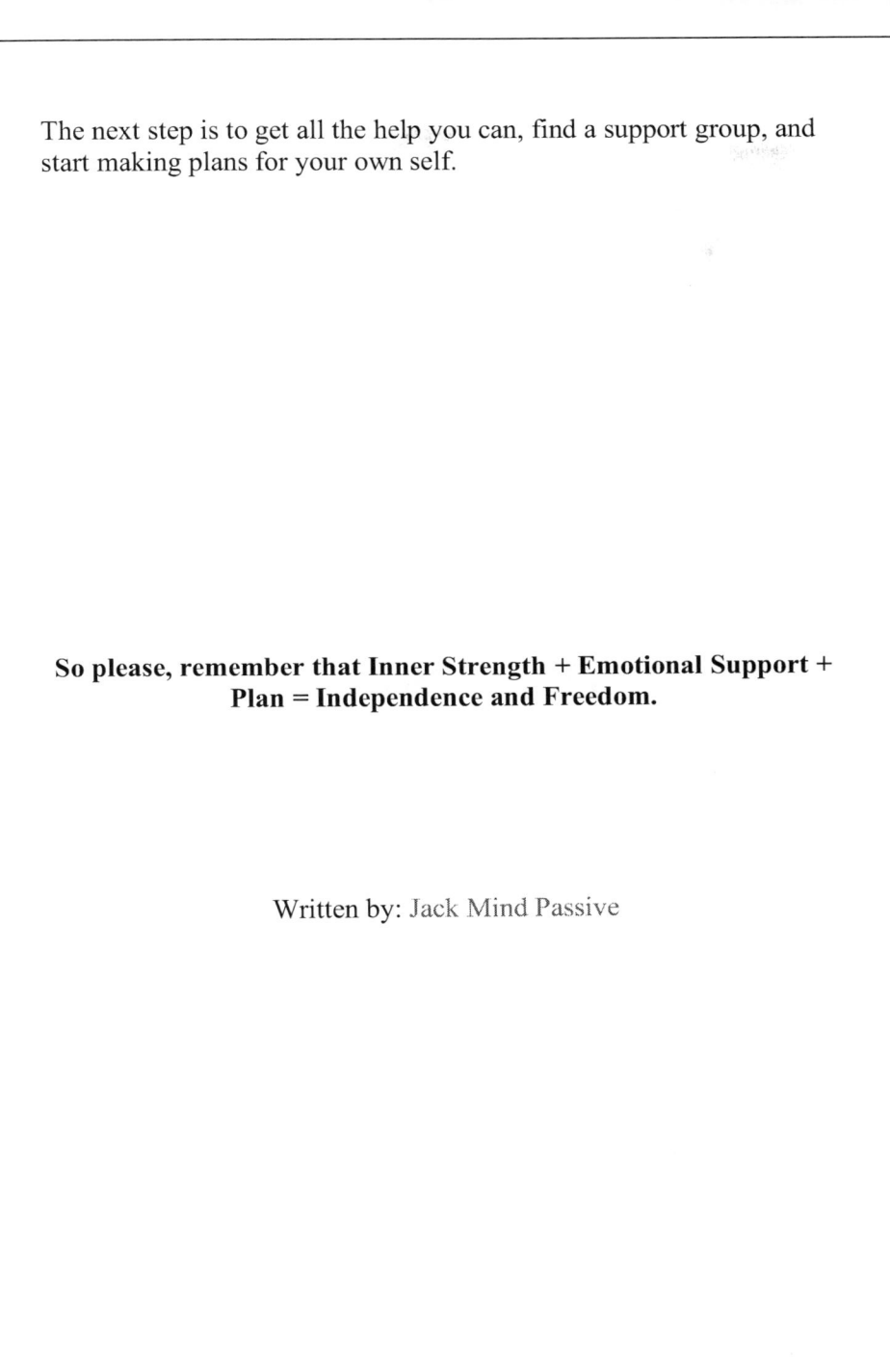

The next step is to get all the help you can, find a support group, and start making plans for your own self.

So please, remember that Inner Strength + Emotional Support + Plan = Independence and Freedom.

Written by: Jack Mind Passive

MASTER YOUR EMOTIONS

SUCCESS AT WORK, AND HAPPIER RELATIONSHIPS. EMOTIONALLY DESTRUCTIVE MARRIAGE, AND EMOTIONAL INTELLIGENCE. (EQ 2.0)

CAROLINE EMPATHY

Master Your Emotions

Success at Work, and Happier Relationships. Emotionally Destructive Marriage, and Emotional Intelligence

© **Written by:** Caroline Empathy

Introduction

Congratulations for downloading this book.

This book is the result of years of providing therapy to couples, families, and individuals in trouble with their relationships. When I began my practice, I noticed that people who displayed good communication skills in normal interactions with others could change drastically when they interacted with family members or their spouses. There was a distinct difference between how people acted when calm and how they acted when upset.

People who become emotionally reactive, can't access communication skills. Emotional reactivity (ER) short-circuits a person's capacity to think clearly and act rationally. This is particularly true when a person is interacting with a loved one and has a history of emotional reactivity with that person. The main requirement in mastering one's emotions is to overcome emotional reactivity.

You should consider that this book is a guide and its major aim is to help you get to know your emotions, help you master them so that they do not become a hindrance but instead a fuel source that powers your creativity and initiative.

Let's get started!

Chapter 1: Emotions

In every moment of our lives, there is always a conversation that takes place in our mind. It is usually one of the most integral conversations we could ever see ourselves engaging in. this conversation is usually a silent, mostly subconscious and limitless conversations based on emotional signals between the brain and the heart. The motive behind this conversation is usually quite imperative as the emotional signal sent from the heart to the brain determines the type of chemicals that get released into our bodies. The moment we feel emotions that we typically term as negative such as anger, jealousy, rage and hate, the heart quickly sends to the brain a signal that expresses our feelings. These types of emotions can be chaotic and irregular and this is clearly shown in the signal patterns received by the brain from the heart.

How emotions transform into stress
To break this concept down, let's have a look at the stock market and liken these emotions to it on a volatile and wild day. Imagine what the data charts show with signals going up, down and haywire. This is the type of signals we make in our hearts when we experience such emotions. What the body does is to interpret such signals as stress and that certain mechanisms which help us to appropriately respond are set into motion. The stress gotten from negative emotions tends to have an adverse effect on the amounts of adrenaline and cortisol present in our bloodstreams. These hormones, typically referred to as stress hormones help prep us for a powerful and quick reaction to the thing that is actually creating stress for us. This reaction also consists of blood being redirected from our organs to the parts of our bodies that require it more at that time. These parts are the limbs, extremities and muscles which we are able to use to either confront our stressor or to run away from the stressor as quickly as possible. This is our instinctive fight or flight response to stimuli.

Fight or Flight
There are moments in our lives when we need to respond quickly to outside stimuli without thinking. This is something innately in us and

it stems from a time where there were so many dangers to our existence. If you take our prehistoric ancestors, for example, they used this response to deliver them from any dangerous angry animal that stumbled upon their camp. When the threat passed, their emotions transformed and the higher than normal levels of stress hormones in their bodies reverted to the average levels associated with everyday life. The major point here to note is that any stress response you receive has been designed only to be brief and temporary. The moment our stress hormones kick in, we provide our body with the required chemistry to powerfully and quickly respond to whatever threat we face. A great thing about having extraordinary amounts of stress hormones in our systems is that we develop, albeit temporarily to do extraordinary feats. We become superhuman, we gain extra strength and things that we ordinarily wouldn't have done become so easy for us to do. If you ask anyone running away from danger if they thought they do what they did to escape on a normal day, most people would say they couldn't. They were able to do all of this without considering it. It is in these sorts of cases that our innate fight or flight response becomes activated. The feelings of do or die cause a surge of stress hormones to pour into the body and cause you to run faster than you have ever run. Another side of this superhuman gift, however, is the fact that whilst the benefits are amazing and can prove to be of help during a time of crisis, that stress triggered surge effectively clamps down on the release of other essential chemicals which support integral bodily functions. When these vital bodily chemicals are released growth function and immunity are improved, it also helps to reduce the occurrence of anti-aging. Every one of these positive properties are reduced when the stress hormones are triggered due to a fight or flight response. What this is means is that it is only possible for the body to simply be in on mode. It cannot be in more than one at once. It could be said that our bodies and by extension our minds were not meant to live with consistent stressors on a daily basis. However, this happens to be the situation quite a lot of us find ourselves.

Living in a World of Stress
In our present time of data overload, speed qualitative analysis, multiple consecutive double cappuccinos, and also the often-heard sense that life is "speeding up," it's inevitable that our bodies will feel that we're in an exceedingly constant state of unending stress. folks that cannot notice a unharness from this sort of stress notice

themselves in sustained fight-or-flight mode, with all of the implications that accompany the territory. a fast shop around associate degree workplace or a room, or maybe a look at our members of the family over Sunday dinner, confirms what the information suggests. It's not stunning to seek out that folks with the best levels of sustained stress also are within the poorest health. The upsurge in rates for stress linked conditions, such as stroke, heart disease, immune deficiencies, certain forms of cancer and eating disorders in the Us, is no surprise given the amount and likelihood of stress-related activities that numerous individuals face over the course of their daily life. Thankfully, the exact same system that makes and prolongs our stress response, usually on a subconscious level is the same can be regulated in a bid to help relieve stress from our bodies in a manner that is healthy. What is great about this is that this is something we can do intentionally and quickly Just the way our hearts send our brains the signals of chaos when we feel negative emotions, positive emotions send another kind of signal to our brains that is more regular, more rhythmic, and orderly. In the presence of positive emotions, such as appreciation, gratitude, compassion, and caring, the brain releases a very different kind of chemistry into the body.

The Key to Personal Resilience
When we feel a sense of well-being, the level of stress hormones in our bodies decreases, while the life-affirming chemistry of a powerful immune system with anti-ageing properties increases. The shift between the stress response and a feeling of well-being can happen quickly. Our feelings or emotions are a significant part of our inner lives. Our emotions are generally speedy primitive reflexes freelance of our thoughts, however, at different times, our feelings mirror our psychological feature assessment of our current scenario. Our feelings involve each our emotions and our urges to act bound ways that.

The intensity of associate degree feeling isn't such a lot determined by the present scenario because it is by the number of actual or expected amendment. Thus, the spider seen fifteen feet away isn't as scary as an oversized one suddenly solely half dozen inches away. Since emotions appear to be designed naturally to assist us to adapt --to solve a problem--we tend to urge "used to" positive conditions (a romantic, giving spouse) however our fears and hostilities continue on and on disconcerting and urging us to "do one thing." As it has been observed that the human mind was apparently not created for happiness, except for survival. Happiness is feasible; however, it should take intentional thought associate degreed effort; it's not forever an automatic method. But anger, grief, insecurity, and jealousy are automatic, generally even unstoppable. The desire to get rid of serious emotional hurts from our life will become thus primary that our robust feelings over-ride reason, shut our minds to different viewpoints, and dominate our actions. Suicide may be a way to escape pain and hurts. Likewise, the angered ex-spouse will consider something else, never any explanations for the previous spouse's wrongdoings. The badness of the adult becomes associate degree obsession, associate degree unshakeable conviction which is able to usually last forever, despite different peoples' opinions. This resolved read may be a characteristic of emotions: the fearful flyer can't take into account the high chance of his/her flight incoming safely; the jealous person is totally bound the lover is fascinated by somebody else; the insecure better half feels certain his/her partner does not extremely take care of him/her. Yet, there generally looks to be thought of as the probable consequences at some semi-conscious level as a result of the fearful rider sometimes does not get off the plane and that we do not forever now dump the "unfaithful" lover or "indifferent" better half. Indeed, several "healthy" individuals tend to distort their read of a scenario in such how that their negative feelings and dangers are reduced and/or their positive feelings are maximized. As luck would have it, beneath favorable conditions, there are reasons that will facilitate us to see different possibilities, see the possible long-run consequences of associate degree action, see the implications of a code of ethics, etc. Reason (cognition) will modify the impulsive actions of the additional stiffly mechanistic emotions. One among the important points is that emotions, still as behavior and reason, are lawful and comprehendible (but not logical). The additional you recognize regarding those laws, the higher your possibilities of dominant your unwanted emotions.

Chapter 2: How to Handle Your Emotions In Relationships

You may be aware of certain situations that cause you to feel more negative emotions than positive ones. You may be aware of a certain circumstance under which it seems like, no matter how hard you try, you can't keep yourself from feeling negatively in it. Here are some steps you can utilize to help you to take control.

Identify What Emotions are Unwanted

Think about the emotions you wish to avoid the most. Think about how it makes you feel afterward, to know that you weren't able to control that impulse at that moment.

Narrowing this down might take some time, but that's okay. Putting a lot of thought into this is a good way to make sure you're on the right track and pinpointing the right emotions to address.

This could be done by taking a pen and paper and thinking about the emotions that you experience the most loudly. Are there any emotions that cause you to have outbursts? Have you had any outbursts of emotion that you came to regret? What emotions were those?

If you're unable to pinpoint what emotion it was, think about the situation and try to remember how it made you feel. Use the pen and paper and do your best to put those feelings into words.

If you're having trouble putting those feelings into words, a good strategy is to pretend like you're telling a five-year-old about it. Break it down to its most basic, simple terms, and move up from there.

Pick the Changes

Now that you've pinpointed what emotional responses you would like to change, it's time to identify the situations that cause those emotional responses. What was happening directly before the outburst occurred?

Being able to see what stimuli brought on what emotional states and responses are the keys to the steps below. The very basic principle behind managing your emotions is "Cause & Effect."

If you know that you've had an outburst or a period of negative emotion every time you're stuck in traffic, you have a living example of the principle above. The cause: traffic. The effect: outburst or period of negative emotion.

Noting cause and effect is a very scientific approach to a problem that can provide the path to figuring out what the deeper roots of the cause are, as well as the key to neutralizing or lessening the effect that cause can have on you and on your life.

Now that you've been able to isolate the situations, stimuli, or "triggers," for these occurrences, what is the next step?

Make Modifications

The next step is to make modifications to those situations so they have less of an impact on you. By nature, when certain stimuli are recognized, their power over us begins to shrink.

So let's run with the example presented above. You know that traffic causes you to have unreasonable outbursts and you would like to change that. How can you make changes to such a situation? Surely you can't shift traffic patterns so they aren't an issue. What you can do is modify the way that traffic affects your day.

Listen to music that calms you down, take a less traffic-heavy route if at all possible, leave about 15-20 minutes earlier each day so you have extra time when traffic slows down your commute in the morning, see if there's a carpool you can join so you don't need to navigate the traffic yourself or take public transit, or have less caffeine before your commute so you're not as easily agitated.

Regardless of the situation, there are solutions available. It may take some creativity, but in most cases, you will find that you're able to make changes that make all the difference in how you're able to respond to situations.

We may not be able to change the things that we're dealing with in some areas of our lives, but we have control over how we respond to it. That's a big responsibility in some cases.

So how else can we make positive changes to situations with a negative emotional impact?

Shift Your Focus

Shifting your focus to be centered more on the things that you would like to accomplish is a huge step in the right direction.

Going back to our example of being in traffic, your focus is generally on what is right in front of you. That wisenheimer in front of you who doesn't seem to think turn signals are a necessary part of the lane-changing process and this other guy on your left seems to think the boundaries of each lane are merely a suggestion. You need to have your wits about you when you're in traffic, or accidents can happen.

This doesn't mean, however, that your focus can't be on your overall goal. What are you usually trying to do when you get into traffic? You're usually trying to get where you're going, which can cause stress in itself. So where should you put your focus? Try to put your focus on something that doesn't inspire a sense of urgency, but a sense of positive determination.

What kinds of things does that leave you? Maybe there's a goal you're trying to accomplish financially by going to work every day; that's a great place to focus. It's a goal you're trying to accomplish and actively working toward since you're on your way to work, but there's no sense of urgency about getting there right away.

If you've got your calming music on the radio, you're running early for work, you're not hopped up on caffeine, and you're thinking about that goal you're working toward. Who could be mad while doing that!

There is an adage that comes to mind in this situation as well. "Energy flows where attention goes." If you're paying attention to a goal and working toward it with purpose, you're more likely to achieve it and to make steady progress over time. How is that for hitting two targets with one arrow?

Change Your Thought Process

The next step is to change the way you think about the situations that cause those recurrent negative emotions. This one is, like a lot of things in this book, easier said than done.

If you're dreading getting into traffic every day, you are already entering the situation with a negative mindset and emotion. Going into something in that mindset is basically a guarantee that you will get "proven right," for being mad, as things to be mad about will inevitably cross your path.

If you're looking for a reason to be upset, you will always find one!

So how should we go about changing the mindset on our example? "How is it even possible to feel positive about traffic?" Well, let's take a look, shall we?

What is your new focus when we're getting into traffic? Your new focus is that financial goal and you're working toward it with purpose. So when you get into your car in the morning and your focus is on that goal, your mindset should be one that's positive.

Now, to be clear, this doesn't mean that it's unnatural to be mad in traffic if you get cut off or if someone pulls some maneuver out of an Evel Knievel stunt. It just means that you shouldn't take that one guy's ridiculous driving as a license to hop out of your car and start a fight or to even let it ruin your morning.

Take Action

When these situations that "set you off," present themselves, it's important to make a conscious effort to chance those seemingly automatic responses. The next time something makes you angry to that point, realize it is happening, stop for a moment and think about whether it's worth it to have that outburst over this situation.

Chapter 3: Methods for Mastering Your Emotions

Understanding your emotions--behavior, feelings, physiology, and thoughts--will assist you set up ways that to vary them. First, do not forget that strategies that specialize in the behavior of changing the surroundings can even cut back on unpleasant emotion, e.g. cut back your worry by golf stroke higher locks on the doors or by avoiding somebody you're mad at. Fears can even be reduced by modeling somebody World Health Organization is a smaller amount afraid than you are. You will develop different behaviors which will counteract the unwanted emotions, e.g. activity counteracts depression, assertion counteracts anger, facing the worry counteracts it, relaxation counteracts the disorder of the compulsive, etc. Contrary to the notion that "time heals," there's proof that fears, grief, memory of a trauma, etc. do not simply dissolve. These feeling do decline if we tend to repeatedly expose ourselves to the disconcerting situation or memory over and all over again whereas relaxed or beneath less stressful conditions (yet, changing into terribly agitated whereas reproof friends regarding the "awful" scenario does not sometimes help). However, changing the results of a behavior will alter emotions conjointly, e.g. ask your friends to praise your healthy self-assertiveness and challenge your mousy conformity. Second, do not forget that our thoughts powerfully influence our emotions. And, since we are able to generally amendment our thoughts and since scientific discipline is during a "cognitive" era, there's nice stress on cognitive strategies at now.

The strategies here alter basic raw emotions: anxiety or fears, anger, and unhappiness. Of course, these same strategies are used on the emotional half (level II) of the other drawback. Passive-dependent problems tend to be handled with cognitive-behavioral strategies and new skills. Emotions are an important part of our lives and that they are fascinating. Several recent books can assist you to perceive. A case can be made for how emotions are aroused and their effects, including the impact on our health. It can be argued that we amplify educational ratio and neglect emotional ratio (knowing and handling our gut feelings and impulses, self-motivation, people skills). You would possibly gain more insight into your feelings from many other books

Relaxation Training

Being able to relax whenever you want is a wonderful skill to have. Majority of people can learn to do so. There are many numerous methods but they all have quite a lot in common. No one relaxation technique is best for everyone. There are numerous bits of evidence that provide a reason to believe that there are so many practical, detailed guidelines to many relaxation exercises. Your first task, then, is to find a method that suitably works well for you. Three methods will be described here: (1) deep muscle relaxation, (2) recorded relaxation instructions, and (3).

After learning a good method for you, the major problem is taking the time to relax when you need to. Be sure to see desensitization and meditation later.

Purposes

- To overcome feelings such as anxiety and reduce tension

- To aid other purposes, such as concentrating and increasing

- learning efficiency, overcoming insomnia and improving sleep, and improving one's general health.

- To counteract panic reactions and to counteract the constant activity of a workaholic or social addict

- To counter-condition fears and phobic reactions, as in desensitization (method #6).

Steps

STEP ONE: Select a relaxation method to try; decide how to give you the instructions. Consider these three ways of relaxing and pick one to try:

1. Deep-muscle relaxation is easy to learn. It is a simple routine: first tense the muscles, and then relax them. This procedure is used with many small muscle groups all over the body. Most of the anxiety and tension you feel is in your muscles. So, by focusing on relaxing your muscles, you can calm and comfort your entire body (and mind) by excluding distressing thoughts (since you are concentrating on groups of muscles). This method is based on the simple principle that muscles relax after being tensed, especially if suggestions to relax are also being given. So, the mind and body can be calmed by starting with the muscles. The detailed steps are given below.

2. There are a large number of commercial cassettes that provide relaxation instructions. Usually, it is better to make your own tape. In

this case, you start with the mind and send relaxing messages to the muscles.

3.   Meditation can be used as a relaxation procedure. The idea is to free the mind from external stimulation, which slows physiological functions and reduces muscle tension...and that reduces impulses to the brain...and so on in a beneficial cycle. Like meditation, the calming effects of all these methods last beyond the time doing relaxation.

STEP TWO: Learn how to do the relaxation method you have chosen. Below are detailed instructions for the three relaxation methods:

1.   Deep-muscle relaxation involves focusing on a small group of muscles at a time, e.g. "make a fist" or "make a muscle in both arms." With each set of muscles, you go through the same three-step procedure:

a.   Tense the muscles. Notice each muscle. Tighten the muscles until they strain but not hurt. The muscles may tremble which is okay but be careful with your feet and other muscles that tend to cramp. It does not need to be rigorous exercise. Hold the muscles tense for 5 to 10 seconds.

b.   Suddenly, say relax to you and let the muscles relax completely.

c.   Focus your attention on the marked change in the muscles from when they are tense to when they are relaxed. Enjoy the pleasure and relief that comes with relaxation. Give yourself instructions to relax more and more, to feel more and more comfortable all over. In this way, you replace muscle tension with soothing relaxation all over your body. At first, this three-step procedure may need to be repeated two or three times for each set of muscles. With practice, however, you can relax in a few minutes. Use groups of muscles something like the following (don't get overly precise about this, any group of muscles will do fine): Arms Hands and forearms--"make a tight fist" and bend it down towards the elbow. Start with one arm, move to both arms. Biceps--"make a muscle." Both arms. Triceps--stretch the arm out straight, tensing the muscle in the back of the arm. Both arms.

Upper body Forehead--raise eyebrows and "wrinkle forehead Eyes--close eyes tightly (careful if wearing contacts)

STEP THREE: Arrange a private place and schedule a specific time for relaxing. A private place is crucial: a bedroom, a private office at work, even a bathroom might be the best place. You should take 10-15 minutes twice a day. Ideally, it should be a comfortable place with no interruptions. A bed or a chair with arms and a high, soft back is good (as long as you don't go to sleep). Many people get sleepy if they meditate after a meal. Drown out distracting noise with a neutral sound: a fan, air conditioner, or soft instrumental music. Turning off the lights helps. Perhaps you had better tell your roommate, co-workers, family, etc., what you are doing, if there is any chance, they will walk into the room.

STEP FOUR: Relaxing on command Most people can relax easily in comfortable, familiar, quiet surroundings. But that isn't where we have the stress. It is harder to relax when called on to speak to a group or when taking a test. What can you do then? One possibility: pair a silently spoken word, like "relax," with actually relaxing. Do this thousands of times, as in the relaxation exercises above or by mentally thinking "relax" as you exhale. In this way, the internal command--"relax"--becomes not only a self-instruction but also a conditioned stimulus, an automatic prompter of a relaxation response (like a cigarette,). So, when you get uptight, you can silently say "relax" and feel better. It is no cure all but it helps.

STEP FIVE: Relaxation--a routine or as needed many people would say that relaxation should be practiced faithfully twice a day, seven days a week. That is certainly necessary if you hope to establish a more relaxed level of physiological functioning on a continuous basis. Other people use a relaxation technique anytime they have a few minutes to rest. Still, others use relaxation only when tension is getting excessive and/or they need to slow down, such as at bedtime. Any of these uses are fine; however, they all require practice in advance, i.e. you can't wait until a crisis hits and then decide you want instant relaxation. Time Required: It may take 4 or 5 hours to learn the method, practice it, make the recording, or whatever is involved. Thereafter, the technique may be used 15 to 30 minutes a day or only occasionally. Common problems with the method many can't find the time to relax twice a day, especially the people who need it the most. Although 10 to 15% of students are reluctant to try a relaxation technique in class, almost everyone can become deeply relaxed with practice. A few people fall asleep while relaxing. If you do, you may need to set an alarm.

Effectiveness, advantages and dangers:

All the above methods, if used faithfully, seem to be effective during the relaxation session. Some research has suggested that meditation works a little better than the other methods, at least for reducing general anxiety. How much the relaxation continues beyond the session is questionable, however, regardless of the method used. Seeking calm in a storm is a difficult task. In many of us, the stress reaction is just too strong to be easily overridden; we may need to withdraw from the stressful situation for a while. One would think that relaxing would be the safest thing in the world for a self-helper to do. It probably is, but several therapists have reported panic attacks in patients when relaxation is tried in therapy. This negative reaction has been observed primarily in persons suffering from very high anxiety. For most people, this shouldn't be a concern. In a class setting, I have found that 5- 10% of the students do not fully participate in a relaxing exercise in class. Some don't like closing their eyes; others are reluctant to publicly "make a muscle," "suck in your stomach," "arch your back" (thus, throwing out your chest), etc.

However, almost everyone can learn to relax. Imaging relaxing visual scenes (a warm sunny day on the beach) works best for some people; repeating calming sayings and self-instructions works better for others; sitting in a warm bath reading a magazine works wonderfully for some. Moods by suggestion: calm scene, relaxation, elation In the Western world we are preoccupied with the external world-- the world of work or TV or interpersonal relations. In Eastern cultures they are more concerned with the inner world--fantasy and thoughts. They use meditation and seek an inner serenity, partly as a way of coping with harsh external realities and partly for the benefits an inner life offers. There is a stigma against daydreaming in our culture. It can be a way of avoiding reality or a way of rehearsing for the future. Fortunately, there is a connection between thoughts and feelings, so emotions can be influenced via fantasies. Harry Truman said, "I have a foxhole in my mind," meaning he had a place in his mind where he could escape the explosive issues bombarding him from the external world. Purpose to supply a desired feeling or mood: relaxation, elation, nostalgia, larger awareness and concentration, and increased motivation.

STEP ONE: Prepare the directions for no matter feelings you want to supply four ways of adjusting feelings are illustrated below: (1) a relaxed scene, (2) self-monitoring for relaxation, (3) positive affirmation statements for a positive noesis, and (4) elation and expanded consciousness. A calm scene. All folks have recollections of being somewhere and feeling carefree, calm and happy. Imagining such a relaxed or pleasant moment in your life will arouse calm or happy feelings. For relaxation, it ought to be a scene within which you're inactive (it's arduous to relax whereas thinking of climb a mountain or swimming a river). Examples: lying in the heat sun on a beach or a ship, resting ahead of a hearth and look the flames, walking leisurely in a very wood on a stunning fall day, sitting on a mountain prime and looking out at the luxurious, peaceful valley below, or sitting in your space, looking the window and resting, simply look the planet fade. Choose cosy, peaceful, pleasant scene that has special which means for you.

My calm scene is walking alone by a little stream that wind through a hayfield ahead of my childhood home. I bear in mind minute details: the clearness of the spring-fed water, the softness of the grass, the rolling hills, the heat of the sun, the minnows and water spiders, the large sycamore trees, building a dam with a crony, mud crawling, dreaming regarding the long run, being alone however not lonely, perhaps as a result of the beckoning heat of my house close. Self-monitoring. It's straightforward. Use the senses of the body as a biofeedback machine. Sit down or lie. Get relaxed and shut your eyes. Concentrate to each sensation, everything that goes on in your body. Don't try and perceive or make a case for what's happening, just observe. categorical in words what's happening. Scan the body and report everything you notice. associate degree example: Eye lids grow heavier, shoulders slump and back bends, respiration deep, abdomen growls, throat swallows, ringing in ears, muscles in face appear quiet and heavy, etc. This is associate degree previous technique. it's sensible for general nervousness. Somehow the nerve-wracking sensations decline and peace follows. Positive affirmations. many folks believe that imagining doing something well will increase actual ability and certainty. therefore, athletes imagine touch a home run, different imagine an executive dive, a speaker imagines a superb delivery.

Supposedly, the brain doesn't recognize the distinction between a true expertise associate degreed an imagined one. So, your vanity grows. Likewise, if you say, with feeling, positive things to yourself, a positive noesis can develop. Image in your mind precisely what you wish to try to or be. Feel positive and assured as you imagine the specified behavior. The statements ought to be recurrent many times every session and during three or four sessions every day. samples of positive affirmations (notice they describe within the present what you may be doing -- "I am calm" or "slim," not "I need to be calm" nor "I am not tense" or "I am not fat"): For a much better self-concept and positive mental attitude -- • daily in each manner, I'm convalescing and better. • I succeed as a result of I feel I will. • I'm stuffed with caring kindness. • I'm happy and content. To encourage some achievement-- • I'm happy with my body (visualize however you may check out your ideal weight). • I'm a superb student; I really like to find out. • I will hoodwink and undo well. To relax and be healthy-- • I'm healthy, happy and relaxed. • Pain free, happy me. To reduce worry-- • forget the past and therefore the future-- I'm within the here and currently. • I settle for any challenge; I will handle it. Expanded consciousness. This fantasy methodology was meant to create increased awareness, larger concentration, better problem-solving ability, and feelings of competency. Have a retardant in mind to figure on before you begin the exercise. It's not a decent fantasy for folks with a worry of heights or of flying. you will have the experience additional absolutely if all you have got to try to is listen, therefore record these abbreviated instructions: "Get comfy and shut your eyes. Imagine you're within the gondola of an outsized hot air balloon. You resting and look what is happening with interest. Let your imagination go free, have vivid images of the items I counsel to you. it's a stunning day. The balloon is filling. See the hayfield around you. You have got nothing to try to however relax and skill the fun of the ride. The balloon is sort of full. Before long, you may start up and as you go higher, your awareness and concentration and thinking also will become higher. I'm reaching to count from one to ten. With every count the balloon can go higher and your mind will expand larger till it's ready to bear in mind of everything. You may become far more responsive to reality and have a larger appreciation of truth and sweetness.

Now, the balloon gently and quietly takes to the air, I begin to count and your consciousness starts to expand.

1. As you float higher, you may have a brand-new experience...pleasant, exciting feelings of increased awareness and sensitivity.

2. a bit higher. You're getting into a better level of consciousness. You're comfy. You're feeling sensible regarding using your full brain.

3. You relish the quiet, swish ride, the superb read, the excitement.

4. You vary of awareness is regularly increasing. Your perception is keener. Your attention and concentration are even more below your management.

5. Rising higher and better.

Your confidence will increase and you feel higher and better.

6. Your consciousness will increase however your awareness isn't overloaded. You're feeling joy as your senses reach their highest level.

7. Your expertise a unleash, a brand-new freedom as your intuitive and intellectual potentials reach their peak. As you go still higher, your heightened talents can change you to check causes and relationships you never accomplished before.

8. You're terribly high currently. Before long, you may enter a brand-new dimension, wherever your insight is very keen and innovative.

9. All the far to the sting of house. You able to experience and concentrate and reason higher than ever before. Ten currently you're at the highest. Your talents, awareness and understanding are able to disclose new which means and new solutions. You're desperate to use

these skills to unravel your concerns. Take as long as you wish. As you specialize in real problems, take time to grasp the causes. Don't skip or run off from any cause--consider it rigorously. are you able to see things otherwise now? Are you able to discover new feelings you had not been responsive to before? Are you able to perceive the sentiments of others better? Next, take time to create new and higher solutions to your problems.

Imagine however every course of action may compute. Consider uncommon solutions and combos of solutions. Decide on the best approach. If different insights return to you, settle for them however goes back to determination the most downside. Now, close up the electronic equipment till you're able to 'come down' and awaken. Start tape once more after you are able to stop: "OK, we have a tendency to be able to descend. I will count from ten to one. When I get to one you may be back in a very traditional, everyday state of consciousness. You will feel sensible and rested and grateful for the special time to think. You may bear in mind everything that went on and every one your insights.

10. Getting down to drift downward and back to a standard state of awareness.

Coming back down. You may bear in mind everything.

Gently floating down. You're feeling terrific.

Enjoying the expertise. Continued down. Down. At the count of one your eyes can open. You see the bottom slowly approaching. Before long, you will be back relaxed and rested. Virtually down. A rush like hayfield below. it will be a delicate landing. You're feeling nice. You're down. Open your eyes. You're feeling terrific."

STEP TWO: notice a quiet place and obtain ready Use a quiet, comfortable, personal place, sort of a bedchamber. Make your recording if required. Place the player close to your hand therefore you will simply turn it on and off.

STEP THREE: Have the fantasy as vividly as potential Have the expertise. Get into it as deeply as possible; have detailed and vivid imagination, victimization all of your senses, and place your feelings into it. it's going to be useful to record every expertise and compare your reactions over time. Preparation time might take from quarter-hour to associate degree hour. However, most of those mood-altering exercises should be recurrent for 10-15 minutes, 2 or additional times each day to be effective. Common issues with the ways in general, they promise an excessive amount of, particularly distended consciousness. Take a "try-it-and-see" perspective. Another downside is that some folks have poor visualization talents. If you don't visualize well, strive another modality, i.e. have your fantasies additional in words and feelings. Through follow you will develop an additional vivid fantasy. Effectiveness, advantages and dangers: Fantasies do generate feelings. There are few experiments during this area however several clinical reports of distress brought on by unpleasant memories and thoughts concerning doable disasters. Some actors produce tears by thinking of a tragic event. it's cheap that positive emotions are often created within the same method. As mentioned earlier, some individuals are reluctant to relax or shut their eyes in school. The advantage is that these ways are easy, easy, and done on your own. There are not any known dangers. How to be happy—determinism Many people would say, "I simply wish to be happy." it's a worthy goal however few individuals who are shrewd enough to seek out happiness do so. Some would say they want to own an honest education and a remarkable career. Others would say they require a in love domestic partner and a pleasant family. Others desire a career, a family, physiological state, smart friends, a pleasant house, 2 sharp cars, good relationships with each family, associated enough cash to require an extended vacation every year and to be comfy. What would you say you wish to be happy? In our culture, nearly everybody encompasses a list of wants or wants. We want pleasures--good appearance, an honest relationship, friendships, fun experiences, etc., etc. we wish possessions--a smart sound system, a jazzy automobile, nice garments, etc., etc. we have a tendency to all would like some pleasure in life. But the matter is after we begin to believe that pleasures and possessions are the thanks to be happy. Once we start to think that method, we have a tendency to begin to mention "if I simply had _ (an education, a boyfriend, a good job, a contented wedding, enough cash to retire, a good relationship with my family...) _, I'd be happy."

Our achievements and acquisitions became the supply of our happiness. we have a tendency to are presently in trouble: we don't get all that we want; we always wish a lot of; not matter what proportion we have got. Recent pleasures lose their thrill; possessions quickly become associate recent inferior model. There is always one thing excitingly newer, better, faster, bigger, and more expensive. Once you say "I would like visited be happy," you have got created a self-destructive mind game. Happiness can't be supported having possessions; cars break down, homes deteriorate, garments quickly go out of fashion, etc.

Finding Happiness
Happiness can't be supported pleasures; marriages fall apart, friends alienate, power fades, intake and drinking build us fat, etc. OK, what will happiness are primarily based on? Associate acceptive frame of mind; a tolerance of no matter is as a result of whatever is, is right. Whatever happens in life is lawful. It takes time to know this viewpoint. Consider it fastidiously. A belief in philosophical theory isn't a helpless-hopeless position; it's not being while not goals, preferences, opinions, or values. In fact, it is important to own a revered mission in life and to have high values; they are nice sources of enjoyment. It's necessary that you just use the laws of behavior to try to your best, that you just facilitate others, which you try to build the planet higher.

However, when you have got done your best, you must settle for the result, despite what it is. Do your best while at work or in a great relationship, however settle for being fired or rejected, if that's what happens. settle for reality. Unconditional positive regard of others and of yourself may be a major consider finding happiness. Other factors contributory to happiness embody learning to own some influence over your world, to be ready to build your state of affairs better, and to own confidence in your self-control. To become happy, it is necessary to be ready to handle sad feelings once they return along. You can't be happy and sad (or angry) at the same time concerning an equivalent specific issue. You can, of course, be happy concerning bound aspects of a difficulty and sad about different aspects. This section helps to build the purpose that the event of a particular emotion, like happiness, is usually terribly complex and involves several aid ways. Obviously, all the methods for reducing depression would possibly apply to generating happiness, but happiness is far over the absence of disappointment. You see the point. (If you're thinking that this methodology is extremely psychological feature, I agree that it's closely associated with the ways in.

Purposes• to know a way to accomplish happiness. • To avoid futile tries to realize happiness via pleasures, possessions, or indifferent and freewheeling behaviours.

Steps

STEP ONE: learn to just accept reality and therefore the quality of life. This is not a simple task. It takes time to shake off our consumption ("Give me") orientation towards happiness. There is a special analogy: Suppose you lived one thousand years past and were asked if you'd prefer to board 2020 with heat homes, cars, aeroplanes, TV, free education, smart medical aid, etc. Of course, if you were living in one thousand A.D. in an exceedingly dirt-floored hut, with very little education, with many kids dying from diseases, with starvation all over, and with no amusement, etc., you'd suppose 2020 would be fantastic. You would assume that everybody in 2020 would be joyfully happy! But all of our benefits, knowledge, possessions and pleasures have not created the country happy. Hopefully, in 3000, we will grasp far more about being productive, moral, and happy.

You will be able to begin creating realistic plans for dynamical some things you don't like, however, settle for and "understand" the method things are. Most importantly, this acceptive, tolerant perspective reduces rancour and frustration with others and together with yourself. This is known as its "unconditional positive regard. "

STEP TWO: Learn to own some management over your life. Even if you're well cared for at this point, nobody is often entirely comfortable realizing that they're unable to support themselves, should the necessity arise. a private or social downside is usually possible; the one who feels unable to address freelance survival should feel uneasy. Learning a lot of concerning handling normal problems for individuals such as you provide a basis for bigger happiness. Self-help reading ought to facilitate.

STEP THREE: Work on reducing the emotions, largely disappointment and anger, that are incompatible jubilantly. Of the four major emotions, depression and anger are the foremost inconsistent jubilantly. they need to be unbroken at a reasonably low level. the opposite emotions aren't as crucial, i.e. we are able to be moderately stressed and still be happy; we have a tendency to can be quite passive-dependent and be happy.

STEP FOUR: There must be some pleasures in each life. The pleasures could also be few and straightforward, however, we'd like some. There are actually an infinite range of linked choices. Develop some, if you don't have any. But, keep it absolutely clear in your mind that these pleasures are not the supply of happiness in your life. If a pleasure becomes unavailable, you will be able to notice another.

STEP FIVE: Your life ought to have a purpose, it ought to have important assuming to you. As chapter three within the starting of this book argues, we have a tendency to all would like a philosophy of life that we have a tendency to are pleased with and willing to follow day by day. Finding happiness may be a major enterprise taking several, many hours, perhaps years. the hassle is really never-ending, as a result of most lives experience a series of nice losses that aren't simply accepted, e.g. death, failure, mental disease, etc. Common issues My expertise is that folks resist the settled notion.

The American belief that there's a fast answer to each downside is extremely strong. It transforms into the concept that we have a tendency to don't need to tolerate anything we have a tendency to don't like, we are able to simply get eliminate the matter. Thus, the idea that we should always settle for our circumstances-of-the-moment becomes viewed as a weak, incompetent, fatalistic position. however, the reality is that many of life's downers are unavoidable-- and irreversible once they have happened. unhappy events are inevitable. So, in these instances, we have solely 2 choices: settle for it as lawful or hate what went on. In no way, ought to philosophical theory result in a fatalistic, hopeless read of tomorrow, however. Effectiveness, benefits and dangers Seeking to be happy is such a fancy method that science is decades aloof from objectively assessing the effectiveness of all the steps concerned. Being happy may be a worthy goal (if it involves facing life as it very is), however. Shared experiences and science can help facilitate this. I don't grasp any dangers from attempting to be happy, as long as we have a tendency to face reality and are accountable.

Effectiveness, benefits and danger
The method is as recent as recorded history; thus, it's withstood the test of your time. It conjointly illustrates the human tendency to avoid testing the effectiveness of mystical processes. Recently, there are a lot of scientific studies. In general, the mixture of meditation, the accompanying philosophy, and therefore the suggestion-placebo effects look to yield these results: relaxation, higher self-control and self-evaluation on, a lot of confidence in self-control, reduction ("desensitization") of scary concepts and issues, and bigger awareness of internal and external stimuli. However, the effectiveness of meditation was compared with easy resting, there were no important differences found. Subjects relaxed (as measured in many ways) equally well mistreatment meditation or relaxation. what is more, fully-fledged meditators became just as physiologically aroused in nerve-racking events as did nonmeditators. that's not stunning, except that meditators would love to believe their methodology is best. there's no magic methodology.

Meditation's long association and similarity with faith makes it just as exhausting to gauge as faith. the assumption that meditation provides a sense of identity and communion with everything within the universe is based on the beliefs and testimony of legion Hindus and Buddhists and different practitioners. however, does one challenge that? maybe, the inner peace and tolerance of all things, claimed by such a large amount of from meditation, can be scientifically incontestable eventually. (On the opposite hand, the value of tolerance, once it's tolerance of mental object, injustice and problems, must be questioned.) We, as a society, ought to demand more exhausting proof from our soft sciences. Like faith, the promise of most is each meditation's strength and its weakness. Simply don't expect it to cure physical diseases or offer long-distance messages. These are often higher accomplished by fashionable medication and a telephone.

Chapter 4: Embracing Our Feelings

Feeling an Emotion
In order to change the difficult behaviors that occur when we are emotionally reactive it is necessary to replace them with new and more functional behaviors. This may result in an increased awareness of our feelings. Habitual behaviors serve to take our attention away from underlying feelings that seem overwhelming. When these behaviors stop, the smoke clears and the underlying feelings become more apparent to us.

To handle the feeling component of an emotion, take the opposite approach. Instead of stopping the feeling, allow it. Instead of changing the feeling to something more positive, embrace it as it is.

The healthy response to feeling is to not change it, move away from it, or distract attention from it. Instead, embrace the feeling with awareness. Feeling is a natural response of our bodies to a situation, or at least to how we perceive that situation. Problems that we have with our emotions lie in distorted perceptions, not in feelings. Feelings demand to be fully felt. If we push the feeling away, we replace it with numbness and repression or with self-destructive actions that distract from feelings. Avoidance of feelings is the source of painful symptoms and defenses. This is why it is so important to embrace feelings, even when we are being emotionally reactive.

Many people run away when confronted with uncomfortable feelings. They are unpleasant; they seem negative. To embrace them is like doing a 180-degree turn. Why embrace unpleasant feelings--like the feelings that accompany emotional reactivity? It is important to understand that they are not destructive. Rather, the behaviors that are used to avoid these feelings are the destructive element. For instance, a person may feel sadness over the loss of a friend, and instead of feeling the sadness will drown his sorrows in drink. In this scenario, drinking is destructive. Embracing the feelings of grief, however, will eventually lead to their transformation.

Over the course of a lifetime we develop numerous, unconscious methods to avoid painful feelings. By embracing our feelings, the compulsion to act these strategies out is short-circuited, and we take the wind out of the sails of defensiveness. If one's tendency is to avoid feelings of hurt by becoming angry, once that hurt is embraced and allowed, then the strategy of avoiding hurt by getting angry has no more purpose. The underlying pain and hurt is faced and transformed.

Painful feelings often become associated with painful events. We believe that if we allow the feelings to arise, we will be vulnerable and hurt again. But the feelings we experience now are not those of past experiences. They are merely changes in our physiology and are not necessarily harmful. What is harmful is running away from our feelings. By embracing painful feelings instead of pushing them away, we can heal.

A feeling is made up of sensations in our bodies as nerve cells become activated. Blood flow changes, adrenaline increases and other chemical changes occur when we are emotional. Feeling is the awareness of these many sensations being stimulated, along with an evaluation of pleasantness, unpleasantness or neutrality. Negative feelings in themselves cannot be horrible or overwhelming, only unpleasant. The true negativity resides in our beliefs and thoughts about them. Understanding this can be a powerful reminder that feelings are okay and are not monsters to be avoided.

Learning to Soothe Ourselves
One analogy we can use is to compare our emotions to the responses of an infant, because infants are highly emotional and have not yet developed the defenses or intellects of adults. They are very sensitive on a feeling level. When an infant is upset and runs to her mother, the mother needs only to hold the infant and attend to her to calm the high emotional arousal of the infant. Being held by a loving caregiver creates a situation in which the original emotion changes, sometimes to its opposite. The child may be laughing and smiling within a few minutes. Feelings require similar attention. We need to soothe ourselves by holding the feeling and staying with it until it changes - until we feel soothed and calmed down.

The ability to soothe ourselves emotionally is a principal skill in mastering emotions. We learn this from our caregivers when we are infants. Those unable to soothe themselves may experience distressing emotions for longer periods of time. Often dysfunctional behaviors serve as distractions from these uncomfortable feeling states. By learning to embrace the feeling component of our emotions and to soothe ourselves, the impetus for these negative behaviors decreases dramatically. The troublesome behaviors may remain as a habit, but the compulsion to act them out loses much of its power.

It is of primary importance that we change our view of our emotions. We need to stop trying to change them or avoid them, instead, let them come to full awareness. If we can make this discovery — that feelings are our friends and have important information for us — we can build the necessary skills to master our emotions and our reactivity.

Steps for Embracing Our Feelings
1. Move your attention to the feeling rather than away from it.
2. Bring your awareness fully to the feeling without backing away or getting distracted. Stay with the feeling.
3. Explore the feeling. What does it feel like? Are there images that occur to you as you explore the feeling? Note the images but keep your attention on the feeling.
4. Notice the specific parts of your body that are affected by the feeling. Where in your body are you feeling this? See if you can break the feeling down into its component parts. Notice what specific sensations are in your body.
5. Let your breathing relax. Take a deep breath. As you do this, imagine that you are breathing directly into the area where you are feeling the emotion.
6. Be aware if the feeling changes, and notice its energetic quality. Whether the feeling is anger or sadness, it is just energy. Stay with the feeling and see what changes take place.
7. This exercise should be soothing. If it is not, there may be some fears or memories holding this feeling in place and not allowing it to move.

By staying with the feeling and experiencing it in our bodies, we contain it and own it. It does not own us. Knowing that feelings are sensations in our bodies allows us to form a container around them.

Awareness is the container that surrounds the emotion and it is larger than the emotion. Awareness contains everything that we are experiencing in the moment: sights, sounds, thoughts, sensations in our bodies. We may be feeling extreme anger in every cell of our bodies, yet our awareness is greater. We can see the trees and the sky, and they have nothing to do with our anger. Instead of seeing anger as a force that sweeps us away, reduce the anger to its true size. Notice how the emotion appears in your body whenever a strong emotion occurs.

As we learn to embrace and experience feeling, a significant transformation takes place--the feelings change. Our feelings have one basic need — to be felt. When we receive this message, it fulfills its task. The feeling may then move to calmness or some other more positive emotion as long as there is no distorted thinking to support its continuance.

Another thing that takes place as we embrace feeling is a change in our deep belief structure. Negative beliefs about experiencing intense feelings fade. We realize that we have embraced the most intense feelings, yet nothing horrible has happened to us, and this helps us break the deep associative ties between these feelings and previous experiences of abuse and distress. We learn that by feeling the feelings, we may soothe ourselves and calm ourselves down. Embracing our feelings now leads to a positive and healing outcome. This is a key method of healing faulty emotional learning that occurs during abusive situations and comes to the surface when we are emotionally reactive.

Numbness and Embracing Feelings
As cited earlier, there are three basic ways of expressing emotional reactivity--through conflict, caretaking and avoidance. All three of these methods avoid feelings to some extent. Let's explore how avoiders can come into greater contact with their emotions.

The avoidant style can be so pervasive for some that it becomes part of their personality style. Because it is difficult for them to experience strong emotions, they avoid them altogether and rarely allow themselves to feel. It may appear that they are not emotionally reactive because they seem calm and peaceful, but this calmness is due to an avoidance of situations that trigger their emotions rather than true peace of mind. They are engaged in a pre-emptive strike; their avoidant behavior itself is their emotional reactivity.

The avoidant person needs to learn to identify avoidant behaviors and to stop them. Awareness of these behaviors is difficult because the rationalizations behind them are so complete. The individual engages in excuse making, judgments and other defense mechanisms not only to justify avoidance, but to disguise it. A person may even get so far away from his emotions that he no longer feels them, even in situations that would typically trigger intense emotions. Some people talk about serious abuse in their childhood as if they were reporting on someone else's childhood. Sometimes a person may express incongruous behaviors, such as laughing when they describe how they were physically abused as children. This dissociation from one's feelings occurs in many people who have had overwhelming trauma.

Facing Areas of Discomfort Gradually
To reclaim the emotional territory that he has lost, the avoidant person must develop a risk-taking philosophy for his emotional life. Many people fit the avoidant personality style--they are driven by fear and have high anxiety. For example, Mary had a difficult time standing up for herself. She had a series of bad relationships with men who did not treat her well. When someone asked her out for a date, she was unable to say "no" even though intuitively she knew the person was not good for her. So she always accepted, fearing she would hurt someone's feelings or cause conflict if she didn't. After getting involved with someone, she would make excuses to avoid having to break up with him, telling herself that the man had potential, that he would change, that she couldn't find anyone better. All these excuses occurred so that she did not have to experience conflict or loneliness.

For decades, behavioral therapists have used a technique called systematic desensitization, or gradual exposure, to help people cope with anxiety and phobias. This set of techniques has proven to be highly effective. Those with anxiety are taught to gradually expose themselves to the situations that cause them fear. Instead of being overwhelmed by facing their fears all at once, they take on their fears a little bit at a time. By facing fears slowly, they don't become overwhelmed.

Discomfort and distress

An avoidant person lives within a circle of comfort. Everything outside this circle is uncomfortable, and is avoided. Some of the situations outside of the circle may indeed be overwhelming and beyond a person's present capabilities to handle. For instance, an agoraphobic person may be tired of being limited by her problem, so she decides to go shopping at the mall despite her agoraphobia. She takes this risk, but then has a panic attack and runs back to her circle of comfort — her home — and vows never to do that again. Taking risks that are overwhelming can easily backfire. However, taking small risks works wonders. In the picture below, there is a circle of low risk drawn around the circle of comfort. This outer circle allows growth, but it is not so far outside of the comfort zone to be overwhelming.

By continuously taking small risks outside the circle of comfort, the avoidant person can slowly face the fear and expand the circle of comfort. After a period of time, the circle of comfort may expand to the outer edge of what was the circle of small risks. They then must identify a new circle of small risks to expand their lives and their capabilities even further.

Each time the avoidant person takes a risk, they are brought face-to-face with an emotion they have been avoiding. This creates an opportunity to uncover emotions that were buried. Taking risks creates opportunities to bring up emotions that are difficult to contact any other way. By adopting this strategic risk-taking philosophy, an avoidant person may transform his life and expand its bounds appreciably. Consistent risk-taking can lead to facing psychological fears that have no basis in reality. If these feelings are embraced, then deep emotional healing can take place and can therapeutically transform the person over time.

For instance, Jerry had a difficult time admitting mistakes at work, defending himself even when he was wrong. He decided to confront this issue by taking small risks. He began by admitting mistakes to Al, his friend at work, whom he trusted. He found this uncomfortable at first because he felt shame about not being perfect. But he realized that although the emotion was uncomfortable, it was not overwhelming. This started Jerry on a journey of feeling more comfortable while admitting his mistakes, and led to many positive consequences in his life.

Everyone uses the strategy of avoidance at times to deal with uncomfortable emotions. It is not solely the province of the avoidant personality type. Facing areas of our lives that we avoid by taking consistent small risks is a tool we can all use. Those who are conflict-oriented may be avoiding feelings of vulnerability. A risk for them would be to check their anger, and allow their hidden, more vulnerable feelings to arise, thereby expanding their emotional range. Caretakers may need to face their fears of abandonment and the fear that arises when they trust that their loved ones can care for themselves. All of us need to take emotional risks; we can do this if we identify our avoidant behaviors and stop avoiding. This will bring us face to face with our unfelt emotions.

Using Fear as a Guide

Fear may be used as a guide to the areas of our lives in which we need to take risks. There are two types of fears. One is physical. We are afraid of heights for good reason--we could fall and hurt ourselves. The other type of fear is psychological: We may be afraid to speak in front of a group, but we are not in physical danger. Attuning ourselves to our psychological fears, and noticing them as they arise, gives us a handy navigation tool that tells us where we need to take risks in our lives. Learning to deal with our emotions also means that we are no longer held hostage by fear and avoidance.

Over the course of our lives we lose areas of feeling because of our defenses and avoidances. As children, we were open and in contact with our feelings and the world around us, but because of painful experiences we shut down to avoid further pain. As we grow older, we lose touch with our feeling nature, and whole areas of our lives suffer. Most notably, we lose intimacy in our families and in our romantic relationships. If we embrace our feelings, we may recover this lost territory of feeling. This will affect our happiness in many unsuspected ways. We may respond more to the world around us, because we can feel it more profoundly. Not only do our relationships improve, but so does our sense of being in the world. We are more connected to our bodies, our loved ones, other people and the culture around us. This heightened awareness of our emotions and feelings has political implications and is one of the main paths for humanity to heal as a group. When we are more emotionally sensitive, we are less likely to act out our aggression on other people. We also gain the capacity for more compassion. If others in our world are being hurt, we can be more responsive to them. We become more responsive to all human relationships.

Mindfulness
A technique that is helpful in embracing emotions is mindfulness. This is a Buddhist practice that is used to enhance and develop awareness. A Buddhist monk may practice mindfulness while he is cooking dinner or washing dishes. It is a helpful technique for spiritual development that is well-suited to busy Western lifestyles. It is also a great practice for anyone who would like to be able to handle their feelings more effectively. Our point of attention is usually focused on the content of our thinking. We think all day long and are absorbed in this thinking. Most of the time, we are not even aware we are thinking. The problem is that the content of our thinking is the source of our problems, at least psychologically. When we examine our thinking, we find that we utilize different kinds of thinking during the day. There is the practical, problem-solving kind that helps plan our day, such as "I need to stop at the bakery to pick up some bread on the way home," and there is the creative kind that supports these practical ideas and makes them happen. Neither of these is involved in psychological problems.

Ego-centered thoughts are what create suffering for us. Worry, for instance, is ego-centered thinking that has an adverse effect on our bodies because it creates stress. Here are some examples of this type of thinking, "I wonder how I'm doing compared to Joe." "I really need to have more money to be happy." "I can't stand that guy at the gas station." We may unfortunately engage in this type of thinking all day long. Ego-centered thinking focuses on protecting the concept of self or attacking others in order to feel better. If we think we are perfect and someone criticizes us, then we become indignant. We may also judge others to make ourselves feel better, or may even attack ourselves and put ourselves down. This type of thinking causes pain, creates stress in the body, and reinforces a separation between us and the world.

Mindfulness is a method to diminish this thinking and to focus our attention on something besides the stream of incessant thoughts that go through our minds all day long, causing us stress. The technique teaches us to attend to other areas of our experience. One of these areas is our sensations. While you are reading this, many sensations are occurring in your body. If you are sitting, you may feel the chair against your back and the lower part of your body. The air in the room may be felt on your face and the exposed parts of your body, and you may feel your feet on the floor. All these sensations are occurring constantly, but because they are so constant we do not pay attention to them. They become part of our background experience. We can bring them to our awareness at any time, however. When we do this we take some or all of our attention away from our thinking — the source of our psychological woes — to a place inside of us that is neutral psychologically. Focusing on our sensations allows us to experience peace and calm.

Another helpful area to become mindful of is our breath. Our breath is a constant background sensation that we rarely pay attention to. While breathing, many sensations are occurring — the rising and falling of our chests, the cool air hitting our nostrils. Breathing can be useful to focus on because it occurs in the part of the body where we feel the most intense emotions--between our nostrils and our stomachs. We describe emotions with such phrases as a "sinking in my stomach," "a tightness in my chest," "a heaviness in my heart," etc. In an effort to control our emotions, we may constrict these areas of our body, and consequently restrict our breathing. Deep breathing helps us to relax. By becoming more aware of our breath, we can make these automatic defenses more conscious. Then we have choice.

Mindfulness of sensations can be practiced anytime and anywhere — whenever your mind is not engaged in activities that need all of your attention. A good time to practice mindfulness is when there is nothing else to do and you would like to do something productive. For instance, waiting in line at a grocery store is a good place to practice, or while being stuck at a stoplight while driving. While walking or jogging or during any exercise, we can attend to the sensations in our bodies as we move.

By mindfulness of sensations, we become more aware of our bodies. This awareness prepares us to be more in touch with our feelings when they occur, since feelings are made up of sensations occurring in our bodies. If we practice mindfulness at times of the day when we are calm, then we are more prepared when a strong emotion does occur. Due to the deep relaxation that accompanies mindfulness practice, our baseline physiological state becomes less tense and more relaxed. We create the habit of bringing awareness to our bodies. This greatly improves our capacity to embrace our emotions and to contain them. We also experience a greater sense of being centered, and of not losing control of our behavior. We learn to soothe our own feelings by embracing them with our mindfulness.

Awareness When We Are Emotionally Aroused
By becoming more aware of our bodies we may learn to recognize when we are getting angry, fearful or distressed. Many people have a difficult time identifying these feelings until it's too late and the emotions have already become extreme. Intense emotions are much more difficult to handle. By having a greater sense of our bodies, we are more aware of the field in which these emotions express themselves. This gives us an edge. We experience these feelings arising in our bodies before they get unwieldy. When we become aware of an emotion as it is arising, we are more capable of soothing ourselves, and of acting more appropriately. It creates a space in which we can see how we are thinking about the situation and to see if our thinking is accurate.

Jeff and Sue have many petty arguments about how they plan to redecorate their house. They each have strong ideas and squabble over their differences. Jeff finds these arguments painful and a waste of time. He decides to practice mindfulness to focus more attention on his body, and to tune into his feelings. He begins to be more aware of when he is getting angry.

When he does this, he notices changes in his level of arousal, and this helps him to change his behavior when he and Sue disagree with each other. His presence of mind helps him change his communication and calm the situation rather than contribute to emotional reactivity. Sue was not able to do this as easily as Jeff. She had a more difficult time, but she did appreciate that Jeff was learning to do this, and she found herself less reactive because Jeff was less reactive.

Awareness and Choice

By practicing mindfulness, we not only help transform our uncomfortable feelings, we also increase our capacity to act more constructively. The behavior that is expressed during emotional reactivity is pre-programmed from the past, and is subconscious and automatic. But this automatic expression may be modified if people are aware of their body. Awareness gives them a choice--they can choose a behavior based on the current situation, rather than one that was learned as a child.

If a friend walks into your room speaking in a loud voice with his fists clenched, you assume he is angry or very excited. He may be so angry or excited that he is not aware he appears threatening. If you ask him, "Are you angry?" he may say "yes" or "no" depending on his level of awareness of his emotions. If you ask him why his fists are clenched, he may stop to realize that they are clenched. At this point, he has a choice to keep his fists clenched or not. Before you pointed them out, he was unconscious of his fists. We have more choice once we bring a behavior into our field of awareness. When our attention is limited, partial, and focused on something else, we have less awareness and therefore fewer choices. Strong emotions can limit our awareness to a narrow field. Mindfulness and awareness of our bodies will help keep the field of awareness open or even expand it.

People Vary in Their Capacity to Experience Their Feelings

For some people feelings are readily accessible. Others, however, have a more difficult time getting in touch with their feelings, possibly due to different family backgrounds and cultural experiences. Some people grow up in families where both parents are mature in dealing with emotions. They learn to be in touch with their feelings from their parents. Other people grow up in families in which the parents are out of touch with their feelings. These parents are unable to teach their children this awareness. Others have traumatic things happen in their lives. This pain leads them to shut down their feelings. This is unfortunate. People who bury their feelings need to re-contact them to handle their emotions successfully. It is difficult to have successful relationships without this skill.

The ability to feel our emotions is a skill that needs to be relearned. We have it as a child. However, it is important to understand that people may differ hugely in their emotional expression. Some people are very effusive with their emotions and others are less expressive.

Some of this is due to inborn predisposition. However a person expresses them, it is important that they can feel their emotions fully.

The Subtle World of Emotional Communication

As stated before there are two levels of communication — the rational verbal level and the emotional level. Even though people have little awareness of emotional communication, they end up responding to it much more than they think. Greater awareness of emotions helps you identify the emotions of people around you, and the emotional influence others have on you. When emotions become strong enough, rational thinking recedes into the background of awareness, and our emotions move into the foreground of consciousness.

We are influenced emotionally all the time by the environment and are mostly oblivious to this influence. Experts in public relations and propaganda understand the power of the emotional level of communication and our susceptibility through our emotions. Advertising influences our desires; political messages influence our fear and anger reactions. The most potent emotional communications come from those that are closest to us, however. They know us the best and we have history with them. The challenge is to catch these emotional communications before they affect us and make us act in ways that are counterproductive. Because people we are closest to know us so well, they also have greater ability to manipulate our emotions.

It is helpful to become aware of these influences before we get emotionally reactive. This can be difficult for a number of reasons. A person's words and "rational" communication may be at odds with what they are communicating to us emotionally. We get lost in the words and don't sense what is happening on the feeling level. It may be hard to identify when people are manipulating us emotionally, because they have no conscious desire to manipulate us; they are caught in their own emotional reactivity and have no idea what affect they are having on us. We may also be so wrapped up in our reasons for what we are saying or doing that we are not paying attention to the emotional level of communication.

Here are some questions we can ask ourselves to help discover this more subtle, emotional level of communication. You may want to consider a relationship that confuses you emotionally while you ask yourself these questions:

--What emotional pattern are we enacting together right now?

--Has this pattern occurred before? Is it habitual and difficult for us to extricate ourselves from?

--Am I feeling pressure emotionally from this other person to feel a particular way or to do something?

--What is the major emotion that I am feeling with this person? Is it anger, fear, guilt, shame, anxiety, hurt or another emotion? How does feeling this emotion make me want to act? How would this action contribute to the habitual pattern I have with this other person?

--How are we affecting each other with the emotions that we are expressing? Are these emotions affecting me in a manner that diverts me from what I really want?

--Can I remain aware of my feeling without acting or saying something according to the old script?

Attending to this hidden emotional level of communication can be a challenging task. However, becoming aware of this is one of the skills necessary to be able to master emotional reactivity and to insure we are not emotionally manipulated by others. Being mindful of our body not only helps us with emotional reactivity but with many other problems, also. Studies of mindfulness have shown it to help alleviate problems such as anxiety, depression, and personality disorders, as well as providing a general sense of well-being.

Chapter 5: The Benefits of Emotional Intelligence

Emotional intelligence is believed to be one of the fastest growing job skills, and for a reason. Those with high emotional intelligence have an advantage over others in the workplace mainly because they cope better under pressure, find it easier to work in multicultural environments, and being good listeners, make emphatic colleagues and potentially great leaders.

Therefore, developing emotional intelligence makes it easier to cope with the demands of a stressful and fast-paced life of the 21st century. This is particularly important for those who see themselves in high-paid, prestigious, or leadership positions.

Therefore, the main benefit of having high emotional intelligence is that knowing how to effectively manage emotions, and being able to easily understand and cooperate with others, you stand to be an asset to whomever you work for.

Besides, emotionally intelligent people process their emotions before responding to them. In other words, they think before they speak. This may not seem very important but chances are if you have a habit of making ill-informed comments, you will sooner or later come to regret them.

This is perhaps particularly relevant for the Western culture where people usually don't like silence and tend to answer questions or make comments without thinking. Or even worse, believe that every silence has to be filled with a witty comment or a remark.

Words can both help and hurt, and your choice of words says a lot about you. So, one of the ways of rising your emotional intelligence is to become more conscious of the implications of what you are saying.

What makes people talk without thinking?

On the one hand, information overload has made us overstimulated and we find it more and more difficult to stop the inner chatter. On the other, prolonged silence easily opens the door to feelings we may be trying to keep buried, eg emptiness, hurt, frustration, etc.

However, if on the other end of the scale you have an emotionally intelligent person who can manage their emotions and use words appropriately, it's no wonder they are so often headhunted by the most reputable companies.

10 main benefits of having high emotional intelligence:
People enjoy working with/for you

Emotionally intelligent people don't harass their staff or bully their colleagues. They know how to get others to do what they want without resolving to arrogance or aggression. Being flexible and open to suggestion, they make great colleagues or leaders.

People easily open up to you

Being empathic, emotionally intelligent people can tune in to others' emotions, so they easily understand others' point of view or the circumstances which may have led them to do certain things.

You are a master of your emotions in any situation

The ability to identify, understand, and manage your emotions means you'll always be a step ahead over others when it comes to responding to challenging situations. Besides, being in charge of your emotions helps you manage stress better.

You easily resolve conflicts

The trick to successfully resolving conflicts is to deal with them before the situation gets out of hand. Your ability to manage your emotions, and easily understand those of others, as well as triggers that may have led to them, makes it possible to respond to someone's behavior in a way that will diffuse a potentially difficult situation.

Because your interpersonal skills are good, you feel relaxed around people and are not easily thrown off balance in unpredictable and difficult situations, or with unfriendly or openly hostile individuals.

You easily become a leader

Emotionally intelligent people have most of the traits of highly effective leaders: they are empathic, confident, communicative, positive, and supportive.

You can work anywhere, with anyone

Great people skills, empathy, and social awareness mean that you will be able to work well and get most out of every situation even under challenging circumstances or in a foreign culture.

You easily get a high-paid job

Being one of the most sought-after skills in the workplace, high emotional intelligence can help you get the job of your dreams.

You don't do or say things you later regret

Knowing that you have to understand and process your emotions before releasing them, means that you will only act once you've had a chance to consider the situation. Sometimes, all it takes is having a few minutes to think things over and give yourself a chance to calm down and assess the situation, before making the final decision.

If there are occasions that you are too embarrassed to think about because of what you said, or did, it's probably because at the time you didn't have or didn't use your emotional intelligence, as a result of which you made decisions you lived to regret.

You are a valued friend and confidant

Emotional intelligence skills are just as valuable outside work, as some of your most important decisions and emotions take place outside the workplace, eg with your family, in your romantic relationships, with your friends, children, etc.

You are fulfilled

Having a successful career and being accomplished personally means you will have lived your life to the fullest.

So, through affecting your emotions, behavior, and interpersonal relations, emotional intelligence has a major effect on the quality of your life.

To continually cultivate and enhance these skills, you should never stop working on your:

Self-awareness

Be constantly in touch with your feelings and learn to tune in to them.

Social skills

Cultivate your communication skills and never underestimate the power of words. Besides, to become highly empathic, you have to try and develop humility. Although being humble is not easy in a society which encourages competition and individuality, ability to openly admit your limitations and mistakes, are traits of a true leader.

Emotional regulation

Learn to control your strong emotions, particularly negative ones, and never act on impulse. Practice this by thinking of something that will make you feel hurt, angry, or exploited. Sit with the feeling, feel the humiliation, or anger, "digest" it, and only after you have calmed down "respond" to the person or situation that made you feel that way.

How Emotional Intelligence Can Really Help Out In Relationships

Have you ever made a snarky comment to your boss in a moment of anger during a heated discussion? Did you ever have a fiery argument with your spouse about a small issue blew up into something huge? Have you ever regretted making an important decision when you were upset? Don't feel bad if the answer is yes! All of us have gone through this. Why does this happen? When you are unable to recognize and understand your emotions, you are controlled by them and react hastily. These are all problems of poor or low emotional intelligence.

People with high emotional intelligence are associated with the following:

- Increased creativity
- **Change acceptance**
- Good team worker
- **Excellent work performance**
- Retention at work

All of these are linked to a professional career. The best part is, people who do well in their career enjoy better interpersonal relationships at home. Dr. Nicola Schutte conducted a study in the early 2000s with her team where she was able to show that people who believed their partners to be emotionally intelligent were highly satisfied with their marital relationship and expected more satisfaction in the future.

Emotionally intelligent people can understand four crucial, critical things:

- They can understand other's emotions, as they are smart in recognizing them. This particular skill is extremely tough when you are dealing with people who aren't emotionally open. You can easily identify that someone is sad when they are crying, but how do you understand the grief in the person if he or she is trying to hide it? People with high EQ can do it, and if you practice EQ, you can do it too.

- They are aware of their own emotions and feelings. They are always in touch with their emotions and know what they feel, how they feel and why they feel. They don't push away the emotions by brushing it aside or giving it a wrong label. Regulating emotions is key, as there is a difference between showing your frustration during an official meeting or waiting for the meeting to finish to show your irritation. Consequences for the former can be dangerous and even spoil your relationship with your boss, while the latter gives you time to think over it so that you put it across in a much better way.

•   Thoughts create emotions! Emotionally intelligent people understand this and work towards clearing and controlling the thought. Doing this can decrease the power of your emotions. Sometimes, your thinking process is affected by your feelings and mood, i.e., over-thinking. For example, your decision-making skills will begin to waver when you are upset, but when you are calm, you make decisions that handle the conflict much better.

•   These people understand the correlation between their actions and the emotional reactions it can cause in other people. For instance, an emotionally intelligent man will know that breaking the promise he made to his wife can result in her feeling hurt.

Building emotional intelligence is a great way to improve your relationship with others – it can be a tough task, but it is doable. How do you build your emotional intelligence? There are many ways to do so, but we will look at the easiest and practical way.

•   **Observe your thought process.**

•   Watch the way your thoughts connect with your emotions throughout the day.

•   **The chemicals released in your brain will change the way you feel about things.**

•   Thoughts release these chemicals.

•   **Notice the connection between your thoughts and emotions.**

•   Work on decreasing negative emotions by not giving the power to the thoughts that create those emotions.

- **Focus on increasing your thoughts towards positive emotions.**

You will need to find out ways to calm you down. Going for a run? Walking around the block for few minutes? Making a call to a friend? Doing some yoga postures? Closing your eyes and clearing your head for 5 minutes? Hugging your pet? Watching funny videos of your kid? Find out what works best for you and put it into practice.

If you are going to be in the vicinity of a negative person whom you are trying to avoid, focus on the positives that might come out of the conversation before you speak to him or her.

How To Determine Whether My Emotional Intelligence Needs Improvement

The act of loving someone calls for emotional intelligence – yes, you read it right! You require emotional intelligence to love, as you need to empathize, recognize problems and should be able to connect with the person on a much deeper level. The way you solve issues at home and your choice of partner indicates a lot about the connection between emotional intelligence and love. When you can harness the power of emotional intelligence successfully, you tend to see an improvement in your relationships.

The conflicts that occur in your relationships mostly rely on your emotional intelligence, which is the ability to observe, identify and respond appropriately to the emotions. Individuals with high emotional intelligence are better at processing their feelings and that of their partners healthily. Emotional intelligence plays a major role in romantic relationships – your EQ can influence whom you fall in love with and how the relationship will play out over a period of time. A series of failed relationships or having a hard time connecting with people (in general) will mean that your emotional quotient needs improvement.

The following are some of the classic signs that will tell you that you need to boost your emotional intelligence.

• Bursting into laughter or lashing out in anger in a moment signals your lack of emotional quotient. This is because you are finding it difficult to control your emotions.

• Having a tough time in building and maintaining healthy relationships with colleagues and friends may indicate your problems with emotional intelligence. Lack of social skills.

• Are you finding it difficult to sympathize or empathize? If you want to have a lasting relationship, you should be able to empathize with the feelings of others. It is an essential part of a healthy relationship.

• You have an issue with your emotional quotient if you are unable to connect with media, movies or books. Tragedy, comedy and horror – all these genres are meant to stimulate your emotions, but if media, movies or books don't move you, there is something wrong with your emotional intelligence.

It is crucial to understand that emotional intelligence plays a major role in every part of your life – it helps dictate a range of things, from a successful career to a contented personal relationship. For some people, emotional intelligence is naturally high while for some it is low. If you feel you have low EQ, don't hesitate to take steps to work on improving it. Self-improvement is a necessity in everything! Mindfulness is the basis for emotions – try meditating or getting into yoga sessions to improve your mindfulness.

The following simple steps will help you work towards improving your emotional quotient:

• Practice self-control. Pause, breathe (deep breath), count (for few seconds) and compose (think) a response. Don't react immediately.

• Abstain. If you are the one who responds indifferently to situations or makes inept jokes, give yourself time to listen to the opposite person before you frame a response. For example, making jokes at a funeral or other tragedy to lighten the grief.

You have so many different ways to improve your emotional intelligence. Choose the best and work on it!

Strategies to Improve Emotional Intelligence
How do I set things right with my partner? Why do I make a big issue of small things that spoil my relationship with my husband? Why am I unable to control my anger when she points out my negatives? Why do I get frustrated with my kids when they go overboard - after all, they're just kids?

These are few of the many questions that keep popping up in your mind whenever you're upset about your strained relationship or your inability to control your emotions. How do you work on it? We will look at a few strategies to develop the emotional quotient for better and healthy relationships.

- Observe your reactions to people. Do you jump to conclusions? Are you judgmental? Do you stereotype people? Look at yourself. Be honest with yourself. Question how you think and interact with people. Be open-minded. Accept their version. Look at their needs and perspectives.

- Think about how you behave in your workplace. Are you an attention seeker? Do you look for an opportunity to shine, and grab it the moment you see it? Don't be bothered too much about praise. Shift your focus towards others. Offer them a chance to shine.

- Self-evaluate. Do you accept that you are not perfect? Will you accept negative feedbacks on your behavior? What are your weaknesses? Are you willing to work on certain areas to make yourself better?

- Study the way you react to stress. How do you react during a stressful situation? What are the series of emotions you go through? Do you easily become upset when things don't turn out the way you want them to? Do you look for a chance to blame others even when they are not at fault? Do you always keep bubbling with anger? You will need to keep your emotions under control when things don't work in your favor. Staying calm and composed in a difficult situation is highly valued not just in the professional world, but also in a personal life.

- You are responsible for your actions. Take responsibility. If you hurt someone's feelings, don't hesitate to apologize. Do it directly. Don't avoid the person or ignore what you did. When you make an honest attempt to set things right, people will be more than willing to forgive and forget. They feel happy when you apologize. They respect you when you accept your mistake.

Emotional intelligence is necessary to turn your intentions into action. If you want to make important decisions on things that matter to you the most, you must do it with utmost care. Connect with people, nurture your feelings, react after thinking and most important of all, empathize!

Chapter 6: Communications Skills in the Workplace

If there is one place that cohesive, clear and precise communication is needed, it's in the workplace. So many decisions hinge on what is communicated within an organization – staff to team leader, team leaders to upper management, management to owners or CEOs and communication to a company's client.

Communication is the core of any business. Deals can be made with clear, concise and logical communication, or broken because of an unclear, muddled miscommunication. And the manner of how something is communicated is just as important.

Communicating effectively with superiors, associates and staff is indispensable no matter what type of industry someone is employed. People who are working in the digital age must have the knowledge of how to successfully send and receive messages via email, phone, social media and in person. If you have good communication skills, they will benefit you throughout your career, help you in getting hired for a position, and lead to subsequent promotions.

Workplace communication is the method of information being exchanged in verbal and non-verbal within an organization. There are many avenues of communication in the workplace. In order to be a valuable and effective member of your organization, it is critical that you are skilled in all the various methods and means of communication that your organization uses and deem appropriate.

The organizational objective needs to be achieved by effective communication in the workplace. Communication is extremely important to organizations because it boosts efficiency and productivity. When there is communication that is ineffective between employees there, it causes wasted time, confusion, and decreases the organization's productivity. Effective communication between staff members can prevent misunderstandings that may cause friction.

Communication needs to pass from sender to receiver. This has to happen regardless of the method of communication.

Communication can be effective if it is understood by the receiver and there can be a response in return. All types of communication include listening, speaking, reading, and skills involving reasoning.

When a communication passes from the originator to the receiver, the opportunity for the original meaning of the message to change is quite possible. Listening, reasoning and feedback is a critical part of the procedure, as it is a chance for the sender to ensure the receiver understood the message.

The Importance of Effective Communication - there are three important points associated with effective workplace communication:

- There is an improvement in productivity with workplace communication

- Employee job satisfaction increases with workplace communication

- A positive effect on turnover rates and absenteeism is seen with workplace communication

Communication in the Workplace – this should happen in a way that has a positive response to individual differences. Think of the following:

- Treat all individual with respect, sensitivity, and courtesy and value them

- Cultural differences should be recognized

- Develop and support trust, confidence and positive relationships with constructive communication

- Use basic tactics to overcome any barriers in communication

How you communicate effects your ability to be compatible and work well with people and get the tasks that you want or need to be done. Communication can be conveyed in positive and negative ways regardless of whether it's verbal, written or visual. People need to get feedback on how others may perceive or decipher how they are communicating and find out how they're communicating and whether it needs improvement or is it misunderstood. There are times our communication may be perceived as dictatorial or aggressive although that was never the intention.

Verbal Communications

When we verbally communicate, we should speak clearly and listen carefully making sure what was said is understood. If you need clarification of the meaning of the information, confirm the meaning by asking questions to avoid any miscommunication and misunderstanding.

One of the best was to be a good communicator is to be a good listener. There isn't anyone who likes communicating with a person who only cares about talking about her two cents and doesn't extend the courtesy of listening to the other person.

Not being a good listener will make it hard to understand what you're being asked to do. It would be a good idea to practice active listening. How you practice is to listen very carefully to what another person is saying, ask questions to clarify the message and intent, rephrase what the person is saying to make sure there is an understanding. Active listening allows you to better comprehend what the other person is saying and can properly respond.

Allow for others to speak. Conversations are a two-way event. If there is a difficult conversation, involve yourself in it when it's necessary. Avoiding a difficult conversation by not saying anything can usually make things worse. And check the tone that you use is one that is open and non-confrontational and encourages feedback.

Clarity and Conciseness

Saying just what you want to say and being brief is another way to exhibit good verbal communication. You're not talking too much or too little. This means to state your message in just a few words, clearly, precisely and distinctly whether you're on the phone, or in an email. If you speak in a jumbled, rambling manner, you'll possibly be tuned out by the listener, or they will not be sure what you want.

Sociability and Friendliness

It's important to have a polite and nice demeanor with your coworkers in the workplace. This is significant in both written as well as face-to-face communication. When you exhibit a friendly tone, or simply smile, you can persuade your coworkers to engage in honest and open communication with you. Personalizing an email or a note at the beginning of an email to your coworkers or staff can make the receiver of the email feel appreciated.

Self-Confidence

When you're interacting with others, it's vital that you exhibit self-confidence. Confidence lets your coworkers know that you have certainty in what you're saying. Displaying confidence can be done by making eye contact or having a firm but friendly tone of voice. Don't make your statements sound like you're asking a question. Don't act or sound aggressive or arrogant. These are two traits that are not welcomed in the workplace. Always listen and empathize with the other person.

Empathy

Being empathetic to others by saying "I understand how you feel" and putting yourself in their position will exhibit that you are listening to the other person and respecting their viewpoints. Important to note – even if you may disagree with a team leader, manager, coworker or staff member, it is critical to respect and understand their opinion and point of view.

Having an Open Mind

A good communicator is open to listening and comprehending the other person's viewpoint instead of getting your own message across. When you're willing to enter into a dialogue, and entering a conversation with flexibility, even with someone with whom you disagree, you will have more constructive and honest conversations.

Nonverbal Communication

The message that you convey is colored by your eye contact, body language, hand motion and voice tones. An open posture that is relaxed (arms open, not crossed and legs relaxed) and a calm, friendly tone will give you the appearance of being accessible and encourages others to speak with you openly.

Your eye contact is important in communicating with others. When you look at a person you are making eye contact with; you want to exhibit that you're focused on them and the conversation, you are engaged and attentive. However, don't stare at the person. This may make them feel uncomfortable.

While you're talking, notice the nonverbal signals that you're receiving from the other person. As an example, if the person is avoiding making direct eye contact with you, they may be feeling uncomfortable or possibly concealing the truth.

Communicating via Email and Other Written Communications

When reviewing an email, read and then re-read the email before sending it out. Make sure the grammar, tone, and spelling are correct before it's read by others. Make sure the subject of the email is pertinent and has a subject heading that corresponds with the content of the email. Contact information should be clear and available for those who read the email can contact the author if necessary. Write emails that are professional and polite, concise, using well-founded points and doesn't have lengthy unnecessary, inconsequential ramblings. Avoid copying anyone on the email that has no relevant connection to the topic or content. Also, an extremely important point is not to discuss confidential information in an email. Ever.

There is a professional environment in the workplace that means every kind of communication that is written as a professional standard that is expected. The expectation that all communication that is written

- Is easy to understand

- Avoids unnecessary repetition, gets to the point and isn't written with sentences that are long, jumbled or muddled and rambling

- Do not use slang, sexist or racist language, or language that is discriminatory or offensive. A sure way to be terminated

- Don't write in an onslaught of technical terminology. Unless it is necessary for the purpose of the email specifically requiring technical terms, plain, simple English will suffice.

Being Respectful

People will want to have open communications with you when you exhibit that you have respect for them and their ideas. Remembering a person's name and greeting them personally, listening to them when they are speaking, and making eye contact makes a person feel recognized, respected and appreciated. When you're speaking on the phone, remain focused on the conversation and prevent distractions.

When you send an email, you can convey respect by reviewing and editing your message. Sending an email that is written in a sloppy and jumbled manner will confuse the recipient. They will probably feel that you don't respect them enough to process and think out your content and communication to them.

Giving Feedback

You may be called upon to give and/or receive feedback. Being able to do so is a skill that is very important in order to be viewed as a way of bolstering morale or showing appreciation for someone's performance in the workplace. Supervisors and managers should always provide their staff with feedback that is constructive and empowering. Whether it be by a weekly status report, email or phone, if an employee is doing a good job, or you thank them for the efforts they put into producing the final product of a report or a presentation, praising them is a great motivator for them to continue to thrive in their position.

Conversely, be open and accepting of feedback from others. Listen to what, if any, issues are being told to you, ask questions to clarify any portion of the information you are unsure of and endeavor to implement the feedback you receive. If it's praise for your performance in the workplace, remember to thank them and let them know their praise is appreciated.

Choosing the Right Form of Communication

Understanding what form of communication that you need to use and apply to certain situations is an important communication skill. As an example, there is going to be a review of the salaries of some staff members, or there are going to be layoffs from one of the company's departments. This type of communication should be done one-on-one in person.

There may be an issue you need to relay to a particular person in management who is the only person that can address the issue and correct it. However, they're pretty busy, so an email will probably be the best way to communicate with them. The person will appreciate that you recognize their busy schedule and get back to you positively and in a timely manner.

Ways of Communicating to Avoid

During the course of a busy workday, there may be ways of communicating that are really not acceptable to use.

- Don't talk about personal issues when communicating with others who you have a friendship in the workplace. Save those conversations and/or emails AND texting for your lunch break or after business hours. The company computer shouldn't be used for your personal email life. Planning a camping trip with your work buddy? Save that communication to do on your own time.

- Don't yell across an office floor. Politely walk over to the other person's office or cubicle to speak with them. It's disturbing to others and frankly, downright rude.

- Don't put your call on speaker unless you have your own office and can close the door. It's disturbing to others working around you who may be trying to concentrate on writing a report or may be on the phone themselves with a vendor or a client. Be considerate of your coworkers.

- Don't gossip. This is a form of communication that is a time waster and is counterproductive to maintaining a harmonious work environment. This is not to say that a workplace should be perfect because it can never be when inhabited by people. It is to say that gossiping, backbiting or being uncooperative with other people is immature and doesn't belong in the workplace. The workplace is for professionals. Communicate and treat one another accordingly.

Communicating with Customers and Clients

You provide a service, sell a product or finish a job for a customer or client outside your company. Conveying a respectful and polite demeanor when using both verbal and non-verbal communications to reply to a customer or client request appropriately is extremely important.

There are times that miscommunication can happen in numerous ways and can develop problems in the workplace. What is heard by your customer or client can be misinterpreted and miscommunication can occur.

- How you phrase what your saying can be misinterpreted

- Body language that doesn't line up with your words can be confusing in communicating with a customer or client

- The customer or client may not be focusing on what you're saying, or you are not listening to them properly

Here are ways to aid your communication skills effectively when interacting with customers and clients:

Speak concisely and clearly. Don't rush your words and speak at a rate that can be understood to provide the correct information

Acknowledge the customer by their name – this gives the customer the feeling of being valued and special

Acknowledge non-verbal messages. Display positive and fitting body language at all times.

Don't be judgmental. Don't judge the way a customer presents themselves or how they're dressed. Be open and have an open stance and a congenial tone.

Always be professional and respectful of a customer's feelings. Be aware of your words and tone.

Show interest in people and take a real interest in a customer's needs. This builds trust and a positive relationship with the customer.

Ask questions and be accepting of feedback. Ask your customers questions that are open-ended to find out what they are exactly seeking.

The workplace is a professional environment that you spend quite a bit of time in on a weekly basis. Communicating with your coworkers, management, customers and clients is extremely important for you to learn and understand. As you grow in your professional life, your mastery of communicating in your profession will help you on both a personal and business level. Implementing these communication guidelines correctly will surely get you noticed.

Chapter 7: Secrets of Building Healthy Social Relationships

Yes, when you listen keenly to people, empathize with them, and try to understand things from their perspective, it paves the way for healthier and more rewarding relationships. We must understand that emotional intelligence is not a static skill that we acquire and will last a lifetime. It is a lifelong process and skill that keeps evolving as we navigate various relationships. However, there are a few established tips that will help you sharpen your emotional skills and help you relate to other people more effectively, thus helping you build strong relationships. Here are a few tips for using the power of emotional intelligence to build healthy relationships:

Isolate One Skill

If you are looking to improve emotional intelligence and social skills, rather than trying to be good at everything, isolate one skill that you want to develop at a time. For instance, you may want to work on your listening skills or develop greater empathy. Don't try to work on too many aspects at a time. Identify one component of social-emotional intelligence and observe someone who is particularly good at it. If you know a friend is really good at listening to people and making them feel comfortable, try and observe how they manage their emotions, react, and speak. How does their body language reveal that they are keenly listening to the other person? How do they acknowledge what the other person is saying? What are the usual words they use to make the person feel comfortable?

Day 16: Open Yourself Up to Establish a Connection

One of the fastest and most surefire ways to build a connection with people is to listen to their experiences with empathy and link it with a similar experience you've undergone. This exchange of similar experiences strikes the right chord in people and makes them open up to you. Don't be afraid to open up a bit and share a similar experience when the other person is sharing theirs. For instance, someone may talk about how painful it has been to grow up in a single parent home. You may be tempted not to share that information about yourself too early on or open up before knowing the person really well, but it can help establish a connection. You can add how you completely understand how it feels because you had been living in a single parent home all through your teens. This is a quick way to set the foundation for a lasting relationship.

Develop a sense of curiosity when it comes to strangers. Emotionally intelligent folks are intrigued by strangers and always have an insatiable hunger to know more about them and understand their lives and views. They make an attempt to understand how the opinions and perspectives of these people are different from theirs. You know what to do next time you're on the train or at the airport. Immerse yourself in a different culture by traveling to various destinations whenever you can. It broadens your understanding of people and cultures. Sometimes, the only way to have an open mind is to go to a different destination and establish connections with locals.

Spend Time Away from the Social Media

Though this is the age of the social media, try and balance your online time and connections with offline relationships too. It is important to maintain face to face relationships with people since it paves the way for developing better social skills. Don't go messaging people. Instead, meet them over dinner or drinks and have a real, face to face conversation. Emotional intelligence goes beyond social media confines and needs real-world connections. Our ability to identify, process, and manage emotions is impeded by instant messaging and social media. Emoticons don't build emotional intelligence. It expands when we actually get out there and interact with people face to face. Staying in the constricted space of social media doesn't allow you to experience real emotions that can increase your emotional perception and intelligence.

Avoid Complaining

Complaining is a huge sign of low emotional intelligence. It happens when a person believes he is victimized and that the situation is beyond his or her control. They will pass on the blame to the next person or situation before thinking it through.

Emotionally intelligent people think in a constructive manner to resolve the issue rather than blaming someone else or complaining. They operate from a mindset that seeks to resolve the problem rather than working from the perspective of just making complaints.

Complaining is a huge sign that people believe they are mere victims of a situation and that the solution is beyond their reach. We consider ourselves victims of other people or circumstances and therefore are unable to find solutions to pressing issues. We believe that the solutions to the circumstances enveloping us are beyond our realm of control. An emotionally intelligent person seldom believes himself or herself to be a victim. They rarely feel that problem resolution is beyond their control. In place of blaming something or someone, they approach the matter in a more constructive manner and look for a solution quietly. Emotionally intelligent folks will peacefully contemplate an issue and look for a resolution through reflection and consideration of all possibilities in lieu of the current circumstances. There is a sense of maturity in their thinking and manner of approach.

The next time you are tempted to blame your alarm clock for waking up late and showing up late at work, resist the urge and focus on what you can do to wake up on time each morning. Can you cut down on post work partying? Can you watch less television and go to bed early instead? Can you set the alarm on two clocks, so you have a back-up if one conks out? There are many ways to resolve the issue if you get out of the victim zone and start looking for proactive solutions that are within your control.

Focus on How You Say it

What you say is important, but how you convey it is even more vital. There are multiple ways to say the same thing or handle a situation. Non-verbal communication can have a massive impact on how you are perceived by people.

Eye contact, voice, tone, expressions, and body language all contribute towards creating an impression about you among other people. It conveys to others how you are thinking and feeling emotionally. Think whether your body language and emotions complement each other. Are you able to articulate your emotions or feelings without offending the other person?

Keep in mind that few things destroy an individual's morale quicker than an overly critical person. Think of different ways to say something without affecting the other person negatively. I always recommend learning something about the other person or understanding them before attempting to communicate with them. For instance, if someone is particularly sensitive, they may not appreciate a direct, straightforward approach. You may have to get your point across in a more diplomatic and tactful manner.

Similarly, straightforward folks may not appreciate you beating around the bush. You may also have to employ a more frank and forthright approach. Thus, knowing an individual's personality will help you communicate with him or her in a more effective manner.

How you say it makes all the difference while communicating, especially on slightly tricky topics. For example, let's take a scenario where you think an employee is not suitable for a specific department and has consistently underperformed there despite receiving the best training, development, and mentoring.

As a manager, it is your responsibility to inform him that he or she is going to be shifted to another department. Now you are placed with the conundrum of telling them the truth without affecting his or her morale. What approach would you take as an emotionally intelligent person to accomplish the same?

Instead of telling the person that he or she isn't good in 'XYZ' department and that he or she is being shifted to another department, you can focus on the positive of the situation and change the angle or approach to give it a more positive twist. You can say something like, "We think you have the ideal skills for (new department) and that your skills or qualities will be utilized to the fullest there." You are still telling the employee that he or she will be transferred to another department, but you are putting across your point in a manner that doesn't offend them or lower their morale. You are simply telling him or her that their skills aren't being utilized to the fullest in the current department instead of telling him or her that their skills are not good enough for the current department. The words, body language, and approach make all the difference.

Also, active listening is a huge component of emotional intelligence, especially during conflicts. Often, while arguing with people, we have our responses ready even before the other person finishes speaking.

During heated discussions, arguments, and conflicts, we only listen to reply but not to understand the other person. How many times have you heard the other person out to truly understand them and not to prepare your response to what he or she is saying? Resist the urge to come across as too overpowering during a disagreement and try to understand where the other person is coming from. Deal with issues in a respective, productive, and assertive manner, without an element of defensiveness. When you actively and empathetically listen to the other person, you are also creating a space for your feelings and emotions to be heard. When you listen intently to the other person's views, you drain all the toxic energy from the situation and instead focus on arriving at a beneficial solution.

I always recommend practicing your non-verbal skills at home to make yourself even more clear and transparent in social situations. Start at your home because it is a space that doesn't make you feel overwhelmed, unlike an alien setting. Make a video of yourself interacting with a friend or relative.

Watch it so you can know what areas you can improve in when it comes to non-verbal signals. Another super way is to practice before a mirror. Pretend that you are interacting with a person and watch yourself in the mirror. Enlist the help of trusted folks when it comes to gaining valuable feedback. They can offer helpful insights about your voice, posture, expressions, and more. You'll be in a more private, low-stress setting, which reduces your shyness and preps your confidence for more important interactions. It's actually enjoyable to try out multiple gestures, expressions, signs, and postures.

When you can read non-verbal signals passed by others, you can quickly spot the disagreement in their feelings or emotions and words. Even a subtle mismatch in verbal and non-verbal signals will help you understand the other person's feelings and behavior.

Notice how sometimes you pick up some clue and call it a "hunch" that something isn't right about what the person is saying. What we like to call or think of as a gut feeling, or hunch, is actually a subconscious notice of the mismatch between the person's body language and words. The person didn't intend to communicate it, but we tuned in to their body language and "listened" to it.

Practice Assertiveness and Expressing Challenging Emotions

An essential part of being who you really are is asserting or being able to speak frankly and openly about things that truly matter to you or are important in your life. Practice taking a clear position on where you stand when it comes to vital emotional issues. Draw clear lines about what is acceptable and not acceptable in relationships.

Setting boundaries in relationships is also a huge component of emotional intelligence. It isn't restricted to being empathetic and being nice to others. Emotional intelligence is also about being fair to yourself.

Set clear boundaries so others can know more about your position which leads to lesser misunderstandings in relationships. This can include anything from disagreeing with someone about establishing priorities, to saying no, to protecting yourself from physical harm or mental duress.

Use the "I feel…when you" technique to assert yourself in tricky situations. For instance, "I strongly feel that I deserve a promotion from the organization based on my performance and contribution."

Similarly, when you are not comfortable doing something for someone over your own priorities you can assert yourself saying something like, "I don't feel comfortable that you expect me to do everything for you over my tasks and priorities." When you feel disappointed that someone doesn't follow through or listen to your instructions, you can articulate it with something like, "I feel really upset or disappointed that you didn't update me about the project despite being instructed to do so."

The trick is to say how you feel when something happens. Refrain from beginning your sentence with "you." It makes you sound accusatory and judgment. The moment the other person hears "you," he or she will subconsciously slip into a defensive position. You are quickly allowing the listener to assume a defensive position, followed by a bunch of excuses. If you want people to listen to you, talk about how you feel when they do something.

Reduce Stress and Practice Staying More Lighthearted

Stress rears its ugly head in all ways of life and completely consumes us following a range of negative emotions. From relationship breakdowns to being laid off from work, there are plenty of emotions that can overwhelm us. When you are stressed, it is challenging to behave reasonably. It will be tough to be emotionally intelligent when you are under tremendous stress.

Find what your stress triggers are and make a list of everything you can do to relieve yourself of that stress. What is it that helps decrease your stress? A long lonesome walk in the midst of nature? Listening to soothing music? Talking to a trusted friend? Having lunch at your favorite café?

Enlist the help of a professional therapist if it feels too overpowering to handle it by yourself. A psychologist, counselor, or therapist can help you cope with the stress in an effective and professional manner, while also helping you raise your emotional quotient. It is easier to establish rewarding interpersonal relationships with people when you are not under stress.

I personally love to combat stress by maintaining a lighthearted atmosphere at work, home, and other social scenarios. It is simpler to appreciate the joy and beauty of life when you take on a more humorous or lighthearted approach. It makes others around you feel less stressed too. Optimism and positivity not just lead to better emotional health (for yourself and others) but also more opportunities. (Who doesn't like being around a positive and optimistic person?) People are naturally drawn to optimistic, lighthearted, and positive people. Negativity, on the other hand, builds defenses. People with high emotional quotient use lots of fun, jokes, and humor to make the atmosphere for others (and themselves) safe, joyful, and happy. Laughter is indeed the best medicine to get through challenging times in our life.

Chapter 8: Tricks & Techniques for Overcoming Negativity

Being overcome with negative thoughts can make it seem like success and happiness are impossible. They can take over your entire mode of thinking and give you a rather grim view of everything in your life. The key is that you can turn it around by interjecting some positive decisions. Decide for yourself that you will do something causative, in spite of not feeling like doing it.

When you make this positive decision, move forward with one or more of the tips and techniques in this chapter. This will start you back onto the path of positive thinking. The first step is to pull your thought process to a stop, pull a U-turn, and head back in the right direction.

One of the first things you will need to do is:

- Recognize a Pattern of Negative Thought

Negative thought patterns are repetitive negative thoughts that recur over time. Their nature is such that those thoughts aren't comfortable or helpful. These thoughts and the pattern of them will generally inspire a less positive emotional response, which can manifest in a number of ways. You may feel stressed, afraid, unworthy, ashamed, or even depressed. There are more emotions you could feel as a result, but these are examples.

Learning to recognize and identify a negative thought pattern as it is unfolding is the key to being able to turn the process around and change it for the better. A lesser-known term for the process of pulling yourself from an active thought process is cognitive defusion. Utilizing this process means realizing that the thoughts in your head are not anything more than just that: thoughts in your head. They aren't the reality and, in many cases, they aren't even an accurate picture of what is the reality.

We tend to grant our thoughts a lot more power and significance in our lives than we may realize on a cognizant level. When we make use of cognitive defusion, you won't take those negative thoughts in your mind as seriously as you might otherwise. When we're stuck in our thoughts, we'll obey them, follow them, and take them as fact.

Cognitive defusion helps us to take a step back, see those thoughts and what they're doing, and choose a better direction for ourselves. Remember that a lot of negative thoughts are not cooked up on a cognitive or rational level. This means that you, as a cognizant and rational person, can evaluate the situation as it really is. You can do so alongside that thought and see if it's something that has any real merit or bearing in your life.

Utilizing cognitive defusion to evaluate what thoughts to keep and what thoughts are holding you back, gives you a lot of power. Because you're looking at them honestly, you can decide for yourself what the best course of action is. You can decide if you need to do something about that thought that is creating an emergency in your mind, or you can choose not to even respond to it. The beauty of it is that the choice is yours. If you completely disregard it and focus on something else, that negative thought is able to fade into the background.

If you're looking for an example of how cognitive defusion could help you to see a situation differently, think of the following. You walk into a room and find that there are several empty bottles on the table. This may make you think that the house is a huge mess and that everything is terrible because no one ever helps you to clean. Now, if you take a step back, you'll see that all those additional conclusions simply came from within. The only real fact in front of you is that there are several empty bottles on the table.

Remove those bottles from the table and take a look around the room with a clear head and what do you see? The same room you saw before, minus the bottles that were there a moment ago. It is simple leaps that our subconscious makes to form negative thoughts and conclusions. It may not feel simple, as the conclusions may seem insurmountable and terrible. Just realize that you can have a small bridge to a big mountain.

Now, if you were to simply clean up the bottles in the living room without addressing your thought process, you might be liable to stay in that bad mood and stew in those conclusions. Erroneous they may have been, you didn't take that initial step of debunking them.

Below, we'll go into how you can go about pulling yourself out of a negative thought process. We'll go into recognizing those processes as they happen, evaluating how helpful those thought processes really are, and how to move forward from there.

It's important to note that it's completely normal to have negative thoughts, as it would be inappropriate to think of everything in a positive light. There are negative things around us, and we should react accordingly. It is also perfectly natural to have a negative or adverse response to general environmental stimuli. The important thing is to know how to pull yourself out of that negative response once a reasonable amount of time has passed.

If you're in the middle of a negative thought process and you're coming up with thoughts that aren't true, it's imperative that you be able to distinguish which of these thoughts are untrue. Once you can identify those untrue thoughts, you can take a look at the thought process and defuse from it, and simply drop the thoughts that don't warrant any further attention, is that they're based in misinformation or blatant falsehood.

We're going to go back to the example of the empty bottles in the living room, we'll take a look at that thought process one more time. When you walk into that living room, you see those bottles and you have those thoughts about the house being a complete mess and that you don't have any help in the house. Of course, with thoughts of that nature, you're going to be in a terrible mood. However, you're not connected to that thought by any physical means. That thought is not embedded in your mind and you're not stuck with it.

Take a look at that thought and remove any connection you have to that thought. It was fused in your mind, and now you're defusing from it. This makes it that much easier to kick that thought from your mind and move forward, clean the living room, and move on with your day. This is what makes cognitive defusion so liberating.

There are some common patterns of negative thinking that may come up in your mind. Below, we'll lay out what types they are, and how they can make you feel. Be sure to keep a close eye on your thought process, and your history to see if any of these processes strike you as familiar.

- Anxiety or Worried Thoughts

Being preoccupied with what could go wrong, or how badly things probably went in our interactions with others, is such an exhausting waste of our time and energy.

This can come up while imagining or looking at hypothetical situations or scenarios. We can sometimes give ourselves a sense of dread about those situations, thinking that there's some way in which those things will go awry. In this pattern of thinking, you can find yourself biting your nails and losing sleep over things like your health, credit, finances, job, and more in spite of nothing negative actually having happened.

When you're in the middle of this pattern of thinking, it's hard to shift your focus to something more positive and it's even harder for positive thoughts to occur naturally. This is why it's important to be able to spot a negative line of thinking and stop it in its tracks.

- Harsh Criticism of Self

We are often told that we are our own toughest critics. In situations in which we weren't completely successful, this pattern of thinking can come about. This is a pattern of thinking that leads us to hold ourselves completely accountable to a point at which we're somewhat cruel to ourselves about it.

It is possible to feel as though this level of criticism is actually coming from others, whether or not it may be true. In those situations, you might find that you have a good deal of turmoil in your personal relationships. Thinking that others perceive us badly can lead to telling ourselves negative things that lead to low self-esteem and low self-worth.

Part of the harsh self-criticism line of thinking is that it can feed into a vicious circle. In order to compensate for this feeling, we have on inadequacy or low self-worth, we launch ourselves into these quests for recognition or status. We figure—no matter how subconsciously—that if we can get others to tell us that we are good, or that we are worth something, we will feel better about ourselves. The high of that recognition from others is usually short-lived, as the negative thought process continues on within you. So, whether you get that recognition from others or not, you're bound to burn yourself out by trying constantly to get it.

Of course, there is nothing wrong with being a perfectionist or someone who strives for excellence. This differs from having a negative thought process, which doesn't allow you to see the successes that you do have, or which is constantly berating you for every little thing that goes wrong. Such a thought process that can lead to depression and some severe effects of depression, which is why it's important to stay vigilant.

This negative line of thinking can make it harder to identify successes as they occur, much less to validate yourself for them. It can seem like you're stuck with failure and like "you can never win."

- Chronic Regret or Guilt

This thought process is similar to the one above, but there are some key differences. This type of thought process can come from becoming stuck with thinking about failures or mistakes we've made in the past. From this thought process, we can derive a lot of feelings that contribute to low self-worth, low self-esteem, and even low expectations for our capabilities. In extreme cases, this line of thinking can leave you feeling worthless or even sinister.

This line of thinking can convince us that we're actually evil or bad for the people around us, no matter how untrue that may be. This line of thinking will leave you thinking on decisions that you've made, thinking they were the wrong ones, or that you were wrong for having made your decision based on certain factors. This line of thinking nitpicks at the choices you make and why you made them.

It is important to note that this thought process is distinctly different than taking a look at past experiences, evaluating what you could have done better, and learning from your mistakes. This is a thought process that mires you down in the details of what occurred and can feel utterly unshakeable. When you get stuck in one of these mental quagmires, it's best to start looking for ways and methods to change it.

- Problem-centric Thought Process

Have you ever been trying to work through something, only to be stopped at every turn with a new problem that makes it impossible? This is an example of a fixation on problems in your environment. Someone dealing with a negative thought process that is stuck on problems will have difficulty even finding a starting point in working through the things that they're up against in life.

Let's consider this example. Charlie is thinking of buying a house and starting a family because it's what she wants. However, when she thinks about how to get started, she might think her credit isn't good enough. Someone might tell her that her credit combined with her significant other's would be sufficient. From there, she would think that maybe it's not a buyer's market right now. From there, she might think of reasons why the timing isn't right, then why they can't afford it, then why it's not a good decision in today's economy. Before you know it, the whole idea has been scrapped and now Charlie is left trying to push her life in a completely different direction.

It may be true that Charlie could do with a better credit score and that the economy isn't as healthy as it has previously been. These things, however, are not impassable obstacles and can be navigated with positive efforts in the right direction, a good strategy, and the advice of professionals in those areas. This thought process of producing a new problem or a reason why not at every turn, is keeping her from pursuing some of her largest goals in her immediate future.

Knowing the risks of a situation before committing to it is a smart thing to do. Understanding what obstacles you'll need to navigate is a prudent part of planning. Getting stuck on every single aspect and seeing each one as a massive brick wall will keep you from getting anything you want out of this life.

- Know Thy Enemy

The first step toward resolution of these issues is to know what sort of negative thought process you're dealing with. When you can identify what your mind is doing and how it's getting you off track, you can more effectively work to get it back to where it should be.

Once you figure out what thought process you're dealing with and how it's affecting your ability to get what you want out of life, take a look at what that thought process is doing. Once you've isolated that thought process and the things about it that are irrelevant or untrue for you, you can start to initiate and interject a positive thought process.

- Treat yourself like a Friend

When you're dealing with a lot of negative inner monologue, there's a rather poignant question you can ask yourself. If you ask yourself this question, you may find that it will put a stop to, or at least slow down, the harshly critical thoughts and jabs.

Would you talk to a friend like this? If you wouldn't say these things to someone you know and love, who found themselves in the midst of this same situation, don't talk to yourself that way. You are important and you are worthy of compassion, understanding, and a second chance here and there.

Conversely, if you would accept it if a friend told you that you are a good person who deserves positive things in life, accept it when you say it to yourself. You are your own friend and you are allowed to accept reassurances and compliments from yourself.

Take a moment to think about what your closest friend would say to you about your current worry. Take a moment to think about how you would advise a friend in this same scenario. Write it down somewhere and refer to it regularly if that will help you to remember that you're a good person.

Acknowledge Your Feelings

If you're working on getting out of a mental jam, the first step to take is to acknowledge how the situation is making you feel. Acknowledge how you're affected by the subject matter of those thoughts. Ironically, when we're trying to resist feeling a specific way about things, we end up backing ourselves into a corner with those feelings. It causes more long-term stress and issues.

If you allow yourself to let those thoughts run their course for a few moments and feel what your mind is telling you to feel, you have a better chance of moving on from those thoughts and opening the door for new, better feelings and thought processes.

Ask the Hard Questions

When you ask yourself these questions and answer them honestly, it can give you some pragmatic perspective on what's really going on around you in life. If can correct those thought processes or patterns that can lead to further difficulty down the road.

Using a journal to answer these questions is great because you'll have access to your answers as you continue to grow emotionally. Even if you just write down your answers on an index card or type it in a notepad document and save it for later reference, it could do you favors.

Ask yourself:

- Is this line of thinking helpful?

- What do I stand to gain from thinking this way?

- Does this line of thinking lead me to a resolution for this problem?

- How can I change the negative statements in these thoughts into positive ones?

- What should my next step be?

Once you've asked these questions, you can start working toward a positive resolution for the current problem. Additionally, it can lead you toward a better pattern of thinking that will make things easier for you in future situations of this sort.

Journaling

Journaling has come up in this book previously as a way to change your emotional pattern. Journals or diaries are great because they can cover a wide range of topics that you need to monitor or about which you have thoughts. Going back through your journal from time to time is a great way to gauge personal growth, progress toward goals, and the overall state of mind.

Writing in a journal gets thoughts out of your mental space so you have room for other, more current thoughts. You would be amazed how much clarity is possible simply after talking about or writing down what you're thinking.

Using a journal for this purpose gives you the opportunity to puzzle out which of the above patterns of thinking you're experiencing, to answer the hard questions above, to speak to yourself as you would to a friend, and to give yourself a plan for the future you're working toward building for yourself.

Find Reasons to be Grateful

Gratefulness is, as mentioned previously, a great way to gain perspective on the things that you have in your life. Thanks to a lot of devices in mainstream media that we see daily, we are constantly being reminded of the things we do not have. We're being advertised to nearly constantly and being told to buy new versions of the things we do have, to buy bigger and better things than those around us have, and to generally make more purchases.

This can, after some time, begin to wear on a person. This can give you the concept that you do not have enough, that you should be comparing everything you have and have done to the possessions and feats of others. Thanks to social media, we are constantly under barrages of posts about amazing accomplishments made by those who are younger, smarter, or more attractive than we're willing to let ourselves believe we are.

All this pressure coming at us from seemingly every direction, can start to give us the sense that we just don't have much of anything, we have accomplished nothing, and that we will always want for more in life. This is a terrible spot in which to find oneself because it will almost never lead anywhere positive. It's imperative to be grateful for the things that we have, the things we've been able to accomplish, and for the people, we have in our corner in life.

Take a moment and think or write about the things for which you are grateful in life. Coming up with even five things per day, to put on that list will drastically change your outlook. It's a great way to gain perspective on how lost you could be, and it's a great way to acknowledge and congratulate yourself for the work you've done to get to this point. It's no small feat to be alive, in good health, with food in the cupboards.

Focus on Your Strengths

This exercise has a lot of similar properties to the previous item in this chapter, with a little bit of a different focus. A lot of anguish can come from being focused on the things that we lack, the areas in which we are weak, and the troubles that we have. This is not to say that being aware of and working on our weaknesses is a bad thing.

Indeed, improving upon our weaknesses would only serve to give us the upper hand on situations in the future. There is a large difference (mainly in tone and focus) between recognizing and improving weaknesses, and dwelling upon those weaknesses to a negative result. In the case of recognizing and improving upon our weaknesses, there is a good deal of effort being expended to actively improve the situation. Dwelling simply means that we're overtly aware of their presence and we feel overwhelming like they will be our downfall.

List out, either on paper or to yourself mentally, what your strengths are. These don't have to be Herculean strengths or talents that could land you a spot on a daytime talk show. These are simply the things in which you excel. For instance, some good strengths to have could be, "I am great at communicating. I am very punctual. I'm good at creative problem-solving. I am more organized than I used to be." These are things you can use to your advantage in a number of situations within your life. Those are also strengths that aren't overwhelmingly common, so don't sell yourself short!

If you find yourself having trouble getting started with this exercise, ask the people who are closest to you for a little bit of help. Simply ask them, "Have I ever impressed you? How did I do it?" This can be said in another way would be, "What strengths do you think I have?"

This is a good way to start this exercise, and it's also a good ego boost.

Establish New Habits

Our patterns of thinking and the ways in which we approach situations can become a habit. In fact, most of the time when we get into these thought processes, we don't even realize we're doing it. Establishing new habits begins with the personal decision and declaration of what habit you're changing, and what the new habit will be.

Not to sound like a broken record, but it's highly recommended that you write this down. Being able to refer back to the habits we're trying to adopt can make it easier to keep them in mind and to bear them in mind. Remember the phrase "out of sight, out of mind," and put these things insight if it's possible to do so.

If you are journaling on a regular basis, make a list of the habits you'd like to adopt and consider implementing a "habit tracker" within your journaling. These can be found on social media with a simple search and you can pick a layout that works best for you and the routine you want to set!

The key to forming a new habit is repetition, so give yourself sample scenarios to work through with the new habit you're working into your life. Take the time to think about how it could work in your life, take time to think of any obstacles that might present themselves in your path to creating it and come up with solutions to those obstacles. Being determined is essential to creating a new habit, as it will require the purposeful opposition against what is currently involuntary or reflexive.

Use Affirmations

You may be aware of some affirmations that people typically use in an effort to self-help. If you have any reservations or objections to using affirmations in your daily life, forget them. We are a species that thrives on reassurance, hope, and security. Having daily affirmations that we are good, we have the capabilities to achieve what we want in life, that we are on the right track, and that we can make it through the rough patches, does a world of good for keeping our chins up and our eyes on the prize.

Affirmations, in short, are positive statements that help you to get over those mechanisms of self-sabotage and negative thought patterns. They thrust a positive line of thinking right into the center of all that and can be helpful to derail that negative train of thought. It's important to note that "affirmation," is a pretty wide umbrella term that can encompass a great many statements. There aren't any rules as to what they need to say, so long as they are positive and challenge a negative line of thinking.

Whatever speaks to you the most is the sort of affirmation you should be looking for when doing this exercise. Some people may have found, "I'm attractive, smart, and good enough," to be the perfect phrase. Others may have found, "I am the chief executive butt-kicker. I stop at nothing for anything," to be better suited to their needs. Everyone is different and a large part of managing your emotions and your personal growth is being absolutely true to yourself.

Using these exercises and affirmations is never meant to change who you are. Using these is about helping you to live a life that is perfectly true to who you are, without all the anxieties and negative emotions that may be keeping you from getting the most out of your experiences and your relationships.

In some cases, drafting your own affirmations is the way to go, because you know what you need to hear each day. If you're feeling a little lost for what to say in these affirmations, try searching for various affirmations around specific topics, or just in general, that you can print out or write down to keep your chin up in spite of the obstacles.

Practice Mindfulness

This is a subject that has gotten a bit more attention lately, and you may have heard of it before this book. What is it, though? To put it as simply as possible, it's a state of mind that's achieved by shifting focus to the current moment, and your awareness in it. Mindfulness is being able to do this, while also calmly acknowledging and accepting the thoughts, physical feelings, and emotional feelings that come along with it. It's a therapeutic technique and it's been more or less utilized in some of the other items in this list.

It can mean taking a moment to see what's going on, acknowledge it for what it is, feel the way you feel about it, then putting yourself completely in the here and now so you can evaluate how you feel right now. You may have practiced this or something that is similar to it. You may also see some similarities between this state of mind, and what meditation aims to achieve.

This is a benefit that many people get when meditating. They feel that it helps to ground them, bring them back to the here and now, and put everything they've been thinking and feeling into perspective.

There are myriad questionnaires throughout the web and self-help materials that specifically help you to be mindful. Bear in mind that not all the questions you can find will inspire you, or even particularly help you to be mindful. This exercise, like affirmations, requires that the questions be of a personal significance to you. If you think of questions that would be more relevant or poignant, go with those to start!

Channel Your Thoughts into Something Positive

In times when you find yourself to be in the middle of a negative thought pattern or process, stop what you're doing and take the time to focus on a project that you're really interested in, or which gets you excited. Imagine if, every single time you started to beat yourself up, you stopped and channeled it into productivity on a project that held personal significance for you. How quickly do you think those projects would get done?

To start, it may not be possible for you to stop everything you're doing and move right onto a project. For instance, if you're at work and this kind of thought process hits you, it could be difficult. However, you can channel that energy into something you're doing at work, or take notes about how to be productive on that personal project once you return home, or once you have time to address it. Put it to the test!

Consider Cognitive Behavioral Therapy

Cognitive Behavioral Therapy or CBT is a therapeutic technique that is geared toward helping to change thought patterns. If you're having difficulty with utilizing any of the tips and techniques listed here, CBT could be a good step for you to take.

There are books on doing CBT, how it works, how it could affect you, and how to do it. If you're able to get the help of a professional who is skilled in CBT, that would be the best course of action to take. However, if you don't have access to a professional, CBT is something that you can do on your own with the help of materials on the subject.

Keeping a journal throughout the processes is a great way to monitor your progress and to ensure that you're getting a good result from the therapy that you're doing.

Chapter 9: Unleash The Empath In You!

When you want someone to see things from the other person's perspective, the first thing you will tell him or her is – put yourself in his shoes before you stand on him! This ability to look at something from the other person's perspective and trying to understand what they go through is referred to as empathy.

Empathy is the ability to interact with and lead by comprehending other people's views, feelings and thoughts. When you work on improving your empathy, you become a better human being. Empathy is strongly connected to the emotional quotient in a person. It can lead to a series of advantages such as:

- Succeeding in a professional environment (workplace)
- Stronger and more meaningful personal relationships
- Better quality of life and good health

Around 90 percent of top-performing individuals in most workplaces are said to come with a high emotional quotient. When people are self-aware of their thoughts, emotions and feeling, they are better in understanding the others' too. Listening plays an important role in this. When you listen better with an open mind, you tend to become a better person!

Lack of Empathy and its Negative Effects

Lack of empathy has been linked to criminal behaviors such as murder, robbery, drug dealing, etc. Multiple studies have proved this and claimed that most people in prison lack empathy. These prisoners who have been charged guilty never really cared about their victims. They didn't make any attempt to understand the emotions and feelings their victims were going through. If they had empathy, they wouldn't be in prison in the first place. When a person can empathize with another person, it is quite impossible for him to do anything rash or brutal.

Honesty and Trust

When you empathize with others, you are unconsciously placing your trust in the person. It gives you the ability to trust. When the person feels that you care for him or her, you are successful in earning his or her trust. Trust is important to build a healthy relationship. If your friends trust you, they will be more than willing to take risks for you and the most important of all – they will be honest and open with you! Your friends will talk openly only when they know they can trust you.

When trust builds, exchange of information increases and they will start sharing their thoughts and feelings with you. The trust they have in you might even make them open up the darkest secrets of their life. Gaining such a trust is a blessing nowadays as you hardly see such people around. This doesn't refer solely to friendship – it extends to personal relationships and professional relationships too. If your colleague can trust you such that she doesn't mind sharing her disturbing thoughts with you, you are working pretty well on your emotional quotient. Empathy and trust go hand in hand. Openness and honesty come only when the trust factor is strong.

Being Considerate and Understanding

You are busy playing a game on your mobile when a colleague of yours comes over with a worried look on her face. You stop for a second, look at her and ask her what is wrong. She tells you about a client call that went bad and is worried about the issue escalating. Instead of actively listening to her, you go back to your mobile game and respond to her with hmm's, aha's and oh's. How do you think she would feel? Will she come back to you ever again when she needs a compassionate ear? No, absolutely not! You just showed her that you are not interested in listening to what she has to say. You lost her trust, and you were pathetically inconsiderate and thoughtless.

The basic and simple thing you have to do when someone approaches you to talk about their worries, ideas or interests is to stop whatever you are doing and listen to them. When you are empathetic, you are aware of the feeling that is being shown. When you are approached for help, try to comprehend and understand what is not being said (nonverbal cues) along with what is being said (the verbal conversation).

Most important emotions in a conversation are conveyed through nonverbal signals such as body language, gestures, facial expression, tone of the voice, etc. You may not realize that every single movement in the body sends a message. The most important part of empathy is to understand nonverbal messages and show consideration for the feeling they are going through. You become an effective communicator when you can empathize and understand what the other person needs from you. Learn to comprehend nonverbal messages to discover more about the other person's thoughts and emotions.

The most common examples of nonverbal communication are:

- Facial expressions
- Eye contact
- Physical touch or contact
- Bodily appearance (physical)
- Hand gestures or physical actions
- The different sounds a person usually makes (depending on the emotions).

Empathy lays the rock-solid foundation for better emotional intelligence, and it is possible to improve your empathy through regular practice. You need to follow the right process and religiously practice them to take your empathy to the next level, which will help increase your overall emotional intelligence. You don't have to go through an expensive course or a complicated process to learn empathy. Choose the right resources and tools!

Why Practice Empathy?
Practicing empathy will help you with greater success professionally and personally, as it is one of the fundamental factors that are required to improve your emotional intelligence. The more empathetic you are, the happier you become! Why is it necessary to specifically work toward enhancing your ability to empathize with others?

- You will begin to treat people the way you want to be treated and more importantly, you would treat the people you care about exactly the way they wish to be treated.

- You will be smart enough to understand the wants and needs of the people around you.

- You can understand the perception others have about you based your actions and words.

- You can comprehend the unspoken words of people and respond similarly.

- You can successfully adhere to your customer's needs, as you are aware of what they are looking for.

- Interpersonal conflicts – both at work and at home - will be fewer as you can deal with them in a better manner.

- Your accurate prediction of people's actions and reactions will be helpful to work on your next course of action/

- You will be self-motivated and make extra efforts to motivate the people around you.

- Your convincing skills will improve, as you can influence your ideas and suggestions effectively.

- You will always allow two-way communication as you start looking at the perspectives and perceptions of the people around you.

- Handling negative people will no longer be an issue as you are better at comprehending their fears and motivations. You begin to empathize by putting yourself in their shoes and work towards a constructive solution.

- You not only become a better leader or a better friend but on the whole, you become a better person!

How to Practice Empathy?

There are a few simple ideas you can follow to develop your empathy, and they are,

- Stop and listen
- Observe and marvel
- Recognize your enemies
- Be the third person

Stop and Listen

Listen with rapt attention when people talk to you. Active listening is important; stop whatever you are doing and get into listening mode. Most often, conversations are often only talking with no listening – this happens when there is a heated discussion or arguments on sensitive topics. Often, people keep talking back and forth with each other, listening enough to reply to the other person's argument or statement. Sometimes, they don't even pause to listen; it is just back and forth talking at each other.

You will also be able to recognize such a pattern within yourself when you think deeper. You will have the response formulated in your head waiting to spit it out the moment the other person has finished with his or her sentence. It will look like you are in for a war of words where each party wants to make sure his or her word is the final.

When you find yourself being part of such a conversation, don't rush - slow down. Push yourself hard to listen to the words the other person is speaking. Gauge the motto (reason or objective) of the speaker behind what he or she is saying and why he or she is saying so. Think what led to this thought process in him – maybe his work experience and the way he was brought up has led to his current viewpoint.

Don't be a mute spectator; respond visually with body languages and gestures such as making eye contact, nodding your head, etc. You can also respond with sounds such as oh, aha, hmm, ok, etc. but let the second pass before you respond verbally. Before you respond with your reply, ask follow-up questions to make sure what the speaker intended and what you understood are the same, which will also help you understand their current emotional state.

Since you were completely focused on the speaker, you will need some to time to speak or respond, as you are yet to prepare your response for the same.

Observe and Marvel

Don't always stick your head into your mobile or iPad. Instead of checking your Facebook or WhatsApp while waiting for your train or when you are stuck in traffic, look around! Observe the people around you and imagine who they might be, what they might be feeling, what might be running in their head, where are they headed to now, etc. Is the person on that yellow bike happy? Is he frustrated? Is he humming the song he is listening to through his earphones? Does he have similar problems as me? Is that lady worried about some meeting she is expecting this noon? Is that why there is a worried look on her face? Just gaze around. Try to observe and marvel!

Recognize Your Enemies
Enemies might be an exaggerated word here, but think about an ongoing dispute you are having with someone – maybe your team member who is trying to disrupt your work routine to prove she is better. Or maybe a particular family member who is constantly coming up with conflictive arguments for whatever you do or say. You always have this thought in your head that whatever they do or say is wrong and you are right – whoever it is (maybe a colleague or family member). Because you are on the opposite side of the war field, you tend to disagree with them on anything and everything, irrespective of what they are arguing for!

Now, reverse the roles – imagine the entire scenario from the other person's perspective. The person isn't evil or a complete fool. Maybe they aren't wrong about whatever you disagree about. The problem here is more to do with the basic philosophical (ideological) difference between you than about the particular conflict that is taking place between both of you.

How does the other person feel when you disagree with them? Are they affected emotionally by the way you respond? What is causing the fear in the other person to accept or reason out with you? How do you worsen those fears in them instead of calming them? Are there any valid agreements for the person to make against your viewpoint? If so, what are they? Does this person hold any good intentions for you? Do they have any positive motivations behind what you think to be negative? If so, what are they? Do you agree with them? Do think these motivations hold more importance than the particular conflict between you two?

When you do this exercise a couple of times, you will feel your irritation and anger reducing – especially with the interpersonal situations which is stressing both of you. It may look clear, but it is different when you do it.

Be the Third Person
It can be difficult and tough to side with your enemy, so it is best to choose the other side – the third side. Look at the entire scenario from a third person's perspective. This step will require a lot of discipline, as you will already be stressed about your own emotions and thoughts. To make things easy, try it with an actual third person.

All of us have loved ones and friends who come to us to complain about that person who has been treating them badly. It is common for humans to complain, as it is the basic nature of the species. It is also the duty of the friend or loved one to listen to the complaints and be sympathetic or compassionate toward the complainer. The general assumption is that the listener will side with the complainer and support him or her. And psychologically speaking, a person who is caring and supportive will side with the complainer, but will also point out the arguments of the other person!

Try practicing this – complain about your opponent to the third person. But don't go with your default reaction immediately. Vent your emotions and then start reflecting. Once you finish with your side of the argument, you become the opposite person and start complaining about yourself. State points from the other person's perspective. Work your way back. This way, you force yourself to hear and speak for your opponent.

All this finally comes down to one major factor – empathy. Though we read a lot of articles and hear a lot of speeches about this, I wonder if people practice empathy – including myself. But if you want to bring a positive change to your emotional health, practicing empathy for even a short period should do the magic.

Tips to Improve Empathy
Research and studies show that empathy is partly inherent and partly learned. It is indeed possible to improve your empathy. There are eight ways to strengthen it, and they are:

Get out of your comfort zone and challenge yourself

When you stick to your comfort zone, you find fewer opportunities to learn and grow. Take up more challenges and experience the change you are undergoing, especially when you are no more in your protective and comfortable zone. Learn a new skill maybe – playing the piano or learning a new language or developing a new competency. When you do such things, you will become humble as you are pushed to stay grounded to learn new things – things that you have no clue about! Modesty enables empathy!

Travel and change of place impart new vigor to the mind (Seneca)

Move away from your usual environment. Travel to new places and explore their culture, since it will make you appreciate even the little things in others.

Ask for Feedback

I know I've been repeating this for quite a while now, but it is important – getting feedback is the only way for you to change and grow. Get feedback on your relationship skills from colleagues, family and friends. Listen to what they have to say and work on improving your lagging areas. Check with them to see how you are doing on a periodic basis.

Explore not just the head, but the heart too

Read books that talk about emotions, read literature that explores romantic relationships or personal connections. This is said to improve empathy – a study conducted on young doctors proved that reading literature showed improved empathy in them.

Put yourself in other's shoes

Initiate a conversation with people and find out what it's like to walk in their shoes. Talk about their concerns and ideas. Check how they handled the situations. Sometimes you will feel like your problems are much better compared to the others.

Inspect your partiality

Everyone has hidden biases within them and sometimes it is not so hidden. When you are biased or partial toward a party, you will lose the ability to decide rationally. It interferes with your ability to empathize, and most often these biases are centered on evident factors such as race, age, gender. Are you partial to a particular group? No? Think again – all of us are!

Be curious

What can I learn from a fresher? What can I learn from a client who is always self-centered? Cultivate the habit of asking curious questions. The right questions can lead you toward a stronger understanding of people.

Ask thoughtful questions

Don't ask questions just for the sake of it. Even if your questions are provocative, let them be thoughtful.

How to be Empathetic
A recent discovery by the neuroscientists has proved that the multiple systems of mirror neurons in human brains are responsible for experiencing empathy. These mirror neurons reflect the actions we examine in others, causing us to imitate the same action in our brains. For instance, when you see someone in pain, you experience the same emotion to an extent. Similarly, when you are with a person who is in an extremely joyful mood, you reflect the same emotion within you to a particular extent. The fundamental physiological bases of empathy are the mirror neurons. They produce a neural Wi-Fi that helps you to connect with people's feelings around you.

Though the majority of the people are naturally empathetic, there are the others who are not. But fortunately, empathy can be learned – research shows that this particular trait, even if not inborn, can be cultivated through regular practice. But to achieve this trait and to practice, you will need to overcome few potential blockades. They are:

Barricade 1 – Not focusing

Your mirror neurons kick in strongest when you notice and examine a person's emotions – eye gestures, body position, facial expressions and physical appearance. Most often people are distracted by their thoughts or other stuff that they fail to pay attention to a person – especially when you multitask.

Solution

Remind yourself of the importance of empathy and how it can lead to success in your personal and professional life. Motivate yourself to empathize with the scenario and people. Put away electronic gadgets and get into active listening mode. Fine-tune your observation skills, especially the nonverbal cues such as a quick change in facial expressions, uncomfortable body postures, trying to read the eyes of the person, etc.

Try to improve your nonverbal understanding by watching subtle dramas or movies with low volume. Make an effort to understand what each character is saying and read what the character is emoting.

Barricade 2 – Communication Issue

Not knowing how to communicate empathetically even after feeling his or her emotions.

Solution

Work on your nonverbal expressions; make a conscious effort to notice what you do (nonverbally) while interacting with people. Check your micro-expressions, hand movement, body postures, etc. Ask your friends to give you honest feedback on your nonverbal communication, especially in situations when you are overwhelmed by emotions.

Check if you have difficulty in being empathetic with specific people. If so, observe and understand why it happens. Concentrate on your tones. When people like teachers, friends, politicians, etc. are empathizing with others, listen to their tone.

I am sorry that you had to go through this. – Try saying this sentence in various ways with different voice tones. See if you feel empathetic when you hear yourself say it.

Be smart enough to leave people alone when they want to be left alone. Don't force your presence and empathetic words upon them. They might not want it at that particular time. For instance, if your friend who is going through a terrible phase because of her divorce proceedings is sending you signals to say that she doesn't want to talk now, respect her feelings and leave her alone.

Barricade 3 – Not able to show empathy

There are times when you do not feel the same way another person is feeling, but your brain is instructing you to be empathetic and hear the person out. This is referred to as cognitive empathy.

Solution

You can always disagree with someone and yet understand the feeling they are going through. Sometimes it is more important to listen to someone and not judge them since this will help them realize that you are empathetic towards them. Communicate honestly in a way that makes the other person feel that you genuinely understand what he or she feels.

Articulating Your Emotions or Feelings

Extroverts usually have the natural gift of being better at letting go of their emotions and feelings, because they are good with words. But concentration, practice and perseverance can help the others who come without this natural gift. When you can express the emotions then and there through body language or writing or by talking with other people, you are giving no chances for your health to dysfunction.

Researchers have found that it is beneficial to release and let go of emotions. Multiple studies have proved that repressed negative emotions or bottled up emotions can lead to increased stress. These researches also suggest that writing about feelings will give better health outcomes for people who have experienced traumatic events, asthma patients and breast-cancer patients. There was also a study conducted on people who lived for 100 years. The result of the study was their positive attitude towards life, and healthy emotional expression has led them to live for many years.

Therefore, it is better to articulate and express your feelings and emotions to maintain physical and emotional health. If you are someone who often finds it difficult to let go of these emotions, it is time you work on the emotional quotient in you. That being said, the solution is not to pop the top off that bottle of emotions and allowing it to spray all over the place. If you do that, you can never identify the cause of a problem or situation!

Conclusion

Thank you for making it through to the end of Mastering Your Emotions. We hope that this material has been informative on the topics within and helpful to you in achieving your goals, whatever they may be.

Your emotions are here to guide you. Learn as much as you can from them, and then let them go. Don't cling to them as if your existence depends on them. It doesn't. Don't identify with them as though they define you. They don't. Instead, use your emotions to grow and remember, you are beyond emotions. How could you not be? They come and go, but you stay. Always.

© **Written by:** *Caroline Empathy*

How to Deal with Difficult People

How to identify and manage difficult, irrational and toxic people in your life

Katerina Griffith

How to Deal with Difficult People

Smart Tips on How to Handle the People Problem and Get the Best Out of Your life

© **Written by: Katerina Griffith**

Book Description

Have you ever encountered someone who is frustrating to the point you feel like pulling your hair? Has someone ever driven you so crazy that you feel like screaming out loud?

Look around you – there are people in your life that are difficult to work or deal with. **You are not alone!**

One thing that I have encountered over the years is a fair share of difficult people – friends, family, and coworkers alike. These are people who don't bother to turn in their work within the agreed timelines, people who hold on tightly to their views that no one else's matter at all. People who do not want to collaborate with others in a team. Those who push back on work they are supposed to do in the first place – so much more!

Here, we will discuss;

- How to identify a difficult person: The big five
- Types of difficult people
- Common traits of difficult people
- Why you must deal with a difficult person
    - At the workplace
    - Home
- Identifying the issue
- Three lenses to look at the world
- How to manage your reactions
- Leveraging self-control
- Steps on how to deal with a difficult person
- What do you do when all this does not work?
- Expert techniques to handle difficult people
- Actionable Tips and Trick

So, what are you still waiting for? It is time to handle those difficult people in your life gracefully and survive the drama they attract.

Read on and find out more!

Introduction

Are there difficult people in your life? I guess that's why you are here. If you have not encountered difficult people before, then it is high time you start preparing for when that happens – because it will!

The thing with difficult people is that they often defy logic. Unfortunately, some of them are blissfully unaware of the kind of damage their attitude has on the people around them. Others are aware of the negative impact their actions cause but yet choose to derive their satisfaction from stirring up chaos and pushing people's buttons hard to know how far they can go. Whichever the case, their actions create unnecessary complexity, stress, and strife.

I run a business where we have over 200 employees. As we collaborate on various projects from time to time, there are instances where we encounter difficulties in getting a unanimous agreement on something because each member of the team is strongly opinionated. When I just started the company, I used to get bothered and so worked up in such situations. Each time I'd think, "Why are these people too difficult to deal with? What an irresponsible group...I don't even want to work with them anymore; I will fire them all!"

After some time, I realized that difficult people are everywhere. Even at home, I was dealing with a difficult teenage daughter who thought that she knew everything, and nothing you told her made any sense at all! The truth is, no matter where you are at or where you go, you will never be able to hide from such people. While it might be possible to avoid the first 1 or 2 of them, what of the 3rd, 5th, ...n^{th} ones out there that you have not met yet? Avoiding these people is not a permanent solution unless you are willing to quit your job or move away from your home and never have anyone around you.

I don't know about you – but I think that this is not possible! Instead of running each time and trying to find solace where you will never find it, why not learn some incredible skills that will help you survive difficult people with so much ease and grace?

According to research, it is evident that difficult people can cause those around them stress. What is even more disturbing is the fact that fear has been shown to have a lasting negative impact on the human brain. When you are exposed to stress even just for a few days, the effectiveness of the neurons in your hippocampus – the part of the brain that is responsible for memory and reason – becomes compromised. If the stress goes on for several months, then the neurons are likely to get damaged. In other words, anxiety is one of the formidable threats to achieving success. If it gets out of control, then the chances are that your performance is affected.

The good news is that some of the common causes of stress are very easy to identify. For instance, if your company is working towards getting a grant for you to function, there is a high chance that you will feel stressed and learn how to manage it. However, when the source of stress is unexpected, then chances are that it will take you by surprise, and this is what causes the most harm.

According to research from the Department of Clinical and Biological Psychology, Friedrich Schiller University, and exposure to a stimulus that causes a negative emotion is the same as when one is exposed to difficult people. The two experiences cause one's brain to have a massive response to stress. In other words, when one is negative, crueler lazy, that alone is enough to drive the mind into a state of anxiety.

It is important to note that your ability to manage your emotional feelings and stay calm even when you are under so much pressure has a direct association with your performance. According to findings by TalentSmart, over 90% of top performers in any organization are skilled at managing their emotions during stress periods. What is interesting is that the reason why they have control over these stressful situations is that they have learned how to neutralize difficult people.

While there are several strategies I have learned over the years from some of the top performers – who are my role models – on how to effectively deal with difficult people, I choose to share them here with you. If you are going to deal with difficult people effectively, then you need an approach that cuts across the board to the things you can eliminate. What you need to understand henceforth is that you are in control of how you respond to different situations more than you can imagine. Take charge today with the following strategies, and your life and experiences with people will never be the same again!

Keep reading!

Chapter 1 How to identify a difficult person: The big five

It is important to note that difficult people come in all forms and sizes. There is a wide range of ways in which difficulty can manifest itself. This can be someone spreading false rumors, seeing negativity in everything, lack of cooperation, and those who don't see value in others' contributions and views, among others. The thing with difficult people is that they see an opportunity to create trouble. They tend to use passive resistance to bring down your efforts to move your goals ahead.

Note that at the end of the day, the definition of 'difficult' is something rather peculiar to every individual. In other words, what you consider challenging to you may not be the same thing to someone else. Therefore, you must understand your personality, triggers, and preferences so that you are better placed to take note of situations and people that get on your nerves.

Emotional Stability

This is also referred to as neuroticism. You may be wondering what this is. Well, neuroticism is one of the factors that go a long way in determining one's level of emotional stability. How do you react or respond to a stimulus? If your score is high, then this indicates that you are no stranger to such emotional feelings as anger, anxiety, and depression. There is a high chance that you experience these emotions on an ongoing basis. In other words, if you score highly on neuroticism, this indicates that you are emotionally reactive as opposed to those who score lower.

The thing with emotional stability is that it indicates how prone you are too intense stimuli. However, what is important to note is that these emotional outbursts often tend to erode one's ability to think logically, make complex decisions, and cope with stress effectively. A high level of neuroticism manifests with a high level of negativity – which exacerbates the slightest setback resulting in one having a bad mood.

On the other hand, a low neuroticism level is indicative that you are emotionally stable. You are less prone to emotional outbursts and are calm. However, what you need to note is that having a lower level of neuroticism does not mean things will always be favorable on your part. Extroversion has a direct correlation with positivity. If you are going to deal with difficult people, then you have to learn how to break free from emotional setbacks.

Extraversion

The chances are that you are already aware of introvert-extrovert binary, right? What part of the scale do you fall? Well, one thing you need to note is that extraversion is a factor that determines how you interact with the world around you.

If you rank highly on the Extraversion scale, you are an extravert. The good thing with this trait is that you tend to possess a can-do it spirits. These are the kind of people who are always beaming with so much energy. They do well in social gatherings and when having physical experiences with the outside world.

On the other hand, are introverts. These are the ones that rank low on the Extraversion scale. An introvert is someone that is more laid back with a very minimal need for social interactions. While they are not so positive minded as the extraverts, the truth is that they are not depressed or shy, universally. However, you must note the fact that they find physical and social stimulations somewhat overwhelming. This explains the reason why prefer solitude – to process their emotions – but also a little bit of social intimacy.

Openness

Each one of us has a certain level of transparency. It is our level of openness to experience that goes a long way in determining how one embraces new ideas and experiences. When one is open to experience, they are said to be artistically curious, intellectual, and with a very keen sense of beauty. The good thing with openness to experience is the fact that people with this trait excel in creative roles often seen in people in the upper echelons of designs and academia. However, these kinds of people tend to stay away from tasks that require adherence to a set of guidelines, rules, and regulations.

Well, this is not to say that there are closed-minded people. The truth is that those who do not rank high on an openness to experience tests are often termed as "closed." These are the people who often have very few common interests to others. This explains why they tend to oppose ambiguity and subtlety – mostly in conversations fiercely – and do not respond well to change.

While people who are "Closed" don't often light the world with innovations, the truth is that they have superior roles and performances in such areas as police work and sales, among others – where protocols, rules, guidelines, and regulations are what takes precedence over all else.

Agreeableness

This is a measure of one's willingness and ability to engage with others in social events. While people tend to think that this trait is a universally beneficial feature from the outset, this is not always the case. Several people believe that agreeableness is something positive, but the truth is that just like all other traits, this also has its downsides. For instance, agreeable people are often racked with indecisiveness – especially when they are trying to complete high-stress or complex tasks.

The good thing with people with this trait is that they understand the importance of getting along with others. They hold a high consideration for others' emotions and goals – even higher than their interests. They are very friendly, relentless, helpful, and optimistic. To the onlookers, they are trustworthy and honest.

On the other end of the spectrum lie the disagreeable people - known to elevate their interests above anything else in this life. The thing with them is that they do not concern themselves with the wellbeing of those around them. Instead, they choose to pay attention to advancing their agendas and goals. Disagreeable people are very unfriendly, uncooperative, and does not give a rat's ass about anyone else. Such people are often found in science, business, military, among other professions.

Conscientiousness

This is a trait that measures the extent to which we can control our emotions. The truth is, our conscientiousness determines the scope of our success, possible experiences, and the best way to attain them.

According to research, there is evidence that shows that highly conscientious people often have been shown to have better control over their emotions. Even though such people tend to come off as dull and rigid, the truth is that they do well in whatever they put their minds to – with proper planning and motivation. The good thing is that they often try as much as they can to stay away from trouble and making erratic decisions. However, the problem arises when plans don't fall into place as anticipated or fail to meet their set high standards.

On the contrary, those who have low conscientiousness can delay their gratifications. This makes them more prone to adhering to their emotions. While this is something so much fun during parties and is something that people find valuable when situations arise, the problem is that they prove to be complicated. This explains the reason why they often get in trouble with people in authority.

That said, you may be wondering whether these big five traits are universal. According to a research study that looked into different people from over 50 cultural backgrounds, there is evidence that shows at least five dimensions can be used in accurately describing personality. This is the reason why several psychologists believe that the five personality dimensions are not just universal but also have a genetic link. According to David Buss, a psychologist, personality traits are a representation of the key characteristics that shape our social landscapes.

But what factors influence the big five personality traits?

According to research, it is evident that both environmental and biological factors go a long way in influencing and shaping our personality traits. Two studies suggest that both nurture and nature have a central role to play in personality development. One of the studies examined 123 pairs of identical twins and 127 of fraternal twins. What was interesting was that 53% of the heritability pointed at extraversion, 44% conscientiousness, 41% each of neuroticism and agreeableness, and finally 61% for openness.

On the other hand, longitudinal studies suggest that the five personality traits tend to stabilize as one goes through from childhood to adulthood. According to one study involving working-age adults, there is evidence that personality traits stabilized over four years and very minimal change brought about by adverse life events.

Studies also show that maturation dramatically impacts the personality traits. As we progress in age, there is a tendency for one to become less extraverted, open, and neurotic. However, features like conscientiousness and agreeableness tend to increase with age.

That said, what is essential to bear in mind is that behavior is something that comes as a result of interaction between one's personality and other situational factors. The situation in which you find yourself in has a role to play in how you respond. However, these kinds of responses are consistent with one's personality traits.

Wrapping it up

The five personality traits that we have just discussed – extraversion, agreeableness, neuroticism, openness, and conscientiousness – account for the difference between people.

For instance, when researchers have studied the personality traits of such animals like chimpanzees and dogs, the same features are also observed, plus more. Take a minute to think about dogs, you know – keep at home or within your neighborhood. What you will notice is that they are different from each other. Some are more friendly, active, and outgoing than others. Some are emotionally stable, while others are not. Some are friendly and agreeable, while some are vicious.

The chances are that you already know dogs that are very conscientious than others – in other words, they try too hard to do what is required of them just so that their master is happy. On the other hand, you probably know other dogs who don't even care what their master wants. Dogs also vary in terms of how open they are to new experiences, while others are more explorative and curious.

The sixth personality that we do not have but animals have is the ability to be dominant while others are more submissive. While human beings differ in terms of dominance, humans are more reflective of extraversion than independent.

Several people wonder how possible it is just, to sum up, personality traits in only five features. Well, if you think of all the people you already know, you might realize that they differ much more than the five personality traits. However, take a minute to think of this; if you take one character at a time rather than a collective personality, you will start to appreciate how diverse we all are.

People differ in personality ranging from low to very high on each trait. Even though each of the personality traits involves a large number of possible scores along the spectrum, you can choose to simplify this by thinking of it on a scale of 5. Now, if someone scores from very low, moderately low, average, moderately high, to very high, this means that we can give each one a score between 1 and 5.

Now that we have five traits, each one of them has five possible score levels starting from very low to very high. If you do that, then you can get at least 3,125 possible combinations on all five traits. That means 5 x 5 x 5 x 5 x 5. This means that if you were to classify people into all possible unique combinations of the five big traits, you would have to use all the five levels of each trait.

Additionally, it is essential to note that based on one's standing, the traits will manifest in quite diverse ways. A character like neuroticism appears to be different based on where a person stands on that trait. Let us consider another simple example. If one is high in neuroticism and agreeableness, they will have more unpleasant emotions - even so, they are still pleasant to be around. In other words, the fact that they are neurotic means that they tend to be clingy, annoying but does not necessarily affect other people much. If that very person is highly neurotic but has low agreeableness, then you had better watch your back!

When someone is highly emotional and is disagreeable, the truth is that they will tend to make their problems your problems too. They will be very difficult to deal with. While neuroticism manifests itself in various ways depending on their level of agreeableness, what you need to note is that such combinations change how our behaviors manifest outwardly.

Chapter 2 Types of difficult people

Perfectionists

When I first started my company, it used to take me at least 12 hours to produce an article that I thought was worthy of being published. My writers would send in their work, and I spent sleepless nights trying to edit and come up with the "perfect" piece. The thing with a perfectionist personality is that nothing will ever be good enough. You will find ways to look for mistakes, even where there aren't any.

One thing that is important to note is that being a perfectionist is something that is crippling. There may be that person in the office that is so passionate about their work is bursting with ideas but unfortunately cannot express them with unbridled freedom. It is the same thing with perfectionism – it holds you back because of anxiety, a sense of haunting unfulfillment, and depression.

Well, so many people think that being a perfectionist is about harboring the desire to be perfect alone. The truth is that it goes beyond that. You are merely choosing to derive your self-worth from the world around you. That explains why you end up being overly sensitive to criticism or rejection, and you end up believing that you are a stupid worthless failure or bad.

If you are a people-pleaser, then that is a sign of being a perfectionist. The thing is, seeking perfection often causes people anxiety because all they are thinking of is how they can be the best. You desire to control the outcome of your actions just so that you can gain approval, acceptance, praise, and rewards.

But do you think that the perfectionist in your office knows that they are obsessive and cynical in their behaviors? Certainly not! Just like I was, they may not even know that they are perfectionists, let alone putting in efforts to stop.

So, how do you deal with them?

Well, the thing with a perfectionist is that they are often detail-oriented, negative towards others, and sticklers for the rules. If your boss, subordinate, or colleague is this kind of person, the ways to handle them vary widely.

Dealing with a perfectionist subordinate

There are different types of perfectionists based on the personality types that we have discussed in the previous chapter; neurotic perfectionist, narcissistic perfectionist, hyperattentive perfectionist, and the principled perfectionist. The thing that these people have in common is that they all notice details and have very high standards that an average person cannot even breath close. To deal with them, you must;

Avoid giving them large project scopes

One thing that is important to note is that most perfectionists have admirable qualities that many people find worthy. However, there are quite a few of them who choose to hone skills on a small component of a project instead of paying attention to the bigger picture. If you work with these kinds of people, it is helpful to assign them to select tasks based on their skillset.

In other words, you can opt to give them projects that are limited in scope but are detail-oriented. The truth is that most of them are not willing to delegate tasks, and the best thing you can do is allow them to work on projects independently – as long as the project requires a unified vision to complete.

Appeal to their sense of vanity and empathy

What if your employee is a neurotic or narcissistic perfectionist? Well, these kinds of people have a powerful desire to please others. The most effective way to motivate them is to explain to them how their style of work affects those in the team. Ensure that you phrase it in such a way that they realize you already know they have high standards – and that you appreciate these high standards they hold.

You may say things like, "Mary, you have very high standards, just like me. That is what this company is all about. However, remember that good morale is essential for good productivity." What you are merely telling them is that the best way forward is to give a compliment even where they feel like there is something to criticize.

Appeal to their self-interest

What you will note is that several perfectionists want to be so perfect – either because of internal or external motivation. If you find that a subordinate is treating their colleagues poorly in the workplace just because they are perfectionists, remind them that such kind of people struggles hard to climb up the ladder. Remind them that the more they raise the ranks, the more they have to learn how to compromise for the sake of the whole team. Say something like, "I know you have been trying to ensure details of the project have been attended to, and the book does everything. That is great because if one is going to get the big things right, they will have to start by getting the little ones right. You are on the right track to the big things. However, what you need to remember as you progress is that the upper rank is about looking at the bigger picture. This means that if you focus too hard on getting 100% success, that will only bog you down. Have a vision for the next phase and not just a tunnel vision that might cost you more than you can pay for."

When you put it like that, they will start to realize that 100% is not all that counts, but achieving the primary goal, however, the approach you take is what counts at the end of the day.

Dealing with a perfectionist colleague

Choose your battles wisely

When you are dealing with a perfectionist colleague, it is paramount that you know when to take a stand and when to let go. While this is something difficult to attain, you must take time to think about how important the issue at hand is so that you know when the time is right to take a stand.

The first thing is for you to keep a perspective. Agreeing with what your boss says does not mean that you have to follow their suggestions to the letter. While this seems at first as being passive, simply say yes and move on with your life. This will reduce the chances of stirring up conflict and stress. Saying yes to what they say does not mean that you have given away your power. It is quite the opposite because this will set you free from paying attention to their demands.

Ask them what it is they would like to do differently

Did you know that criticism is one of the best ways perfectionists use to hide their insecurities? While this is upsetting, it always helps to remember that this is their defensive mechanism. They may just be lashing out because they feel insecure about one thing or the other.

When you take time to ask them what their preferred methods of going about something is, you are merely disarming those insecurities. Try telling them that you care about their emotions. When they realize that you understand their feelings, they will start to feel secure – and less critical in the future. Say things like, "I see that you are upset about the outcome of this project. Would you like a chance to talk about it?"

Stick to your guns

Think about it, is the issue you and your colleague have relevant? If so, then you are right to stick to your guns. There is a chance that no one at the office is aware that your colleague is a perfectionist. If there is something you consider relevant to you and disagree on, then realize that it is your right to spit it out.

Don't get me wrong- by disagreeing, I don't mean that you should argue about it. Simply state what it is that you disagree with and then move on. You don't have to let that disagreement to define the kind of relationship you both have. Simply say things like, "I understand where you are coming from. I just think that our perspectives are quite different on this one."

If they stir up an argument, simply walk away. No one will blame you for walking away from a case.

Keep distance

One of the simplest ways you can stay away from conflict is keeping a safe distance from it. If you have to work together on a project, simply remind them that each one of you has their roles and responsibilities and that you will do yours to your supervisor's satisfaction and not theirs.

You always have the choice of disengaging. If they keep going on and on about inconsequential details, all you have to do is remain noncommittal. Simply make your escape with such statements as "Huh, I didn't know you felt that way."

Dealing with a perfectionist supervisor

Manage your manager

This is simply what I often refer to as 'managing up.' The main aim of doing this is to help you identify the personality of your boss – their strengths and weaknesses – so that you can effectively tailor your conversation to match theirs.

The problem with a perfectionist boss is that they always desire to be in charge. At first, this may be self-evident, but the truth is that it is not. Ask them what their expectations are. When you do this, you are giving them an enhanced feeling of being in control. This also protects you from providing an arbitrary response. While perfectionism may be unreasonable – inherently – you must try as much as possible not to be. The trick is for you to pay attention to their start points, endpoints, or boundaries to lower the chances of getting them angry.

Push information their way

Once you know what it is that your perfectionist boss is looking for, simply give them – don't wait until they ask for it. The more you offer them a wealth of information they are interested in, even before they can ask for it, the less likely they will think of you as a flawed person. This way, you escape conflict by being in the right place, at the right time doing the right thing. Remember, out of sight, out of mind!

Be at peace with the fact that there is only so much you can do

The fact that you are a subordinate means that you have very little influence on your superior's personality traits. There are times when they are critical and others overly-critical. But the good news is that you can still earn their trust and respect. The only downside to that is that you might have to endure too many interactions that are draining. Just do what is right and let the rest be decided by fate!

Seek mentorship and support elsewhere

Now, you have a perfectionist boss who is supposed to be your mentor, but the truth is that they have set unreasonable standards you cannot attain. This means that if you take them as mentors, you will strain yourself too much just to earn their praise.

Perfectionists make very poor mentors!

While we all need support at one point or another, you cannot find it from your perfectionist boss. The truth is that such people tend to hurt your self-image even more. The last thing you want is having your self-worth determined by people who already think that everyone but them is worthy.

Jump ship when you have to

Consider that dealing with such a boss is something that you have to adapt to and not accept it indefinitely. You must know when to cut the cord. The trick is for you to earn their recommendation and move on. This might mean that you seek employment elsewhere.

Start planning your exit strategy as early as you can.

Control Freaks

Let us consider the following situations;

You want to hang out with a friend you met recently, but then your long-term friend insists that you should not because you have not known them well enough to hang out with. This friend asks that if you are going to hang out, you must tell them where exactly you will be meeting when - date and time.

Does this sound familiar?

Well, the truth is that this has happened to us – whether by partners, friends, or family members.

Such kind of people is referred to as control freaks. Dealing with such types of people is not fun – no matter how much they mean to you. It could be that they are doing it because their heart is in the right place, or they mean you no harm, but this is entirely lethal force you don't want to mess with.

You may be thinking, but who exactly is a control freak? Well, a control freak simply refers to perfectionists who feel vulnerable to anything that seems to them as uncontrollable.

The term "control freak" is a psychology-related slang. It describes a person who wants to dictate what everyone does and how everything is done around them. People who have an extremely high need for control over others are considered as control freaks.

Their main attempt is to hide their vulnerabilities by ensuring that everything within their surroundings is under their control. They try hard to manipulate people and put so much pressure on them just so that they don't have to change themselves. Everywhere you go, you will spot a control freak – whether at home, school, or workplace.

With the right strategies up your sleeve, you can deal with them and live a happy life.

Get rid of turf wars
So many control freaks often feel the need to retain control of each aspect of their work just because they do not want to lose their status. It could be that there was a time when they were the only employee in the office and were used to doing all things by themselves. The problem with these kinds of people is the fact that they are very difficult to handle because of their resistance to change – especially growth and expansion.

The real problem is that they feel that the person who has just joined the workplace is out to get "their" job. At first, they did not need any help, and now, they still think that they don't need any help whatsoever. It does not matter how competent the other person is because the control freak will not welcome any ideas or suggestions that are not theirs.

To deal with such a person; what you need to do is get rid of turf wars by ensuring that you engage them fully during role allocation. Allow them to create their projects so that they feel as though they have a sense of tenure. If it is possible, you can separate their duties from those of other employees. Once they see that their roles are highly valuable to the company, they will ease off on their controlling attitude – giving the others ample space and time to go about their duties with minimal interruptions.

Stroke their ego

According to research, there is evidence that shows control freaks are often very insecure. The thing with such people is that they often fight just so that they can retain control, considering that they are not sure of themselves. Such people hate trying new things and desperately are afraid of new situations and events. They feel that by retaining control over their work surrounding – something familiar to them – they can keep their insecurities in check.

Well, unfortunately, the approach they use in controlling things and people around them depicts their domineering and overbearing attitudes. This is precisely what stands to undermine their self-esteem and confidence further – especially if they spent the time to evaluate their behaviors honestly.

To deal with such kind of people, you need to find a way to help them regain their control so that they can feel secure. The best way to do this is for you to appeal to their ego. While they may come off as confident people, the truth is that inside, they are fragile. They are just hiding under that assertive shell so that they can win others' approval. Before they can offer you any help, go to them and ask them to help you with a difficult task. Even when you feel as though things are not looking up, simply compliment them on anything so that they can relax and make it easier for them to relinquish control over small things.

Stand your ground

There are instances when you feel that there is nothing you can do to appease someone who is controlling. This is because they firmly believe that they know best. They will even go as far as throwing tantrums if they don't get their way.

The best way to handle them is to try and assess what it is that you disagree on. If it is something important, you should stand your ground. While this may stir up conflict and friction at the workplace, it will help them know that not everyone can toy around. The trick is that you choose your battles with caution. If it is an issue of how the office should be cleaned, ask yourself whether it is something you would want to die for.

Take note of the little things

Just like stroking their ego, taking note of small things is about paying attention to what their needs are. Whatever it is, ensure that you pay attention to these tendencies. Reassure them that they are doing an incredible job. Tell them that the place would not be as excellent as it is without them. Praise them for their underlying qualities, and before long, you will realize that their controlling attitude reduces significantly as they soak in praise!

Give a little

Is there someone in your office or home that thinks they know so much more than anyone else? Does it even matter that they believe this? Well, the truth is that in the grand scheme of things, the question that truly matters is if this person is involved in all your daily activities and your ability to do your job. If they don't stand in the way of you getting your job done, the best way to tame them would be to give to her selfish and immature attitude – and simply move on.

Ask questions

One thing you will note about a control freak is that they often are obnoxious. Several people around them dismiss them because of their bossy attitude and desire to control every little thing. Well, the truth is that in reality, they just desire to be part of something – and can offer valuable input – if only people would listen.

Therefore, the next time you encounter a control freak at home or in the office, and they want to boss you around, ask them pointed questions about how they want this or that to be done. If they insist on installing the lights in a specific manner, ask them why they think it cannot be done differently. It could be that they have a phobia for heights, and that is why they insist that it be done a different way than that avoids falling. This allows you to realize that these control issues do not hurt and have the potential of affecting their security in the workplace or at home.

If they are adamant that stationeries go to the right side of their desk and then picture frames on the left, demand for an explanation, there are times when you will realize that they don't have a valid reason for that. If it is not their desk, then that is unacceptable. However, if it is their desk, the best thing is for you to oblige. The point is for you to help them confront their obsessions so that you can know whether there is an actual control issue going on or there is something else subtler that goes beyond stationeries.

Spending time with them talking about these issues will help both of you resolve the problems amicably so that you can both get back to what matters and be productive at it.

If necessary, enlist the help

What if you are not able to reach a point of compromise with someone who is a control freak? In such a case, you can seek advice from your superiors or line manager. You must try to explain to them that your intention is not to cause disharmony in the office. Instead, what you are interested in is creating an atmosphere where each one of you can thrive.

This will also go a long way in helping the boss understand that you are not there to complain but that you have the company's best interest at heart. You must tell your manager that the other person's tendencies are getting in the way of you working and reaching your goals. Ask them to clarify what your roles and responsibilities are at the office. There is a chance that the management has no idea of what the situation is like, and asking them to step in will help a great deal to clear things up.

It is also essential that you are always ready to offer possible solutions to the issue so that your bosses are aware that you are also a team player. While working with someone who is controlling can be difficult, realize that it does not have to be impossible! Just a little effort aimed at understanding their motivations and alleviating their insecurities will go a long way in helping you work together in harmony.

Narcissists

Narcissists are people who are ready challenging to work mainly because of their big ego and vanity. The problem with them is that they pretend to know it all. If you have such a person at home or the workplace, you must determine where they are real experts and where they are pretentious.

If they are real experts, then your research should prove that they are knowledgeable in that area because of the validity of their ideas and information. You must not subjugate their ideas or permit any condescension. The trick is for you to be respectful when dealing with them. Where you feel they are wrong, simply correct them without being confrontational or overly aggressive.

Gossips

With the advent of technological devices, gossiping is no longer restricted to the water cooler. Today, people gossip with ease of emails and social media platforms. What is interesting is that in spite of all these technological innovations, chatting today at the office or home can be traced back to one single individual who always knows and shares information – whether true or false.

If you have such a person in your life, the best way to deal with them is to avoid sharing information with them or someone close to them. You must practice remaining cordial when around them. Whenever they try to pry into your life or that of others, gently pull away from the conversation and change the subject into something more productive and useful.

Bullies These people are a fact of life, and the most unfortunate thing is that by the time they are graduating high school, if they will not have changed, then chances are that they will never change. These are the kind of people who end up taking their insecurities to the workplace, marriages, and friendships. The problem is thinking of others as weak and susceptible and hence use that to be vindictive. They will always try to get other people to gang up against one or more people around them.

When you are dealing with such a person, you must try as much as you can to hide your weaknesses. Stand up to them, and don't tolerate them being respectful to you. Don't get me wrong; I don't mean that you get aggressive with them. However, you must not allow them to interfere with your life. If they try to bring their attitude to your place of work or home, simply ask them to leave.

Slackers

These are the kind of people who are not motivated and are unreliable. They are the kind that cannot carry their weight. If you have never worked with one of these, thank you, God! They are the kind of people who will leave all the work to you. When you are asked to partner with them, ensure that the job assigned to them is done to completion. If not, then you should be prepared to take on their portion of work.

Trust me; they are out there to let people down – beware!

Pessimists

 Some people view the world through shades of gray. They are the pessimists whose primary agenda is to dismiss every idea someone comes up with without necessarily offering an alternative. Much of their time is spent complaining about this or that. If you have such a person in your team, the trick is to remain positive. Remind them that you cannot just sit and do nothing; instead, they should give their contributions as well.

Oh, and be prepared to shoulder much of the work!

The hostile or bossy

The one thing I have learned when dealing with these kinds of people is that strength and tact goes a long way. People who feel as though they have been wronged tend to be violent.

The other trick is for you to try as much as you can to help them meet their needs without necessarily being aggressive or discriminatory about it. Try to stay away from any interaction with them that stirs up intense emotions like violence – as they say, don't hang out with the enemy when they are carrying a weapon or drinking! Check your actions to ensure that they don't stir up anger. In short, try not to be a pushover.

The worst thing you can do is strongly retaliate against an aggressive person. Remember that hostility often begets hostility. The best thing you can do is try to divert their attention to something more meaningful. This way, their anger tends to go down. Try to explain to them more about the situation pointing out common interests so that they are open to calm and rational ways of resolving the issue at hand.

The chronic complainer

These are the kind of people who will always find fault in everything you do. They will go to the extent of blaming you. They pretend as though they know all that should be done when, in fact, they are never open to correcting the situation themselves in the first place.

If you want to cope with these kinds of people, the first thing is for you to pay attention to all they have to say and then ask questions to seek clarification – even though you have been falsely accused or are guilty. The secret is for you not to complain, apologize, or be overly-defensive. If you do, then you are causing them to restate their concerns in a more heated manner. You must be severe and supportive of it. Accept the facts and get all the complaints in writing. Involve them in the process so that you all actively find the solution. Rather than dwelling too much on what is wrong, try to get them to think of what should be done.

The Super-Agreeable

Has anyone ever agreed with everything and anything you say to the point that they make you angry? Well, these are the super-agreeable people. While it is a good thing to get along with people at home and the workplace, some people agree with every idea you give, and then when things suddenly go south; they back down.

What you need to note about these people is that they are after approval. We all come from different family backgrounds with diverse upbringings. Some learned that the best way to get love is through pretense. In the same way, those people who are super-agreeable tend to promise heaven on earth but cannot deliver that. They will tell you, "I will submit the report tomorrow, or I will help you run errands." Don't be fooled; all they are doing is buttering you up.

The best way to handle them is to assure them that it is okay to say "No" when they feel like they will not be able to deliver. It is okay to speak the truth even when it is hard to spit it out. You must take time to ask them to try and be candid so that they can find it easy to come out and be frank about anything. When you support them overcome this habit, they will stop making promises they know they couldn't possibly keep. Show them that you value the relationship you have, and the truth won't hurt. Ensure that you let them know you are ready to compromise, considering that they will be fair and just.

Critics

"It's hard to kiss the lips at night that chew your butt all day long."

- Former Congressman Ed Foreman

Criticism is not all that bad, but the truth is that there are times and places for it. Debates are where the most effective solutions are birth. This is where some of the best minds challenge every point of view in the room.

But is that always the case with criticism? Are there demanding critics?

Indeed, there are so many demanding critics whose criticism is destructive. They are not seeking answers. They are not even concerned with the give and take that leads to a strong team and a consensus. They are the people who behave like politicians. I like to think of critics as spectators and not players.

Look around your office; is there is a critic there? Is your spouse or friend a critic?

Often, you will notice that critics are the kind of people who will always be quick to point a finger, and yet when their help is needed, they will not lift one. They are the kind of people who will not cooperate within the project, and it is their negative attitude that makes it hard to work and achieve the set goals in a team.

Liars

"Honesty pays, but it doesn't seem to pay enough for most people."

- Kim Hubbard

This saying is sad, but it is probably right. Think about it, if you have a project you are working on, and the members of your team don't want to cooperate and are dishonest, will the project mandate be fulfilled?

The chances are that you will not even have a team to work in the first place. Honesty goes a long way in fostering cooperation, teamwork, and productive working relationships. If you lack trust, then you can't work together peacefully. You cannot be productive.

If you think about lies, the truth is that they come in so many different forms. It could be that little white lie you tell a client to impress them or those you say your spouse so that they are not upset. They could be the lies you show potential employers when you are trying to get them to hire you. One recruiter once said, the closest anyone comes to perfection is when they are trying to fill out a job application. There are three kinds of lies, according to the former Prime Minister of Great Britain; statistics, lies, and darned lies.

Whatever kind of lies you tell; the truth is that it is difficult to deal with a liar. The thing with lying is that it is rarely necessary. It does not matter how distasteful the truth is, the truth is more comfortable to accept than a lie. Once you tell one lie, it spirals and continues for as long as you take it. By the time you realize it, you have caused so much harm than good. The thing with liars is that they will always tell a lie to cover up the first lie.

If there is someone that is always lying, simply talk to them about the value of the truth. Don't try to look down on them. Help them always tell the truth by holding them accountable for their word – bitter or sweet.

Chapter 3 Common traits of difficult people

Everything is about them

Have you ever noticed that there are people who are masters at spinning things – conversations and situations – so that it is about them? Such people often have a way of doing all it takes to bring the discussion back to them when they realize that it has veered off, and the spotlight is no longer on them.

The truth is, interacting with such people is boring. The reason is that whenever you start discussions with them, you are almost sure that the story will be tied to them – how they spent the weekend, what their thoughts are, what ideas they have, or everything else going on in their lives.

Many people ask themselves why they even do it in the first place. Well, the truth is that difficult people are not necessarily cruel. The thing is that they are experiencing a slight immaturity in their personal growth.

They are so used to unabashed attention such that everything is about them and have no time to think of what others think or have to offer too. In worst-case scenarios, everyone that is around them is only there to boost their ego and make them the center of the universe.

They are verbally toxic

Difficult people always have something nasty to say about almost everything. If they are not gossiping, then they are blaming or whining or busy shouldering off responsibilities to the next person they want to bully or use.

In short, these people don't even know when the right time to shut up is. They will always run their mouths about this or that – a typical master storyteller. If someone at home or the workplace experience something even in private, they want to be the first ones to break the news to the whole world – especially those who might be interested.

However, if the news does not seem so unusual, they choose to stand on it on their own two feet. What is worst is that they try to add in salt and sugar just so that the story is compelling – talk of fiction!

Just like the first trait, this reason why they choose to do this is so that they can be the center of attention. What is funny is that instead of making the whole story about them, they choose to be the traveling poet who is busy distributing the news everywhere. They do this so that they can control everything that people know.

They paint themselves as victims

The other trait you will notice with difficult people is that you cannot tell them anything because they tend to portray themselves as less-than-charming. For instance, if you call them out on something, they will suddenly become emotional and start apologizing profusely. As they do this, they give people a million and one reasons for their actions.

It could be that they are behaving in this manner because they were not brought up in a loving family, or that they are insecure about something from their childhood. It could also be that they have an incredibly rare mental disorder that causes them to act this way.

Their behavior is a prime example of what deflection is all about. While there are some of these people who are consciously unaware of what they are doing, there are instances where some have adopted this kind of defense mechanism from their childhood into adulthood, and everything seems reasonable to them.

Often oblivious to the obvious

Whenever you meet someone trying, one thing you need to bear in mind is that you are not the only one that feels that way. Someone difficult to you will always be trying to everyone around them.

The lives of difficult people are filled with several people interested in confronting their challenging behavior. You will find their families sighing about it, people looking at them with sneering at them by the roads, or coworkers having disgruntled faces whenever they meet by the corridors. However, no matter what happens, these signs don't seem enough for them.

They choose to be oblivious about it all so that they can keep behaving in the same way.

The main reason why they do this is that they have an abundance of pride or are simply not aware of their behavior.

They count everything

The thing with difficult people is that they will never do anything and be quiet about it. They have to go on and on about what they have done. Whenever they are asked to do anything that goes beyond their usual roles and responsibilities, they will ensure that you pay them for it. Even once you have paid them, they will remind you over and over again that they did you a favor and will use that to get what they want.

The main reason is that they are too self-absorbed – something that causes them to be too self-serving. Each minute they use doing a task that is not directly linked to their interests; they will live in anguish.

That said, a difficult person is one that will never exemplify all the typical traits we have discussed in this chapter. Instead, they often tend to have a different blend of problematic characteristics that cause them to be complicated.

We all certainly have at least one or two of these traits that make as demanding in one way or the other. By recognizing these features, we can act on them, work on fixing them – whether in us on the people around us – so that we can all live a happy and free life.

Chapter 4 Identifying the complicated issue

What will get you ready and self-aware whenever tough situations involving difficult people arise is if you choose to turn the situation inward and analyze each trigger and reaction. According to Elizabeth B. Brown, there is a wide range of questions you need to reflect on for you to better understand the root cause of issues and why the other person involved is driving you crazy. These questions include;

- What are the emotional tornadoes that the problematic person brings to your life?
- **What is your reaction to the difficult person?**
- How do they respond to your reactions?
- **If the other person in your life is the cause of all problems, have you found ways to grow unhealthy actions and responses towards them?**
- Is it possible that you are a difficult person driving others crazy?
- **If that is the case, how do they choose to respond to your actions and responses?**

When you are trying to deal with a difficult person, the last thing you want is to feed into your frustrations. The truth is that when you do this, you are just continuing a vicious cycle that will not end. The problem with most people is that they tend to see or to hear things the way they want to and then interpret them based on assumptions rather than facts and actions.

Unfortunately, we often lack information on why one shows up the way they are. This explains the reason why often, we fill in the blanks with our theories and assumptions because we don't have the facts or do not want to find them in the first place.

Mitigating These Situations

If you are going to deal with the difficult people in your life objectively, you have to be willing to separate facts from assumptions or theories. It is often beneficial to try and separate ourselves from our negative emotional feelings that we may be experiencing at that very moment. While this may be easier said than done, those who can get to this point can arm themselves with the power of friendly and productive interactions with people who make them cringe.

To achieve this, you must use the three different lenses to have a general outlook of the world. These lenses include;

Realistic optimism lens

To use this lens, you must start by asking yourself two simple questions whenever you feel that someone has unfairly treated you. These questions include;

What is the factual information in this case?

Is there a story I am telling myself about these facts? What is it that I anticipate as an outcome?

The reverse lens

This kind of glass requires that you look at the world around you through a glass of the person that triggered you. Well, don't get me wrong – I don't mean that you should sacrifice your own opinion just so that you can make others happy. Instead, you must widen your perspective. Using the reverse lens, you need to ask yourself;

- What is the other person feeling? How do their feelings make sense?
- What is my responsibility in all these?

You may see this as counterintuitive at first, but the truth is that this is something compelling in helping you reclaim your value. Whenever you feel threatened, you must find a way to appreciate yourself and the other person, too – this is essentially what we refer to as empathy.

The long lens

Did you know that at times the worst fears you have about the other person may turn out to be true? Most difficult people I know often derive satisfaction from unreasonably bullying others. If you choose to see things from their perspective, that might not make sense at all. These are the people that will take credit for your work. When and if this happens to you, the first question you need to ask yourself is, "irrespective of what I feel at this moment, is there a way I can learn and grow from this experience?"

Realize that when you are dealing with difficult people – irrespective of what their personality traits are – there are essential steps that you must take to make the best of the whole situation. You can work hard towards finding a more productive outcome. We will discuss this in detail in the next chapter.

How to manage your reactions

Managing your reactions and emotional feelings are all about taking in deep breaths. According to research, slow and deep breaths go a long way in triggering something below the spine – referred to as the Vagus nerve – which transmits neurotransmitters to the brain to calm down.

You must ensure that you take a moment to reflect on how you are feeling. The most important thing is for you to ask yourself how you would like to respond to those emotional feelings. Is it possible for you to create a good outcome from the situation?

Well, this may feel at first as though it is an overkill. However, realize that this will get your brain out of its automatic response. You will not feel that negativity, sharpness, and defensiveness anymore. When you force yourself to think of ways that create positive outcomes, your brain automatically assumes a positive mode of thinking.

Leveraging self-control

If you are going to handle every difficult situation with a difficult person in an amicable manner, you must know yourself. When you have a clear sense of who you indeed are, what it is that stirs up the tension, and where your limits are, you will be better off socializing with people however difficult they may prove to be. You must learn how to stay calm, develop your awareness and skills in emotional intelligence so that you can effectively manage your reactions to every frustrating situation.

Today, challenge yourself to always start by seeking to understand the situation at hand better. When you have more clarity about the situation – by asking questions – you will not only manage your reactions better but also help you find a mutually satisfactory outcome. Reflect on what it is that you consider a satisfactory result before you can interact with difficult people so that you better place to keep your focus on what truly matters in the first place.

The other trick is for you to ensure that you stick to the facts and acknowledge your emotions. When you make use of examples rather than interpretations, you will be able to keep your interactions with difficult people in check. Before you can respond to what it is that they said, ensure that you paraphrase and check the accuracy of their words so that you have a good understanding of what they mean rather than choosing to make assumptions by hearing what you want to hear. When you check for the accuracy of the information first before responding, this is an indicator that you want to work with others effectively.

When you respond by stating your emotions or what impact their words have on you, this can be a great nudge that will help the other person realize that what they are doing is wrong and hurtful. If there is something you think is not right, it is better if you seek the help of others.

The truth is that you are not alone in this.

Some so many other people have been through what you are experiencing at the moment. Their experiences may have been productive when dealing, working, or interacting with someone difficult. When you seek their advice or coaching from someone experienced, this can go a long way in helping you overcome. Research shows that when you talk about your feelings, you will be in a better position to reframe the whole situation to a place where you can effectively facilitate a positive result.

Where necessary, ensure that you keep records. There are times when things get a little bit more abrasive to the point where you run the risk of hitting an end-state you never intended in the first place. If the interaction gets to the point where it is toxic, you must start making intentional efforts to document them. This means that when things begin to go south, you will have an excellent map to lead you to a place of restoration and peace.

Chapter 5 Developing Coping and Negotiation strategies

As you may already have learned, difficult people are everywhere. There is a chance that you, too, are difficult. The truth is that several people struggle to go through periods where they are not in their best behaviors. If you desire to maintain a healthy working relationship with someone difficult, then it is high time you learned some of the most practical and helpful coping and negotiation strategies that will make your life easy.

Here are some;

Method 1 Approach the problematic person

Step 1 Choose your battles carefully

When you are butting heads with someone difficult, the most important thing for you is to decide when you think your efforts will yield fruit – that is when you go ahead to discuss the issue at hand. Realize that not every fight that comes your way is worth fighting. The sooner you realize that battles are to be chosen wisely, the better you will be.

In an ideal world, both you and the difficult person would simply set your differences aside and make compromises. While this is often impossible, what you need to ask yourself in such a situation is whether the issue is so distressing that you must address it right there and then. Consider your relationship with this person. If you are at loggerheads with your boss or someone in authority, then the sooner you accept the things you cannot change, the happier you will be. If the issue arises between you and a member of your family, then you have to choose between saving your time, efforts, and grief, or whether enabling a bad behavior is a preference.

Take a step back and think whether by fighting the battle, you stand to win. You can only take on someone that irks you once you have assessed the whole situation and consider whether there is a possible resolution to it. If the timing is not right, then take time to formulate a plan, seek help, wait for the right time or find another practical option.

Step 2 Take a pause

Before you respond to any situation, the first thing is for you to take in a deep breath. This will allow you to recollect all your thoughts, calm your mind, and your emotional feelings. If you are dealing with a problematic person via a mobile text message or email or other digital means, try as much as you can not to send anything that might stir up the war further. Allow your stress levels to come down first before you can approach the other person and reason together.

Try also to have a neutral meeting place where you both can discuss the issue. For instance, you could talk over the issue while taking a walk or doing something else. The importance of this is to try and limit one-on-one negative interaction.

Step 3 Clearly state your needs with assertive communications

The thing with difficult people is that when you try to communicate with them and have a reasonable discussion, they will try to manipulate you or twist your words around. The best way you can avoid that is by using the 'I' statement instead of 'you' that may sound accusative.

Let us consider an instance where someone has been consistently late to work the whole week. Now, if their boss is the difficult one, simply say, "I understand that you are mad at me for being late this week. That is precisely how I would feel. Unfortunately, our subway line is under construction, hence the constant delays at the station. My apologies for making you wait every morning this week. "

This is different from saying something like: "You are such an unreasonable person for expecting me to get to work on time when the subway is under construction. You don't care about anything but your work. If you did, you could have already paid attention to the news and known that the line had issues."

The first response is the best one. It shows your remorse for being late, your respect for the boss, and your plan to resume routine once the subway has been completed. You must try as much as possible to sandwich your response while talking to someone difficult. Always start with a positive comment to show how much you value the relationship between the two of you. Then head right into the tough part of the conversation. Finally, complete it with a positive remark like thanking them for lending you a listening ear.

Step 4 Keep being polite

My grandmother always said that being polite is something that will not cost you anything but will earn you every good thing. The same applies when dealing with someone difficult. It does not matter what the difficult person's response is because what truly counts is how you respond to it. If you keep your cool, things will always not escalate out of control.

Several people get in the trap of name-calling and abusive behaviors. The trick is for you to take a step back, take in a deep breath, and then give your response politely. Try as much as you can not allow yourself to sink into the other person's level. The calmer you remain, the higher the likelihood of the other person noticing and trying to mirror your behavior.

It all starts with how you respond!

Ensure that you do it right.

Step 5 Stick to the facts

Have you ever tried arguing with someone whose speech is all over the place – throws around claims and accusations – without really taking the time to substantiate their claims? This can be annoying!

When dealing with a difficult person, the trick is to keep your conversation short, clear, and to the point. It does not add any value bogging it all down with too many unnecessary details that will only stir up negative emotions. The chances are that you will not successfully get to them enough for them to see your point of view. There is no need to convince them. Simply state what took place, and don't try to explain yourself.

You must avoid all forms of triggers. If you always fight about holidays with your brothers, stay away from the whole topic. Instead, allow someone neutral to mediate. Don't try to be defensive. Yes, you might want to argue your point, but if it is with a difficult person, you had better skip the whole argument. It does not add any value trying to prove you are right. Let the situation stay as neutral as you possibly can.

Step 6 Minimize your interactions

It is one thing to be hopeful about dealing with the issues you have with the difficult person and get the desired outcome. However, the best advice you can give yourself is to try and avoid spending too much time with them. If you must interact, then keep it short. You can excuse yourself from all conversations or even bring on a third-party. Throughout the interview, ensure that you stay positive and always try to calm down afterward. Just accept that this problematic person might never be the colleague, neighbor, friend, or sibling you ever wanted to have – and that is okay.

Step 7 Talk to allies

If you are not getting along with someone and you think that you should, then it helps to find a potential mediator to help bring the two of you together. If you are colleagues, then perhaps your boss can help make the situation better. If the conflict is within your family, then you can reach out to a mutual neutral party to help you negotiate. The point is for you always to seek to share complaints with those you trust only.

Method 2 Change your mindset

Step 1 Realize that there will always be difficult people anyway

As we have already mentioned, you will ever encounter difficult people everywhere you go. There will always be people out there who are looking for someone to hurt. The key here is for you to learn how you can deal with such people. While they may be impossible to avoid, you must take time to study their personality traits so that you better place to deal with them.

For instance, if the person is a hostile type, you may notice that they are cynical, think that they are always right, and are argumentative. These are mostly people who do well in authority or power roles. If it is someone that is emotionally sensitive, they will always look for insults – are easily offended, hence choose to use textual approaches when expressing their disappointments and anger. Egotists, on the other hand, are concerned with their selfish interests without really caring much about what others want – often loathe compromise, ungrateful and insensitive. Finally, Neurotic types are those who are anxious, overly critical, and pessimistic.

Step 2 Increase of frustration tolerance

You can control a bird from building a nest on your head, but you cannot prevent them from crossing over your head. In other words, the other person's behavior is something that is beyond your control, but your reaction to them is within your control. You are the one to choose whether or not to engage them. To achieve this, you must be ready to build your frustration tolerance – which involves you taking the lead at challenging irrational beliefs that might contribute to stress, anger, and outbursts.

When you are interacting with a difficult person, you may think that you are unable to deal with them. Those are just irrational thoughts trying to scare you off. The best approach is for you to take in a deep breath and then question the validity of that thought.

In reality, you can deal with anything you put your mind to. If your mother-in-law is trying to micromanage you in your own house, you will not go crazy because you can deal with that. You are stronger than you give yourself credit. The trick is for you to fine-tune your mind to handle it. Instead of stressing over it and causing yourself harm, take in a deep breath and hand her some work to do so that she is occupied. Watch the words you use and ensure that they are rational.

Step 3 Examine your behavior

If you find that people continuously attack you, then the chances are that you are attracting the wrong crowd. If you are overly negative, the chances are that you will attract a group of pessimistic people who will flock around you.

To deal with fire, you have to arm yourself with fire. To attract positivity, you have to engage in positive behaviors. Think back to all the negative experiences that you might have gone through and ask yourself what your role was in them. How did you respond to the other person's behavior? At the office, there may be someone that always picks on you – how you talk, dress, work, or do things at work – how do you respond to them? Do you have the power to stand up for yourself? Take time to recognize all your strengths and weaknesses so that you are better placed to confront the difficult person in a way that puts them in their place.

Step 4 Beware of your perceptions of others

Have you ever thought that maybe the reason why your friend is acting up is that they are going through a rough patch in their lives? While that is no excuse for their behavior, you must not be quick to judge others behavior. Take time to practice empathy. Simply take a step behind and reflect on how you would respond if you were in a similar situation. Your sensitivity to differences in personality might just be the reason why you hand a wide range of conflicts.

The trick is for you to learn how to practice acceptance. Take in a deep breath and look at them with such compassion. Talk to them with so much calm and tell them that you see that they are suffering and in pain. Let them know that you accept the fact that they are scared and anxious, even if you don't understand the reason behind their situation. Let them also know that their situation is making you anxious.

The truth is, when you accept the situation just the way it is, you let go of so much tension that might have stirred up resistance and conflict between the two of you. Yes, you may not understand why your client blew up at you as they did. Rather than becoming angry and snapping back at them, consider the possibility that they may be hurting inside. Whether the reason is valid or not, it will help you stay calm and not yield into the power of negativity.

Chapter 6 Steps on how to deal with a difficult person

If you ask any manager or coach, they will tell you that there is always that one employee that is not so great to work with. As it turns out, management is still there to ensure that within the company's landscape, they are there to oversee the performance of all other employees within their department. This does not mean that being a manager or parent or in a leadership position means that you are not a difficult person to work with. Even those in authority can prove very difficult to deal with, whether at the workplace or home.

The last thing you want is to be held hostage, spend lots of time and emotional energy thinking of how you are going to get your work done without someone standing in the way or trying to make your life a living hell. There are times when you are left debating whether or not to let them go, but you never get around to pulling the trigger.

So, if you are this kind of person that has been pulled by difficult people into the endless vortex of frustration and ineffectiveness, these are the steps you can deal with them gracefully;

Step 1: Listen

Often, when someone is difficult, the truth is that we stop paying attention to what it is that is going on. We get irritated and lose hope in them. We decide what we think of them just so that our focus shifts to something else – because we want to avoid them and protect ourselves from them.

However, if you want to be effective at dealing with them, then you have to be very attentive when they are not doing well or are being hard headed. Your best shot at making things better is seeking to have a clear understanding of the issue – including knowing the other person's viewpoint. In most cases, the first thing that you need to do is simply listen. Listening alone can save the day.

When you listen, you set yourself up to hear what the real problem is, and you may even note that it is not the other person's fault. The truth is that the problematic person might just start acting differently once they know that their concerns have been heard. Not everyone difficult becomes that way just for fun – it could be that there are real issues they are airing, and they need them to be addressed.

Step 2: Offer clear behavioral feedback

If you look around you, you will notice that most people spend weeks, months, or even years complaining about someone in their lives, which is trying. What they don't do is give actual feedback on what it is that they need to change or do differently. You cannot keep doing the same things over and over again, expecting a change each time.

While giving harsh feedback is something that can be uncomfortable for many people, you can choose to do it responsibly. When you change your ways, you will realize that the other person will also change. The approach that you can use to give transparent and honest feedback is first to lower the other person's defensiveness so that you can offer them with the information they need to be better. Whatever approach you choose to use, they must do these two things – and you will be on the right track.

But why do we hate giving feedback, and how can we make it easier?

Well, over the past three decades, my friends and I have worked to train and coach thousands of people to become better managers and leaders, whether at home or in the office. When we asked them what they consider is the toughest part of their daily job, they said giving others corrective feedback – almost without exception.

So many of them said that at work, they find it hard to fire someone – painful or not. But then this is something that they still have to do, however hard it may be. However, this is not to say that everyone is afraid of giving feedback. There are a handful of other people I know who are not afraid to give people harsh feedback.

But really, the question is, why is it hard for you to give your employees, friends, or spouse difficult feedback to tell them that they are doing something wrong and they need to change?

Well, the truth is that we are often afraid of how these people will react. We think to ourselves, they are already complicated, what if they explode in anger? What if they break down? What if they respond by telling me that I am an idiot? What if they become defensive and start blaming me. There are times when we want to tell someone that their attitude is terrible, but we stop and think of what it is that they might say; "you don't even have respect for me. You don't care about what I am going through," - all of which worsen the situation.

With all these myriads of thoughts racing through our minds, we convince ourselves that it is not a big deal at all. We tell ourselves that it will all go away soon. We tell ourselves that if they are the right person, they will realize that what they are doing is wrong, and they will just let it all go away. While this will make you feel justified and self-righteous, the truth is that you are causing more harm than good. There are people I have seen lose their jobs just because their bosses or the people in their lives chickened out and did not tell them what they are doing is not alright. They needed your corrective feedback, but you did not give them. Some people cannot magically know that they are difficult and that they need to change. They need you to be their eyes!

Here are the tips you can use;

Pay attention first

While this might seem counterintuitive at first when you know that you have screwed your courage, you just need to stand up and get it over with. The first thing is for you to listen to what the other person has to say. Walk up to them and tell them that you would like to talk to them about something. Invite them to share with you what their view is about the whole situation.

For instance, you could say something like, "Hey Mary, I'd like to have a word with you about the ABC project. What time are you available for a chat?" Once you meet, you can ask them, "what do you think has been working well, and what has not been working well on the ABC project?"

When you do this, you are merely offering the other person a heads-up on what you would like to discuss. You are telling them that you would love to have a balanced picture of the whole project – not just focusing on the good news but the bad news as well.

Then give them ample time to share with you their opinion. Try not to interrupt – whether in agreement or disagreement - when they are talking to you. This way, you will be able to gather what it is that the other person thinks so that you have all the information you need to give a more objective response. You may realize that the other person will say so much of what you were going to say too. This way, the conversation turns into a coaching session!

Often, you will notice that the other person will see part of the problem and that allows you to pick it up from there and clarify what they have said. Now, if the other person is entirely oblivious to the whole situation, listening first to what they have to say makes the entire conversation less adversarial. This allows them to listen to you better when you start giving them your take on the issue.

Camera check

The other useful tip you must consider is what I refer to as the camera check. This is mainly feedback on people's behaviors rather than on their mental state. Let us go back to the example that we have already used in the previous point where you think that the employee has a bad attitude.

Now, at this point, you know that if you just say it plainly, that will not help, and the chances are that it will make the situation worse than it is. Such a comment is guaranteed to make the other person feel defensive because it mentions that they have a flawed character. You also are giving the other person no indication of what it is that you want them to do differently, which they don't have an idea how. How does the right attitude look like?

Rather than jumping in and making these comments without basis, simply do a camera check. In other words, what you need to do is take a mental video of what you consider a bad attitude and the other person doing it. What is it that you see in your mental tape? You might see them coming to work late, turning in their assignments late, saying negative things about their colleagues or the company, consistently not offering support to clients, among others.

These are some of the things that you can tell them. "Hey Mary, I notice that you have been turning in your assignments late, coming to work late this month, and saying negative things about your colleagues – Mark and Jane." When you frame it this way, you make it a hell LOT more comfortable for the other person to hear, rather than just saying that they have a bad attitude.

The point is, if someone is difficult, you can camera check what you consider to be an evil character or attitude and frame it in that manner. This is reasonably comfortable and skillful when trying to offer corrective feedback. When you let them know what it is they need to do differently for improvement and success, you are not only helping them be better but also yourself and the organization as a whole.

Step 3: Document

I can't stress this enough, but whenever you have significant issues with someone, you must jot down all the key points. There are several times when I have had people in top management levels tell me that they couldn't let go of a difficult employee because they did not have a record of them having bad behavior. It is this lack of documentation that comes as a result of misplaced hopelessness. The manager either thought that they did not want to be too negative about the employee or believed that it would soon go away.

If you are smart enough, then you know the value of documentation. You are keeping a record of each employee or person in your life, and what good and evil they do is nothing negative. If anything, it is something very prudent. What you need to note is that you can solve problems. All you need to do is take in a deep breath, follow it with a sigh of relief and write down everything you like or do not like about the other person – everything they are doing that qualifies as bad or good behavior.

You will thank yourself for it when "enough is enough!"

Step 4: Maintain consistency

If there is a behavior that you consider not okay with, then there should not be a time when you all of a sudden are okay with it. Remember that where you are, people are watching you. The last thing you want has everyone thinking that you are inconsistent or mistreating others. If it is at the employee, what you must remember is that employees are always looking to see what it is that you do more than you say.

For instance, if you tell everyone that they must turn in their end month reports by Friday Midnight and then there are times when you are upset about it, and in other times you are not, the truth is that they will not take you seriously. Those employees that are difficult won't do it at all.

You must learn to pick your shots. Set standards that you are willing to hold to – then hold tightly to them.

Step 5: Establish consequences for when things don't change

If, at this point, you still feel that there is no improvement, then it is high time you start getting specific. There is a saying, "I believe you can still turn this around," and this is where you apply that. Turning things around simply means that if you don't see behavioral change by a specific date, then something will happen – letting them go, initiate corrective actions, disciplinary committee discussion, or lose their eligibility for promotion.

The consequences have to be substantively negative for them to see the seriousness of the whole issue. If difficult people don't believe that their actions have serious consequences, then what makes you think that they will even change in the first place?

Step 6: Work through the company's processes

What you need to note is that when you are a good manager or leader, you will hold out hope for improvement to the point where you can't see any more hope and decide that you are letting go. You ensure that you have dotted all the I's and crossed every T so that you have a clear conscience when you finally make go of the other person. Maybe this is the point where you are in your marriage, parenting, or at work. If this is the case, then what I would advise you to do is to have a clear conversation with your spouse, boss, or child on what exactly you need to do to clear the whole path to termination – if necessary.

Step 7: Don't poison the well

If there is something I have learned over the years I have worked for my company is the value of not poisoning the well. There are times when junior and senior managers alike come to the office and lousy mouth a problematic employee in their department to all and sundry. This is not the right way to address an issue like this. Instead, you must follow all the steps that we have highlighted here.

It does not matter how difficult the person is, how crazy they drive you, or how hurtful their actions are. What matters the most is that you don't talk trash about them – you will only be adding salt to injury. Remember that the people you are telling are the same people that will go out there is talk – with distorted information. This will only create an environment of distrust. You will be choosing to back-stab them, something that pollutes the other person's perception. You will also be opening yourself up for the rest of the people to look at you as weak and unprofessional.

Trust me; this is no way to resolve an issue.

Just don't do it – however tempting it may be!

Step 8: Manage your self-talk

There are instances when someone frustrates you to the point where you end up having an inner conversation about the whole issue. While the internal dialogue is calming, it never should be unhelpfully negative or unhelpfully positive.

You may think to yourself, "what an idiot, Mary will never change" or "I will not worry too much about this. I am certain that things will turn out to be fine. Mary is such a great employee or wife or child, and there is nothing to worry about." These two thoughts are not helpful at all.

You must be willing to take a fair witness stance so that everything you say to yourself on the inside is not only accurate but also possible. You could say something like, "Mary's behavior is stirring up problems for the entire family. As I do everything I can to support them to change, I have to monitor their behavior closely. If the change, that will be great. If not, then I will have to do what I promised to do."

Now, that is helpful because you are taking the facts and using them to make informed decisions that are not only going to make you look good but are aimed at helping the other individual.

Step 9: Have the courage

By this time, you know that firing someone is the hardest decision most managers have to make. If the difficult person you are dealing with is your spouse, then you know that the toughest decision you are going to make is to seek marriage counseling or divorce. Whatever your situation may be like, the most important thing is that you do it right.

Instead of making excuses, putting things off, or making someone else do it, just brace yourself, gather your courage, and do it yourself. Realize that you are the manager of your life, and if you are as good as you think you are, then you are going to make the tough decision impeccably well. If – Hallelujah – things change against what you hoped for, dare to accept them. Realize that sometimes being proved wrong when we have lost hope in someone is as tough as being proved right.

If you learn to use these steps when dealing with a difficult spouse, colleague, employee, or friend, then it does not matter how things turn out because, in the end, you will know that you did the best you could to salvage a tough situation. That alone is enough to reduce your stress levels!

Chapter 7 What do you do when all these do not work?

This is one of the questions that so many people ask. There are times when we feel that we have done all there was to be done, and we still cannot see any improvement. While we may be tempted to think that there is nothing more we could do, the truth is that there is always something new we can do. If you have reached this point while dealing with someone challenging in your life, here is a message for you – there is still more you can do!

Here are some of the things you can do;

Be calm

Sometimes, you may be tempted to lose your temper and snap at other people. Well, I will tell you that this is not the best way to handle a difficult person. If you go around snapping at other people, don't you think that you are difficult for other innocent people yourself? What makes you think that you are any different from a difficult person? You are not going to get the other person to collaborate with you if this is the attitude you choose to have.

One thing that is important to note is that you cannot trigger the other person – unless you are silently using it as a strategy – it is best if you keep your cool.

One thing you will note about someone calm is that they often appear as though they are in control – even when that is not the case. Keeping your cool tends to help you stay centered and respectable. If you are always on edge, no one would be willing to reason with you. If you keep your cool, you will start noticing that the other difficult person gets all your attention.

Understand the other person's intentions

I believe that no one chooses to be difficult just for the sake of being tough. While there are times when the other person seems as though they intend to get you, you have to realize that there are always underlying reasons why they are acting up the way they do.

Well, this kind of motivation is not always something apparent. The most important thing is for you to identify what triggered their actions. Is there something that is making them act the way they are doing? Are they willing to cooperate with you? If not, what is stopping them from working with you? Is there something you can do to help them amicably resolve the issue?

Get some perspective

There is a chance that the people around you have experienced exactly what you are going through now. The truth is that while this may be happening to you for the very first time, some can help you see things from a different perspective and offer you a different take on the whole situation.

The challenge is for you to try and seek them out, share with them your experience, and then pay attention to what they have to say to you. The chances are that they will offer you valuable advice amid your conversation, and you will have overcome what seemed impossible at first.

Let them know where you are coming from

If anything has worked perfectly for me, it is letting the other person know what my intentions are. I always come clear on why I am doing what I do. While there are times when my words face resistance for thinking that is just being tough on them, the truth is that it works. When you let other people in on the reason underlying your actions and what is happening on the ground, they will not only empathize with the situation but will also change their behaviors. This is how you can get difficult people on board!

Do it today.

Establish a rapport

Today, the use of a computer system in messaging and communication has simply turned work into a mechanical process. The best way you can re-instill that human touch when interacting with others is always set aside time to connect with them at a personal level. You can choose to go out with your friends, family, or colleagues for drinks, lunches, or dinners. When you do, don't just concentrate on what you are eating or drinking, always spend time knowing each other – hobbies, families, life in general. Fostering a valuable connection with others goes a long way in helping you appreciate the beauty in diversity and know how best you can deal with situations that might arise between the two of you.

So, how do you establish rapport?

One important thing that you must note is that building rapport is not just about mirroring, matching, or leading the other person's behavior and actions. When dealing with a difficult person, think of it as a therapy session or sales. If you want your relationship to be productive, then you want to pay attention to the building blocks of good rapport. The general idea here is for you to mirror their posture – such that if they cross their arms while talking to you, you do the same shortly after. You can also speak in the same tone, pace, and language they speak in – adding in a couple of unique phrases and words they use while communicating with you.

When the other person starts to notice these similarities in their unconscious mind, the truth is that they will begin to feel that they are on the same level as you are, like you, and tune in to what you have to say. Little by little, you will start to lead them towards the direction you want them to go. You will begin to make them feel relaxed. If the rapport you develop is sufficient enough, then you will start noticing on your end that the other person is slowing matching your behavior without even realizing it. They may lean back, integrate your ideas, and echo their enthusiasm in all the skills you are trying to bring to life.

Does it all happen in one go? Not. Just like every other good thing, establishing rapport with a difficult person is something that takes time and effort. You have to be persistent and patient enough to see this through. Remember, you are dealing with someone difficult, which means that they are not just going to all of a sudden take up your ideas and support you. The truth is that you will experience moments of resistance, reluctance, and lack of focus on what you are saying. The sooner you make the other person feel heard and understood, the sooner you will be able to connect and integrate therapeutic interventions.

But how can you do that? How is it possible for you to instantly connect with a difficult person, build rapport with them, and make them get where you are coming from?

The power of utilization

Each time you want to have a connection with someone, you will need to use the principle of utilization to build rapport. One of the most straightforward approaches is for you to discuss your experiences and interests as you talk to them, even though you don't share them.

My friend Lance serves in the military. He told me that their former commando was such a difficult person to deal with. He wanted for them to get along, and he just knew the right way how – going into a trance. He said that hypnotic trance simply takes advantage of the narrow focus of attention and the passing of time. He simply re-evoke part of his military exercise to his commando and boom – it was all there in his mind. Now, it made it very easy to lead him one step at a time to where he desired to go – leveraging that alert and focused state of mind. This way, the commando started becoming receptive – by integrating his perspective, ideas, and ability to control pain. By the end of the session, they both were getting along like never before.

Effective communication through the utilization

The other trick is for you to utilize the other person's interests when talking to them. This is one of the most straightforward and powerful tools you can use to capture their attention and get them interested in what you have to say. Once you have them hooked, you can then bring up topics that you find interesting – but do it gradually just so that they don't feel overwhelmed and lose interest. While flirting is something that is not recommended in professional settings, you can bring on the game instinctively!

Realize that even the stand-up comedians don't always bring their comedy to people that love it but to those who think that they are not funny too. How do they get them hooked? By employing the power of utilization. The thing that seems to get people to laugh at their jokes if recognizing that what they are saying is true, but the chances are that they have never tried to put them in words. They also seem to exaggerate things to an entirely absurd level. Why is that? They can utilize what the target audience already understands.

Even though the examples I share here are from a therapeutic field of hypnosis, the principle of utilization goes a long way in communications as well as teaching. If you become too professional, you might just lose them.

Flirt instinctively!

Stop the psych-jargon

Occasionally, meeting someone for the very first time, I can tell whether they are difficult or not, and the ideology that is ingrained in them. While there are people who speak like they have swallowed a self-improvement book, every word they say is plainly but psych-jargon.

With the principle of utilization, all this goes out of the window. If you are going to have any influence on them, you must learn to see things from their perspective, learn their language, and understanding instead of dragging them into your thinking.

If you talk to any hypnotherapist, they will simply hand you ready-made scripts. This is not what you want to do. You cannot just dish out ways the other person should get along with you as though to tell them you don't have the slightest regard for their uniqueness. When you understand and practice the power of utilization, they will start to feel respected. You cannot just force your interests or ideas on the other person.

Instead of trying to change the other person from the outside, why not try changing them from the inside? This means that every action and the word you use must appeal to their unique personality traits and interests. This way, you offer them a chance to grow through progression quite naturally while at the same time facilitating a deeper level of rapport with them.

Let us consider a smoker who is always prone to outbursts. Where do you channel that anger? Well, you can make them direct that anger towards the cigarettes. In doing so, they don't dismiss the reality of their passion but then helps a long way in constructively managing their anger until they know the best way how. You could also argue that when anger is directed towards something potentially harmful, this is completely helpful.

Utilizing the gaping problem

According to Milton Erickson, you can use the difficult person's issues as a way of helping them make progress in life. He narrates a time when he treated a suicidal patient that was convinced life had no meaning because she believed that she was unattractive and could never find a partner. But what did she think was making her unattractive? A gap between her teeth!

Now, you don't just tell that person that they are attractive and ignore all their worries and concerns. What Erickson did was to utilize the very things she worried about just so that she could change her thinking. The girl squirted water through her supposedly "ugly" gap on her teeth during a break at the office. The young man thought of this as a provocative act and asked her out on a date! That completely changed her thought process.

In the same way, you can utilize the power of gaping problems when dealing with a difficult person, and you will be amazed at how fast they begin to change their minds and perspective.

It works!

Treat the other with respect

Do you like being treated as though you are incompetent, stupid, or incapable? Well, no one does, and neither do you. The thing with treatment is that it is two-way traffic. You have to do unto others exactly how you would like them to do unto you. You cannot possibly expect others to respect you when all the time you interact with them, you are disrespectful.

Today, ask yourself how you love others to treat you. Then use exactly those requirements when interacting with others. Respect is earned – so earn it!

So, how do you even treat a difficult person with respect, in the first place?

Well, if you want to lay the groundwork for respect, here are some of the things that you need to do;

Stop to see where they are coming from

As we have already established, people do not just choose to be difficult for no reason at all. It is not like this is a default setting – even though there are times when it seems like it when trying to manage and work with them. Think about it, if you have a difficult coworker, do you think that they just found themselves in that job? Someone somewhere must have selected them as a candidate out of all others vying for the same position.

Why is that?

Because they brought onto the job skills and personality that would get things done, if you think about it, they probably fit in well with the rest of the team at the beginning. However, if they no longer embody these traits and skills, the only honest thing to do is stop and find the reason why. Is there something in the job description that has changed? Are they having trouble finding the right balance with their work and private life? Is there someone on the job that keeps irritating them every other day?

When you set aside time to have an honest and open discussion with them concerning all the challenges they may be facing, this could help. While this is a necessary step in addressing the problem, it is something tricky to do. Therefore, rather than getting frustrated, open yourself up for a candid conversation with them.

Trust them first

If you want to build respect with a difficult person, you have to start by building trust. This is one of the most critical steps, especially in an instance where the other person does not trust you. A difficult person that does not trust you at all with always challenge you at every level. To give the benefit of the doubt, choose to believe them first.

While you may have the authority to manage their actions, the truth is that you cannot change their attitude. It does not matter what position you hold in the company; the truth is that the only way out is to try and influence them. Whenever you make promises, ensure that you live up to them. Do everything that you said you would do – and this will earn you trust. Soon enough, everyone around you will take your word for it and know that you expect nothing less from them. When you trust them to do the same, you are opening doors for higher results and respect.

Pay attention to the positive

As you work hard to establish trust and respect with the difficult person in your life, the one thing you must not forget is to offer positive feedback. You can do this by way of appreciation. Are there areas that the difficult person is trying hard to improve? If there are, recognize them in front of the whole team. To make it even better, you can take a step further to ask them what it is that they think is the best trait they possess at work and then recognize it too.

In so doing, you are demonstrating to them that they truly matter, and their contributions are much appreciated. You can understand them vocally whenever they do something commendable. Soon enough, they will realize that they are an essential part of the team. To earn your employees respect or anyone for that matter, you have to show them that you value them.

It all starts with you!

Have a new perspective

What is the bottom line of respect? Well, the truth is that you have to earn it. In other words, you have to give it for you to receive it – it is reciprocal. When you treat someone with respect, however hard headed they were when interacting with you, their opinion of you will begin to improve.

Rather than trying to label difficult people as being impossible, try to change your perspective of them. Always perceive them as an essential component of your team – one that the team cannot do without. It could be that they like challenging every idea, protocol, or project you initiate. When you make that shift in your mentality and perception of them, they will start to change how they talk about you. The point is for you to listen keenly to their feedback and then act accordingly.

Focus on what can be actioned

There are times when your awkward friends, colleagues, or family colleagues put you into a hot soup. For instance, you may have some work to be turned in, but then they fail to do it, or they may do something, and then you are held responsible for it when you don't even deserve that kind of unfair treatment. Whatever it is that the difficult people in your life do to you, the first step towards resolving the matter is for you to accept that it has already happened. Instead of crying over spilled milk, simply focus on what the next steps should be like.

What are some of the necessary steps to take in resolving the situation?

Create the change you want to see.

Ignore

If you have already tried all you could and still thought that nothing works, the other trick is for you to ignore everything. The best way you can treat someone difficult is to ignore them. You cannot possibly argue with yourself, right? They may try as much as they can to trigger you into being angry or acting up. However, when you ignore them, you simply cause them to stop because they are not getting the kind of reaction they are looking for. When you act up, you are giving them the satisfaction that they won, and they will keep on poking until you break.

Think about it, have you done everything you could within your means to handle the situation responsibly? If so, then you have nothing else to give them. Simply get on with your life and try as much as you can not to interface with them unless necessary. If they play a central role in your daily work and it is standing in the way of your productivity, then you can choose to escalate this to the higher authorities to help you resolve the issue. This is often referred to as a trump card. You should not use this unless you have exhausted all other possible options.

In most cases, if you want to get to someone moving, you can do it by employing the top-down approach. You must exercise caution when using this option. Try not to use it every often lest your bosses begin to think that you cannot handle small issues independently. While this works, it is only to be used when all else is depleted. Trust me, I have used it, and it works like magic.

Employ kindness

I get it, when you are dealing with a difficult person in your life, your gut feeling is usually to be difficult as well. When someone is attacking you, the first thought you have is often to try and defend yourself. I have been there, done that. The problem is that when you do this, you get sucked up into a vacuum such that you don't even take a moment to slow down and just breath.

In almost every difficult situation, I have found myself in is that showing kindness goes a long way in helping one calm the case down. When two difficult people are hard on each other, the chances are that the whole situation tends to escalate to the extent that nothing can be accomplished.

However, when you choose to be kind, you will diffuse the whole situation so that you can get all that you want. This is one of the techniques that should be at the top of your list whenever you encounter a difficult person in your life.

Show compassion

If you have been in a problem before, then you know that you must deal with your issues. The truth is, we all have issues, and we tend to think that what we are going through is so harsh that no one can bear.

However, if you sat down to listen to what other people are going through, you will simply take your baggage with you and shove it back into your backpack.

Well, I love that!

My point is, no one knows what it feels like to have another's problems. When you are dealing with someone difficult, this should be your principle – it could be that they are experiencing a very tough ordeal or an enormous problem that you wouldn't even be able to bear in part.

Often, when you choose to show a problematic person a little bit of compassion, they tend to respond positively. Several of us get stuck in our heads and lives that we don't even open our eyes to what the people around us might be experiencing. Your friend might just be looking for a little kindness. The next time you encounter someone difficult – whether at work, home, or elsewhere – show them some kindness, and you will be amazed at how that works magic.

Find something in common

When you are talking to someone for the very first time, what you will note is that sharing something in common with them often makes your connection stronger. Each one of us has been made in such a way that we desire to belong to a group. We are natural beings that want to have a strong sense of belonging.

When you meet someone, it always feels nice to know that you both went to the same college, even if during different years. Having something in common creates a form of kinship. My children are in high school now, and each time I met a parent that has children the age of mine or that our children attend the same schools, I feel like we have a parental connection.

Today, if you have someone difficult in your office, at home or elsewhere, try to establish something that you both share in common. This will go a long way in helping you get along with each other afterward.

Control what you can

There are things in life that we can control, and others out of our control. One thing that is important to note is that we must focus our attention on the things that we can control.

When you are trying to handle a difficult situation with a difficult person, you must start by thinking about what it is in that situation that is within your control. It could be that there is someone else you can deal with instead of that difficult person. That is the person that might just pave the way for you to do things right.

A few months ago, I was trying to work with the sales department on a novel initiative I was trying to bring to life in our company. One of the team members suggested that I should speak to a specific person to seek their help because that has been the tradition. When I first contacted the person, I did not get a response. I kept sending them emails after emails, left several voicemails, but still did not get a response. I finally got frustrated and resorted to speaking to other people in the department.

Several people in the sales department were willing to help with the project with so much joy. That was a difficult person that I managed to workaround. Today, you can do the same – control all that you can!

Look at yourself

The scripture in James 1:23-24 states, "For anyone who hears the word but does not carry it out is like a man who looks at his face in a mirror, 24 and after observing himself goes away and immediately forgets what he looks like...."

If you are going to deal with a difficult person, then you will have to know who you are first. Your focus should be on what you hold inside you. Is there something that you are doing or not doing that is standing in your way of dealing with a difficult person?

There are so many of us who know precisely what kind of people we are. We know that we are always in a good mood and are sociable. Every single day is a smooth one. There are instances where you may have lots of things racing through your mind – solving one problem after the other.

Even when you are having a conversation with a friend, your mind is probably elsewhere. You may come off as though you are condescending, abrupt, and short. It is this kind of attitude that can make someone that is already irritated to get upset quickly. How you choose to respond will determine whether you are adding salt to injury or quenching the fire.

Therefore, spend some time to reflect on how you interact with other people – especially the difficult ones – to ensure that you are not making the situation worse than it already may be.

Overcome Your Fear of Conflict

If there is a technique that I like the most when dealing with someone difficult is overcoming my fear of conflict. You cannot deal with a difficult person if all you do is run away from them. So many people are scared of stirring up strife and conflict with a difficult person, but what you need to realize is that the more you try to run, the more you are giving that person the power to walk all over you.

While the process of dealing with someone difficult in itself is challenging enough, the truth is that if you do not stand up to them and set boundaries, the situation will only get worse than it already is. Each one of us deserves to be treated with respect. Therefore, do not allow them to manage you less than that.

Don't get me wrong; I am not saying that you should intentionally stir up conflict. What is merely asking you to do is that in the event a difficult person treats you less than you deserve to be treated, stand up to them and confront them about the whole situation. Conflict does not mean that it has to be something terrible. In so many cases, it is a good thing – especially when it leads to a resolution of issues and brings to fruition what you desire most.

The bottom line is, if you look around you, you will not miss at least one difficult person. You cannot run away from them. The key is for you to communicate with them gracefully and peacefully so that you can both reach a consensus. It is better to "agree to disagree" so that you can both move past your selfish interests and live a happier life.

Chapter 8 Expert techniques to handle difficult people

Practice reflective listening

Have you ever been upset, and then someone comes in and tells you, "I understand," Did that ever make you feel better?

I didn't think so!

Well, one thing that is important to note is that using such kind of statements will not help you accomplish anything. Let us consider an instance where you have a client in your company. They tell you that they are frustrated because of the budget cuts and the fact that you are not willing to offer them discounts even though they have been your loyal clients for several years. How do you respond to that? Do you just tell them that you understand what they are going through?

The truth is that if you did tell them you understand, that conversation is probably never going to have a good ending.

If you are in such a tight spot with a difficult client, the first thing you should tell yourself is to practice reflective listening. In other words, try to put yourself in the other person's shoes. Understand what it is that they are saying by simply interpreting their body language and words. This will help you to respond by reflecting their thoughts and emotional feelings back to them.

Instead of telling them plainly that you understand, try something like - "So, if I get you correctly, you are saying that our pricing is too high that is becoming a barrier to your business, right? – and because of the tight budget you are working with and the fact that we are not offering discounts. Is that right?"

If you have understood what they are telling you, simply move on with your conversation. However, if you have not yet understood what they are going through, ask them to give you more information so that you can understand their situation better. The trick here is for you to make them feel that you get where they are coming from and that you are concerned. They want to feel your empathy.

Try as much as you can to avoid making promises you know you might not be able to meet. The goal is to make the difficult person feel that they have been heard and that they are greatly valued.

Consider their affect heuristic

This simply refers to a mental shortcut. This plays a significant role in helping you make a quick and efficient decision based on your emotional feelings towards the other person, situation, and the place you are at. In simple terms, our choices are greatly influenced by our experiences and general outlook of the world around us. It is merely because of our bias.

The leading cause of the problem is that we are not objective in such situations, and facts do not matter that much. We choose to run every decision we make based on our mental software and then develop strong opinions based on that.

If the difficult person keeps having a different opinion and keeps asking you what you think is the catch, try not to respond rubbish them off by saying that we have to move on because of ABCD's. There is a chance that this person may be trapped in another information source, contract, or agreement with the previous vendor who failed to deliver what they had promised they would. Based on that very experience, they may be looking at you through the same lenses.

What you need to do is ask questions so that you fully understand what the root cause of the problem is. Some of the questions you can ask them so that they can relax and offer you insight as to why they are resistant include;

- I really would like to understand why you are a little skeptical about this. Would you tell me more?
- **Is there anything we can do to relieve your fears?**
- What can we do to help you feel comfortable enough so that we can all move forward?

When you ask such questions, you are allowing them to simply redirect their thoughts from thinking that you are not trustworthy in considering what is needed for the team to move forward and make progress.

Tap into the beginner's mind

The beginner's mind is often referred to like the Zen mind, and it serves as a strategy of approaching each situation as though you have no prior experience in it. Whenever you adopt this kind of thinking when dealing with a difficult person, every conversation you engage in is made with the "I don't know" mindset. This allows you to try as much as you cannot judge the other person or the situation.

This also goes a long way in helping you not to live with the 'should' kind of thinking. "You should have thought of the budget before the year started. You should have read my email concerning the discount expirations. You should have known that I am a busy person and available only once in a week for consultations."

When you are addressing a difficult person, try not to use 'should' statements. They only set your mind on the defensive and get in the way of your productivity and conversation before it can even start.

The good thing with adopting the Zen mindset is that it allows you to let go of an expert mindset. While you may be an expert in your field or in what you do, you have to realize that you are not an expert when it comes to a difficult person or situation.

For instance, instead of saying things like "You said that you wanted to increase your sales by 30% by the end of the month and the kind of delays am seeing will not make this possible," choose to approach the conversation in a beginner's mindset. Try not to prejudge the other person. Forget what it is that they should have done and perceive the conversation you are both having as a puzzle that needs to be solved.

You can choose to say something like this instead "It seems to me like with these delays, we will not be able to reach our sales goals. But, let's explore strategies that will help us achieve the results that we are aiming for." If you keenly study this statement, you will realize that you are acknowledging the fact that there is a problem, but immediately starts moving in the direction of a possible solution.

Let go of fear

Again, you cannot be afraid of negative results to the point that you allow that to drive your reactions. It is because of doubt that we tend to feel the need to control things and the people around us. If a colleague is difficult, you may feel afraid of challenging them because that might just put your relationship at risk. If a client expresses displeasure in your services, timelines, or pricing structure, you may be afraid because you think that you might not be able to fix the whole situation.

The first thing is to let go of the idea that there is something that needs fixing. When you are having a conversation with a difficult person – whether a friend, child, client, or coworker – remember that your role is to listen, understand what they are saying and then discern what the next steps forward should be. I don't mean that you start dishing out solutions immediately. Take time to go over what they have told you and then think through the possible solutions to find the best way forward.

For instance, rather than trying to validate emotional feelings, slap together common fixes, or apologizing, what you can do is express how unfortunate it is that the situation happened once again. Assure the other person that you get how the whole situation is affecting the business or your relationship and then appreciate them for being patient enough to allow you to work towards resolving the issue.

"Chunk" the problem

You may be wondering what 'chunking' is all about. Well, this simply refers to the process of taking a huge problem and then breaking it down into smaller manageable portions that you can address one at a time. When you break problems into smaller portions, this allows you to handle them. They also make people more willing to start dealing with all the issues at hand.

What I have learned from my mentor over the years is the importance of chunking things and then organizing them into tasks that you can handle every other day. This is the same way you can choose to deal with a tough situation with a difficult person.

Does your employee always find a reason not to turn in their work on time because they cannot get started using the new software?

What you can do is to ask them to help you break down each of the steps into smaller bite-size pieces that you can work on to come up with an easy to follow protocol. The point is for you not to apportion blame or say that they are lazy, but to find the best way forward. When each task is chunked, it becomes easier for the other person to digest what is left to be done.

Remember, anger is natural

We have all encountered difficult people – clients, friends, and colleagues alike – that we get so furious. It could also be that you have been on the other side of things. For instance, if you are a customer at a store and you pay for a new product upgrade, and then you realize that it is shallow that it makes you angry.

The recalibration theory of anger states that anger is a natural emotion that is wired into human beings. In other words, you have to realize that anger is the best way we have been made to get into the bargain. We press our lips together, bite our tongue, furrow our brows, or flare our nostrils just so that we can drive the other person to a place of higher value based on what we have to give.

If you are dealing with a difficult person, the point is for you to try and avoid justifying your actions or position. Realize that the reason why they could be feeling that way is that they think that their opinion is being undervalued or that they want to control the situation. It is advisable that you take the other person's frustrations seriously and not personally. Once you have understood the frustrations and arguments of the other person, thank them for bringing that to your attention. Also, let them know that you will think through everything and get back to them with a solution or a way forward.

When the other person is already furious, the chances are that they will not take any solution you offer at that time. However right the answer might be, they will not feel like it is the best way to go about the whole situation. Therefore, you must allow them some time to calm down before you can pick up the discussions where you left them – this time, with practicality and reason.

But what if the difficult person is already raging with anger, how can you deal with the situation?

Well, there are so many ways you can try to calm the whole situation down;

Keep your calm

This is probably a point you will see everywhere in this book – because it is essential and easy to get wrong. If someone sends you an angry text or email or starts shouting at you on the phone, the truth is that it is hard not to get personal. There is a chance that you will get a bristle of anger, and defensive thoughts will begin to pop into your mind of how wrong you think the other person is. You will start to think about how ungrateful they are for all the hard work you give the company, and before you know it, you are exploding with fury.

The best thing to do is to take in a deep breath. Try to take in what it is that the other person is trying to say. In between those lines, you might note that the other person is in a struggle or is frustrated with the whole process, product or service to the point that they took it out on you or the team. We are all human, and there are times when we are caught in our moments of weakness. If you try to understand this fact, you will not see the reason why you should take their difficulty, comments, or arguments personally or hold it against them.

If the other person is being abusive, rude, or aggressive in their language or intonation, don't tolerate their behavior. If, at some point during the conversation, you feel like they are belittling you, simply feel free to escalate the situation to a third-party that can help you resolve without killing the other.

Let us consider an instance where a client calls the support team in your company expressing how upset they are about the delay in the delivery of their products. They may be agitated and are shouting at the top of their lungs on the phone call. This is where your support team or you should remain calm and try to ask the three what's; what is the problem, what are their goals, needs or desires, and what are the available options. If you are the one on the other side of the phone, keep your cool and find out more details about their issue. That alone will work to de-escalate an angry person.

Practice active listening

Try as much as you can to focus on what they are saying - rather than the anger behind their words and voice. When your attention is on what they are really saying, you will be better placed to determine what it is that is agitating them. This will also help you resolve the issue rather than trying only to de-escalate it to comfort them. When you know what the problem is, you can find a solution, and you will have a satisfied colleague, friend, or client at the end of the day.

Let us consider an instance where a client walks into your store and tells you that the product you sold them stopped working for them a few days after they bought it. They continue to tell you how surprised and disappointed that you could offer such a poorly designed product.

What will you do? What will your response be like?

Well, the simplest way to go is to pay attention to the words they use – surprised, disappointed. Those are the words they used to express their emotional feelings. The point is that they are not angry but surprised by how your product behaved.

In such an instance, you may be tempted to respond with the words "I understand that you are frustrated…" while that is a response, it is not only going to escalate the other person's feelings but will now make them angry. By saying that, you are only giving them a reason to go from disappointment and surprise to anger.

However, if you demonstrate that you are actively listening to what they have to say, you will calm the situation down. You can say things like "that is certainly surprising and disappointing. Let me take a look to know why the product stopped working unexpectedly." With this response, you are acknowledging the client's feelings without necessarily escalating them.

Repeat back what your customers say

One of the key components of active listening is ensuring that your client and you are on the same page. Once you know the root cause of their anger, you can simply repeat what you heard from them so that you are sure you understand what is making them angry. In so doing, you are also letting the other person know that you get hat their concerns are and are working on a resolution or response.

Let us consider an instance where someone badges into your office ranting about the product you sold them not working. You can simply start your response with such words as "What am hearing you say is…" this will simply get the ball rolling. Try to highlight how the issue is standing in the way of them achieving their goals. This will show them that you did not just listen but understood their needs and are going to help them.

Thank them for bringing the issue to your attention

When the other person you are conversing with is angry and is sending negative vibes about the whole situation, you can thank them for speaking out their concerns. This will go a long way in helping you establish a good rapport with them. With just a simple 'thank you,' acknowledging their time and contributions, you will sufficiently calm the situation down.

One of the best ways you can deal with someone who is continuously difficult and angry is to ensure that you thank them each time. When a difficult member of your team starts an inquiry, simply acknowledge their efforts for reaching out. If you have held onto a case file for extended durations of time, thank your team for being patient while you were troubleshooting. When that difficult person shares their negative views about the project, thank them for being bold enough to share their perspective and making the whole team better.

Explain the steps you'll take to solve the problem

When that difficult person at your office raises an issue, you must make it clear to them that you will get started on addressing their concerns. It does not matter whether or not it is a simple issue that you can finish up over the phone or something that requires a whole process that might take days, weeks or even months – the trick is for you to plainly and spell out your intentions and next moves to them so that they feel valued, heard and at ease.

One of the best ways you can achieve this is if you set timelines for their issue to be sorted out. Spell out every single step you intend to take, and when each one of the steps is expected to be complete. This way, you are communicating to the other person that you know exactly what it is that you are doing and the time when you expect to have a resolution ready.

Set a time to follow-up with them, if needed

There are instances when a simple phone conversation cannot resolve the problems that arise between you and another person. Some will require you to sync up with the manager or fill up a request form for the resolution process to be initiated. If that is the case in your instance, then you will need to explain this to the other person. Try to give them timelines of when you expect to have a response for them.

The benefit of talking directly to the other person is so that your client, coworker, or friend has ample time to calm down. At the same time, this will give you sufficient time to seek guidance and feedback from your superiors on how best to proceed. If at all, you will need to follow up with the other person, explain clearly why that break would greatly benefit them.

For instance, it could be that you will need to speak to the product expert for troubleshooting purposes. The point is that you are as transparent with them as possible. Let them stay aware that they cannot take any further action, at least until you can seek clarification with those concerned as well.

If they keep being uneasy about what you propose to them, you can also choose to offer them a contingency plan. Tell them exactly when they expect you to reach out to them and the kind of information you will have for them. This will justify the follow up you will be taking up with them.

Be sincere

The same way remaining calm when dealing with a difficult person is essential, so is sincerity. Trust me, people know when they are being spoken to in a somewhat condescending way or even an angry manner. Choose the right set of words to use and the intonation to employ when communicating with a difficult person. Ensure that your tonal voice is not only intentional but also respectful. No one likes being talked to with an angry tone. Simply take the high road and make the other person feel like what they are saying is being taken seriously.

There are times when that difficult person in your office will call you at midnight with an "issue," but then after reading through or troubleshooting, you realize that it was an error on their part. You may be tempted to poke fun on the other person who did not pay attention enough to pick the error out, costing you your good night's sleep.

What you need to understand is that this other person could very well be you. It is through them that you know whether the services you render are quality enough or not. Even though they may be at fault, it is their contribution that makes the whole product quality. Therefore, ensure that you are politely explaining the reason why an issue arose in the first place and the best ways to prevent them from happening in the future again.

Highlight the case's priority

One of the common frustrations for people who conflict is feeling like their support case is not as crucial to the business as the other person's. This is especially the case when dealing with a company or a situation that has a broader client coverage. The other person might feel as though their case is expendable while the rest of the team is busy providing poor experiences.

To get this feeling out of the way, you must highlight how critical the situation is to everyone involved - whether directly or indirectly. Let the other person know that you are putting in efforts to notify essential stakeholders in the company so that the issue they are concerned about is resolved as fast as possible. This way, they will feel as though the whole company is on their case even if it's only one support team that is working on it.

One last word

Indeed, dealing with difficult people is one of the toughest tasks in life. They are the kind of people who will ruin your perfect day before it can even begin. It could be a colleague, family member, partner, or friend. It could also be anyone random you run into at the street. Whoever that may be, the trick is to ensure that you have armed yourself with the above methods, steps, and approaches to deal with them appropriately.

Realize that difficult people exist all around us, and if you don't do something about them, then you risk letting them hurt others.

The truth is that there is no easy way to deal with these people – after all, they are different combinations of personality traits. They all have different ways to make others' life difficult.

As the saying goes, "It takes two to tango." Realize that these difficult people may not even notice that they are difficult. To most of them, this is their usual way of life. In fact, to a difficult person, everyone else around them is difficult. They don't have your perspective of things.

So, have you been continually dealing with difficult people yourself? If so, it might be time for you to take a look at your behavior. Ask yourself whether you are the one being difficult. Look for such indicators as;

- **Lack of close connections at home, school or the workplace**
- You lack a sense of self-worth in what you do
- **You find yourself being misunderstood too often or complaining about this or that**
- You always think that people are talking ill of you
- **You still are an emotional person**
- You feel like people don't even care or remember you

You might just be the difficult person we have been discussing here. If that is the case, then it is high time you use the strategies above to deal with your behavior. If these traits are what you see in someone around you, then you can also use the techniques we have discussed to help them become a better person.

Remember, a little self-reflection goes a long way in helping us be a better person to the people working and interacting with us daily.

You can help yourself and the difficult person around you to see what they are doing so that they can change for the long-term.

It is a win for all of us!

So, what are you waiting for? Start identifying them around you and help them BECOME!

© **Written by: Katerina Griffith**